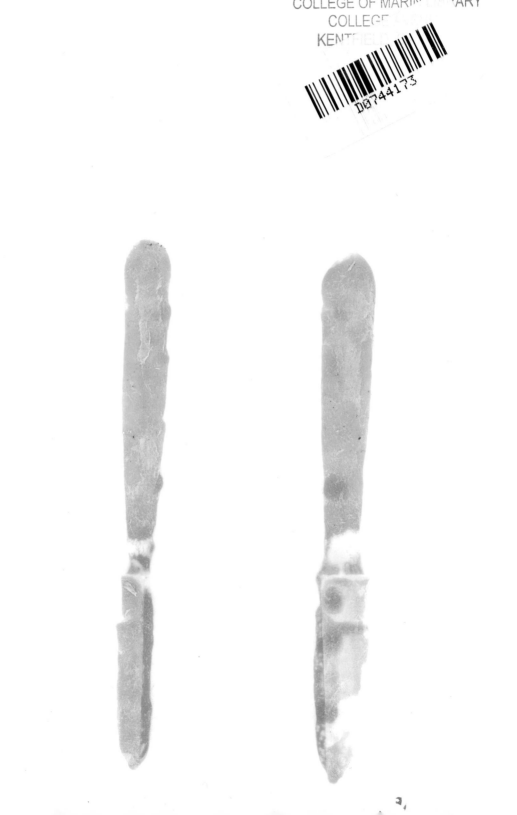

A
HISTORY OF
CHINESE
DRAMA

A
HISTORY OF
CHINESE
DRAMA

WILLIAM DOLBY

BARNES & NOBLE
BOOKS
10 East 53d St., New York 10022
(a division of Harper & Row Publishers, Inc.)

to Mrs Liu Yin-ch'eng

Published in the U.S.A. 1976 by
HARPER & ROW PUBLISHERS, INC.
BARNES & NOBLE IMPORT DIVISION

First published 1976 by Elek Books Limited, London

Copyright © 1976 William Dolby

ISBN 0–06–491736–3

Printed in Great Britain

Contents

List of Excerpts Quoted

List of Illustrations

LINE ILLUSTRATIONS

Preface

For many centuries the varied fascinations of Chinese drama have enthralled all levels of society and all kinds of people. Peasant and emperor, commoner and king, statesman and scholar, general and soldier have acted in plays and delighted in plays. Many Chinese have also been infuriated by plays, and tried to shun or suppress them, but none has ever reasonably been able to ignore them, for, in spite of its many vicissitudes, drama has remained a lively and ubiquitous element of Chinese life throughout the centuries into present times. The playwrights, too, have been a considerable variety of people, including actors, unemployed literati, hermits, priests, imperial princes, ministers, chancellors, civil servants, and generals. An abundant treasure of written drama survives, although it is only a small part of the wealth of performance that there has been. In recent times some of China's theatrical past has been subjected to thorough and comprehensive analysis, but even now the studies that have appeared in print are only a drop in the ocean compared with what remains to be done. Yet generalisation and the elucidation of minutiae must both go hand in hand, to correct, balance and amplify each other. The present history is an attempt at generalisation, and, inevitably, a sketch of a sketch of an exploratory sketch. It attempts the as-yet impossible, but some such endeavour seems overdue.

For the sake of clarity, and because the subject is such a vast one, I have generally kept to the peaks and mainstreams of Chinese drama, leaving the necessary correction and further refinement of the story to other works and future research. For the convenience of a general public, I have translated play-titles, many ladies' personal names, and some professional names, so as to restrict the amount of blank romanisation. The system of romanisation used is the one usually called Pinyin, which is neater to the eye and memory than the Wade-Giles system more commonly used in Western books on China, but for well-known geographical and other familiar names I resort to the customary transliteration. I spell Sông (Sung) dynasty with the circumflex to avoid confusion, since 'song' is one of our main topics.

In approaching such a rich and ancient drama, with its endless ramifications, I have had to rely on the research and opinions of others in many respects. The works of numerous twentieth-century scholars have been of very great assistance, particularly those of such masters as Wang Guowei, Zhou Yibai, Aoki Masaru, Sun Kaidi, Tan Zhengbi, Yan Dunyi, A. C. Scott, and Luo Jintang. In the early days of my studies of Chinese drama, Professors and Doctors H. C. Chang, P. Van der Loon, Gen Itasaka, L. E. Picken, and Cheng Hsi were helpful with advice, bibliographical assistance or inspiration, and Mr Chen Che was a remarkably patient and kindly tutor on modern drama and Peking Opera. In more recent times, Professors and Messrs André Lévy, W. Idema, Donald Rimmington, Michael Kennedy, David Hawkes, John Chinnery, and Angus Russell have been among those who have drawn my attention to useful works or stimulated me by discussions or lectures on drama. To all I express my warm gratitude. This history and any errors it may contain are entirely my own responsibility.

William Dolby,
Edinburgh

Dynasties

Xia	c. 2100–1600 BC
Shang	c. 1600–1028 BC
Zhou	1027–256 BC
Qin	221–206 BC
Han	206 BC–AD 220
Three Kingdoms	AD 220–265
Western Tsin	265–317
Eastern Tsin	317–420
Northern and Southern Dynasties	420–589
Sui	589–618
Tang	618–907
Five Dynasties	907–960
Sông	960–1279
Northern Sông	960–1126
Southern Sông	1127–1279
Liao	947–1125
Xi Xia	1032–1227
Jin	1115–1234
Yuan	1279–1368
Ming	1368–1644
Qing	1644–1911
Republic	1912
People's Republic	1949

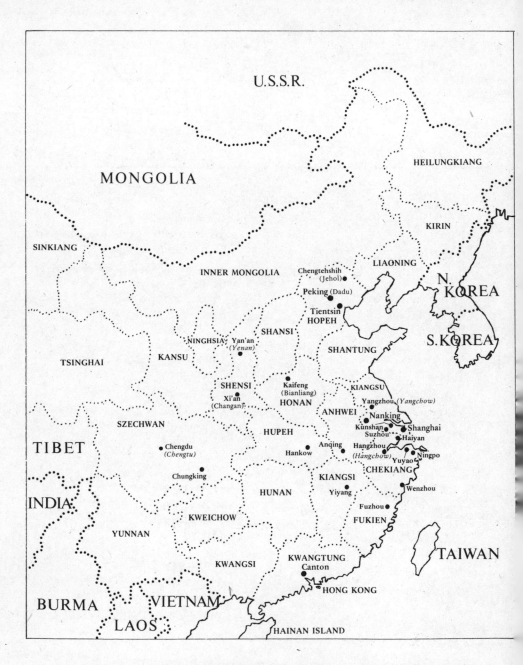

The provinces of China (today's boundaries) and towns important in the history of Chinese theatre. Common alternative spellings are bracketed and in italic type; former names are bracketed and in Roman type

1

Antecedents of Drama and Tang Plays

The earliest Chinese dramas of which we know come from the thirteenth century AD. How Chinese drama first arose has in modern times been the subject of much debate. It seems most reasonable to assume that this drama derived its forms from a variety of sources, and such evidence as there is suggests a great complexity of origins. Much of the evidence has disappeared, lost in the course of time, or never even recorded in writing or other enduring manner, but we can still observe some things which may have gone into the creation of a 'drama consciousness', a mental preparedness for drama or a familiarity with the components of drama, and we can also see other things which seem more directly and more concretely to have contributed to the birth of drama.

The earliest known Chinese drama was a highly synthetic art, embodying a broad range of different kinds of performance, such as dance, song, music, acting, recitation and acrobatics. Very early in Chinese history there is evidence of the synthesis of two or more of these, which, if not directly leading to further elaboration and the birth of drama, may have contributed to the drama consciousness. The step from dance to drama seems a small one. Sometimes indeed the form of drama is dance, as in the dance-dramas of various parts of the world, such as the *ma'yong* of the ancient kingdom of Ligor in Malaya, which includes performances by the *pawang* – a shaman or witch-doctor and intermediary between men and gods – or the dance-drama of ancient Turkey, thought by some to have derived in part from the rituals of the Uralo-Altaic shamans. Greek tragedy arose partly from a lyric that was sung and danced by a chorus and that had religious connections with Dionysus. Again, the step from religious ritual to secular drama can be a very small one, and often the two are found inextricably intermingled.

Religious ritual and dancing both occurred in the shamanistic and court dances of the Zhou dynasty (1027–256 BC) in China. The shamans or sorcerers invoked gods by means of highly erotic wooing songs. They undoubtedly acted, sang and danced, and may well have worn costume and make-up.[1] The court dances, which were refined versions of orgiastic and other religious and quasi-religious dances from furthest antiquity, had set movements that were sometimes almost equivalent to the enacting of a drama-like story and involved acting, singing, dancing, dressing up and other features reminiscent of drama.

With the steady decay of central power during the latter part of the Zhou dynasty, regional rulers and feudal lords set up their own elaborate court establishments, and appropriated and diversified the Zhou court rituals and music. They kept their own personnel for music, dancing and other entertainments, and it was probably from among these entertainers that the specialists in jest-couched counsel arose, the court jesters and wise fools of ancient China. Jester Meng for instance, is known to have started his career as a musician or entertainer.[2] Like Henry VIII's Will Somers, Elizabeth's Richard Tarlton and the other court fools and king's jesters of mediaeval and later Europe, the Zhou jesters had the twofold duty of entertaining and of advising through the medium of humour. Perhaps there is a universal *raison d'être* for them. The safest medium for checking and counselling despotic and arbitrary men of power is disarming humour, the cloak of soft folly or the charm of gentle wit. The Zhou jesters gave their often audacious advice in the form of satirical skits, which sometimes involved singing, dressing up and rudimentary acting.

Acting had a very long history before the advent of the drama in China. Like the Latin word *lusor*, the Anglo-Saxon *plegman* and the French *joueur*, which could be applied to anything from a jousting knight or a monk performing in liturgical music-drama to a keeper of a troupe of acrobatic monkeys,[3] ancient Chinese terms were often loosely applied to a whole range of what to the modern understanding seem quite distinct categories of entertainer. The term *yueren*, for example, could mean minstrel, juggler, actor, or indeed entertainer of almost any kind. Perhaps the modern understanding all too frequently errs in failing to see the essential mimetic unity and singleness of purpose that the terms indicate. Some terms also changed their connotations over the centuries. For these and other reasons, historians of Chinese drama are often led astray by over-ready etymological deductions or by the failure to perceive the changing meanings of one and the same term. An etymological connection between words for 'jester' (which usually contain the syllable *you*) and a number of words used in later ages for the stage actor has led some modern scholars to overestimate or to estimate all too readily the connection between the Zhou jesters' skits and the drama. It is easy to see how the Zhou skits at least could have developed into play-acting, but there is no sure evidence that they *did*, or even that they lay at or near the source of something which eventually developed into the drama. As in the case of the early dances, all we can suggest is that they may well have assisted the growth of a drama consciousness, and in a general manner have helped to pave the way for the introduction of proto-dramatic forms of entertainment that may be linked directly with the advent of drama. Nonetheless, in later ages the performances of very similar jesters, and a variety of dances, were to have a clear connection with the drama.

During the Han dynasty (206 BC–220 AD) the synthetic dances continued in an abundance of forms, as almost certainly did the jesters' acts. The enacting of a story was one of the most vital elements of early Chinese drama, and in the Han dynasty a certain very simple story-sketch, now generally referred to as *Mr Huang of the Eastern Ocean*, became popular. This is said to have been about a magician, a certain Mr Huang of the Eastern Ocean (Japan? Korea?), who in his youth was able to tame tigers and snakes by his magic. As he grew old, the effects of too much wine-drinking reduced his magic to impotence. One day, towards the end of the Qin dynasty (221–206 BC), a dangerous tiger appeared in his vicinity, so he set forth with a red turban round his head and a gold sword in his hand to try and deal with it. Alas, his spells were no longer effective, and the tiger devoured him. This tale was made into a popular play (*xi*), and the Han emperor also adopted it, and made it into a game (*xi*, same character) of Horn Butting (*jiaodi*).[4] One can imagine that this simple story-performance, with its acting, use of costume and humorous climax, could easily have developed into a whole range of plays, but there is no direct evidence of its having done so.

It is possible that this sketch may have been performed as a satire against the sorcerers and magicians who plagued and duped the Martial Emperor, Wudi, who reigned 140–87 BC. More important, for our present considerations, however, is the manner in which it was performed, probably as a contest between two players taking the parts of magician and tiger. It was classed as one of the Horn Butting games. The Horn Butting game seems originally to have been an actual fight. Could it have been, like the Mumming plays of the British Isles, a survival of the rites of some primitive folk festival, some contest in which masks or head-pieces like the Dorset Ooser were worn, or a trial of strength like the old Ashanti game of 'butting heads' between two contestants as to who could make the other fall first?[5] Probably it became a wrestling combat, and was as such included in what were known as the Hundred Games (*baixi*).

The Hundred Games were entertainments in the nature of circus or fairground spectacles. No doubt current among the populace at large, such spectacles were adopted by the Han imperial court, which referred to them as the Hundred Games, or as 'Diverse Music' (*sanyue*). The latter term, opposed to 'Refined Music' (*yayue*) which covered the more formal and time-honoured dances and other entertainments of the palace, was also applied to an acted play and to actors in later dynasties – another example of the catholicity of ancient terms or of the unity that lay behind the various entertainments. 'Horn Butting game' came to be a generic term applied not solely to games involving a combat but also to a wide range of feats and shows, including tight-rope-walking, weight-lifting, pole-climbing, sword-swallowing, fire-eating, somersaulting, tumbling, equestrian acts, ball-juggling, sword-juggling, balancing on poles, conjuring tricks allied to 'sawing the lady in half', multiple balancing acts, acts similar to jumping through the fiery hoop, dances in supernatural and animal disguises – and *Mr Huang of the Eastern Ocean*. Acrobatics played a very prominent role in later Chinese drama, and in the Horn Butting games they came under the same general heading as the 'play' of Mr Huang.

As indicated above, the old Chinese words for 'game' and 'play' were one and the same: *xi*. This word could refer to virtually any entertainment, acrobatics, sport, jest, or children's amusements, and was similar in its ambiguity, or rather in its all-embracing nature, to the Latin *ludus*, the Anglo-Saxon *pleg*, or the English 'play' and 'game'. Another word for 'play' or 'game', *ju*, had a like breadth of application in ancient Chinese, sometimes being interchanged with *xi*, or united with it as in the Chinese word for 'drama': *xiju*. This breadth of application of *xi* and *ju* has often proved an etymological red-herring for drama historians who, analysing the origins of drama with simplistic retrospection, have sometimes tended to assume that anything called *xi* or *ju* must have been a stage play or drama, whereas it might have been tightrope-walking or sword-swallowing. There are also instances, of course, where time has created a present ambiguity difficult to resolve.

The centuries that followed the Han dynasty were largely a period of national disunity, decentralised power, invasions by Turkic and other non-Chinese peoples, frequent non-Chinese political domination, bitter wars, internecine strife and widespread devastation. Such conditions undoubtedly favoured the influx of ideas from foreign sources and the creation of new attitudes and interests. One major import was Buddhism. This entered China as a fairly minor influence during the Han dynasty, and by the sixth century had established itself with millions of adherents all over China as the major religion of the country and one of the most powerful spiritual, intellectual and economic forces in the land. The spread of this foreign religion from India and Central Asia suggests the tantalising possibility that with it may also have come a knowledge of Sanskrit drama.

The Sanskrit drama of India came into being at a very early date. Traditional literature attributes its maturity to a period as early as the third century BC, but it is quite certain that by about the year 300 AD it was a fully-fledged drama. Surviving texts bear witness to this. We know that in the early seventh century AD the famous Chinese Buddhist pilgrim Xuanzang visited the capital of an Indian prince who was one of the most celebrated Sanskrit dramatists.[6] An old manuscript of part of the Sanskrit play *Shakuntala* has been discovered in the twentieth century in a temple near Wenzhou in Chekiang province.[7] Wenzhou was the original home of a form of play that played a considerable part in the growth of Chinese drama. Sanskrit drama may very well have influenced and inspired the manner of Buddhist preaching, for we know that during the Tang and later dynasties preachers and story-tellers were fond of using dramatised sermons and stories strongly marked by the use of vivid dialogue. This almost certainly influenced early play-acting in China. All the same, there is no even vaguely reliable proof that Sanskrit drama became generally known or ever played a direct part in the rise of Chinese drama.[8]

There is fairly detailed mention of puppet shows during the centuries of disunity and during the brief Sui dynasty (589–618 AD). Some form of puppetry existed as early as the Han dynasty, wooden models being used for dancing and singing acts at wedding and other auspicious banquets.[9] These may have derived from mortuary figurines installed with mechanisms to allow movement similar in some ways to the mobile-limbed statues of ancient Greece and Egypt, to certain mediaeval church figures in Europe and to some African idols, all of which are sometimes also associated with the antecedents of puppetry. It is recorded that elaborate automata were made for various rulers, during the years 227–39, 559–60, and 605–17.[10] All these automata seem to have been mechanically or water-operated and were rather in the nature of intricate toys for the monarchs' amusement; they went through a limited sequence of movements, sometimes possibly enacting brief scenes as a kind of mechanised pageant, but as far as we know they had no connection with any widespread development of a puppet theatre performing actual plays. For certain evidence of puppet plays we have to wait till later ages. No doubt, however, at least at the palace level, the automata contributed something towards an acceptance of the idea of acting.

A penchant for actors is in Chinese histories often associated with a ruler's decadence. An early example of this is the case of the last monarch of the Wei dynasty (220–65), Cao Huan (r. 260–5), who would daily order two of his jesters, entertainers or actors to sport or perform naked in front of his palace. He would also take up a position at some high vantage-point and have his entertainers perform the *Witch of Liaodong* down below. This they did with such excessive levity and indecency, we are told, that passers-by covered up their eyes.[11] Unfortunately we have no precise idea of the nature of the *Witch of Liaodong*. It may well have been an acted sketch, but equally well may have been a dance or some other kind of performance.

With the Tang dynasty (618–907), surviving literature gives a strong impression of a profuse burgeoning of complexly synthetic entertainments – although records of many other aspects of this dynasty are also comparatively rich. The first century and a half or more of the dynasty saw China at one of the zeniths of its power and cultural abundance, and many works and commentaries have survived as a rich testimony to the civilisation of the period. The relative lack of literary records for some of the earlier periods may possibly give a false impression of steady growth in complexity, when the only growth may have been in enduring records. Nevertheless, one has the feeling that the records do reflect something of a reality, that the relatively peaceful conditions of the early Tang most likely did allow a blossoming and a coalescing of various aspects of the culture, and that the appearance of a strong centralised government for the whole of China may well have encouraged such tendencies.

A number of dances flourished, some of which had their roots in earlier ages.[12] The *Melody of the Prince of Orchid Mound's going into battle*, which originated in the period 550–77, concerned the story of a prince who, because of his effeminate features, wore a mask into battle. The dance seems to have involved the martialling of troops, some form of combat and the wearing of the mask.[13] It is also referred to as a 'play'. The *Botou* dance, or 'play' (*xi*), came from non-Chinese Central Asia or India. It was about a non-Chinese who was eaten by a tiger and whose son sought out the beast and killed it.[14] The theme recalls that of *Mr Huang of the Eastern Ocean*, but the similarity of the combat with a tiger could easily be no more than coincidence.

A dance-sketch called *Stepping and singing woman* was also popular during the Tang dynasty. It had first been performed during the sixth century.[15] A certain ugly scholar who lived during the period 557–81, a failure in his career and a habitual drunkard with a red nose, would illegitimately adorn himself in the rank of Government Secretary. He was forever coming home drunk and setting about his beautiful wife. She would air her grievances and lament to the neighbours, expressing her sorrows in songs which she composed and sang with great beauty. Their contemporaries made a skit on this, in which a strapping man in woman's clothing would dance or 'step' slowly on stage or into the area of performance, singing the wife's songs as he went. The songs were accompanied by string and woodwind instruments. At the end of every stanza bystanders, presumably players but quite possibly the audience, would chime in with the chorus, 'Stepping and singing come with us,/Poor suffering stepping and singing woman, come with us.' When the person playing the husband arrived and the couple had a fight, it was the occasion for great merriment among the audience.

In Tang times the wife's part came to be played by a woman, the title of Government Secretary that her husband assumed was dropped and he was simply called Uncle A, and a treasurer or storeman was added, 'entirely losing the old significance and form of the skit' according to an early source.[16] The husband was portrayed with a hat, red clothes and a crimson face to convey the idea of his drunkenness. One account says that he wore a mask. Sometimes the title of the skit was changed to *Tân Comely Maiden*. It was, at least on occasions, performed on a round stage or other area surrounded by the audience.[17] The red nose or red face and the wife-beating are regular universal stocks-in-trade of coarse farce, and the skit must have been akin to a very simple stage play, although the plot seems gossamer-thin. In one Tang work, together with *Botou* and *Melody of the Prince of Orchid Mound's going into battle*, it is placed in the same section as pole-climbing, fire-eating, sword-swallowing, juggling, tumbling and other dances.[18] In all three dance-sketches we note an element of conflict or combat.

Jester skits with two or more actors depicting all kinds of satirical and comic themes were very frequent during the Tang, and by their sheer frequency must have made the advent of more complex popular play-acting all the more probable. During a festival in 832 actors were driven from the palace for satirising Confucius.[19] In about 847, boy servants dressed as women presented a skit on the shrewish mistress of their household, causing her husband almost to faint with mirth.[20] During the period 860–74 a duo act,[21] for the emperor's entertainment, set out by means of quotations and puns to prove that Confucius, the Taoist philosopher Laozi and Buddha were all women. This time the emperor showered the leading jester with gifts and promoted him to the post of Clerk to the Inner Palace Guard. Skits also served to make fun of harsh warlords.[22] Such 'plays' seem mainly to have been in the nature of duologues between a comedian and his stooge, somewhat akin to the modern *xiangsheng* acts of Hou Baolin and Guo Qiru, but probably much less elaborate.

A kind of performance known as *canjunxi*, 'Adjutant play', was very popular during the Tang. Basically there are two accounts of its origins. According to one it was founded on the story of Shi Dan, a magistrate of Guantao during the period 89–105, who was found guilty of accepting bribes. As he valued his services the emperor pardoned him, but for years afterwards at every feast he made Dan wear a white smock and commanded the players to ridicule him.[23] Another account gives the magistrate's name as Zhou Yan or Zhou Ya and declares that he was in addition an Adjutant (*canjun*), assigning him to the period 319–33. He was convicted of misappropriating some thousands of bolts of government silk, and thereafter obliged at every big banquet to dress up along with the comedians in an official's hat and an unlined yellow silk robe. A jester would ask him, 'What sort of an official are you, roughing it with the likes of us?' 'I used to be the magistrate of Guantao', was his set reply, and then he would shake his robe and add, 'and I was had up for pinching this. That's why I've joined you lot.' This drew forth great guffaws.[24] Part of the joke must have hinged on the assumption that the players were of lowly status.

The reason for calling the Tang performance of this sketch an 'Adjutant play' may have been that the ridiculed official was an Adjutant, but one Tang source emphatically states that it was because the player Li Xianhe (Li Immortal Crane) so excelled in the playing of it, some time during the years 712–56, that the emperor awarded him the salaried sinecure of Adjutant.[25] Adjutant was regularly used as an official title only after the Han dynasty.

The Adjutant play was clearly very popular during the eighth and ninth centuries, and must have constituted a genre rather than just one act on one theme. At least it underwent alterations of its form. One variation was known as *Adjutant Lu (Lu canjun)*. The celebrated poet Yuan Zhen (779–831) witnessed a performance of this in Chekiang province – which indicates that it was widely performed in China, not only in the capital in the north but also in southerly regions. The players on that occasion were two men and one of the men's wives, a certain Liu Culling Spring, who played the Adjutant and to whom Yuan Zhen presented a poem.[26] From this poem and its context we gather a number of insights. The performance involved acting, speaking, singing, costume and make-up. Moreover, the variation known as *Adjutant Lu* was common enough for it to be referred to without further elucidation of that title. The witty recluse-poet Lu Yü (d. 804, subsequently deified as the God of Tea!) seems to have written words for an Adjutant play.[27] It is possible that the *Adjutant Lu* or *Lu Adjutant* play had something to do with him.

Another poet, the minister Xue Neng (d. 880), wrote a poem about a woman or women performing the Adjutant play in Chekiang province, to the accompaniment of strings and woodwind and possibly drums.[28] This indicates that Liu Culling Spring was not the only woman to play the Adjutant. Indeed there is further, clear evidence that women often played the role. At a feast given by an emperor during the years 756–63 actresses performed the *jiaguanxi*, 'false official play' – most probably another name for the Adjutant play, the actress who wore green clothes and held a bamboo tablet of office being called the *canjunzhuang*, 'Adjutant Pillar'. Yuan Zhen's poem also mentions the tablet. Shortly before 756 a Tatar general was executed and his wife was sent to join the ladies of the imperial palace. An excellent actress or entertainer, she was assigned to the musicians and her performance of the Pillar at a banquet amused the emperor and the other guests. Her part was termed that of the 'chief of the false officials'.[29] Besides providing proof that women performed in Adjutant plays these scraps of information prompt a discussion of the set kinds of role found in Chinese drama.

Throughout the centuries Chinese drama of most kinds has apportioned roles in a number of generalised categories. Essentially the object of this would seem to be to facilitate the organisation of the actor's training. Of course a particular part in a play would demand its particular individual characteristics and the actor's own individual stamp on its performance, but if certain characteristics were recognised for a particular range of parts, this would make it easier to organise the actor's training along particular lines and to indicate which particular skills he should concentrate on in his general training, and easier for a pupil to be assigned to a particular teacher, and for that teacher's acting and other special skills to be passed on in concentrated and enduring form. It would also give the audience a feeling of familiarity and connoisseurship, in that they would to a considerable degree come to know what to look for and expect of the actor.[30] Some parallels can be drawn with the masks of the *commedia dell'arte*,[31] but the comparison should not be taken too far. As far as we know, such role categories first arose with the *canjunxi*. A poem by Li Shangyin (813–58) mentions 'learning the Adjutant and subduing the voice to call the Grey Hawk [*canggu*]'.[32]

During the Five Dynasties period (907–60), we find the Adjutant play still being performed. An official history records that Xu Zhixun (d. 918) was always cruelly humiliating the heir to the throne of the Wu dynasty, Yang Longyan, a delicate child unable to stand up for himself. In the year 918 they were on one occasion drinking together in a wine-house. A player was ordered to join them in their drinking, and, presumably with his assistance, Zhixun played the part of the Adjutant while Longyan had to don a patched worn-out robe and arrange his hair in a hemp-strewn hair-style and play the part of the Grey Hawk.[33] Another history gives a slightly different account, declaring that Zhixun, an arrogant bully who lacked all proper deference, would torment the prince, feeling no sense of respect for his superiors. Once he went upstairs with him and subjected him to grossly familiar sport and mockery. He himself wore 'lotus robes' and held a wooden tablet of office, calling himself the Adjutant, while he ordered the prince to wear a hemp-strewn hair-style and patched, worn-out clothes and attend upon him as his Grey Head (*cangtou*).[34]

The Pillar ('post' or 'pile') seems to have meant the Adjutant part, or at least the 'chief of the false officials', which can scarcely have been anything but the Adjutant. Does the notion of 'pillar' imply the foundation, the pile, so to speak, upon which the play was built, or does it have some meaning like 'butt', something to be subjected to verbal or physical blows?[35] Or does it have both or other meanings? Clearly the performance involved some butt, like the harlequin of *Scaramouche a philosopher*, and some knave or victimiser of the butt. A fourteenth-century writer, Tao Zongyi, attempting to explain the etymology of the role categories *mo* and *jing*, says that in the past the *mo* was called Grey Hawk and the *jing* was called Adjutant because as the hawk is able to attack all the other birds so the *mo* may beat the *jing*.[36] A treatise on drama and song which was written in 1398 states that the *mo* grasps a *kegua* to beat the *jing*, 'which is why of old the *mo* was called Grey Hawk'.[37] *Kegua*, meaning something like 'knocking gourd', was some relatively harmless soft cudgel used for raining comic blows, the equivalent of the English clown's bat, the slapstick, the wooden sword or dagger of lath of Vice in Elizabethan times and the mediaeval fool's bauble, marotte or bladder filled with dried peas. Whether it was used as early as the Tang we do not know, but the later use is suggestive of some characteristics of the earlier performances.

It would seem, from such scanty evidence as has been outlined, that the Adjutant was the butt and the Grey Hawk the knave who maltreats the butt or gives him his rough deserts. Yet the example from the Five Dynasties describes them the other way round, with the Grey Hawk at the receiving end of the abuse and mockery, and clad in the rags often associated with Western traditions of the butt. Butts often evolve into knaves, and perhaps that is the explanation of the puzzle here. Perhaps the Adjutant and the Grey Hawk changed places, on that occasion at least. Grey Head (*cangtou*) is most likely a mistake for Grey Hawk (*canggu*), but normally means, as it stands, a servant who wore a grey or green hat as a decoration or an aged servant. The apparent contradictions are not easy to reconcile without some bold assumptions.

The Adjutant play, which survived into the Sông dynasty (960–1279),[38] was clearly a humorous performance. If we can rely on them at all, perhaps our brief scraps of information would suggest that people in the earlier days of the Adjutant play set some store by the finesse of singing and quieter humour, and that later there was a growing tendency towards slapstick. Both men and women specialised in the playing of the Adjutant. The likelihood is that this entertainment had a considerable effect on the nature of other stage performances during the Sông dynasty.

In the last throes of the Tang, in the year 901, the imperial palace presented a form of entertainment with seemingly more elaborate story content than the Adjutant play. It was called the 'play' (*xi*) of *Fan Kuai rescues his monarch from distress*, or the 'play' (*ju*) of *Fan Kuai pushes open the palace door*, and was written by the emperor to celebrate the defeat of a rebel, and to entertain the general who had accomplished the defeat.[39] It was based, most appropriately, on the story of the founder-emperor of the Han dynasty and his meeting with his arch-enemy in 206 BC. At the meeting his faithful henchman, former dog-butcher Fan Kuai, bravely intervened to save him from a plotted assassination. Unfortunately we have no idea how this 'play' was performed in 901, except that it was at an imperial banquet. It may, for instance, have been narrative song with dance, but the rare use of the word *ju* perhaps suggests it may have been an acted performance.

Puppet shows were popular in both palace and market-place during the Tang. One kind of show presented a jolly, rotund figure called Mr Guo or Baldy Guo, based on a certain real-life jokester. Puppet shows about Baldy Guo had been a favourite hobby of a monarch who reigned from 565 to 577, and during the Sui dynasty became so popular that the term Baldy Guo came commonly to be used to refer to puppet shows in general. The nature of the Baldy Guo shows proper was a puppet dance involving song and joking.[40] The eminent official Du You (735–812) was fond of another kind of puppet show, and once declared that his ambition after retirement was to eat a hearty meal and then, clad in an ordinary coarse-clothed jacket, ride into the markets of Yangzhou and watch Plate Bell Puppets to his fill.[41] Plate bells were a kind of cymbal deriving from the non-Chinese of Central Asia or India. Probably they were used in dances at one time, and Plate Bell Puppets may well have been a puppet dance show using such instruments. Clearly they were a common entertainment current among the ordinary populace.

The Emperor Xuanzong (r. 712–56), better known as Minghuang, 'Resplendent Emperor', had puppet shows performed by the Imperial Academy of Music (founded in 714) in the inner palace. Later, during the miserable twilight years of a forced abdication, he must still have watched puppets, and he even composed a quatrain upon them:

> They've made an old man, wood-carved, string-pulled,
> chicken-skinned, crane-haired, like the genuine thing;
> The show over in a flash, lonely, loose-ended,
> once more I am back in this dreamlike human life.[42]

The poem draws a parallel between himself and the marionettes. There are various other accounts of puppetry during the Tang. Cui Anqian, a governor in Szechwan province during the years 878–80, would hold puppet shows in front of his residence with completely free access permitted to all the soldiers and common people.[43] A rebel general would hold public puppet shows whenever he came to a new district in order to spy out the disposition of the local people.[44] Elaborate, lifelike automata or fantoccini depicting a fight between a Chinese and a Turkic general and also the famous meeting that gave the theme to *Fan Kuai rescues his monarch from distress* served to dry the tears of the bereaved at the funeral of Imperial Commissioner Xin Yunjing in 768.[45]

It was the Emperor Minghuang who established the famous Pear Orchard Conservatoire for the training of very large numbers of men and women entertainers in the Tang capital, Changan.[46] Although he came in later ages to be apotheosised as the founding father and patron deity of the Chinese theatre and the term 'Pear Orchard' came to refer to the acting profession of true drama, this conservatoire was concerned with musicians and singers rather than stage actors. One of Minghuang's main motivations in establishing it was his fondness for a kind of song, the *faqu*, which in 744 he had performed to the accompaniment of an orchestra of flutes, bells, cymbals, gongs, chiming-stones, *pipa*-lutes and other instruments. This point reminds us that in pursuing evidence for the kinds of performance more readily associated in our minds with the drama we are not necessarily looking in the right directions. Music played a very important part in the advent of the drama, and the existence of the Conservatoire must have encouraged music and the arts in general, and at least indirectly fostered latent cultural propensities towards play-acting and drama.

Many other entertainments may also have been significant in the development of drama, such, for instance, as the lavish dance devised by the imperial actor-jester-musician Li Keji (fl. 860–74) on the death of a princess.[47] He composed a lament or dirge, which brought tears to the eyes of all who heard it. Then, using the same music, he trained several thousand dancers, taking jewels and pearls from the imperial treasuries to fashion into jewellery for their hair and painting eight hundred bolts of government silk with patterns of fish, dragons and waves to serve as a carpet for them to dance upon. As they danced, the whole floor would be covered with the precious stones. Elaborate spectacles such as this may well have encouraged a taste for novel visual entertainment.

Circus-like performances of the Tang included, in addition to such common skills as tightrope-walking and pole-climbing, a variety of rarer arts: horse-riding through an alley of sharp knives;[48] rope-dancing by two pretty girls, later joined by two boys, on a tightrope a hundred feet long and nearly as high;[49] a woman balancing a pole on her head with purportedly as many as eighteen people on the pole;[50] and other breath-taking feats of balance and sword-handling.

The story is a vital element in the drama of ancient China, and we should certainly not neglect to take into consideration various forms of narrative art which flourished, and in some cases first came into existence, during the Tang. Short stories in a literary style and known as *chuanqi*, 'marvel tales', were often of a very high quality, and later served as material for the plots of many dramas, as well as no doubt giving impetus to the development of narrative techniques and entertainment habits in their own times. One of these stories, the erotic *Trip to Fairy Paradise*, was written largely in dialogue form.[51] More immediately important, one imagines, in their effect on the structure and form of play-acting, must have been the more popular and vernacular styles of story-telling.

Popularisations of Buddhist sutras and other scriptures as a means of oral preaching sometimes referred to as *sujiang*, 'popular sermons', are represented by the *bianwen*, 'Mandala texts', of the Tang and Five Dynasties.[52] The *bianwen* include both religious and secular writings, although we should not too rigidly regard these two compartments as mutually exclusive. By the early Tang dynasty the bulk of important Buddhist sutras had been translated into Chinese, and already during the preceding period of disunity the needs of popular proselytisation had called into being various hymns, psalms, parables and other means of disseminating Buddhism at a non-literary level. This process flourished under the Tang, and the *bianwen* are the written embodiment of it. In such circumstances, when the vital problem is to present a subject to a lay public in as vivid a way as possible, the line between religious and secular treatments is bound to be very thin. First came expositions of the scriptures, then Buddhist sermons or stories not directly connected with the formal canons, and finally more or less predominantly secular pieces. The secularity no doubt arose from two different tendencies: on the one hand, the preachers themselves could easily and humanly have been tempted into the secular by a quest for certain kinds of vividness and in the attempt to interest the less religiously inclined of their audiences, and, on the other, non-clerical people very probably admired the genre and imitated its form for secular themes. During the years 821–4 a priest called Wen Shu preached publicly, using the sutra fables as a pretext for 'spouting nothing but lewd filth and vulgar smut', and 'filling the monastery with doltish oafs and loose women who came to listen and pay their respects'. His style was adopted by entertainers for their songs.[53]

Among the more religious of the *bianwen* were such as the *Great Maudgalyāyana saves his mother in the Underworld*, which was current in some form at least as early as the period 806–20. There are several surviving versions.[54] The most complete one is in the British Museum and has a copyist's date of 921. The story concerns a certain Maudgalyāyana, whose mother is banished to the tortures of Hell at the end of her life because of her deceit. As a hungry demon she receives no food and is all skin and bone. Maudgalyāyana seeks her out and after appalling setbacks is able, with the help of Buddha, to save not only her but all hungry ghosts from their miseries by establishing the Avalambana festival of offerings on the fifteenth day of the seventh month. This theme was a favourite one of dramas, stories and popular ballads throughout subsequent ages. The secular story of the *Qiu Hu bianwen* was also a common theme of later tales and dramas.[55] Among the secular *bianwen*, besides those which deal with traditional and historical themes, there are some that take seemingly contemporary political and social material for their framework.

The form of the *bianwen* may well have had more effect on subsequent literature and entertainment than their content. They were often a mixture of literary and vernacular styles – prose, song, verse, rhymed proverbs and common sayings – akin in many ways to the heterogeneity of the drama, with the same sandwiches of prose between verse that one finds in the drama. Their vivid eclecticism and exuberant imagination could also have provided inspiration towards dramatic presentations. They sometimes used a mixture of different line lengths in the verse, again somewhat like the songs of early drama. It seems probable that they influenced the form of the tales of vernacular story-tellers of the Sông dynasty, and they may have sired or inspired various kinds of popular ballad. Some of them were very long, and, in their length and other stylistic characteristics, remind one of the Chinese vernacular novels. Their many drama-like features may well have set minds thinking along the path to drama. As so often in consideration of such matters, we can only say 'may'.

Tang culture flourished in many directions. Poetry knew an unprecedented age of glory, and music and song reached new heights, all no doubt pushing the arts and entertainments towards that complexity which is a fertile field for the mushrooming of drama. Yet at best we have only a lopsided picture. Surviving literature on play-like performances leans heavily towards the activities of the palace, and may only represent a small slice of the reality of the times. Village festivals and market shows must have abounded in entertainments, but were left by and large to oblivion by the writers of the times. Apart from the *canjunxi* and one or two other separate genres of literature and forms of entertainment, there is little surviving proof, however tenuous, of anything like an irresistible movement towards the creation of a theatre world. That was not to come until the Sông dynasty.

2
Sông and Jin Plays

Any conception of drama as something readily distinguishable and basically distinct from other forms of entertainment is a highly misleading one with which to approach emergent drama almost anywhere in the world, at a period before that drama has established itself as an independent art with its own distinctive institutions and traditions. In the Elizabethan period, for instance, and well into Shakespeare's heyday, drama must often have still been regarded as only one of a kaleidoscopic range of sports, pastimes and entertainments. In 1586 when Leicester's Men visited the court of Denmark, they were called 'singers and dancers'. Actors not only acted, but also 'jumped' and performed 'activities' or 'feats of activity'. That turncoat playwright, the Puritan Gosson, declared that the Devil in his seductions sent the theatres not only the beauty of their houses and stages but also: 'in gearish apparel, masks, vaulting, tumbling, dancing of jigs, galliards, moriscoes, hobby-horses; shewing of juggling casts, nothing forgot that might serve to set out the matter with pomp, or ravish the beholders with a variety of pleasure'.[1] From queen to village people shared this taste for mixed bills, for the 'medley' or 'gallimaufry' entertainment. Three, four or five plays in one was a popular formula, and clowns' vaudeville acts and spectacular afterpieces were included in otherwise solemn or lofty plays.

For all the obvious differences, the situation in China during the Sông dynasty at first sight seems startlingly similar – though the system of multiple entertainments and the social conditions favouring them persisted much longer in China, in some respects right up to the present day. There were the same multiple bills from palace to market and the same 'heterogeneous' entertainment quarters, with story-tellers, balladeers, puppeteers, medical men, mountebanks, fortune-tellers, singers, acrobats, actors, singing girls and musicians elbowing and jostling for custom together, reminding one of the famous picture of the Pont-Neuf of ancient Paris. And there was the same apparent vagueness or transferability of terminology and the same casualness about describing or recording in any detail the nature of the entertainments. After all, who was to know that drama would appear, and radically alter entertainment possibilities? It is a fairly general tendency for people to chronicle popular entertainments only when the entertainments are waning or finally disappearing.

By the beginning of the Sông dynasty most of the components of the drama already existed as established traditions: the telling of tales with drama-like plots, the singing, musical accompaniment, rhythmic backing, choruses, recitation, dialogue, dance, dressing up in costume, make-up, female impersonation of men, male impersonation of women, men and women acting their own sexes, acrobatics, clowning, song interspersed with speech, and other features were all there. During the Sông period there is ever-increasing evidence of their combining or coalescing in what we may now see as distinctive new forms of entertainment and as close forerunners to the drama.

The Sông dynasty divides into two periods: the Northern Sông dynasty began in 960 as the government of a united China with its capital at Bianliang, the present city of Kaifeng in Honan province in the north of China. It ended in 1126 after the non-Chinese Jurched people, ancestors of the Manchus, conquered the north of China and set up their own Jin dynasty (1115–1234), with present-day Peking as the site of one of their capitals. The Southern Sông dynasty (1127–1279) then came into being, and ruled the middle and southern parts of China, establishing its capital at Hangzhou in Chekiang province to the mid-south-east of China. It is during the period when the Jin and Southern Sông were sharing most of China between them that we see the greatest growth of theatre and allied entertainments.

When drama appeared in the thirteenth century it was of the kind usually referred to as *zaju*, 'miscellany play' or 'variety play'. The term *zaju* and the alternative form *zaxi* were used as early as 832, to refer to the skit on Confucius, and 829, to refer to unspecified entertainments, and also during the Five Dynasties, when the Emperor Zhuangzong (r. 923–6) often performed *zaxi* with his actors,[2] but before the Sông dynasty the recorded instances of use are fairly rare. In the Sông dynasty they refer to various kinds of sketch or play or dance-and-song presentation. In some the farcical or comic act predominated in the show or possibly even constituted the whole of it. In others the music and singing were more prominent. In addition, some were puppet plays, some were 'dumb *zaju*' (like the dumb shows of *Gorboduc*), some were called 'little *zaju*' and some were called 'big *zaju*' and some may for all we know have been acrobatic acts – for they appear listed among the Hundred Games of the Sông dynasty. On one occasion a dumb play involved two or three emaciated players powdered all over and made up with 'golden eyes' and white faces to make them look like skeletons. They wore brocade and embroidered stomachers, held 'soft staffs' in their hands and, making comic gestures and rushing around, comported themselves as if acting a play. In this instance the dumb play came during a Hundred Games show and was sandwiched between a dance duo, one of the dancers being masked and dressed in the part of Zhong Kui the fearsome ghost-catcher, and a gruesome sword-fighting act of seven people in costume lunging realistically at each other with real swords. Each item was preceded by fireworks. Other shows were called 'supernatural *zaju*' and 'rake *zaju*', the former no doubt concerned with ghosts, demons and divine beings, and the latter perhaps with romance and naughty sex.[3]

Although the records of all these kinds of *zaju* reveal differences of theme, it is quite possible that most of the *zaju* contained the same range of ingredients. Indeed, the very term that was used, *zaju* – *za* means 'variety' or 'miscellany' – surely distinguishes the genre from other more clear-cut and unambiguous entertainments such as sword-swallowing and fire-eating. If our literary records only mention one aspect of a particular instance of performance, does it necessarily mean that there were not other aspects? Most *zaju* seem, anyway, to have entailed some form of play or sketch.

Most of our records of Sông and Jin *zaju* concern performances for emperors, in the palace and elsewhere, often as one of numerous items in an extensive multiple bill of entertainments, as one of the items of a mammoth Hundred Games show, or at lengthy banquets in between goblets of wine, the serving of food dishes, and a variety of other entertainments. One Hundred Games programme lists *zaju* immediately after cock-fighting and along with Horn Butting, football, juggling and other games.[4] At other times it might occur between singing and instrumental music.[5]

There were *zaju* performed throughout the Sông dynasties, during the Jin dynasty, and also during the Liao dynasty (947–1125) – a dynasty founded by non-Chinese Khitan people in the north-east of China. Essentially the *zaju* seem to have been the same under all these dynasties. Under the Jin there was also a kind of play known as the *yuanben*, which was closely connected with the birth of the drama.

The meaning of *yuanben* is not certain. Most probably it is an abbreviation of words meaning 'texts or books of the entertainers or of the entertainers' quarters'. According to some it simply means 'brothel texts', since the actresses who performed the plays were very often singing girls and whores as well.[6] Essentially the *yuanben* and the Sông *zaju* seem to have been very similar, and it is generally convenient to treat them together, but although it also spread to the south the *yuanben* was really a northern phenomenon. Both were performed at all levels of society. They were composed by members of the imperial Music Academy and it seems that at least one emperor wrote words for *zaju*.[7] Writers' guilds or cooperative associations, known as *shuhui*, 'writing societies', wrote *yuanben* and other plays during the thirteenth century and most probably had also done so previously.[8] There were various amateur clubs or societies in Hangzhou known as Hundred Games clubs: the Level-with-the-Clouds Club for *cuju*-football, the Horn Butting Club for wrestling, the Brocade Target Club for archery, the Soaring-to-the-Clouds Club for a kind of balladry, and the Brocade Body Club for the tattooing that was so popular in those times. One called the Crimson and Green Club, most likely for young amateurs from the gentry or of 'respectable families', wrote or at least performed *zaju*.[9] It is fairly certain that uneducated players also created and improvised such plays. The households of ministers or high officials kept private troupes of players or engaged them to perform in their homes – and both of these customs have endured into recent times.

Much of the life and growth of the plays must have been at the lower and lowest levels of society. In Bianliang the 'musicians' of the theatres would perform the zaju *Maudgalyāyana saves his mother* from the Seventh Night Festival in the seventh month right up to and including the fifteenth day of the month, which was the day of a traditional Chinese festival and also of the Buddhist Avalambana Festival.[10] Almost certainly, to judge from later Maudgalyāyana plays, this too was a gallimaufry. There were no doubt numerous acrobatic and other spectacular interludes to which the vivid story and the gruesome excitements of Buddhist hell and demonry would readily lend themselves.

The Sông dynasty was a period of booming handicraft production and teeming commercial activities, with ever-increasing populations and growing cultural and social diversification in the big cities.[11] Entertainment in them became correspondingly varied and intense. Bianliang, Hangzhou and the Jin capital Zhongdu (present-day Peking) were all bustling cosmopolitan cities with huge populations. In Bianliang there were amusement quarters resembling vast fairgrounds or little towns of amusement arcades. These quarters were known as *wa*, 'tiles', *wazi*, 'tiles', *washi*, 'tile market', or *washe*, 'tile booths', and within them were a number of theatres, known as *peng*, 'awnings', *kanpeng*, 'watching awnings', *gousi*, 'hook booths', or *goulan*, 'hook balustrades'.[12] Most probably these were fairly solid enclosures with a raised stage open on three sides and hemmed in by a low railing or balustrade. There were as many as fifty or more such theatres in two of the Bianliang *wazi*, and the bigger ones, called Lotus Flower Awning, Peony Awning, Yaksha Awning and Elephant Awning, were capable of holding several thousand spectators.

When the Sông court moved south there were probably few if any *wazi* in Hangzhou, but entertainers moved there from Bianliang and after a decade or so *wazi* were established, first of all round the military camps to cater for the pleasures of the mainly northern soldiery, and then later within Hangzhou to provide places for itinerant artistes to concentrate themselves[13] (and perhaps also, one wonders, to facilitate the control and talent-spotting of artistes for imperial sprees?). There were many more *wazi* in Hangzhou than there had been in Bianliang. One list gives no less than twenty-three.[14] Besides the theatres of the old designations there now appeared some which included the word *lou*, 'tower' or 'storied building', in their names, perhaps indicating the rise of some more modern kind of theatrical structure. One theatre of the period 1266–74 was called by the composite name Sheep Awning Tower, rather as a theatre in Britain might call itself the . . . Hippodrome Theatre or the . . . Playhouse Theatre. In the last decades of the Sông dynasty a decline seems to have set in for the *wazi*. Of some our sources state, 'now abolished for commoners' dwellings', 'only the theatre now survives' or 'only one theatre now survives'.[15] Possibly some flourished at the expense of others, or perhaps the theatre was sometimes tending to monopolise the custom. We do not know.

To these amusement cities and their theatres all kinds of performers came daily to display their skills: puppeteers, shadow showmen, balladeers, comedians, tightrope-walkers, story-tellers, and an endless variety of others. Prominent among them were the players of *zaju*. These included some Music Academy actors, which shows us how unreal rigid analytical divisions into palace and populace may often be.[16] As in Elizabethan England, court and fairground were sometimes very close to each other and shared each other's entertainers.

Temporary stages were also constructed for itinerant players. We hear of an all-day competition on the opening day of spring festivities in Szechwan when stages were erected and players vied with each other to provoke the most laughter.[17] And, of course, itinerant players performed with stages anywhere they could draw an audience. Buddhist temples may also have had raised stages in front of the temple, although this point remains a matter of controversy.[18]

Whether the Sông *zaju* was a mainstream derivation from the *canjunxi* plays is open to debate, and difficult to prove one way or the other, but certainly it inherited features from them.[19] No full libretti or scenarios of Sông *zaju* survive, and what do survive are skits very much in the nature of the jester duo acts of earlier dynasties. Perhaps it would be unwise to over-emphasise the distance between skit and story, since layers of elaboration can easily transform the one into the other. Yet somehow one expects more than the skits suggest. We know of one household that would struggle through the cold weather by hugging the fire, calling for singing and dancing and *zaju*, and drinking to a high degree of inebriation.[20] Another source uses the simile 'both delighted and afraid – like a dog eating hot butter and like children watching *zaju*'.[21] A celebrated poet declared that composing poetry was like performing *zaju*: you must first set your scene, then as you near the end of it you must come in with your punch line or comic dénouement.[22] All these casual allusions perhaps suggest more than simple satiric skits, and possibly such skits are simply the only parts of the performance that have been quoted in writings, quoted casually for the sake of their point in another discussion rather than for their own sake as stage entertainment. It is clear from other indications that *zaju* in actual performance were rather more varied and complex.

In palace performances *zaju* were generally sandwiched between other entertainments on multiple bills at imperial banquets, often between dances and other shows by girl troupes, or by boy troupes made up of boys of eleven or twelve. The *zaju*, as well as the other items, were introduced by verse prologues composed by many of the intellectual luminaries of the age, such as the sparkling poet and powerful minister Su Shi (1036–1101).[23] These indicate that the *zaju* themselves were a mixture of music and comedy. By the Southern Sông it is clear that *zaju* were performed in three main sections, with the main comedy part in the middle.[24] The introductory section called *yanduan*, 'glamour section' or 'flame section', seems to have been a play too, a curtain-raiser, but much simpler and briefer in form than the main *zaju*, sometimes a one-man comic act.

The final section or afterpiece called *sanduan*, 'dispersal section', was often, if not always, made up of another comic act or play of the kind known as *zaban*, 'miscellaneous playing'. *Zaban* originated during the Northern Sông, in Bian-liang, as a comic entertainment, being then a joke-act about yokel gaffers.[25] It became very popular, and players of it from the common entertainment quarters were hired for banquets and like occasions. Attaching itself to the *zaju*, it remained comic, with some kind of story or sketch and probably dance and song. Most likely it was a slighter and briefer envoy to the main *zaju*. The stage names of *zaban* players were particularly vivid, including such as Iron Brush Soup, Rabbit Head, Dried Orange Peel, Silvery Fish, Golden Fish, Sweet Flag Head, Dimple, Vegetable Market Funster, Yangtse Fish Head and Spring Welcoming Seal. Fish Gets Water, Spontaneous Cuteness and Wang Longevity Perfume all specialised in female roles.[26]

One standard formula for the performance of the *zaju* may be reconstructed as follows. The *moni* (actor-director) would direct the show, beginning with dancing to the dance tune known as *qupo*, 'melody break'. There may have been other items at this stage such as acrobatic turns. Then the *yinxi*, 'play-leader', would lead on the main play, performed by four or five players and concentrated around the comic antics of a knave and butt. This was in the form of a story, sketch or incident, the stress being upon farcical comedy, singing, speech and recitation, with a connected theme and logical dénouement. It was expected, we are told, that it would convey a moral and that good advice would be casually given in the course of the play. This formula certainly underwent variations. It was a conven-tion that even the emperor would take the moral advice and innuendoes with a benign smile, regarding them as part of the function of the players and not deserving of punishment.[27]

It is clear that the *zaju* was not an isolated, watertight compartment but that it was allied to, involved with, and influenced by other genres of entertainment and other acts. Competition, as well as natural affinities and the quest for novelty, encouraged the different entertainments to coalesce with each other or to approp-riate features from one another. Among those which had a strong influence on the *zaju* were the *qupo* and other dance-songs such as the *daqu*, 'great melody', and the *zhuanta* or *chanda*. These dances often had story content, and must have been almost dance-dramas. Some of them were composed in suites of songs rather in the manner of the later, northern dramas.[28] The *sanyue*, 'diverse music', play also had very close affinities with the *zaju* and may even partly have merged into it. It seems originally to have been associated with non-Chinese Central Asian drum music.[29] Like the *zaju*, the *sanyue* plays inherited features from the *canjunxi* plays. This *sanyue* was a specific type of performance, not the generic *sanyue* mentioned in the first chapter.

For the Southern Sông a list survives of 280 *guanben zaju*, 'official-text miscel-lany plays'. The *guan*, 'official', is of uncertain implication.[30] It may mean 'of the government', but clearly a large number of the titles simply represent Sông *zaju* in general, some of them Northern Sông. In themselves these titles tantalisingly fail to determine beyond all doubt how full the stories of the Sông *zaju* were. Some indicate themes that were later to be treated as very extensive and complex stories in the early dramas, but those that include in them tune titles or the words *zhugongdiao*, 'key medley', *faqu*, 'dharma melody', and so on strongly suggest absorption from other entertainments and a wide motley of form and presentation. Some were most likely the simple duo acts in which slapstick farce and quickness of tongue were the main appeal. A number of coloured tiles and pictures concerning *zaju* and *yuanben* have survived. One of these pictures depicts what is undoubtedly the play *Eye-medicine Suan*, which was both a Sông *zaju* and a *yuanben*.[31] It shows two characters on stage, one an eye doctor and the other a *jing* clown who is having his eyes seen to. Very probably this was a simple butt and knave situation, though one can by no means be sure.

The earliest account of a *yuanben* performance – and indeed the earliest detailed account of a visit to a theatre in China – is probably the merry, robust long poem by Du Renjie (c. 1190–c. 1270) entitled *Farmer's first visit to the theatre*.[32] After a good harvest the farmer takes a trip into town, and, attracted by a gaudy poster with a crowd around it and by the shouts of the man keeping the theatre door, he pays his money, and goes in. The seating is arranged in a slope, presumably benches, with perhaps a pit for standing audience around the stage. On the stage are women musicians playing drums and gongs. After an introductory act the first play begins, a *yuanben* called *Fixing the romance*. It involves at least three characters: a wealthy man, a waiter and a pretty girl; and there are probably a magistrate and one or two other characters too. Catching sight of the pretty girl, the rich man sends the waiter to try and seduce her into marriage by fair promises. She has a sharp-edged and nimble tongue, and at last the exasperated squire lashes out, presumably at the waiter, and smashes his 'leather baton' in two. This may well have led up to a court scene, one of those beloved episodes of humorous Chinese plays, but at this point laughter, bringing on the pressures of nature, forces the farmer to leave the show, much to his regret. He misses not only the end of the *yuanben* but also the drama to which it is the curtain-raiser.

Another poem, by Gao Andao of the thirteenth or early fourteenth century, also enacts a visit to the theatre, where it turns out that a thoroughly decrepit and maladroit troupe are performing.[33] Among those present are a rough-tough chucker-out or doorkeeper, a ruffian audience, a most unsavoury flautist and drummer, and a peppermint vendor. Women musicians seated on the *yuechuang*, 'music bench', are ugly and sluttish, their eyes sweeping the audience for whoremongering customers. The bill is introduced with singing, then comes a fiasco of clod-hopping dancing, followed by acrobatics during which the performers become entangled in their flags and streamers, a stilt-walker (or stilt-walkers) nearly comes to grief, a back-flipper seems about to break himself in pieces, and various other players equally fail to impress. A demon act is a complete flop, utterly unable to chill any spines. Then follows what must surely be a *yuanben*, insipidly presented, and this in turn gives way to an execrably executed drama, murdered by an uncouth bunch of actors led by an unsightly female role who clutches her book of words in her grubby fingers. A *sanduan* rounds off the dismal bill.

These and other Yuan and Ming descriptions provide invaluable insights into the *yuanben*, but they are all rather late. Even Du Renjie's poem was almost certainly written after the end of the Jin dynasty. Our earliest and fullest direct source of information on the *yuanben*, the scholar and compiler Tao Zongyi, is also very late for our present discussions. Tao Zongyi, who lived in the middle of the fourteenth century, left some brief but important comments on the genre and a list of over seven hundred titles of *yuanben* plays.[34] This information no doubt reflects the situation in Tao's times, but does it represent what was performed under the Jin? A number of titles are the same as those of the *guanben zaju*, and a further number seemingly indicate the same themes. This helps to confirm the basic identity of the *yuanben* with the Sông *zaju*. Some of the other titles are identical with those of the drama to come; these *yuanben* and many others may well have had stories, however briefly sketched. Other titles suggest performances more in the nature of modern *xiangsheng* comic duos, in which the appeal lies in the cleverness of the smartly skipping tongue. In some singing, dancing or acrobatics was prominent. As in the case of the Sông *zaju*, some clearly derived from or utilised other forms of entertainment, the *daqu*, the *faqu* and others. The *yuanben* must have included a wide variety of formal nuances, if not some major divergencies in presentation.

Plays termed *yuanben* or named by other synonyms continued to be acted well into the Ming dynasty (1368–1644). Sometimes, as we have seen, a *yuanben* was a curtain-raiser for a drama or one item on a multiple bill. At other times on country stages, in private residences, and in generally more casual circumstances a number of *yuanben* may have been performed together. Basically a northern phenomenon, though closely allied to certain nation-wide traditions, the *yuanben* came to·be incorporated within the dramas of both north and south as comical or farcical intermezzi. Only a few reliable examples of the *yuanben* survive, one or two incorporated into plays and one or two independent ones, all from the fourteenth to sixteenth centuries. The earliest actually marked as a *yuanben* is found in the drama *Meeting of immortals* by the imperial prince Zhu Youdun (1379–1439). The theme of the whole play is the conversion of the aberrant Angel of the Peaches of Immortality to the virtues that merit immortality. The angel is banished to earth and there incarnated as a courtesan, so that she may experience to the full the four cardinal vices of 'wine-drinking, sex, greed for money and wrath', and overcome them. Several gods are sent to assist her, incognito. Four of these gods, Han Xiang, Zhang Guo, Li Yue and Lan Caihe, all disguised as itinerant entertainers, provide a *yuanben* as part of the entertainments at a party thrown by the courtesan for the birthday of her beau, Scholar Shuang. The *yuanben* occupies approximately half an act, and is basically an expression of the customary birthday wishes for long life. The four entertainers assume the roles of *fumo, jing, moni* and *jieji*, all acting the parts of Star Gods of Longevity who come to convey their propitious wishes and to present auspicious gifts. The *fumo* and *jing* have the major parts, but the *moni* opens the play, and the *jieji* also seems to have some prerogative of introductory functions early in the play. None of these terms has a very clear etymology, but perhaps they may be translated as 'assistant man', 'adjutant', 'leading man' and 'captain' respectively.[35]

Yuanben from *Meeting of immortals* by Zhu Youdun

JIEJI.	As the sound of song dies away,
MONI.	and strings and wood a while shall pause,
JING.	we four together now advance
	with our histrionic masterpiece.

FUMO.   And what divine diversions of pure genius are we about to deliver?

JIEJI.   It is Scholar Shuang's birthday today, so we must each provide a line of poetry conducive to long life.

	Green of pine and cypress all four seasons perseveres,
FUMO.	Gifts of divine fungus borne by fairy cranes and deer,*
MONI.	Peaches of immortality at Gold Mother's feast by Jasper Mere,†
JING.	And may you live every day of one thousand eight hundred years!‡

FUMO.   (*Beats* jing) That's not poetry! Let's have something better than that!

JING.   Well, may you live every day of two thousand nine hundred years!

FUMO.   That's not poetry, either.

JING.   I've got it! I've got it!

> And may you live thirty-three thousand three hundred years,
> with white moustache and eyebrows, and white whiskers round
>   your ears!

FUMO.   Excellent! Now you really are speaking like a Star God of Longevity!

JIEJI.   Now I shall ask each of us to give him a birthday present in token of our wishes that he may enjoy a long life.

> I give a pair of pictures
> whereon three people you may see:
> Star Lord of Joy, Star Lord of Wealth,
> and Star Lord of Longevity.

FUMO.	I give a pair of pictures
	whereon four plants you may see:
	green pine and kingfisher cypress,
	dwarf bamboo and mushrooms of longevity.
MONI.	I give a pair of pictures
	whereon two creatures you may see:
	a Yellow Crane bringing gifts of wine,
	a deer bearing flowers, to wish longevity.

---

*The cypress, pine, fungus, cranes and deer were all symbols of longevity or conventionally associated with longevity.

†The Gold Mother of Heaven traditionally presided over feasts by the Jasper Mere or Jasper Pond, at which the Pan-peaches of Immortality were eaten.

‡The customary wish is always a round number, a thousand or ten thousand.

JING. (*Capering to and fro*) I've got a present, too!
>> I give a pair of pictures
>> whereon a 'target'* you may see:
>> I don't know, but everyone says
>> they're 'spring pictures'† and good for vitality!

FUMO. (*Beats* jing) What sort of a birthday present is that to give someone!

JING. I only wanted to wish him a '*sex*tra' long life!‡ (*Capering to and fro*) Now each of us must give Scholar Shuang a birthday present of two musical instruments, one string and one woodwind, to embody our best wishes for a long and happy life.

JIEJI. I give him a jade mouth-organ and a silver zither, and here is just one little ditty to the tune '*Drunk in days of great peace*' to wish him a happy birthday and long life:
>> (*Sings*) Jade mouth-organ and silver zither,
>> as birthday gifts I bring you hither,
>> to wish you long and happy life,
>> their propitious tones a-ringing
>> like phoenixes a-singing
>> in sweet harmony together,
>> beguiling gods with their blessings to fall
>> into this dwelling, into this hall.
>> With this mouth-organ of jade
>> you may blow forth tunes of cheer and ease,
>> Upon this silver zither
>> you can pluck the latest melodies.
>> Come now, all you Star God players,
>> let us join our birthday prayers
>> to wish him a thousand years of life
>> free from trouble, free from strife.

MONI. I give him a dragon flute and a brocade psaltery, and here is just a little song, to wish him happy birthday and a long life:
>> (*Sings*) Finger the dragon flute
>> and you shall hear a phoenix trill,
>> Pluck the brocade psaltery
>> and there shall flow a lilting rill.
>> Star Gods, as at this party you entertain,
>> wish him ten thousand springtimes
>> and ten thousand more again.
>> Come, psaltery,
>> you 'silkworm of ice',§ spit forth your strands clear and pure,
>> Come, flute,
>> you bamboo of purple, tune forth in harmony steady and sure.
>> Bearing this dragon flute and brocade psaltery,
>> I wish you times of peace and calm prosperity.

---

*Some pornographic depiction.

†The usual term in Chinese for pornographic or titillating pictures.

‡At least there seems to be some such pun in the Chinese, with the sentence semantically splittable in two ways.

§The term refers to a fabulous, beautiful silkworm. Stringed instruments and their notes were often referred to by images of silk and ice, alluding to the smoothness and purity of the music.

Now let my toast to you be made
in fragrant liquor from jugs of jade.

FUMO.   And I give a mandolin and a violet piccolo, with just a little song to wish him a happy birthday and long life:

(*Sings*) Strum the mandolin and its graceful rhythms glide,
blow the purple pipe and its even tones coo and slide.
With mandolin and piccolo
we come to entertain,
For your pleasure at this banquet
we tune this dulcet strain.
With mandolin you may convey
your yearnings for eternity,
With piccolo you can commune
with celestial divinity.
Come now, Star Gods of Long Life
and offer your congratulations,
to wish him now a ripe old age
mid laughing jubilations.

JING.   (*Capering to and fro*) Don't forget little me. I've got a one-string banjo and a one-hole pipe, and here is just one song to wish you a happy birthday and long life:

(*Sings*) Twang this wooden cotton-fluffing bow,*
and with this blow-pipe† your firewood blow!
These two instruments are a very special treasure
that afford this merry-andrew‡ pleasure beyond measure.
If you go cotton-fluffing with this cotton-fluffing bow,
you can make a fluffy downy, keep you cosy frost or snow.
If you go puffing faggots with this blow-pipe good and strong,
it will furnish you with cooked meals your whole life long.
Yes, with these two gifts, all winter through
he'll get a proper meal and never freeze.
My gifts are much more use, I tell you plain and true,
than your whistles and guitars and tweedledees.

FUMO.   (*Beats* jing) You clown with all your blarney and clever tommy-rot.

JING.   Let us now proclaim the cast and bill, just run through all the lot:

FUMO.   Lan Caihe§ claps castanets of sandalwood in his hand,

JING.   Han Zhongli bears the True Words¶ so all may know and understand.

FUMO.   Iron-Crutch Li blows his fife with skipping whistle and skirl,

---

*A bow-like instrument used in the cotton-spinning industry for fluffing out the cotton and separating cotton from cotton-seeds.

†A pipe used, like a bellows, for blowing air into a fire and increasing the heat, to help light fires.

‡He directly refers to himself here as *fujingsedi*, '*fujing* role'. See below, pages 26 ff.

§The ten people named here and below are all Taoist gods, being the usual Eight Immortals, minus, for some reason, Angel-maid He, and plus Gaffer-god Xu, the jester Dongfang Shuo, and White Jade-Toad. Four of them are acting in this *yuanben*. Perhaps the others are mentioned with reference to the play as a whole. The Eight Immortals appear in Act One as scholars, and in Acts Three and Four as Star Gods of Longevity. Scholar Shuang is in fact the mortal disguise of Lü Dongbin.

¶Literally, 'The book with the truth' – perhaps taken here in the double sense of the immortal truth and of the true words of the script, the prompt book?

JING.	White Jade-Toad flutters in dance, sleeves and skirts a-whirl.
FUMO.	Master Han Xiang reels off lines, flawless flowers of wonder,
JING.	Zhang Guolao pounds his drum with booms like peals of thunder.
FUMO.	Imperial Uncle Cao great songs in mighty tones resounding sings,
JING.	Gaffer-god Xu leisurely strums, caressing his dulcimer strings.
FUMO.	Dongfang Shuo is learning the player's comic arts,
JING.	And Lü Dongbin is director* to run them through their parts.
FUMO.	Immortals one and all, perform their play upon this stage
JING.	To wish you a thousand autumns, a merry life and ripe old age.
FUMO.	But what role, might I ask, is your choice, buffoon boy?†
JING.	Comptroller of Artistes in the Court of Ample Joy!
FUMO.	(*Rounding off*) Worldly wealth and comely women, and wine in sumptuous bowers,
	all these are things that bring mortal men delight and joviality.

How far this example from the early Ming is typical of Jin and Yuan *yuanben* is difficult to tell. One strongly suspects that its material is somewhat less vigorous and more decorous than the *yuanben* performed as a more independent unit of a bill of entertainment, but even here one finds the characteristic occurrence of bawdiness and coarse suggestion. Formal features are, for our present purpose, much more interesting than thematic ones. In form this example must have been generally recognisable as a *yuanben* during the first decades of the Ming dynasty. Apparently introduced by music and song, it was a short play that could be used for a brief interlude of entertainment at an informal occasion, although we cannot assume that that was its only use. Verse and song occupy a large proportion of the words: of the total 722 Chinese syllables, 502 are found in rhymed verse, 108 in other poetic forms, and only 112 in prose speech. The style of language ranges from concise, and sometimes difficult, classical Chinese to looser colloquial. The *jing* tends to speak and sing most colloquially. The verse forms are quatrains of generally even lines (*shi*, seven-syllabled *jueju‡*), *qu* of uneven line lengths and making liberal use of *chenzi*, 'padding words'§ and seven-syllable couplets. Distinct sections may readily be perceived in this *yuanben*. After an introductory couplet, unrhymed, the first section consists of each character submitting a line for a quatrain. The second section consists of each giving a picture, explained in a quatrain. In the third section each of them gives two musical instruments; these are presented in each case by means of a *qu* song describing the virtues of the gifts. In each of these first three sections the *jing* makes his contribution last of all, and his comedy or folly in each case earns him a beating from the *fumo*. The fourth and final section is a rapid-fire duet between *fumo* and *jing*, each alternately contributing a line for a continuous series of eight couplets, all the alternate lines in

---

*Or perhaps 'prompter to remind them of their [singing] parts'.
†Again the reference is directly to the role category *fujingdi*, i.e. *fujing*.
‡The *jueju* was a verse-form having four equal lines, of five or seven syllables each, to the stanza.
§See page 56.

the Chinese rhyming in the same sound. Finally, the *fumo* concludes the *yuanben* with a conventional *yuanben* couplet of conclusion, unrhymed. Immediately following the *yuanben*, Scholar Shuang remarks, 'I thank you most gratefully, sir actors, for your impromptu play. Indeed it was a splendid, saucy piece, rendered most eloquently.'

Certainly much of the form and some of the content of this *yuanben* must have been typical of the earlier *yuanben*. The introductory piece, the bawdiness, the slapstick, the comical or slapstick dénouement, and the rounding off recitation using stock phrases are also features in evidence in the few other Ming examples of *yuanben* and probable *yuanben*.[36] These few examples are very late, but we can be reasonably confident that they were akin in much of their spirit and form to earlier *yuanben*. There is a fair amount of singing in this *yuanben* and a similar amount of singing is found in one or two other surviving examples. Certainly *yuanben* must often, although not always, have included some singing, but they tended to be thought of, in contradistinction to the drama, in terms of speech, recitation, acrobatics and comic antics.

During the Ming dynasty there arose a short, more especially literary play form also termed *yuanben*, typified by the *Wolf of Mount Zhong* by Wang Jiusi (1468–1551). While this bore certain features in common with what we know of the earlier *yuanben*, principally its shortness and its tendency towards humour, it was in other ways very different in form and spirit and is definitely to be regarded as a different genre. In the late years of the Ming dynasty, however, the Music Academy was still performing a few traditional *yuanben*, and there were also plays called *guojin*, 'intermezzo brocade', performed in the palace at imperial entertainments.[37] The *guojin* were lusty farces, a mixture of finesse and vulgarity, very close to the *yuanben*, regarded as such, and probably no more or less than the old *yuanben* under a new label.

There can be no doubt that comedy was the prime characteristic of the Sòng *zaju* and the Jin and other early *yuanben*. They were acted by very few players, generally no more than four or five.[38] The central role categories were the *fujing* (*jing*) and the *fumo*, direct descendants of the *canjun* and *canggu* respectively. The *fujing* was the clown with his painted face, and the *fumo*, his partner in comedy, would belabour him with his *kegua*, a piece of felt-padded wood wrapped in soft leather, or with some other cudgel.[39] Although the *fumo* had physically the upper hand, his tended to be the more serious role of the two, and the *fujing* was the main comic attraction. Sometimes, however, the butt and knave may have reversed roles, and the *fumo* have suffered the blows. In addition there were a *moni* and a *yinxi* (and in the *zaju*, a *xitou*, 'play-head'). They took part in the performance, and sang and danced, but as far as we can tell they were not part of the central story, having rather prologue and introductory duties. Perhaps they should be regarded as stage functionaries rather than as role categories, although the *moni* in particular may have played an increasingly active part in the play itself.* (In one later southern drama '*moni*' was used as an equivalent to the leading, young male role.) In addition there could also be added a *zhuanggu*, 'act-official', playing dignified government officials or gentry parts, or a *zhuangdan*, 'act-female', playing female roles. There were a large number of other terms for what may sometimes have been role categories, but were probably often type characters. The line between the two is sometimes fine, and in fact the *zhuanggu* seems to have failed to hold its place, and in the early drama to have fallen back to the status of type character. The *baoer*, 'bustard', included bawds, veteran whores and middle-aged and old women in general, and the *suan*, 'sour, intellectual-looking one', played scholar types.

. Also during the Sông dynasty there existed in the south what is known as Wenzhou *zaju* or Yongjia *zaju*. It originated during the years 1119–25 under the Northern Sông in the Wenzhou area of Chekiang province.[40] It did not become widely popular till the Southern Sông, when it broadened its appeal by including a wider variety of songs and tunes in its repertoire, creating a mixture of *ci* tunes† and common melodies. Its popularity was secured during the years 1190–4 by the appearance of two plays, *Zhao Chaste Maid* and *Wang Kui*, and it probably flourished until around the 1270s. Thereafter the northern drama came to predominate, but it continued to be performed, and in the 1360s its fortunes were revived, its nature somewhat altered by the successful appearance of the play *Lute* by Gao Ming, who also came from the Wenzhou region. Besides the names Wenzhou *zaju* or Yongjia *zaju* the genre is also known as *nanxi*, 'southern play', and as *xiwen*, 'play-text'.

The plays *Zhao Chaste Maid* and *Wang Kui* both concerned scholar heroes who proved unfaithful to their virtuous wives and were in the end destroyed, in the one case by thunder and lightning and in the other by ghostly retribution. The first of these plays seems to have been banned by the government, along with a number of others.[41] Was it because of its treatment of the scholar gentry? Or is that too fanciful or too simple an explanation? The earliest surviving play of the *nanxi* is *Top Graduate Zhang Xie* by an anonymous author most probably of the mid or late thirteenth century. Its theme, too, is the scholar unfaithful to his wife. He even wounds her with his sword, in a dastardly manner, yet in the end the two are happily, if surprisingly, reunited. The play is comic in style and it is tantalising, although unwarranted, to imagine that it may have been written as a partly tongue-in-cheek response to the ban, with the scholar allowed to survive but in a somewhat ridiculous manner. This play, too, was written in Wenzhou, by a *shuhui* ('writing society') or a member of one. For a glimpse at the vigour and richness of this play, which may well have been equalled or surpassed by many others of the period that have been lost to posterity, let us take a look at its prologue. This

*The *jieji*, who in the late fourteenth and early fifteenth centuries seems principally to have provided a comic prelude, may have performed functions similar to the *moni* and *yinxi*, but the nature of the *jieji* during the Sông and Jin is not clear.

†See page 55.

prologue is in *zhugongdiao* ballad form,* and is followed by other genres of entertainment, again illustrating the medley nature of drama and the intercommunion of various kinds of performance in the times under consideration. Most of the prologue is actually in *ci* verse, but here the spoken verse, apart from the two *shi* poems, is written as continuous prose in order to give a clearer visual picture of the alternation of speech and song. The *sheng* mentioned in this excerpt is a role category in southern drama, that of the leading young male role.†[42]

Top Graduate Zhang Xie: Prologue

PROLOGUE.   Time hurries our hair white, and years change our ruddy cheeks. Life in this drifting, shifting world wholly resembles stems of duckweed driven hither and thither. Along the path the scarlets and purples vie in splendour. Outside the window, orioles trill and swallows chatter. And when the flowers fall, the whole garden is empty. Such is the way of the world, and let it be. For what use is toil and fret!

But amongst us here, though scions of patrician families we be, everyone is versed in the strumming of strings and the blowing of woodwind; not only do we spill song and poesy of gay romance, not only are we thoroughly accomplished in miming, gestures, and quick-fire repartee, but neither do we stint the painted clownery and farce by which we fill the hall with song and laughter. Yes, just like the Yangtse with its thousand-foot waves, we are a very different, quite a special 'stream' of tradition!

Cease now your hubbub, pause a little in your merry conversation, and let us take a look at another, unique line of entertainment. In the manner and style of the Music Academy, and worthy of mention in the same breath as the Crimson and the Green,‡ we entertain you with our endless flow of lyric charm, our banter and joking repartee, and when you hear our disquisition all present will be filled with wonder. For we are no whit comparable to those upstart learners who wantonly boast fictitious fame! Previous performances have enacted the story of *Top Graduate Zhang Xie* for you, but now this writing society wishes to bear the palm, and to reign supreme for prolific achievements in all Eastern Ou,§ we shall sing forth the motive of our play in a *zhugongdiao*. The golden basins¶ resound, so, noble sirs, I bid you pray be silent, and we shall let you hear our minute exposition.

(*Sings*) Zhang Xie had pored through all the classics
              yet still not risen to the fame that was his due,
          So to take the spring exams and win his laurels
              alone a while he left his home, and bade his parents fond adieu.
Yes, he regarded 'all things in this world as inferior, and only study a noble enterprise'. And what of Zhang Xie's home? He lived in Xichuan,** and who in Chengdu prefecture did not know the man? Who was there who did not respect and admire him! For truly he was at the classics and histories from morning till evening, reading them in the daytime,

---

*See page 35.
†See page 86.
‡This was the name of a Hangzhou *zaju* 'club' or 'society' (*shuhui*). See above, page 16.
§Eastern Ou being the region of Wenzhou prefecture in Chekiang province.
¶A term meaning 'gongs', based on a dialectal pun.
**i.e. Szechwan province.

and revising them at night, his mouth never pausing in its chant, his hands never ceasing the unfolding of the pages. Ah yes, indeed, 'In the furnace for refining medicines there is no resting fire, and beneath the student's window the lamp flickers ever on.' Suddenly one day, he went into the main apartment, and announced to his mother and father: 'This is the year of the Great Competition.* Your son wants to go to the capital to take the examinations, and requires some travel expenses for his upkeep on the journey that faces him.' Anything else would not have disturbed his parents so, but when they heard these words two rows of tears at once descended their cheeks. 'For ten years,' their son said, 'I have been studying the civil and military arts, and now this year I shall sell my studies to the Imperial House. I am going to give our family a change of dwelling, a higher station in life. – Why weep?'

(*Sung*) 'Some while ago I dreamt a dream that rent my heart,
   that cast me into gloomy meditations:
   You have never wandered far in all your student days,
   – how will you bear such trials and tribulations?'

'Since ancient times,' their son replied to his mother and father, 'it has always been said, "If at the first watch you muse, and at the second watch you ponder, then at the third watch you'll be dreaming." In general life's circumstances and human nature are not susceptible to external constraint, and dreams are illusions, not reality. Life and death as a whole are decided by predestined fate, and wealth and splendour derive from Heaven. So what is the point of worrying?' His mother and father, seeing their son so desperate to go, had no alternative but to give him several taels of gold and silver to serve for the costs of his travel. Repeatedly they enjoined him, saying, 'It is not yet late, so first find some lodgings for the night, and do not cross the pass until cock-crow. Whenever you come to a bridge, you must dismount from your horse, and when you come to a ferry, do not strive to be first.' Assenting to his parents' loving commands, their son took his leave of them.

(*Sings*) Loath, from his village he wended his way,
   turning his face to keep home in sight
   there beneath the clouds of white,
   and secretly brushed his tears away.
   As far as the eye could see the wild land lay,
   no travellers' inn far or near,
   and all that he could hear
   was the plashing of flowing streams at play.

But we must not digress long-windedly! That day, as he journeyed on, his heart felt sore and heavy. At home, he had never been conscious of the ploughing in springtime, nor aware of the harvesting in autumn. Truly a tender loving mother she was to spoil him thus! The classics of poetry and history had ever been his companions, and his writing-brush and inkstone had been his only tools of trade. If his path had kept to level ground, well and good, but how of all things was he to tramp a high mountain, the one called Five Chickens Mountain!

'How can it be so tall! Towering into the blue sky, looking as if it soars straight into azure Heaven. Wild geese and swans could not fly over it. Apes and gibbons would fear to try and climb it. Craggy, jagged, steep, sheer, how on earth can a man tread the tracks of ravens! Wheeze, heave, puff, pant, for this place you need your rattan staffs made with

*The triennial Civil Service examinations.

sharp points! Yes, others mount on the smooth – why do I alone have to clamber up through the clouds! Even though I have never attended a feast by the Jasper Mere of Heaven,* you would think I was some unemployed deity adrift in the world! The wild monkeys yell to their young, and from afar you can hear their moaning, moaning, howling and yowling. Falling leaves take leave of their stems here all around, fluttering, fluttering, whispering, rustling down. Ahead of me lies no wanderers' tavern, and behind me stands no human habitation.

> (*Sings*) 'In the north wind that scours the land
> loose specks of willow-floss streak,
> High on the mountain no tavern stands,
> the scene is desolate and bleak.
> Where shall I curl my limbs now day is done?
> Darkly I brood: my road has still so far to run.'

But before he reached the end of his road, he suddenly encountered a weird wind softly whistling, that set reeds and leaves stirring, floating, wild birds calling in alarm, and mountain monkeys vying to outyell each other. And all at once appeared a wild beast, with flashing golden eyes like two copper bells, with a brocade body of exquisite hues and patterns just like half a span of some sunset-cloud damask, and with a set of teeth like rows of keen blades and eighteen claws closely spread like steel hooks, that leapt from the waves of the forest, and raced along the wild and grassy path straight towards him. So filled with dread was Zhang Xie that his wits fled from him and his senses ebbed, and he flopped in a faint upon the ground. An instant later, he heard the sound of shoes, the ring of footsteps, and, raising his head, perceived straightway that it was no beast but a man. And why, the man was dressed up in tiger-skin helmet and tiger-skin robe! But what for? His two eyes burning bright, the man roared in bold fury: 'Lay down your gold and jewels, and I'll spare your life. But if you refuse at all, I shall have no mercy on you!'

(*Prologue makes gestures or actions.*)

Zhang Xie with deference declared:

> (*Sings*) 'A student I am, pray have pity,
> I'm going to take the Examinations,
> I'm bound for Changan city,
> And with these trifling provisions
> I hope to pay my way along the route.
> I beg your mercy – do not rob me,
> do not leave me destitute.'

The robber paid no heed to his words, but, anger surging from his heart and vicious malice rising from his gall, with his left hand wrenched hold of Zhang Xie's hair, and with his right hand grasped a shining, gleaming, cold, whistling, rat-tail shaped sword. He turned the sword over to its blunt edge, and hacked at Zhang Xie's flesh, right and left, beating him until he was mute with agony, then snatched from him his baggage, gold and jewels.

---

*A lake in the Taoïst Jade Heaven by which feasts are held and divinities partake of the 'peaches of immortality'.

At this juncture, what fate lies in store for Zhang Xie? The crow and the magpie share the same branch* – there is no telling whether it will go ill or well for him. And now, rather than thus narrate and sing of these things in a *zhugongdiao*, why not perform the story? You actor-gentlemen behind, attune your drums in sprightly fashion and throw in a stirring concert prelude for good measure, and let our leading man† give us a dance into the bargain.

(*Enter* sheng.)‡

SHENG.   Are you in tune yet?

(*All say they are.*)

SHENG.   May I trouble you, I would thank you now for the gift of an overture.
ALL.   Not at all, 'tis we who are troubling you, young sir.
SHENG.   Well, young gentlemen-entertainers to the rear, let us have a 'Candle-shadows sway their red'§ as our overture to send us on our way.

(*All sound their musical instruments.* Sheng *goes through the movements of his dance.*¶)

SHENG.   Ah, lovely! What truly gay and fascinating skills I do possess! Now I find there's no fun in wielding the clappers or 'fire-leaping'; polo and 'ball-shooting' are a sheer waste of energy; and I feel no zest for playing the flute or pipes, and I'm sated with quipping and smart repartee,** so for my entertainment I shall rely on song. As I come and as I go, I must requite you with a poem, and in between I'll slip in some laughter for good measure, so that this audience may be merry and mellow. Just now I heard a strain of music. I wonder who was playing it?
ALL.   'Candle-shadows sway their red'!
SHENG.   Might I have the loan of a ritornel?
ALL.   Certainly.
SHENG.   Very well then, I shall assume the likeness of a Zhang Xie.
ALL.   Much obliged.
ZHANG XIE.
          (*Sings*) In the gay boudoir the quiet conduces intimate pleasures,
                    the broidered curtain drapes to shield the vernal bed,
                    Glittering its ripples the passing cup brims verdant liquor
                    Deep in the night the candle shadows sway their red.††

---

*Traditionally the crow was the harbinger of ill, and the magpie the harbinger of happy news.
†The Chinese has *monise*, thus associating the functions of *sheng* and *moni*.
‡It is this *sheng* who plays the part of Zhang Xie in the play proper. Here he is still appearing as the actor and not as the part. For a discussion of the role category of *sheng*, see pages 86 and 105.
§The title of a *ci* song. Wedding candles were red, and the title itself is somewhat suggestive.
¶Possibly a rhythmic pacing, accompanied by patter, but this prelude by the *sheng* contains a number of cruxes.
**These are presumably all entertainments that could normally be used to 'send off' the main play. Polo was a full formal court game, but here must imply some stage game using balls. 'Fire-leaping' and 'ball-shooting' must likewise have been some such stage entertainment.
††This is a spoken, even-lined *shi* verse. The text says that it is sung, but is almost certainly mistaken.

(*All respond.*)

ZHANG XIE.   (*Sings, to the tune 'Candle-shadows sway their red'*)
                            Candle-shadows sway their red,
                            congenial to our wanton straying,
                            – What delights now lie ahead!
                            Things weird and wonderful well worth your viewing
                            are woven in the splendours we now spread.
                            Truly in the Pear Orchard Academy style,
                            and who but our tutors could match our wit and guile!
                            The Nine Mountains* Writing Society is all the rage these days,
                            with a very special savour, a unique flavour to its plays.

(*Applause.*)

                            Smear on your zany's black-face, and lime your skin clown-white,
                            caper forth, hop to and fro, for everyone's delight.
                            Especially since all present are gents of celebrated sort
                            whom we've seen here before to give us their support.
                            But now behold, a novel marvel we unfold,
                            – Let fresh lyrics spill, and fresh tunes come trill!
                            And you, kind sirs, I bid you hush, by your leave,
                            watching eyes are not easy to deceive,
                            we wait your verdict to receive.
                  (*Says*) In Xichuan dwelt Zhang Xie's family since days of yore,
                            there many years by 'cock-window'† over books he was wont to
                                  pore.
                            His mind was set on the emperor's court, to assist his illustrious
                                  lord,
                            but glory's hour eluded him, and sorely fretting, his lot he deplored.
                            From the one-inch tip of his writing-brush, that was steeped with
                                  ancient and modern lore,
                            often across the walls a-winging his cloud-trail calligraphy would
                                  soar:
                            'Success, fame, wealth and splendour, such are human desires,
                            but now I know that everything comes only when Heaven
                                  requires.'‡

---

*Jiushan, either the town in Anhwei province, or, more probably, referring to the famous Nine Moun-
tains of China, or to something unknown. This writing society must have written or revised this play.

†i.e. in his study. This term derives from the story of Sông Chuzong of the Tsin dynasty (265–420),
who acquired a Perpetually Crowing Cock-bird, which he placed in a cage at his study window. The cock
spoke in human fashion, and would converse all day with Chuzong in a manner that enabled him to make
remarkable progress with his studies.

‡As well as sandwiching the 'Candle-shadows sway their red' song between two even-line spoken *shi*
poems, this poem serves to introduce the play proper, as the *sheng* embarks upon the start of the actual
story, and begins to abandon his role as compère and fully to assume the identity of Zhang Xie

Last night Zhang Xie had a dream that boded ill. I must just look out a few friends, and ask their advice about it [. . .]*

A few other whole *nanxi* of the thirteenth and fourteenth centuries survive besides a large number of fragments. The titles of a number of these correspond to those of the list of *guanben zaju*. What was the relationship during the Southern Sông between the Wenzhou *zaju* and the general run of Sông *zaju*? It is most likely that they were intimately connected, either because at first they were essentially the same thing, or because the Wenzhou plays were a local offshoot and development of the mainstream *zaju*, an offshoot which itself eventually became the most popular kind of play.

In concentrating on obviously drama-like entertainments we inevitably once more neglect others that may have had as much or still greater effect on the drama. Puppets, for instance, were a considerable vogue during the Sông dynasty. Among them there were rod puppets (*zhangtou kuilei*), marionettes (*xuansi kuilei*), various kinds of automata, and shadow shows (*yingxi*).[43] Puppet shows were performed in the streets, in the *wazi* and in the palace. In the palace they entertained the emperor and also foreign ambassadors. Some puppeteers performed both in the *wazi* and in the palace. One puppeteer of Bianliang would be up by, or before, five o'clock every morning putting on 'little *zaju*' in the *wazi*.[44] There were guilds or societies of puppeteers in Bianliang, and in a certain two lanes there were simultaneously twenty-four puppet shows, with puppets dressed in bright and gay clothes. The fine lady puppets wore flowers, embroidered cloaks and bejewelled and emerald-clustered headdresses, and, with their slim, willowy waists, were as lithely graceful as real women.[45] Many of the puppeteers achieved considerable fame. Music was certainly used in the shows; various songs, and sometimes a *pipa*-lute accompaniment. Some puppeteers performed a very broad range of plays, about beautiful ladies, spirits and monsters, stout and valiant knights, and court cases. Sometimes their material resembled the *zaju*, at other times the *yaici*, 'cliff lyric', a narrative ballad, and, at other times again, the stories of the popular story-tellers concerning figures, events, battles and so forth taken from China's history, literature and legend.[46]

Shadow shows most probably arose during the Northern Sông dynasty, though some writers claim that it was earlier.[47] There is an amusing account of a young man, son of a wealthy father, who was orphaned, and came into much money early in life. This attracted the friendship of rogues, who led him astray in every conceivable way. The young man became very fond of watching shadow shows, and, whenever a particular show came to the point where the famous hero-general Guan Yu (later the Chinese God of War) was to be slain, he would burst

---

*There now ensues a fairly lengthy comic interlude between *moni* and *jing* as a clowning duo, before the play moves into its real substance.

out crying and enjoin the puppeteer to postpone it for a while.[48] The shadow shows had a wide choice of themes, similar to those of the other puppet shows, and likewise including many very similar to the tales of the popular historical story-tellers. Initially the figures were cut out of plain paper, but later they were made of coloured leather. Good characters were given obviously upright and worthy appearance, while evil characters were made emphatically ugly.[49] In the Southern Sông, at least, there was a 'great shadow show' (*da yingxi*) performed by human actors.[50]

One kind of puppet was called a 'flesh puppet' (*rou kuilei*),[51] and there is much dispute as to what this name implied. One interpretation is simply hand puppet or glove puppet,[52] but another view is that a flesh puppet show was a show acted rather than manipulated by humans. The main proponent of the latter opinion has used it, supported by a large volume of evidence, in an attempt to prove his thesis that human-acted drama in China derived from and imitated puppetry.[53] It would be unwise to dismiss the proposition as a whole too readily, especially when one recalls what has been the role of puppetry in Japanese drama, what a dynamic force puppet shows have sometimes been in Europe; that, for instance, in the time of Charles II the theatre owners of Drury Lane were worried by competition from a puppet show, and that in eighteenth-century Venice the impresarios and actor-managers dreaded the puppet theatres. Puppets can some-times say things that live actors could not. They excel in particular kinds of exaggeration. Beau Nash used marionettes in Bath for a lampoon against the fad for wearing high boots, a use remarkably similar to the skits of the *zaju*; and Punch and Judy shows, and the still more violent Guignol shows, demonstrate how ideally suited puppets are to the slapstick comedy that was so typical of the *zaju* and *yuanben*. We should not underestimate either the appeal of puppets, or their possible closeness to the living stage in Sông times. Puppet shows were performed in the *wazi* and the palace, cheek by jowl with the human-acted *zaju*. From surviving evidence, however, it does seem unlikely that the live play origi-nated from the puppet show in China, but almost certainly both exercised a powerful influence on each other, and were closely interwoven in the tartan com-plex of entertainments.

A wide range of songs and tunes contributed to the form and content of the early drama. As its backbone the drama had a kind of song known as *qu*. The *qu* tunes derived from a multiplicity of sources. A large number came from the *ci* tunes of the Tang and Sông. Others came from ballads such as the *daqu* ('great melody'), or from some source shared with such ballads. The source of most *qu* tunes is unknown, and certainly many foreign tunes were incorporated, but it is clear that popular ballads made a contribution and were an inspiration to the drama – and not only musically. Some ballads arranged their tunes in a way characteristic of the drama. Many interspersed speech, even direct speech and dialogue, between their songs in a manner very similar to that of the drama.

Many told quite complex and drama-like stories, and in a boisterous, supple, heterogeneous language like that of the early dramas. Most important of the ballads was the *zhugongdiao*, which itself drew on a broad range of other kinds of song, traditional music and story. The genre originated in Bianliang during the second half of the eleventh century, and its creator was a certain Kong San-chuan.[54] Zhang Wuniu (1131–62) composed one on the love story of Shuang Zhan and the singing girl Su Xiaoqing who is torn away from him by the wicked tea-merchant Feng Kui. This was based on near-contemporary actual situations. It became one of the most widely loved tales in subsequent centuries and served as the subject-matter for many songs, stories and dramas, as well as for the allu-sions of many other compositions. Shang Dao (1185–1231) composed a revised version of Zhang's *zhugongdiao*. Fragments of only a few *zhugongdiao* survive and only one whole example, the '*West wing*' *zhugongdiao* composed by Dong Jie-yuan, 'Top Graduate Dong', some time during the years 1190–1208 of the Jin dynasty.[55]

The tale of Dong's ballad is taken from a Tang *chuanqi* novella by Yuan Zhen, and concerns one of the two most famous Chinese love stories. Through the ages it directly and indirectly gave rise to much literature on the same subject, including the early drama *West wing* by Wang Shifu, written in the thirteenth century, the most celebrated of Chinese plays. This play derived much of the manner of its treatment of the theme from the ballad, as well as much of its language. The early dramas in general no doubt likewise owed a great deal to Dong's and other *zhugongdiao*. The first dramas arranged their songs in suites or song-sets, and such arrangements are also found in the *zhugongdiao*, where, as in the dramas, each song-set uses one rhyme sound running through it. There is reported dialogue between the song-sets and songs, another feature reminiscent of the dramas. The *zhugongdiao* did much to popularise the *qu* form of song and the bold, robust, flexible language that were both such basic elements in the early drama. For centuries after the Jin dynasty the performance of *zhugongdiao* was closely associated with the drama. Its composers were sometimes also play-wrights and its performers, frequently women, were sometimes also actors or actresses. It seems to have disappeared, as a genre under that name, during the fifteenth or sixteenth century. A number of non-extant examples were also tales used in the drama. In these and many other respects the importance of the *zhugongdiao* in preparing the ground for the drama was clearly very great. The dramatic stance, the tendency to use exchanges of direct speech rather than reported description, and the alternation of song and speech are but some of the latently theatrical features which may be seen in the following extract from the '*West wing*' *zhugongdiao*. The monastery where the hero and heroine of the play are staying has just been surrounded by a menacing army of mutinied soldiers now turned brigand, and the abbot and his monks are in a quandary as to what to do for the best.[56]

From '*West wing*' *zhugongdiao* by Dong Jie-yuan

(*Sung*) The abbot declared: 'What course is right?
The mutinied soldiers are camped at our gates,
and we cannot oppose them in fight.'
A monk among the crowd, in a voice thunder-loud,
called out stern and clear:
'Grand Master, have no fear!
We are bonzes three hundred and more,
yet all we can do now is natter and jaw!
What's the use of our corporal munificence?
– eating our dough wasn't worth half a pence,
if it's filled us with so little gumption and sense!'

He hitched up the hem of his one-sleeved habit,
and raising in his hand his three-foot knife
(sworn to harm no plant and take no life),
he roared:
'I'm ready to butt with the brigand horde!'
Who was this monk? Why, none other than Dharma Acuity. Acuity was, you see,
descended from Mongol warrior tribes to the west of Shensi, and as a youth had been
very fond of archery and fencing, and delighted in hunting expeditions, and would often
sneak off into those foreign lands to engage in robbery and plunder. So he was a bold and
warlike man. One day, when his father and mother had suddenly perished, he awoke to
the fickleness and shallow insubstantiality of the ways of the mundane world, and left his
home to become a monk at this monastery.

'Any man worth his salt sticks to his ideals come what may! Now we've encountered
this rebellion, we can't just sit back and watch it, can we! That's not the attitude that a
goodly man of virtue takes! I would like those of my brother monks who have the
courage, to join me, and if we unite our strength in the endeavour to destroy the
brigands, we shall find it as easy as "striking the withered stalk, which severs of its own
accord". In all their great host, there are only one or two of them who are actually
making the rebellion. All the rest have gone along with them willy-nilly, greedy for the
gain they can see in front of their noses, but forgetting how easily things can swing to
other, disastrous extremes. If we put it to them quite plainly what they have to gain and
what they may lose, it is bound to damp their martial ardour, and make them contribute
to their own collapse.'
(*Sings*) He cannot read the holy scriptures,
his penances he cannot recite,
He is neither pure of error,
nor clean of sullying spleen and spite.
– All he has is sky-high pluck and fight!
A pair of unblinking eyes there stare
that can take away life without touching a hair!*
Since he vowed the Buddhists' abstentions

*The Chinese text has a pun on the word *zhan* which can mean either 'to blink' or 'to slay'. For Dharma
Acuity not to slay is, of course, to maintain his Buddhist principles!

the iron quarterstaff he holds
has stayed many years unpolished,
and dimming grime its gleam enfolds;
the thou-shalt-not-kill cleaver slung at his waist
was once a tiger-chopper, a dragon-lopper, death's taste,
but after he clove to the law
that 'all living things abhor
a destroyer of life',
that knife
hung on the wall, there lingered long unfingered,
its ram's-horn hilt, solid, tough, now cased in dust,
its snowy blade and frost-sharp point, jagged, rough, now laced in
     rust.
He bellows: 'Monkish ranks,
who among you will join me in arms?
I only beg you to have no qualms
– you'll suffer no slightest hurts or harms!'
Inwardly he muses with much relish:
'When my pacifist knife comes into play,
it'll not be salad on the menu today,
and my iron staff should acquire a good polish!'
He stations himself at the end of the cloister,
and proceeds his monkish men to muster:
'Daring, dogged, doughty lads, which of you will dare?
We're going to rend the rebels asunder,
reduce their rabble to surrender,
Just you roar battlecries like thunder,
– Surely you see no danger *there*!'

'When I open the gates, all *you* need do
is assist with your bellicose yelling
While my gentle knife that cherishes life
will be busily bandits a-felling;[. . .]'

Murderous mettle became the mind to succour mankind, and highwayman's heroism
turned instead into rebel-vanquishing valour. Acuity called out in a loud voice: 'Our
creed commands, and we monks serve. If there be any among you who dare to help me
repel the rogues, come out to the bottom of the hall.' In a trice, there were nearly three
hundred men down at the end of the hall, all holding their white staffs and their 'no-
killing' knives, and responding to his call with the words: 'We are willing to follow you,
sir bonze, and fight to the death!'

(*Sings*) Submit them to your careful scrutiny:
there's Dharma Acuity, a sight to be seen!
bristling brow, grim air, and grotesque mien;
His buffalo shoulders are spacious,
his tiger loins long and thick,
He grasps a three-foot sabre
and wields an iron stick;
Mounted on his charger stout,

he looks a living icon, with its teeth knocked out!
He has only a tunic of padding to wear,
no helmet or armour of iron-plate,
He's a strapping eight-footer of heroic might,
like some swashbuckler Zilu* turned cenobite,
or some Vajrapani† with tonsured pate.
And his followers . . . over two hundred, all bearing
weaponry odd and unique,
Men with deepset burning eyes,
of limber limbs and fierce physique.
Some grasp a kitchen salad-knife,
some hold a pastry rolling-pin,
They thump their great temple-drums like thunder,
their dinner-bells clang with resounding din.
Armourless, they wrap round them instead
altar banners, baldachin banderoles,
and for helmets they pop on the top of their head
their clerical begging bowls!
(Some untonsured novices with wild flowing hair,
don iron-brown cassocks, the sole iron they wear!)
They march away from their beadsman cells,
measureless valour in their air revealed,
and declare, 'We gladly volunteer
to war with might and main upon the battlefield.'

One of the reasons for the northern drama's predominance in the thirteenth century was no doubt its wide choice of themes. *Nanxi* seem to have been more restricted in this respect. One explanation of this difference may be that *nanxi* underwent a steadier, more narrowly organic growth, whereas the creation of the northern drama may have been a more sudden amalgamation of various arts and entertainments. The drama was able to draw on a vast variety of stories already made familiar to the public by *yuanben,* narrative ballads, puppet shows and popular story-tellers. This widespread familiarity with tales ancient and modern was an enormous advantage to the dramatist, a springboard largely denied to the modern Western dramatist. Able to assume an audience's familiarity with the basic story, the Chinese dramatist could proceed with freedom to embroider upon and juggle with the story for dramatic effect. Being familiar with the stories, audiences would be highly receptive and sensitive to his treatment and also, in beneficial ways, highly demanding. This was all to the general good of the drama.

There were market story-tellers in China at least as early as the eighth or ninth centuries and probably much earlier.[57] In the absence of solid evidence, one can perhaps nonetheless feel sure that at least amateur public story-telling existed in

---

*Zilu refers to Confucius's disciple Zhong You, who was famous for his fighting nature and activities.
†The Vajrapanis were mace-bearing, giant demon guards, who, among other things, were depicted as guardian images and divine sentinels of temples.

furthest antiquity. Some of the *bianwen* may well have provided the material for secular, professional story-tellers, but it is not until the Sông dynasty that there are sure signs of widespread story-telling as a profession.[58] It flourished in the *wazi* of both Bianliang and Hangzhou and doubtless also in Zhongdu, and already during the Northern Sông was prospering to such an extent that narrators specialised in several different types of story-telling. Some told stories of history, some of fiction, some of Buddhism. There were tales of love affairs, court 'detective' cases, the supernatural, magic, immortals, fighting, war and much else. There were short stories and there were long saga-like novels.[59] Many examples attributed to the Sông dynasty survive from later dynasties, but have probably undergone heavy editing and re-creation or are otherwise of doubtful authenticity. Numerous titles, however, which refer to thirteenth or early fourteenth century oral tales, survive to assure us of the wealth of this branch of entertainment[60] and, since many of them are readily identified with those of the early drama, strongly argue for the influence of the spoken story upon the drama. Not only in their material, but also in their language, the oral story-tellers must have had a profound effect on the drama and provided it with a far richer setting than it would otherwise have enjoyed on its first entrance. Equally certainly, the drama in turn affected the trade and material of the story-tellers.

The huge bustling cities of Sông and Jin China were a constant flow of human intercourse, a ceaseless blending of pastimes and professions. None of the rigid modern compartmentalisations seem applicable to the entertainment worlds there. The puppeteer no doubt listened with one ear to the story-teller a few yards away. Before they went on stage the actors no doubt stood listening to a snatch of ballad. Entertainers poached themes and techniques from one another, consciously and unconsciously, learning and trying to improve both for the sake of their own artistic pride and for the sake of their rice bowls – or simply because that was the most natural and unavoidable thing to do. Entertainers probably did not think of themselves as exclusive experts, or see themselves as performing very different tasks from one another. They might well have combined two or three genres of entertainment in their own repertoire. Most entertainments included music and song. Entertainers gathered in the same quarters, played on the same bills together, and were one and the same phenomenon. It can scarcely have been otherwise. And the drama was to scoop the cream of the entertainment world with equal lack of concern for compartments, for category for category's sake.

The stage was set, but was there a drama?

3

Yuan 'Zaju' Drama

In 1234, seven years after the death of Genghis-Khan, and seven years before the Mongols – already the destroyers of Kiev and victors over an army of Polish and Teutonic knights – stood before Vienna and a surely doomed Western Europe, Mongol forces conquered the Jin empire and gained control of the northern parts of China. It was largely in reaction to East Asian pressures that the fearsome Mongol war-machine arose, and the Mongols viewed the conquest of China as the highest prize. Their most bitterly fought and longest campaigns were against the armies of China, and it was for the Chinese that they reserved their greatest opprobrium and mistrust. In numerous ways China was the pinnacle of world civilisation, incomparably wealthy both spiritually and materially. Marco Polo's astonished admiration testifies at least to the latter. China was the battleground for the conflict between the ultimate refinement of military barbarism and the greatest of settled civilisations.

The philosophy dominating Chinese attitudes and institutions was Confucianism, inculcated through an elaborate system of education. When the Mongols came to power, it was to be expected that they would discriminate against the Chinese people, and more particularly against the scholars who had been moulded by, and who had generally profited from, Confucian education, and who continued to manifest the marks of its teachings.

On the fall of the Jin after many years of war large numbers of literati had died unnatural deaths, become slaves and menials, or were left in poverty and ruin. Some, unthinkably, became 'butchers and wine-vendors'! Numerous Chinese scholars, whose education had hitherto entitled them to expect a post in government service, were left with little or no prospect of employment in their traditional calling. Many were unable to find government employment at all or occupied trivial posts well below their capacities. Others, remaining loyal to the Jin dynasty and disdaining to serve the savage, uncouth conquerors, chose not to take up office even when powerful patrons urged them to do so – for there were still some opportunities for them through the channels of patronage. Some educated men suffered wretched indignity and poverty. Many were obliged to seek careers outside government service, which in some cases gave them a spiritual and intellectual outlet. From being the backbone of the administration, the scholars largely became personae non gratae to the rulers. The Mongols held the traditional civil service examinations only once, briefly, during the thirteenth century and did not revive them until 1313, and then only in a manner very discriminatory against the Chinese.[1] To carry out their government in China the Mongols relied to a very large extent on Mongols and non-Chinese Asiatics, and even welcomed the talents of Europeans such as the Polos of Venice. Very often the administrators were Muslim merchants and tax-gatherers. There were notorious cases of rapacity and maladministration perpetrated by them.

One assessment of the social classes that was current in those times gave the order of the various estates as: members of government, lesser officialdom, Buddhist clergy, Taoist clergy, medical men, artisans, hunters, commoners in general, Confucian scholars, and beggars.[2] This categorisation should not be taken too literally, but it vividly indicates the status of scholars at that time. Merchants and military men, who mysteriously fail to figure in the list, were given the highest position. Buddhist priests, who as a further indignity for the conquered people were often Tibetans, were given much sway, and some tyrannically abused their privileges.[3]

The Chinese concept of reclusion and hermit life needs some explanation. For the Chinese scholar, life in public office was regarded as normality, the 'real world'. There lay his traditional niche and vocational obligations, and to withdraw from an official career was tantamount to 'abandoning the world'. Reclusion of this kind was a particularly marked feature of scholar life under the Mongol régime, and it took two major forms. Either one could live the simple life of the rustic recluse, or one could become a recluse of sorts by sinking oneself into the human sea, by merging into ordinary, non-governmental urban life. Many scholars chose to withdraw, either as an artistically expressed ideal or as an actual way of life, and not a few chose the latter option. Such men of education who sought their living or spiritual outlet or both in the world of popular entertainment could consider themselves recluses of a kind.

It was an opinion expressed by several Ming dynasty writers in a confident, matter-of-fact manner, that many scholars unwilling or unable to serve the Mongols poured their genius and their frustrations into the writing of qu songs and drama, and that their opposition conveyed through these media was a major cause of the quick downfall of the Mongols.[4] There is nothing essentially improbable about this. Drama and song can be among the most powerful stirrers of emotions, which explains the constant interest in drama and song and the constant apprehension about them shown by governments throughout the ages. Some pieces written under the Mongols undoubtedly contain direct political protest. Yet the thesis as a whole is difficult to substantiate by any detailed equation of the surviving literature with known facets and events of political life during the period. Attempts at this often rest upon quotations of excerpts from the late Ming dynasty editions of the early dramas, notwithstanding that these were often very heavily edited during the Ming and that the late Ming especially had its own good reasons for fierce political protest. By and large, we lack the detailed circumstantial evidence needed to interpret with any certainty much of what might have been protest.

Nevertheless, the confidence of the Ming writers carries a strong authority, and the likelihood of their being right is empirically considerable. It would not do to forget, however, that writers of dramas were often long-term professionals and no doubt often desired to entertain, amuse and edify on a plane more general than immediate protest against conditions of the minute or even of the age; it would not do, either, to forget how much scholars would have resented their status and the humiliating position of their civilisation under the Mongols. But some of the scholars were of non-Chinese origin, and many others had non-Chinese friends, so we must always credit them with the possibility of complex outlooks, and make no over-ready assumptions about the nature of their loyalties.

The *zaju* and *yuanben* of the Sông and Jin were no doubt performances that we should easily recognise as plays, and certainly have a place in any discussion of Chinese drama, in the looser sense of the term 'drama' as the totality of theatrical tradition and activities. In this history, it will be convenient to regard drama as having arisen in the thirteenth century, understanding 'drama' in its narrower sense, implying some contrast with the earlier plays. The written records are inadequate to justify a belief in such a contrast with any certainty, but they do strongly suggest that Yuan *zaju* was something radically new in its scope, that, among other things, it brought literary breadth and confidence to the theatre. Where did this drama come from? How did it arise, and would it inevitably have arisen at some time? In the thirteenth century? All or most of the components were there, but do components always of their own accord coalesce into a whole? The constituents of the new drama were living, changing phenomena, part of ever-changing social conditions, and one large aspect of those conditions was the Mongol conquest. Perhaps we cannot say what might have happened without that conquest. It is possible that peaceful social change and some increasing formal complexity and coalescence of proto-dramatic forms would of themselves have called forth playwrights of the requisite literary skills. We cannot tell.

Writers ancient and modern are often vague, sometimes deliberately so, about the chronology of this period. Strictly speaking the Yuan dynasty did not begin until 1271, or by the more standard conventions 1279 or 1280, when the Sông dynasty finally disintegrated. The drama under present discussion is usually referred to as 'Yuan *zaju*', yet some of its important developments undoubtedly took place between the thirties and the seventies. The term 'Mongol period' is often used to embrace the missing decades of Mongol rule in the north, but it is unwieldy. Hereafter the term 'Yuan' will generally refer to the period 1280–1368 or, when northern matters are under discussion, the period 1234–1368. If necessary, further specification – e.g. 'Mongol period' – will be given. 'Yuan *zaju*' will be taken to refer to the northern-style dramas of the period 1234–1368.

The first Yuan *zaju* drama came into being in the north in and around the Mongol capital Khanbalik, known to the Chinese as Dadu, 'the Great Capital', the Peking of present times. We know that the Mongol khans sometimes watched

Chinese plays, as is shown for instance in the following passage from the thirteenth-century Persian of 'Ata-Malik Juvaini. 'Khitai' means China, the conquered Jin empire, and the khan is Ogodai (r. 1229–41). Juvaini wrote his history in 1260.

A troupe of players had come from Khitai and acted wondrous Khitayan plays such as no one had ever seen before. One of these plays consisted of tableaux of every people, in the midst of which an old man with a long white beard and a turban wound round his head was dragged forth upon his face bound to the tail of a horse. Qa'an asked who this was meant to portray. They replied that it represented a rebellious Moslem; for that the armies were dragging them out of the lands in this manner. Qa'an ordered the show to be stopped and commanded his attendants to fetch from the treasury all sorts of jewels from the lands of Khorasan and the two Iraqs, such as pearls, rubies, turquoises, etc., and also gold-embroidered webs and garments, and Arab horses, and arms from Bokhara and Tabriz; and likewise what was imported from Khitai, being garments inferior to the others, small horses and other Khitayan products; and all these things he commanded to be laid side by side so that it might be seen how great was the difference. And he said: 'The poorest Moslem has many Khitayan slaves, while the great emirs of Khitai have not one Moslem captive. And the reason for this can only be the beneficence of the Creator, Who knoweth the station and rank of every nation; it is also in conformity with the ancient *yasa* of Chingiz-Khan, according to which the blood-money for a Moslem is forty *balish* and for a Khitayan a donkey. In view of such proofs and testimonies how can you make a laughing stock of the people of Islam? This crime you have committed ought to be punished, but I will spare your lives. Count that as a total gain; depart from my presence forthwith and be seen no more in this neighbourhood.'[5]

Discounting the obvious notes of propaganda, we may take as thoroughly reliable the mention of 'wondrous Khitayan plays such as no one had ever seen'. Most likely the one described would be a *yuanben* rather than a Yuan *zaju*, although it may have been some other kind of performance. There are other indications of imperial interest in plays, and such interest, and the new conditions of relative peace after decades of warfare, may have encouraged developments on the stage. Early in the Yuan, three leading members of the Music Academy carried out thorough alterations of the *yuanben*, and renovated it as a genre.[6] The precise nature of their alterations is not known. Nor do we know whether they inspired, or were inspired by, the birth of Yuan *zaju* drama. Almost certainly, since the *yuanben* was so closely associated in performance with the Yuan *zaju*, there was some connection between the two genres in these changes. Some of the early dramatists, for instance, were the sons-in-law of a famous Music Academy actor who was probably one of the three renovators of the *yuanben*.[7]

Without actors, public, available wealth, places of performance, and so forth, there could have been no drama. Equally obviously, although one should not underestimate the learning of the actor-playwrights, a strong infusion of formally educated, literary minds was possibly vital in enabling the theatre to avail itself so freely and confidently of such a broad spectrum of China's past literature, or at least to ensure the theatre acceptance at all levels of society. As English drama may have needed a Marlowe, as well as a Kyd, to help it flourish, so the Chinese stage may well have required men of high formal education. The common theory that the Mongol conquest was responsible for scholars' turning to the stage seems over-simplified, but it is difficult adequately to replace. Nor should we neglect the absence of certain prejudices among the conquerors or the positive contribution of Mongol and other non-Chinese tastes in entertainment, which were probably very important for the flourishing of drama, although the records provide little direct evidence in such respects. Many things, such as the large amount of originally non-Chinese music used in Yuan *zaju*, seem to point to the likelihood of initially favourable attitudes to dramatic entertainment among the non-Chinese newcomers. No doubt, too, the conquest was important in removing or considerably mitigating social stigmas against scholarly involvement in the entertainment world.

Another traditional view which meets with some strong objections nowadays is that one individual was the creator, the first writer and the founder of Yuan *zaju* drama. Admittedly ideas can occur simultaneously to a number of people and dramas were sometimes written collectively, but it is at least equally likely that, as the old writings tell us or at least suggest to us, a single individual initiated the process. Of course no single individual was the sole creator of drama: so many of the vital constituents were already in existence centuries earlier, and even such an individual must himself have been a product of the past. But that the vital joining together of the constituents was the work of one man, or was guided by one man, is not at all unlikely. In one sense nothing is new, in another everything, and it is not by any means unreasonable for the Chinese to claim that Guan Hanqing was the father of the Yuan *zaju*, and its first creator.[8]

Guan Hanqing lived from around 1220 to 1300. He may have held some minor medical post or else have been enrolled in the medical census category, thus perhaps avoiding some restrictive fiscal and legal obligations. He was fairly reliably reputed to be a Jin loyalist. The famous courtesan Pearl Curtain Beauty, wooed and no doubt won by some of the leading literary and government personalities of her day, and herself a poetess of renown, was an intimate of his. Among his friends was Wang Heqing, leading poet-wag, with whom he conducted a friendly rivalry of witty digs for a good half of his lifetime.

Guan Hanqing was by far the most prolific of Yuan playwrights, writing over fifty plays, including some of the most popular in his own time, and some which have been performed in revised forms throughout the ages into modern times. *Slicing fish* is a sparkling comedy in which an ingenious wife saves her husband from execution by seducing the wicked lord who has trumped up the capital charge and plans to carry out the sentence. It is superbly plotted and exquisitely witty, the heroine coming out as a delightful epitome of resourcefulness and lascivious feminine guile. *Moon prayer pavilion* concerns people in flight from Zhongdu (present-day Peking) to Bianliang in the year 1213 when the Mongols were invading the Jin capital. In the confusion a mother loses her daughter who meets up with a young man, who meanwhile has lost his sister. The girl and young man travel on together and fall in love, but he becomes ill and they rest at an inn. Her father, a high-ranking minister, discovers them there and angrily tears her away. The young man's sister has met up with the mother, and is adopted into their family. Eventually the young man comes out top graduate in the civil service examinations and the father, unwittingly, seeks him as a splendid match for his daughter. The young man's sister is married to the top *military* graduate, who is also his sworn brother, and all are happily united.

Guan Hanqing's plays were predominantly about love, love with whores, courtesans, maidens and ladies, and mostly include a great deal of scintillating humour. His range, however, was very wide. One of his most enduring plays was *Single sword meeting*. The warrior hero Guan Yu is invited to a feast by the treacherous minister of the rival state of Wu, Lu Su, who has prepared an ambush. His wit, valour and magnificent aplomb turn the tables and Lu Su is forced personally to escort him to safety from the middle of the sprung ambush. The hero does not appear on stage till half-way through the play, and his appearance is preceded by awe-inspiring descriptions of him that create enormous dramatic excitement and expectancy about his eventual entry. Another play, *Dream of two on a journey*, is pervaded by a masterfully evoked spectral gloom and foreboding. Liu Bei, Emperor of Shu, longs for his sworn brothers, generals Guan Yu and Zhang Fei, and sends a messenger to recall them from their outposts. The messenger learns that they have both met their deaths through foul treachery. Meanwhile in the palace the wise minister Zhuge Liang reads the astrological signs of this grave national disaster, but cannot bring himself to burden his monarch with the terrible news, fearing that Liu Bei's wild reaction may bring further calamity to the nation. The ghosts of the two dead men, however, are making their way back. They meet on the road, and in tragic grief recognise one another. Together they enter the palace, and reflect with bitter nostalgia upon the scene of their former eminence and splendour. They present themselves before Liu Bei, who lies alone in his bed-chamber. He greets them joyfully, but when he realises they are only ghosts his anguish knows no bounds. Dawn drags them away, and they leave him, exhorting him to exact a mighty revenge upon their enemies. As far as we can tell, this play is a fine example of the way in which Yuan playwrights used their sources with superb freedom for great dramatic effect. In known earlier accounts the two deaths were years apart, but by bringing them together and adjusting other details Guan Hanqing created a compact and dynamic plot.

Besides his plays Guan wrote many excellent non-dramatic *qu* songs, including one that seems to convey personal experiences of Hangzhou around the year 1280. In his poems, too, the main theme is that of love, often illicit love described in a highly erotic manner.

Another outstanding playwright was Bai Pu (1226–post-1306), who along with Guan Hanqing, Ma Zhiyuan and Zheng Guangzu was hailed as one of the Four

Great Men of Yuan *zaju* drama.[9] His background and mood in some ways contrast with Guan's. Son of an eminent official under the Jin, he saw his family torn apart by the Mongol invasions. A family friend, Yuan Haowen (1190–1257), who was the greatest orthodox literary figure of the age, fostered him with warm kindness, and educated him to a high level of erudition. In spite of this kindness, Bai was grieved by his separation from his parents, and was marked by a certain melancholy for the rest of his life. Very loyal to the Jin dynasty, he turned his back on government service and embarked upon a life of wild pleasure-seeking. A powerful local governor valued him so highly that he wanted to recommend him for employment to the imperial court, but again and again Bai rejected the chance of an illustrious career, indifferent as he was to fame and wealth. His son, however, may have attained some position of distinction, which may explain why Bai was awarded very lofty posthumous titles. After 1280 Bai moved south to live in Kiangsu province. Although he composed poems for people of humble standing and frequented singing girls, many of his friends throughout his life were orthodox literary men and high government officials. His surviving *qu* and *ci* poetry is somewhat more restrained in mood than Guan Hanquing's songs, and his plays stress the difficulties of love.

Most famous of Bai's plays is *Rain on the paulownia tree*, the immortal love story of the Tang Emperor Minghuang and Lady Yang. The emperor conceives an affection for the coarse frontier general An Lushan and gives him to Lady Yang as her adopted son. Lady Yang's elder brother, a powerful minister, offends the general by sending him off to a frontier command. One night the emperor and Lady Yang swear vows of eternal love beneath a paulownia tree. The following day comes news that the general has rebelled. Forced to flee his capital, the emperor makes for Szechwan. On the way his guards mutiny, and demand the death of Lady Yang, whom they regard as responsible for the disasters. He is left with no choice but to allow her to commit suicide. Later, when the rebellion has been crushed and the emperor obliged to abdicate in favour of his son, he returns to live in the capital, where he yearns miserably for Lady Yang. One night he dreams that she invites him to a lovers' party, but at that point he is woken by the insistent sound of rain pattering mournfully on the leaves of the paulownia tree outside. The endless sorrows and nostalgia that this evokes leave him weeping brokenly.

After the unification of China in about 1280, another of the Four Great Men, Ma Zhiyuan (fl. c. 1280) of Dadu,[10] held a fairly minor post, possibly in charge of taxes, in the administration of a region covering the area of the southern provinces Kiangsu, Anhwei, Kiangsi and Fukien. If we may judge from his poems at all, he seems to have retired from his official career and to have led a reclusive, rustic life. Many of the poems are in praise of such an existence. A large number of his non-dramatic *qu* songs have survived, and they are among the very best of the genre, showing brilliant wit and whimsy, and a mastery of laconic evocation. His most moving and deservedly most famous play is *Autumn in the Han palace*. Again the theme is an emperor's love. Seeking a wife, the emperor sends his evil minister

Mao Yanshou on a tour to pick beautiful girls for the imperial seraglio. The father of the ravishing Wang Lady Splendour fails to slip Mao the required bribe. As the emperor chooses whom to favour from his harem by consulting portraits of the ladies, Mao is able to avenge himself on Wang by making the daughter's portrait an ugly one. All the same, the emperor eventually discovers her and is enraptured. Mao escapes to the Hunnish khan bearing a true portrait of Lady Splendour. As intended, the khan is so struck by the portrait that he demands her as his wife as the price for peace with the Chinese. The grief-stricken emperor is forced to acquiesce, and he and Lady Splendour take the saddest leave of one another. She later throws herself into the River Amur. Meanwhile the emperor dreams a dream of her, but in the dream she is snatched away from him, and he wakes to hear the mournful calls of migrating wild geese, which remind him how far away is his beloved. The news of her death arrives with Mao Yanshou, whom the remorseful khan has sent in chains to be executed.

Such plays as *Dream of two on a journey, Autumn in the Han palace* and *Rain on the paulownia tree* raise the perennial question of whether early Chinese drama ever contained tragedy. The question might seem rather odd to anyone acquainted only with European drama and its traditions. Certainly Chinese drama contains nothing quite like Racinian tragedy with its pure earnestness and flawlessly attained, ineluctable, unmixedly sad destinies. Most early Chinese plays are either comedies or include humorous parts. When the three unities are observed it is by coincidence or dictated by the plot or by the specific desire for entertaining and forceful effect, not in conformity with any preconceived general set of structural theories. *Rain on the paulownia tree* ends on a purely sad note, as we have it, but it is a rare exception. Even the consistently gloomy *Dream of two on a journey* ends with an 'optimistic' note of revenge, as the text survives. Humour does not prevent a play from being sad, tragic in the looser senses of the word – indeed it is arguable that it may intensify sadness by contrast or by rendering it more profoundly human and moving – but the overall sadness of a fair number of Chinese plays is quite strongly negated or mitigated by a sudden optimistic or would-be happy ending. Whether this overrides or detrimentally contradicts the sad note of the rest of the play may well be a matter of personal judgement. One suspects that for the audience the sad feelings would often provide the main impression while the happy endings would often just be a convention to round off the play. Yet undoubtedly there is more involved in such endings than mere conventionality. Probably the question is linked with a broader range of Chinese attitudes, and with various concepts of existential harmonies.

The matter is complicated, and space does not allow a full discussion here. *Dream of two on a journey*, for instance, has a 'happy ending' of sorts, or at least ends on a forward-looking note, but the dialogue is missing from the extant edition, and in such cases we cannot be certain how the plays were concluded in performance. In addition, although the prospect of revenge seems to constitute a 'happy ending', the Yuan audience would have been only too aware from their general knowledge of the historical and legendary background of that particular play's subject-matter that this revenge was actually embarked upon, and ended in national disaster, as is feared or predicted by Zhuge Liang in the play. The audience reaction to this play must have been very complex, and perhaps the irony of the concluding 'optimism' may only have served to intensify the 'tragedy' of the play.

Another celebrated play of the early Yuan is *Yellow millet dream*. Ma Zhiyuan wrote the first act, another playwright the second act, and two actor-playwrights the third and fourth. This is an interesting example of cooperative authorship of plays, and we find similar instances throughout the history of Chinese drama. It is also an indication of the close liaison and intimate connections between dramatists and the acting world in the early Yuan, and of the closely knit theatrical society that existed then.

As already mentioned, the most famous Chinese play through the ages was *West wing* by Wang Shifu (fl. late thirteenth century). Very little is known of him.[11] He wrote some fourteen plays. *West wing*, perhaps in response to the established popularity of its theme and to the length of the '*West wing*' *zhugongdiao*, is five times the length of a normal Yuan *zaju*. The young scholar Zhang Junrui woos young lady Little Oriole behind the back of her stern widowed mother, Madam Cui, in the Buddhist monastery where they are all staying on their travels. A brigand chief hears of the young lady's beauty and comes in force to seize her for himself, but Zhang contrives to bring his friend, a general stationed nearby, to the rescue. Madam Cui has previously promised to reward Zhang with Little Oriole, but now she tries to go back on her word, as Little Oriole is already engaged to another man. With the sharp-witted maidservant Red Maid acting as go-between, Little Oriole and Zhang are brought together in secret and deliciously described love. Faced with a *fait accompli* Madam Cui is forced to consent to the formalisation of their match, but insists that Zhang first wins his laurels in the imperial examinations. He eventually does so. Meanwhile, the original fiancé arrives at the monastery. His slanders persuade Madam Cui to readopt his claims to her daughter, but on Zhang's return his friend the general intervenes, and the thwarted liar commits suicide, whereupon the two lovers are finally reunited. The whole play is a feast of rich humour, vigorous action, delicate emotion, titillating suspense and plentiful spice. The following extract (we must bear in mind that it is from a Ming edition*) shows something of the roguish humour and complexity of characterisation of the play. It describes how Zhang Junrui, having seen and been enraptured by the beautiful Little Oriole, resolves to try to obtain lodgings in the monastery so that he may be near her. The monk Dharma Acuity has just announced Zhang to the abbot.[12]

---

*And thus possibly very different from its Yuan form, especially in its spoken parts. See below, page 54 for a fuller discussion of the implications of a Ming edition.

From *West wing* by Wang Shifu

ABBOT.   Well, this monastery is a poor place, but we have quite a few rooms. Choose whichever one suits you.

ZHANG JUNRUI.

> (*Sings*) I do not want the refectory,
> nor yet the meditation-cell
> called Hall of Withered Wood.
> No, somewhere far from the southern vestibule,
> away from the eastern wall,
> close by the western wing,*
> Yes, near to the principal cloister,
> beyond the oratories,
> any room there will do.

ABBOT.   Otherwise, how about sharing my apartment?

ZHANG JUNRUI.   What on earth for!

> (*Sings*) On no account must you suggest
> your own fine abbot's chamber.

(*Enter Red Maid.*)

RED MAID.   Madam told me to come and ask the abbot when there would be a suitable occasion for holding a service for the Prime Minister.† She said I was to see that everything was settled and in order, and then report back to her. Off I go then. (*Meets abbot*). A thousand blessings on you, abbot! Madam sent me to ask when it would be all right to hold the requiem mass for the Prime Minister? I was to report back to her when everything was arranged satisfactorily.

ZHANG JUNRUI. (*Aside*) Cor, there's a fine miss!

> (*Sings*) Manners meet for manorial halls,
> fine dignity and etiquette,
> no slightest trace
> of skittish giddiness.
> She greets the Great Master
> with seemly, fervent reverence,
> and, parting lips of fair cerise,
> couches her words befittingly.
>
> This comely maiden's face
> is lightly, tastefully adorned,
> The mourning clothes she wears
> are decorous, plain white silk.
> And those rare, darting peepers!
> as sharp and spry as sparrow-hawks',
> stealing little glances
> from the corners of those eyes
> she sweeps Master Zhang from tip to toe.

*Which is where Little Oriole and her mother are lodged.
†Madam Cui's late husband was a Prime Minister.

> Should I one day share the nuptial couch
> with her passionate young lady mistress,
> how could I suffer her to spend her days
> just folding our quilts and smoothing our bed!
> I shall beg the young lady and pester Madam Cui,
> and if they then refuse to grant the wench her freedom,
> I myself shall write the deed
> to emancipate her from servant bondage.

ABBOT.   The fifteenth of the second month would be a suitable date for the Prime Minister's requiem service.

RED MAID.   Come with me to inspect the Hall of Buddhas, sir abbot, and then I'll go back and report to Madam Cui.

ABBOT.   Please sit down for a while, sir. I shall be back as soon as I have been to inspect things with this young woman.

ZHANG JUNRUI.   Why leave me behind? Why shouldn't I keep you company, too, eh?

ABBOT.   All right then, come along with us.

ZHANG JUNRUI.   Let the young woman go on ahead, and we can follow close behind!

ABBOT.   A scholar with great insight and good sense!

ZHANG JUNRUI.   Might I have a little word with you?

ABBOT.   What on earth's to stop you!

ZHANG JUNRUI.

> (*Sings*) This gorgeous bird from the house of Cui . . .
> Can it be . . . ?
> Could she be out to seduce you,
> my old spotless saint?

ABBOT.   We monks are celibate! We've left such worldly things firmly behind us! How could there be any question of such a thing!

ZHANG JUNRUI.   Well, if not,

> (*Sings*) Then why is she peeping so fondly
> at the glitter of your pate?
> And why is she all togged up
> in such flashy, classy gear?

ABBOT.   What on earth are you suggesting, sir! It is a blessing that the young woman cannot hear what you are saying! If she realised, what on earth would she think!

(*Red Maid enters the Hall of Buddhas.*)

ZHANG JUNRUI.

> (*Sings*) Up the aisle,
> and into the bridal suite,
> Yes, 'Love's bounties drop from Heaven'!

I'll keep a watch at the door. In you go.

ABBOT. (*In anger*)   Sir, your words flout all the precepts and principles of the sage kings of yore! You must be aware that you are gravely insulting a follower of Lord Buddha! How could such an elderly priest as myself indulge in such goings-on?

ZHANG JUNRUI.

> (*Sings*) What a pretty sight you are,
> all worked up and hoity-toity,

> If there's nothing in it,
> what's the flap?
> Why get so hot and shirty,
> Holy Tripitaka* of the Tang?
> Can't blame me for my suspicions:
> has such a powerful household as theirs
> no male servant they could have sent?
> But has to send a pretty maid to do its errands?

ABBOT. Madam Cui rules her household with a rod of iron. No man is allowed to frequent any part of her abode.

ZHANG JUNRUI. (*Aside*) This bald bugger's got an artful tongue.

> (*Sings*) You stand there,
> with your dogged argy-bargy,
> head hard down, and butting with your skull!

ABBOT. (*To Red Maid*) Everything has been arranged for the food offerings and the service. On the fifteenth I shall ask Madam Cui to bring her daughter to offer incense here.

ZHANG JUNRUI. What for?

ABBOT. Because the young lady always felt great affection for her father Prime Minister Cui, and wishes to express her gratitude for her parents' love. It will, moreover, be the day appointed for the removal of mourning, at the end of the stipulated period of three years' mourning for the Prime Minister, and they will duly be casting off their weeds. Those are the reasons why a service is to be held.

ZHANG JUNRUI.

> (*Says, weeping*) 'Alas, alas, my father and mother,
> my birth occasioned you great toil,
> I yearn to requite your love profound,
> but it was limitless as mighty Heaven.'†

The young lady, one of the weaker sex though she is, yet feels moved to express her gratitude for her parents' affection, whereas I, all these years, have been drifting around the backwaters of the country, and since my parents passed away have never once offered up even a few penceworth of sacrificial money to show how grateful I am to them. I hope, goodly monk, that in accordance with your principles of compassion you will allow me to contribute five thousand pence, so that I may in some little way participate in the offerings, and render up prayers and sacrifices for my parents' happiness in their afterlife. I am sure that if Madam Cui comes to hear of my taking part in the service, she will raise no objections, since I do so solely in the desire to fulfil the duties of a loving son.

ABBOT. Allot this gentleman a portion of the service, Dharma Acuity.

ZHANG JUNRUI. (*Secretly asks Dharma Acuity*) Will the young lady actually be present on the day?

DHARMA ACUITY. Of course she will – it's for *her* parents!

ZHANG JUNRUI. (*Aside*) That five thousand pence is going to bear fruit, mark my word!

---

*The famous seventh-century Chinese Buddhist pilgrim, sage and saint.
†A quotation from the classical *Book of odes.*

(*Sings*) Paradise on earth,
a look at Little Oriole
is more blessing than any requiem brings.
She is supple jade,
she is warming perfume,
And – even not to hold her close –
if one could manage one small touch,
it would absolve one from all sinful karma,
all still-to-come calamity. [. . .]

For the Mongols conquest was a *raison d'être*. Immediately they had conquered the north they came into conflict with the Southern Sông. This was their toughest campaign of all. It has been fashionable to depict the Sông as an effete, pacifist dynasty, but such depictions often confuse civilisation with weakness. The Southern Sông was a powerful military giant, well defended by huge armies and advanced weaponry, guarded by mighty citadels and in command of the most developed military skills. It took the Mongols a long time to learn the arts of citadel warfare and to wear down the might of the Sông. After lulls in hostilities, they opened a major onslaught under the redoubtable Khublai-Khan.

In the end it was to a large degree the Sông court's internal disagreements and lack of decision that gave its enemy the victory. In 1274 the Mongol general Baiyan, known by a pun as 'Hundred Eyes' (*bai yan*), forced the surrender of Hangzhou, the city Marco Polo refers to as Quinsai. By 1280 the last effective resistance by remnants of the house of Sông had been eliminated.

The region round Hangzhou was by far the most densely populated in China – indeed in the world – and had for long been the focal point of Chinese civilisation. With the country freed from the disruptions of major internal warfare and at last reunited it was only natural that the centre of cultural activities should tend to swing back to that region. Increasingly after the reunification the leading playwrights were domiciled in or around Hangzhou, being either northerners who moved there or local men who adopted the northern style of drama. After an interim period of adjustment, we find from about 1320 or 1330 onwards that the Yuan *zaju* drama was predominantly based in the south.

Zheng Guangzu (c. 1280?–c. 1330?), fourth of the Four Great Men, belonged perhaps to the middle phase of Yuan *zaju*.[13] Coming from Shansi province in the north, his high level of traditional Confucian education earned him a minor post in regional government in Hangzhou. Rather dogged and sticklerish by nature, he was very cautious and slow about making friends, which led many of the eminent literati to underrate him, not for a long while perceiving the sterling qualities he possessed. His sixteen plays brought him fame throughout China, even in the imperial court, and he was such a popular figure with the acting profession that if anyone ever mentioned 'Venerable Mr Zheng', the actors always realised immediately that it meant Zheng Guangzu. His friend Zhong Sicheng (c. 1279?–post 1360), who tells us all this, curiously considered that he was over-fond of joking and humour in his plays; Zhong claimed that this had produced a lack of consistency and certain other imperfections in them. On his death Guangzu was cremated in the Divine Fungus Monastery on the edge of the scenic West Lake of Hangzhou, and many of the leading literati attended the ceremony, and composed elegies or prose dedications to his memory.

Many of Zheng's plays have survived in some form, and such as *Romance of the Hanlin academician*, *Wang Can ascends the tower*, *Regency of the Duke of Zhou*, and *Qiannü's soul goes wandering* are without exception finely constructed works. *Regency of the Duke of Zhou* tells the story of one of China's political saints. Having assisted the Warrior King to overthrow the Shang dynasty and establish the Zhou dynasty on a firm footing Ji Dan now wishes to retire and lead a simple rustic life, but is persuaded to stay in the government. Fifteen years later the king falls mortally ill. The duke, Ji Dan, prays to the royal ancestral gods, offering up his own life in exchange for the king's renewed health. The written prayer is by mistake placed in a gold-bound casket of divinations. After the king's death, the duke acts as regent, since the crown prince is still a minor, and establishes a just and kindly rule. There is a rebellion, and the rebels falsely claim that the duke intends to harm the infant king. He offers himself for gradual dismemberment as proof of his loyalty, but is instead put in charge of forces to crush the rebels. As he returns victorious, a terrible storm of grit and stones arises, blotting out the sun. An aged statesman chances to open up the gold-bound casket to seek some explanation of this calamity among the divination documents there, and finds the duke's noble prayer. The duke's selfless loyalty to the dynasty is proved beyond all doubt, and he hands over all the reins of government to the young king, fully vindicated. Stressing loyalty to the monarch, this play must surely have been one strong reason for Zheng Guangzu's popularity in the imperial court – or perhaps a fruit of that popularity.

The last decades of Mongol rule were marked by decay of government and of the economy, sinicisation of the rulers to a degree inadequate for any real benefits to accrue from it, and a wave of rebellions throughout southern and central China. The rebellions were Chinese-led, and that they sprang up in the south was significant for cultural as well as political developments. While the Mongol court bickered over internal squabbles, and even erupted into civil wars, the south was asserting its ascendency in no uncertain manner. The culture of the south was becoming steadily more dominant. Yuan *zaju* of northern style were still produced in abundance, but southern elements were being introduced. The late Yuan was another decisive point in the history of Chinese drama.

Many Yuan *zaju* texts survive, as well as the names of scores of dramatists and the titles of hundreds of plays.[14] It was a genre capable of treating any topic, old or new, in great depth – love, war, religious conversion, devotion to learning, political scheming, diplomatic intrigue, criminal investigation, brigand adventures, tales of the supernatural[15] . . . an endless variety of themes – in dramas abounding with seductive courtesans, virtuous ladies, waspish and witty maidservants, rascally monks, saintly hermits, flesh-bound clerics, doughty warriors, iron generals, inspired strategists, demonic villains, sly ambassadors, gods, spirits, devils, and a vast range of other vivid characters.[16]

Many of the plays survive only in Ming editions, bearing clear evidence of considerable Ming editing and Ming additions, particularly in the dialogue. Nonetheless, we can place considerable confidence in the songs even of these Ming editions as representing much of their original form, among other reasons simply because the *qu* songs are such an intricately balanced form of composition that the marks of editing and tinkering are readily perceptible.[17] The Yuan editions pose different problems. Some contain only the songs from the plays. It may be that sometimes the playwrights wrote out only the songs, and that this was what was printed – possibly surreptitiously or illicitly printed – or that only the leading role's song-part was printed, or that the demands of competition required the writing of the plays in only partial texts for the sake of safety, or that the publishers felt that readers would only want the songs. We do not know. Most of the Yuan editions, however, do give some dialogue, though in greatly varying amounts. The action of a play tended to be carried by the speech and dialogue, while the songs were the poetic, spiritual and philosophical heart of the play, the inner reflections, the confidings in the audience, the emotional reactions and so forth; but the songs were so closely related to the action that the plots remain clear even in the complete absence of dialogue or stage directions. The songs were the essential structural framework of the plays, their chief characteristic and in general their most esteemed constituent. This does not, however, make the plays into poetic dramas or operas with neglected plots. The stories are at least as tightly and superbly constructed as those of any large body of drama anywhere in the world.[18]

Nearly always, Yuan *zaju* consisted of four main acts, with sometimes the addition of one or two short 'wedge acts' (*xiezi, xieer*). The songs were, even more than the stages of development of the plot (although, of course, from the true master's hand the two coincided), the delineating features of the division into acts. Each act was built around a song-set. In the case of the wedge act this usually consisted of only one song, one tune with one or two stanzas to it. Each of the main acts included a number of songs to several tunes. The tunes within one song-set were all to one and the same key, with the exception of some permitted borrowings, and arranged in a set order, culminating in what were called *weisheng*, 'coda-tunes'. No Yuan music survives, although some claim that a few of the tunes still exist in the music of later drama.[19] We have no precise idea which distinctive moods the tunes of the various keys conveyed, but for the song-set arrangement to have had any strong significance there must surely have been such distinctions.[20] Each main act used a particular key not used elsewhere in the main acts of the plays. The wedge acts used distinctive tunes in the same key as that used almost invariably for the first main act. Since certain keys tended to be used for certain acts – though the conventions were less strict in the later acts – the effect must have been to reinforce musically the audience's and players' sense of dramatic movement, division and progress for the play as a whole. It also emphasised musically the opening and conclusion of each act, giving each act a musical unity.

Yuan *zaju* used the kind of songs known as *qu*.[21] The three main genres of Chinese poetry are commonly known as Tang *shi*, Sông *ci* and Yuan *qu*. In fact the *qu* had already appeared during the Sông and Jin dynasties, and had been utilised in many kinds of entertainment. *Qu* songs were composed to *qu* tunes. Of course, initially someone would have composed a song to a tune, or a tune for a song, no doubt often basing his work on earlier songs or tunes. Once composed or adopted or adapted into the *qu* repertoire, the tune would then have been generally available for any *qu* poets to compose their words to ad infinitum. There is nothing unusual about this; it is a universal practice to compose new words to well-known and well-loved tunes. That strangely mayfly genre English ballad opera was remarkably similar in some of its concepts to Yuan *zaju*, with its spoken dialogue and its songs fitted to already popular tunes, as in John Gay's *Beggar's Opera*. Song-books in Britain still sometimes introduce their songs with the words, 'to the tune . . .'

By the early Yuan there were already available hundreds of *qu* tunes. One Yuan list gives 335.[22] They had come from a great variety of sources. The vigour of absorption and incorporation was one of the strengths of the genre in its early days. Some seemingly came from the *zhugongdiao* and *daqu*, or from other ballads and dance suites, although we often cannot be certain of the ultimate source of the tunes, nor whence they entered the *qu* repertoire. A considerable number came from the *ci* tunes – though to say that *qu* rose from the ashes of *ci* any more than that *ci* rose from the ashes of *shi* is both an over-simplification and otherwise incorrect. But the over-simplification does suggest a certain truth. The *ci* form of composition had seemingly lost a lot of its energy and universality, at least in the north of China. The *ci* had come to be sung less, and had seemingly become more and more the property of literary men – although one should not exaggerate the extent of these trends, for, especially in the south, it remained a popular and dynamic medium of song. Perhaps one reason why the *qu* partly displaced the *ci*, or gives the impression of having done so, was that new needs of expression had arisen. The *qu* was undoubtedly better fitted for conveying the word-meaning of a song more directly and immediately to literate and non-literate alike. But the vast majority of *qu* tunes came from elsewhere, many stemming without doubt from ordinary popular songs, many being non-Chinese tunes from other Asian countries and nations, and many having been but recently composed by poet-musicians. They continued to be composed during the Yuan.

The *qu* is often referred to as a 'freer' form than the *ci*. Now in poetry, where 'restrictions' are often, in the hands of a master poet, the means to greater powers and refinements of expression, to more concentrated, more musical or otherwise more beautiful conveyance of ideas and feelings, it is difficult to be certain of the meaning of 'freedom'. As always, we must ask, 'freedom for what or to do what?' The *ci* looks free, with its uneven line lengths, but was in fact subject to strict prosodic rules and syllable counts. The *qu* likewise has uneven line lengths, even more raggedly uneven, and does undoubtedly facilitate a greater freedom in certain directions. The prime distinguishing feature of the *qu* – a feature responsible for much of the *qu*'s potential for freedom and immediacy – is the use of *chenzi*, 'padding characters' or 'extra-metrical syllables', which could be added to the prosodic lines with a certain amount of random choice.

Associated with each *qu* tune was a prosodic pattern, stipulating line and stanza lengths and determining much of that alternation of pitch tone which provided the metrical effects. There were certain latitudes. Later at least, lines could be added to the stanza and extra syllables to the line of the basic prosodic pattern, within certain limitations. But the pattern was suited to the tune. If a song-composer wished to alter it beyond a certain degree, he would perhaps have been best advised to write another tune – which is no doubt what he did – or at least to alter the tune and call it by another name. Part of the force of the *qu* was people's general familiarity with the tunes.

Without in any way altering the basic prosodic pattern the song-composer could add *chenzi* to the beginning of the line or in the middle of the line at caesuras or semantic and rhythmic divisions of the line. Generally more *chenzi* were added at the beginning of the line than elsewhere. Groups of one, two, three or four syllables of *chenzi* were common, but they could be much longer, often far surpassing the basic prosodic line in number. They are distinguishable from the wording of the basic line (i.e. the words according with the basic prosodic pattern) in a number of ways, for instance by the elimination of the prosodic pattern and by their meaning. In general *chenzi* are words of slighter meaning than the rest of the song, very often more colloquial words or conventional phrases which are easily recognised as such. Many of them have meanings such as 'You might think he would . . .', 'Do they not say that . . .', 'There is a saying that . . .', and 'By good fortune it happened that . . .'; they are somewhat similar to the story-teller's stock phrases and impart a similar narrative intimacy and directness. Semantically less vital, though often indispensable, these words were probably also sung or otherwise uttered more lightly than the rest of the song. Far from destroying or altering the tune or rhythm, they would contribute to rhythmic suspense, urgency or ease, as in the case of similar devices in many other forms of singing such as Blues and various forms of Chinese singing into modern times.

The *chenzi*, used to a considerable extent unpredictably, gave a great air of casual freedom to the *qu*. In addition they could also help to make meaning more immediately understood and by a wider audience. Remove them, and you often discover a concise poem in classical and abstruse Chinese. By their extra elucidations, their colloquiality and simply the extra sound and listening time they afforded, the *chenzi* facilitated rapid understanding of a song, thus assisting the less literate and less educated to appreciate the meaning. They eased the pressure on the poet, since if he were forced into abstruseness in the basic wording he could always redeem clarity with the *chenzi*.

Another, connected freedom of the *qu* lay in its language. The prosodic form and the customs of its use permitted the *qu* to encompass all kinds of Chinese from the loftiest literary styles to the most red-blooded and vulgar of colloquialisms, and often it cheerfully and superbly presented the two extremes side by side. In the same spirit that Chaucer and many Elizabethans reveal, the best composers of *qu* felt no embarrassment about mixing any levels of speech if it served their poetic ends.

Such are some of what might be termed the 'freedoms'. The 'restrictions' are at first sight most intimidating. The metrical effects of the *qu* are obtained by the alternation of the four pitch-tones, in one of which virtually every syllable of Chinese was pronounced or could be pronounced. The nature of the alternations was stipulated by the prosodic patterns with some strictness, especially towards the end of the line, the end being the most vital part of a line. The *qu* was stricter than other forms of Chinese poetry in this respect, and it was so possibly because it first flourished in one particular region, in the north, and in its rhymes and pronunciation adhered to one particular dialect familiar to song-composers and their audiences alike: this would have facilitated both fine and accurate play upon sounds and also fine connoisseurship and censorship of the phonetic and musical qualities of *qu*. The high demands of rhyming conventions in *qu* no doubt arose from some of the same considerations.

Rhyming in *qu* is extremely dense. Within each stanza most lines end in the same rhyme, and often every line does so. In a song-set likewise the same sound is maintained for the rhyming throughout, so that in a song-set of three or four hundred lines frequently over eighty per cent of the lines will rhyme in the same sound. Prosodic conventions practically always stipulated which lines should rhyme. It was something of a *tour de force* to rhyme a whole song-set in the narrowest rhyme categories, where the available rhyming words were very few.

Yet these 'restrictions' were not imposed for love of fetters, nor accepted for love of them. They were created and flourished because they offered freedoms for more effective and more beautiful poetic and musical expression. The metrical rules created a pleasing language of sound alternations with which poet and audience were familiarised by habit. They assisted the meaning, as did the conventions of poetic parallelism and antithesis so prominent in *qu*, by stressing contrasts and relationships of meaning, or by permitting more beautifully concise expression of ideas. Similarly, it might be thought that the repetition of the same rhyme sound through three or four hundred lines in fairly close succession would be monotonous or oppressive to the listener; on the contrary, this convention, like the 'monotonous' beat of a drum, could produce great tension and excitement, and would give the song-set and thus the act of the play an extra layer of auditory unity. Since, moreover, each main act nearly always used a different rhyme sound from all the other main acts, the rhyming was another means of giving a distinctive mood to each act. We are told that one rhyme category was feeble and lifeless and made one feel dispirited to hear it, while another had a bold resounding tone.[23] I do not know whether such precise distinctions were valid, or always valid, or whether they were ever put to dramatic use.

The *qu* was thus a robust, flexible and powerful form of poetry. To add to the list of its advantages, it was already widely popular at all levels of society when the dramatists adopted it. The public was accustomed to it in entertainments and its prestige was established by its use in such ballads as the *zhugongdiao* and by a number of respectable orthodox literary men who chose to compose some of their verse in it. Most important of these men was Yuan Haowen (1190–1257), but there were many others. The drama gave the genre a further accolade, and it became firmly established not only as the prime medium of non-dramatic song and poetry but also as the basic element of the drama throughout the Yuan, acceptable and loved in the residences of the high and mighty as well as in the streets, markets and villages.

As long as *qu* composition was more or less confined to the north, general familiarity with the standard dialect, which was a language of the north and closely connected with the modern Peking dialect, served as an anchor and ready check for its quality and consistency. Once, however, it became popular in the more southern parts of China and was composed and listened to by people who were not native speakers of the northern dialect, the ready check disappeared, and phonetic and prosodic transgressions of the rules became frequent. Yet in a sense there were no real rules – hardly any written rules as far as we know [24] – and presumably the only real rule for such a literary form was that it should give pleasure or be effective in conveying what the composer wished to convey. No doubt, however, the loss of uniform standards did threaten the general power and beauty of the *qu*, if only temporarily (for a new power and beauty might well in time have emerged from the breakdown of uniformity). It is at such moments of change or decay that the men with the rule-books invariably come upon the scene. In 1324, in piqued and possibly very personal reaction to the appearance of the first, or one of the first, anthologies of non-dramatic *qu*, Zhou Deqing (c. 1270?–post 1324) produced his *Sounds and rhymes of the Central Plain*, a manual of rhyme tables and *qu* phonology, lambasting dialectal and other errors and establishing clear-cut standards, based on the northern dialect and the works of the early northern *qu* poets, for the composition of *qu*.

Once rule-books exist the whole aspect of composition is inevitably transformed. The written standards then always lurk behind the free and casual-spirited poet, ready to be wielded as a cudgel. If Zhou Deqing's rules stemmed decay, as no doubt they did to an enormous degree, preserving a form that without a written exposition of its structural features might well have disappeared in time, then posterity's debt to him is very great. At the same time, once there is a rule-book, sterile or lazy poets can work by rule and produce structurally faultless but dead poetry. The later *qu* poetry, dramatic and non-dramatic, though often still magnificent, generally falls off in vigour and 'naturalness', and it is not unfair to attribute at least some of this decline to the existence of a rule-book.

The speech between the songs of the drama was generally very colloquial and could be very racy when required. Often the more important characters recited a *shi* quatrain on entry. They would generally introduce themselves, too. The speech was frequently a cue to the songs or the songs would sometimes take up the wording of the preceding speech. Speech passages were often extensive and dialogue took up a large portion of the play. The spoken passages sometimes included summaries of the story so far.

4

Performers and the Theatre World during the Yuan Dynasty

From surviving plays, and from a small handful of biographical works and objets d'art, we can reconstruct something of the nature of the acting and actors of the north during the Yuan, although we obtain but the briefest glimpses of many facets of the subject, and none at all of many others. The picture is not by any means a balanced one, but perhaps the surprising thing is that we have even so much material, since much of it seems to have survived by sheer accident or through the nostalgic whim of a single individual.

The role categories of Yuan *zaju* shared certain features with the *yuanben*. The leading roles were the *zhengmo*, 'main man', and the *zhengdan*, 'main woman', who were the only ones to do any singing. They could both appear in the same play and in the same act, but only one leading role would sing in any one act. In some plays the one leading role would sing throughout, in others there would be different leading roles for different acts. The *zhengmo* perhaps inherited some features from the *fumo* and also from the *moni*, but really his function was as different as the Yuan *zaju* itself was from the slapstick *yuanben*. The *zhengmo* (abbreviated to *mo*) roles included young men and old men, often serious and dignified roles, but sometimes comic ones, the scholar, the hermit, butcher, minister, warlord and pedlar. The range was very wide. It was wide for the *zhengdan* or *dan*, too, but rather less so; its roles included anything from maidservants and singing girls to noble ladies, but were generally fairly young women. Lesser role categories were prefixed with the word *wai*, 'secondary'; or sometimes *lao*, 'old', if the character was elderly, or *xiao*, 'little', if the character was young. The *jing* was like the *fujing* of the *yuanben*, a clown or a villain, or both, and embraced such parts as the comically unscrupulous magistrate, the cowardly general, the tramp knight-errant, the clumsy would-be Macchiavelli, the idle and rascally bricklayer. Besides this there were a number of what are best thought of as type characters. The *jia* were emperors and monarchs, the *gu* were ministers and high officials, *buer* were old women, *bolao* were old gaffers, *meixiang*, 'plum-blossom scent', were the soubrettes, maidservants, and so forth.

There were both men and women performers, and men and women played both male and female roles. Some individuals excelled in both *mo* and *dan* roles.[1] If anything, it was the actresses who predominated in Yuan *zaju*, although this impression may be coloured by the wealth of biographical material there is about some actresses, and the paucity of it concerning actors. Around 1354, Xia Tingzhi (c. 1310?–post 1368), a rake-poet and generous patron of the entertainment world, and thus amply qualified for the task, wrote his *Green Bower collection*, which was a collection of biographies of singing girls and actresses from the early thirteenth century to his own times.[2] It is a mine of information on a scintillating galaxy of talents from a whole vivid society.

The actresses were frequented, wooed and taken as wives by the highest-ranking ministers in the land, by top-ranking generals, and by literary men, artists and playwrights of immortal fame. They performed in the palace, in the theatres and at intimate private gatherings and tête-à-tête feasts. Whether exquisitely perfect in their looks or hunchbacked, blind, one-eyed or physically defective in some other way, they were all said to shine in wit, spirit and entertainment skills. One lady was described by the poet Zhong Sicheng, author of *Register recording ghosts*, our main source of information on Yuan *zaju* and playwrights, as having 'a voice as perfect as a xylophone, A body like a xylophone-hammer'.[3] Some of them came from 'respectable families' that had fallen low. Others were non-Chinese, such as the Uighur girl Miliha, as indeed were several of the playwrights and *qu* poets. A number of the girls, in contrast to their professional lives, later became nuns or Taoist priestesses, and often evinced remarkable chastity and fidelity. One beauty, on the death of her husband, a government official, cut off her hair and became a Buddhist nun. Fine gentlemen of high rank often pestered her with visits, so she mutilated her looks to turn the men from the folly of their longings, and chastely lived out her life as a nun.

Accounts of these actresses' love affairs make stirring reading. Any Time Beauty was loved by a lofty academician. Once, when ill, she conceived a yearning for a dish made from horse entrails. Without ado the academician killed his own splendid steed to provide the dish. A yet higher-ranking minister, a Mongol, took a fancy to her and asked her in jest how he compared with the academician. 'You are a government minister,' she replied 'and he is a literary man, a poet. When it comes to balancing the affairs of state, fully implementing the ruler's wishes and organising the people's welfare, he is not a patch on you. But as far as the poetry and wiles of love and romance are concerned, you are quite unworthy to compete with him.' The Mongol roared with laughter, and let her be.[4]

There were most colourful and eccentric characters among the actresses. Vying Heaven Perfume, wife of Li Fish Head, had a hygiene complex, which apart from her flawless body was no doubt her major attraction for that most famous landscape painter of the Yuan, Ni Zan (1301–74), who also had a hygiene complex of which many amusing anecdotes were told.[5] Beautiful Yang Bought Slave, famed for a most unfortunate disease, and loved by eminent gentlemen, was over-fond of tippling. Another lady accumulated a fortune and would scatter gold like dirt. A celebrated actress was last heard of at the age of seventy with hair as white as driven snow, and her finger-nails on both hands over a foot long, a sign of health and extreme leisure. One singing girl was favoured by a high-ranking minister. When he had to leave her for some while, she swore to remain faithful. However, another man of wealth and power forced her eventually to accept his attentions. On the minister's return she confessed to him and, in fulfilment of her vows, stabbed one of her eyes with a hairpin. Alarmed, and filled with admiration, he continued to love her as warmly as ever. This story formed the subject of a Yuan *zaju* drama, a salient example of the liveliness of the genre, and the contemporaneity of some of its themes.

The actresses were astonishingly versatile. Besides the trades of love and stage they often commanded many other arts and abilities. Many were brilliant extempore composers of *qu* songs and other kinds of poetry, their compositions enjoying general popularity and delighting the greatest of contemporary scholar-poets. Others even published their verse in written form, and one or two such poems still survive. One celebrated courtesan, actress Pearl Curtain Beauty, published a collection of her poetry with a preface by one of the most noted orthodox literary men. Indeed the literati dedicated many of their songs to these actresses, in the confidence that they would be worthily received and appreciated by the girls. One excellent actress of *zaju* was very erudite, being deeply versed in the two classical monumental histories: the *Historical records* of Sima Qian (145–86 BC) and the *Comprehensive mirror* of Sima Guang (1019–86). Some had a prodigious capacity for memorising. One actress who excelled in *dan* roles knew over three hundred parts by heart. Little Spring Feast would often post up the titles of the plays she knew by heart all over the theatre walls and beams, and allow the audience to pick whichever play they desired.

Many actresses and singing girls excelled in other entertainment arts. Some performed *zhugongdiao*,[6] or played the *pipa*-lute or other woodwind and stringed instruments, and one ranked among the mere ten or so noted singers of Tatar or Mongol songs to their own string accompaniments in China. Some were fine calligraphers or tellers of riddles, and many combined dancing and singing skills with sparkling wit and joke-telling. One richly talented lady would keep gentlemen amused by her humour all day long. She died at the early age of twenty-two, and for years afterwards admirers would make springtime pilgrimages to her grave. Another was a story-teller, whose narratives tumbled forth 'like balls rolling down a slope and like water flowing from a pitcher on a roof'.[7]

The actresses made their names in all kinds of roles. Pearl Curtain Beauty played emperors and monarchs, and flighty young women or singing girl roles, as well as genteel male roles. Any Time Beauty played yearning and pining maidens, various other female roles, and monarchs. Several excelled in robber and brigand roles, including the actress Pingyang Slave, who was blind in one eye and tattooed all over, and another actress who had exceptionally small feet but all the same bore herself most boldly and martially. Jade Lotus, graceful and witty, singer, dancer and humorist, was accomplished in the acrobatics of weapon-handling. Dragon Tower Scene and Cinnabar Steps Beauty specialised in *nanxi* plays, while Lotus Beauty performed both *zaju* and *nanxi*, a clear indication of the proximity of the two genres and of the inter-influence that no doubt took place. Another actress was famed as 'the tender *dan*' and another as 'the gay romantic *dan*', both of them playing flighty young women or singing girl parts.[8] Apart from the general role categories, the actresses and actors clearly tended to specialise in types, and to be particularly strong in portraying particular human characteristics.

Actresses married not only into the gentry, but also into the entertainment professions. Many of them had actors as their husbands, some of whom performed *zaju* but many of whom were *yuanben* players. This is another reminder of the closeness of the two kinds of play in the acting world. Daughters often followed their mothers' footsteps into the acting profession and achieved fame in their own right. Actor families frequently occur in the history of Chinese drama.

The prominence of women in Yuan acting is further shown by an invaluable coloured mural completed on 24 May 1324 and discovered not long ago in a temple in Shansi province.[9] It depicts a Yuan troupe on stage. The troupe is headed by a woman and there are several other actresses, some playing male parts. There are ten people on stage, but two or three of them are musicians, one playing a flute, one holding clappers and one near a drum. Five or six of the players are wearing elaborate costumes, and one actress has a false beard of the kind still worn in Peking Opera in modern times. They hold fans, a weapon (most say a sword, but is it possibly something akin to a *kegua*?), and a tablet of office. The stage surface seems to be of square tiles. It projects from a back curtain, and seems to be open on three sides. The back curtain is covered in a pattern of symbols, and against it are hung two cloths depicting a man waving a sword at a fierce dragon, probably a scene from a play but not the play being performed. Someone is peeping from behind the curtain through the entry or exit door, known in Yuan times as the *guimendao*, 'ghost door passage'. Over the stage hangs the announcement, written horizontally: 'The Taihang actress Loyal Capital Beauty is now performing here.'

Several poems and plays from the Yuan and early Ming afford us further brief glimpses of the Yuan theatre. We have mentioned Du Renjie's farmer and the multiple bill including both *yuanben* and *zaju*. Gao Andao's song-set* also indicates a very varied and full bill: music, dance, acrobatics, *yuanben*, *zaju*, and a *zaban* or some such *sanduan*. The leading role in the *zaju* is no sister of the actresses in the *Green Bower collection* but a most uncomely *dan*, devoid of all demure seductions, as slender as a water-buffalo, hoarse-voiced, thick-necked, grubby-fingered, and in no way living up to the stage directions that her part should be played 'with graceful dancing posture and mellifluous singing voice'. The other performers are equally unappetising. The *waidan* is 'stinking rank and frowsy', the stage properties are filthy, and there is a miserable hotchpotch of costumes.

*See pages 21–22 above.

It is commonly stated that *qu* were accompanied by the *pipa*-lute. This was certainly very generally the case for the singing of non-dramatic *qu*, but for the drama the drum, gong and wooden or ivory *ban*-clappers were common, perhaps used for rhythmic backing rather than accompaniment. Other instruments were also used, including the horizontal *di*-flute – though most probably the flute was used for introductory or bridge passages of music and so forth rather than as accompaniment. The thirteenth or early fourteenth-century poet Sui Xuanming wrote a *qu* in praise of the drum, which describes its use in the theatre, in *yuanben* and in village plays, for introductory and other purposes.[10] The style of singing associated with northern *qu* was generally described as more bold and vigorous than southern styles of singing; it tended to have one or more syllables to the note, while southern singing was melismatic and often kept the syllable extended, even over several notes. Broadly speaking, this made the northern *qu* more directly comprehensible in word-meaning, while in the south the melody generally had more mastery over word-meaning. Some suggest that the reasons for the differ- ence lie partly in climate, the brisk harshness of the north and the soft lushness of the south, and there may well be something in the theory.* Music in the north used a heptachord, whereas the south used a pentatonic scale. Northern *qu* music seems basically to have been fitted to the *pipa*-lute, whereas drum and *ban*- clappers were the regulating instruments for southern singing.

Costume and make-up were used in Yuan *zaju*. There was a distinction bet- ween ancient and contemporary costume, and different types were given charac- teristic dress – fishermen wore thatched raincoats, for instance – but we have no details as to how far accuracy of costume was carried.[11] Probably not very far generally, and the humbler the troupe the less any such niceties would have concerned it. Stylisation of costume would also have had the advantage of familiarising the audience with types. *Jing* roles were particularly heavily made up. Lime or chalk powder, ink, soot and other substances were used. A number of small stage properties were employed, such as cangues, swords, basins, bamboo- horses (like hobby-horses), fly-whisks, maps, and so forth. The musicians played on stage, to the side on the *yuechuang* ('music bench'), or behind the players. There was, as far as we know, no scenery at all, nor any curtains at the front of the stage, though there were drapes at the back of it.

One late Yuan or early Ming *zaju* provides us with a vivid example of theatrical life. The play is *Lan Caihe*, by an anonymous dramatist, and it concerns a troupe of actors.[12] The leading role in the play is Xu Jian, an actor whose stage name (*yueming*, 'music name') is Lan Caihe. He is the *moni*, the leading actor and man- ager, of a theatre (*goulan*) named Liang Park Awning, which implies something like 'Tivoli Playhouse'. The theatre – as described in the play – is a permanent structure with a lockable door, probably open to the sky. There are loges situated high up and known as 'bowers of the gods' and more general seating known as 'waist awnings', presumably benches. On the stage is a *yuechuang* reserved for the

---

*See pages 73–75 below for further elaborations on this topic.

female musicians. Coloured posters and backcloths and other drapes and advertisements are hung up before the performance, including the announcement, 'The *moni* of Liang Park Awning, Lan Caihe, is now performing here', very similar in wording to the announcement on the Yuan mural. Both *yuanben* and *zaju* are performed by his troupe, having been written by 'kind gentlemen of the *shuhui*'. Sometimes the same play is showing elsewhere and there is sharp competition between troupes. The audiences for this theatre would seem to be rather exclusive, since the hero at one point declares that 'only officials, solid citizens and moneyed gentlemen are allowed to divert themselves in the theatres', but this is unlikely to have been always the case, and is probably not meant too literally even in this instance. Spectators are known as *kanguan*, 'looking officials', and it is the custom to allow them to choose what plays they wish to see performed.

Drum, gongs, clappers and flute are used for the music of the plays performed at Liang Park Awning. Actors too old to act any more sometimes become drummers, and probably other kinds of musician too. The actors live in the theatre, and seem to be a small company sharing profits. The number of persons is mentioned as twenty, but that may be a metaphorical turn of phrase. Some of them, at least, are relatives. As is borne out by many other writings, actors can be called away, often without warning, to perform services for government officials, and for the purposes of providing palace entertainment. To fail to fulfil such duties is a serious crime, punishable by such dire penalties as forty strokes of the heavy rod. Actors are referred to as *luqi*, 'byway men', *yueguan*, 'music officials', *lingren*, 'musicians' (or 'Ling men'), *hangyuan*, 'singsong-house players', and *linglun*.[13] The latter term was originally the name of the music master of the mythical Yellow Emperor of antiquity, Ling Lun. The actors of this troupe seem fairly prosperous.

Many of the features of theatrical life shown in *Lan Caihe* were general ones. A song-set by playwright and poet Tang Shi who lived during the late Yuan and early Ming offers further insights.[14] Written during the reign of the first Ming emperor (1368–98), it nevertheless describes conditions that were almost certainly similar to those of the Yuan. It was composed in response to a request from the Music Academy for a dedication for a newly constructed theatre in the Ming capital, Nanking. After a eulogy of the age, praising the emperor for having 'pacified and annexed China mid a jest and chat', it describes the massive foundations of the theatre, the magnificent planning and proportions, the ceaseless construction work, the resounding of axes and the harsh noise of saws and shovels with sparks a-flying, the floors of flattened tile and rubble base, and the brick or stone walls built with busy haste. The theatre, it says, is one built to last for ever. 'Iron-trunked, frost-barked timber of specially selected trees from the southern mountains' has been felled for the framework, and 'gold-starred snowy-waved rocks have been fished up from all over the eastern ocean' to serve as giant pillar bases. The curving roof-tiles soar into the sky over a splendid, powerful edifice. High up, there are intricately carved and latticed windows and below, possibly leading to them, are steep steps 'a hundred feet high'. Leaning over the balustrade one has a view over vast stretches of the River Yangtse. There are fine tapering tiles stretching aloft in the form of the wings of colourfully patterned mandarin ducks and projecting from the 'wind-barring eaves', while from the corners of the eaves the 'cloud-flying' ridge-beams with grim monster tails stick boldly forth.

Facing the theatre to the south is the famous Phoenix Terrace, a scenic spot of which China's most celebrated poet, Li Bai (Li Po, 701–62) once sang, and winding round the theatre is the Rouge Stream, associated with the love story of a famous poet-monarch of the sixth century and his *femme fatale*. From the southern end of the theatre precincts there is an endless vista of the kingfisher-blue slopes of the Bell Mountains peeping through white clouds. The nearby crossroads commands the way to the ruined palaces of the ancient emperors who once held sway in this same city. There is deep shade from weeping willows and dense clusters of blossom on the trees. To one side of the theatre are wine-houses from which issue the loud noise of music and singing, and on the other side bathing-houses whence drift the titillating perfumes of orchid and musk. The imperial palace is very near, so near that the roll of drums, the rattle of clappers and the sounds of all kinds of other instruments can be heard as some lofty procession enters the palace.

The poem goes on to compare the theatre to various paradises, praising its spaciousness, its generous proportions, its splendour and the air of fine romance and gaiety that pervades it. Then Tang Shi portrays a very different set of performers from Gao Andao's sorry crew. All or most of them are actresses. This time the *dan* has a dancing posture 'as supply wafting as the willows where sleep the sloughing silkworms'. The *zhuanggu* official is mighty and imposing of mien, cockbold and martial in his bearing, and 'spits forth rainbow vapours' – magnificent speeches. The *moni* has a singing voice that 'strews one continuous string of pearls'. The *fujing* is a thorough clown, with a flustered, dodgy face and weird features, body and bones all at odds with the norms of this world.

The other performers are all equally attuned to their roles. No wonder that in the audience the young lords are clutching their gold in their breast-pockets, itching to bestow it upon the actresses, as other young blades, their eyes popping out with eagerness, also prepare to congratulate the stage beauties with their gifts. Successful scholar-gentlemen and laureate doctors of the imperial examinations, professional swindlers and coney-catchers, all alike take pleasure in the proceedings. Wealthy men unload themselves of their lucre, striving to dispense their snow-white silver. Presumably, as was often the custom in later ages, they are trying to buy the favours of the actresses by spilling largesse as they request items of performance? Whore-hunting, would-be squires, their necks straining and eyes bulging, are taking a hard hungry eyeful of the feminine charms. The bustle and excitement is reminiscent of a temple fair. The fame of the theatre is assured and resounds throughout northern and southern China. Finally, presumably in tribute to the emperor's patronage or benevolent interest, or for the sake of expressing pious loyalty, the poem declares that thanks to the emperor's favours the theatre, with its assembly of 'orioles and blossoms', reigns supreme in the universe, unmatchable by even ten thousand Liang Parks. 'Liang Park' means a wondrous place of pleasure, a fine theatre, or sometimes the city of Bianliang.

Large theatres were nothing new by that time, and although there are fewer records of them in the Yuan than in the Sông we can be sure that there were a good number. The end of the Yuan was after all only some eighty or ninety years after the Southern Sông, when Hangzhou alone had seventeen *wazi* and no doubt a much larger number of theatres. There was an accident in the summer of 1362 when a theatre collapsed and forty-two people died.[15] One imagines it must have been a fairly large construction, perhaps of the scaffolding type. A Yuan stage survived in Shansi until about thirty years ago, and various other early temple stages which may have been in use during the Yuan are mentioned in modern writings.[16] In addition, of course, there were the temporary stages of the itinerant players.

Yuan *zaju* drama was played in all kinds of ways and *milieux*, and met with all kinds of reactions. It was welcomed high and low because it brought pleasure, edification and colour to life. At the same time, there were many who partially or wholly disapproved of the theatre, many who firmly held it in moral opprobrium – as there have been at all times and in all countries throughout the history of civilisation. Of course whoredom, illicit love, wild living and broad views of morality were inextricably part of theatrical life. It was easy to forget what the theatre offered and to concentrate attention on its dangers: young gentlemen being led astray, ruined morally and financially; the free and potent dispersal of new ideas; large and potentially dangerous and riotous gatherings; the dangers of sedition; the danger of the theatre's being used by political opponents; the dangers of opening men's minds and suggesting alternatives to the safe cold hypocrisies of respectability.

Yet those who concentrated on such dangers – anywhere in the world in the early history of drama – would ignore the fact that the theatre was often highly moral in its teachings, setting good over evil in a most forceful manner. The fact that the theatre was such a potent alternative to other teaching media was no doubt one of the major causes of opposition to it from the moralists of ensconced respectability, who would have liked to have the monopoly of teaching and to restrict the imparting of knowledge to the narrow range of ideas not inimical or offensive to their own ways of life. Yet the moral disapproval was not limited to strait-laced killjoys, but was felt to some extent by many, possibly by most people. Some would disapprove of some aspects of the theatre and approve of others.

Ambivalence of this kind appears to have been particularly marked in the attitudes of Chinese emperors and their governments towards the theatre. On the one hand was their fear of social change, disorder or political opposition, and, on

the other, their desire to monopolise the fun, to appropriate for their own purposes the powerful, pleasant means of education, to gain control of a potentially
unrivalled medium of propaganda. Yet the attitudes of the Chinese rulers should
not be over-simplified. They were aware that theatre was often more flourishing
in the wilds of ordinary society than in public performance, also perhaps that it
was not wholly eradicable by law, and for these and other reasons they never
monopolised it as completely as one might expect.

Particularly from the Ming dynasty onwards there is ample written evidence of
social and moral objections to the theatre, and of government measures against
players and plays.[17] It must not be thought that evidence of the former is ever
surely indicative of the dominant attitudes of any one group of society: for
instance, a Chinese scholar could often pour condemnation upon a work while at
the same time privately relishing it. Nor were government measures always totally enforceable. The evidence is, however, strongly indicative of the alertness of
orthodoxy and of the watchful, wary eye that governments kept on the theatre.
The severity of some of the prohibitions against it is a convincing sign of the
rulers' anxiety and concern.

A number of surviving Yuan edicts contain prohibitions against various kinds
of entertainer and entertainment. According to one, the composition of ci and qu
songs, which without doubt also covered the composition of plays, was to be
punishable by death.[18] Perhaps that sweeping extreme was produced by a particular moment of crisis, but it was in any case a useful bludgeon for the government to keep in reserve. According to another, young men of the people who
pursued no proper livelihood but for no worthy motives performed and sang
stories and plays (zaxi), gathering crowds in markets and fair-places for the sake
of lewd amusement, were all without exception to be proceeded against. The
performance of puppet shows, beating of 'fish'-drums, enticement of people into
forming crowds, and selling of false medicines were also to be banned, those
breaking the ban to be heavily punished. According to yet another document,
those who in a disorderly manner composed songs to convey satirical advice were
to be deported. And yet another declared that those who sang lewd (the word can
cover a multitude of sins and supposed sins!) songs in market-places were to be
given forty-seven strokes of the rod, and their local mayor and various others
twenty-seven each.

A number of the prohibitions are datable and more specific. In December 1274
an assembly of about a hundred people gathered in a small town in Hopeh to hear
story-telling, amid music and the drinking of wine, brought down punishment on
a mayor and others responsible. The accusation included the charge of allowing
young people to perform masked plays, and it was recommended that all those
peasants, townsmen and young men of respectable families, excluding registered
entertainers, who practised playing and story-telling should be banned from
doing so. In 1281 there was a prohibition against performing demon kings in zaju,
dressing up as certain Buddhist deities or wearing skull masks. In 1319(?) a ban
was imposed on the singing of certain pipa-lute songs to the tune 'Pedlar'. The

singing of this was apparently causing crowds in Khanbalik to block the streets and markets, men and women mixing with one another; this was not only giving rise to fights and litigation but also causing the authorities concern that it might occasion 'other incidents'.

In 1313 came a ban indicative of more general prejudices, when actors and entertainers, along with the incurably maimed or disabled and those convicted of major crimes, were excluded from taking the imperial civil service examinations, which had only that year been reinstituted after many decades in abeyance. A document of 1317 condemned the casual gathering of crowds at fairs, which 'causes agricultural people to practise vagrancy and idleness, their pure simple habits to turn into frivolity and irresponsibility, and there to arise litigations, theft and all manner of awkwardnesses'. In this and other bans the gatherings at village fairs were associated with vagrant salesmen and players. Village festivals were likewise regarded with suspicion. It was feared that such events might corrupt morals and interrupt agricultural work, as well as fostering trades that evaded taxation, but perhaps it was also feared that with the bulk of China's population living in the countryside, which was less easily controlled by military means than the towns, the fairs might be the means of fomenting disorder.

The pressures from authority were clearly very strong and persistent. In 1319 improvements and specifications were made to earlier prohibitions against village entertainments. Penalties were fixed not only for the village heads, but, perhaps as a sign of the seriousness of the issue, also for those regional government officials who failed to bring the offences to light. The officials were to lose a month's salary. It was regretted that it would be difficult or impossible to punish all the vast mass of those involved. Another ban complained that officials were not implementing the prohibitions with due severity, and that this failure was in evidence even in the capital, let alone in the countryside. The author of the document expressed surprise that he had himself witnessed a gathering of crowds in a southern village to listen to ballad-singing. Henceforth performers were all to be arrested, and precise penalties were stipulated for fairground entertainers, for magistrates and other officials failing to pursue the prohibitions with rigour, and for community heads and other responsible persons.

The itinerant players and entertainers at fairs and in the markets were part of the same world as the theatre performers. In the complex of entertainment life mountebanks, puppeteers, story-tellers and players of all kinds still mingled in the same fairs, markets and entertainment quarters. In literature there was a similar lack of rigid compartmentalisation. One and the same scholar might write anything from the most formal of essays or poems to the most colloquial songs or plays. It was in the late Yuan or early Ming that the first long Chinese novels were written, in a language often reflecting the colloquial tongue.[19] They are generally attributed to Luo Ben (fl. c. 1364), who was a composer of riddles and *qu* songs and a *zaju* playwright.[20] They seemingly drew some of their material and many of their ideas from the professional story-tellers of the markets and entertainment quarters, and are yet another example of how closely the activities of entertainers and writers were interwoven.

The Yuan *zaju* established the drama in China, but in doing so it had by the late Yuan lost some of its force and freshness. This, coupled with various political shifts and upheavals, and other more purely cultural factors, was to give the advantage during the Ming increasingly to other kinds of drama.

5
'Nanxi' Drama, 'Chuanqi' Drama, and the Beginnings of Kunqu Drama

Much of our view of the past is inevitably distorted by the bias of what has been recorded in writing, and by the bias of what has survived of these records. How many kinds of entertainment have been lost because no one thought to describe them in writing? How many that are only meagrely recorded were in their day great vogues, flourishing arts that gave delight and stimulation to multitudes? Many even of those that were documented may well have been consigned to neglect by the prejudices and blindnesses of later ages. Most of what we know about Yuan *zaju* playwrights and performers comes from the nostalgic memoirs of one or two playwrights and song-composers who were personally involved in the theatre world. Had those works been lost, as so many were, we should, as far as we know, have remained eternally ignorant of most of the background to Yuan *zaju*. And had not a group of *zaju* printed in the Yuan chanced to survive in the hands of a book collector, we should have had almost no sure basis for saying what Yuan *zaju* drama was like.[1] Even the late Ming editions were the work of a relatively small handful of enthusiasts. It would have been very easy for Yuan *zaju* drama to have vanished without much trace. The offical history of the Yuan devotes no pages to it, and other formal records mention it only briefly or in passing, if at all. Yet, as the most vital form of literary expression of a literary-minded nation, in many ways it embodied the essential spirit of the age.

What might easily have happened is seen in the case of another kind of drama contemporary with Yuan *zaju*. Lotus Beauty acted both *zaju* and *nanxi* plays, and other actresses mentioned in the *Green Bower collection* also acted *nanxi*. Playwright Xiao Dexiang (early fourteenth century) wrote both kinds of play.[2] Zhou Deqing, in defending the purity of northern song, declared that it was shameful to adopt the southern pronunciations used in the singing and recitation of *xiwen* plays, such as *Le Chang divides the mirror*, from the area round Hangzhou, which were the 'play-acting pronunciations of a fallen state', the Southern Sông.[3] Contemporary with Yuan *zaju*, then, there existed the southern *nanxi*, a powerful and in some respects more flexible form of drama, which has until very recent

71

times been largely neglected by posterity, and which has yet to be restored to its proper place alongside Yuan *zaju*, of which it was a by no means insignificant rival.

A hundred and seventy or so titles of *nanxi* are known, some no doubt from the early Ming but many from the Southern Sông and Yuan. For several there are corresponding extant plays, and for over a hundred there are song fragments, ranging from one or two lines to a large number of songs.[4] Very few authors are known, however, which makes for an enormous gap in our understanding of the genre. Nonetheless, enough of *nanxi* can still be seen to hint tantalisingly at the treasure of entertainment and literature which it must have constituted.

Originating, as briefly mentioned above, in the Northern Sông dynasty, this drama developed a music which took tunes from *ci* and from folk-songs. During the years 1190–4 it had a success with the plays *Zhao Chaste Maid* and *Wang Kui*.[5] We have no real idea how far removed in form these plays were from the Sông *zaju* in general, but assuredly they were more than simple skits. During the years 1268–9, only a few years before the fall of the city to the Mongols, a *nanxi* play called *Wang Huan* enjoyed great acclaim in Hangzhou.[6] After the conquest the *nanxi* still remained popular. A villainous and influential Buddhist priest took himself a beautiful concubine, but when she became pregnant he obliged the son of one of his followers to marry her in order to avoid a scandal and so that he might still continue the relationship with her. The son, however, unable himself to bear the whispers of scandal and gossip, ran off with the woman. The priest fabricated charges and the son's whole family were subjected to beatings in court. When they appealed to higher authorities, the priest's bribery secured them more torture. They prepared to take matters to the capital, but before they could do so the ruthless cleric had thugs seize them, take them to an isolated spot and drown them. There followed a public outcry demanding that the priest be punished, but the regional authorities had been bribed, and were slow to take action. These events were made into a southern play, which was widely performed and so intensified public pressures that the authorities had the priest killed in jail, just five days before a special pardon for him arrived from the capital.[7]

After the unification of China, the vigorous northern *zaju* drama spread rapidly and soon gained the ascendancy in the south too, though southern plays still continued to be performed. Three whole plays, discovered as the last remnants of a large Ming collection on a London book-stall in 1920, may well originate from the late thirteenth or early fourteenth century.[8] *Top Graduate Zhang Xie*, introduced in chapter two above, may possibly be as early as the late Southern Sông.[9] *Little Butcher Sun* is the story of a butcher whose brother marries an evil woman. The woman has a paramour who on her instigation murders her maidservant and contrives to have her husband accused of the crime. But the butcher manages to shift the blame to himself and is executed in his brother's stead. Moved by this act of virtue, the Emperor of Heaven restores the butcher to life. The butcher, his brother and the maid's ghost frighten the wife into a full confession of her and her lover's crimes, and obtain justice and the punishment of the guilty pair. *In the wrong career* concerns the love affair of a young nobleman with an actress. They are discovered together by his father, a high-ranking official, and he flees home to escape his father's wrath. His money exhausted, he is obliged to join his beloved's family troupe and act *yuanben* and *zaju* for a living. One day, his father is sent on a tour of inspection, arrives at the area where they are performing and summons actors to amuse him. He recognises his son and the actress among the performers, and, delighted to be reunited with his son, gladly gives his consent to the marriage.

It was in a way strange that the first great drama movement to achieve national popularity, the Yuan *zaju*, should have come from the north of China, since the weight of China's population, and much of its wealth of cultural traditions and its commercial abundance, lay in the regions around Hangzhou in the south. The last decades of Mongol rule produced a shift of power away from the Mongol court in the north, and with the resurgence of Chinese power and political confidence in the south came a general tendency for the south to raise its head again. Partly because of this new general self-respect, and partly no doubt because it had by now undergone certain changes, profiting from the example of the northern drama, from about 1330 onwards the *nanxi* gained a sudden new lease of energy and popularity, with great numbers of playwrights making their appearance. Xiao Dexiang may have been among the early ones. He carved his chief livelihood from medicine. Whenever he came across an old piece of writing, he would 'bevel it into southern songs', which became very popular in the streets and markets.[10]

The 'southern songs' are generally referred to as 'southern *qu*'. Zhu Youdun made the following distinctions:

> Since the late Tang and early Sông, there have been songs entirely based on *ci* form for the main part, which are nowadays referred to as southern *qu*. When, during the Jin and Yuan, barbarian customs became current in China, compositions in the Jurched form arose, and furthermore such musical experts as Top Graduate Dong and Guan Hanqing adapted the form of southern *qu* to northern music, whereafter songs produced in the north became prevalent in the Central Plain [i.e. northern China], these being what are nowadays called northern *qu*. Thus two categories are to be distinguished: the southern *qu* which the southerners sing, and the northern *qu* which the northerners sing.[11]

Zhu seems more or less to equate southern *qu* with *ci* , but they have often been differentiated, 'southern *qu*' referring to the whole repertoire of southern music, including both *ci* and other traditional and folk tunes, that was associated with the southern drama, and that during the late Sông or mid-Yuan, probably in emulation of the northern *qu*, acquired various features, such as the use of *chenzi* and the organisation of tunes in song-sets, which do indeed distinguish it from the earlier Tang and Sông *ci*. Nonetheless, southern *qu* derived a much greater proportion of tunes from *ci* than did northern *qu*, and were clearly closer to it, and generally closer to the more traditional form of Chinese music, than were the northern *qu* as a whole.

Southern *qu* tended to use much fewer *chenzi* than northern *qu*, often none at all, and differed also in their rhyming, which followed southern and traditional *ci* standards and was less sustained than in the case of northern *qu*, and in their manners of organising tunes within their song-sets. The most marked difference, however, lay in their overall musical effect. Since no large body of written music of the period survives, we must largely rely on generalised views of the difference, views, moreover, which for the most part stem from mid-Ming or later. One Ming critic presents the contrast as follows:

Hearing northern *qu* stirs one's mood and spirit, rendering them as fierce and martial as the soaring falcon, makes one's hair bristle and scalp tingle, and is capable of inspiring one to bold endeavours. Yes, truly, the northern barbarians excel in drumming up fury, and just as is said, 'the music by being compressed and staccato creates hatred'. Southern *qu* on the other hand are meandering and slow, drawn-out endlessly, graceful, charming and seductively lilting, floating and drifting one away, so that one loses all firmness of purpose without being conscious of it oneself. Yes, truly the south is soft and beguiling.[12]

Another Ming scholar puts the matter more precisely, although still presenting sweeping generalisations:

The north stresses vigour, urgency, boldness and vivacity, whereas the south stresses tranquillity, insubstantiality, gentle softness and ethereal remoteness. In the north the syllables are many and the tune compressed, this compression giving prominence to qualities of energy. In the south the syllables are few and the tune is slow and extended, this extendedness giving prominence to the rhythmic cadences. In the north the semantic import of the words is greater than the musical import, while in the south it is the other way round. [. . .] The north tends to be too coarse of mood and the south to be too feeble.[13]

These are at best loose general impressions. There can, for instance, be no reasonable doubt that many of the northern songs could be gently lascivious and beguiling, and that southern songs could sometimes be vigorous and stirring.

In performance, northern and southern dramas would have been distinguished from each other not only by, among other things, the overall mood of their music, but also by the arrangement and effect of their singing. The Yuan *zaju* used solo singing. The *nanxi* had solos, duets, songs with three or more people singing separately and in chorus, and songs sung entirely in chorus. In contrast to Yuan *zaju*, the speech tended to follow *nanxi* singing rather than introduce it. With the earlier *nanxi* the songs were not arranged in song-sets or arranged in very loose song-sets. This lack of musical organisation was one of the reasons why the genre was not accorded high esteem by the orthodox literati, although the very lack of tight organisation or musical consistency may well have had charms of its own. During the late Yuan there arose the habit of combining northern with southern *qu* in song-sets or in other kinds of association. The playwright and song-composer Shen He (d. shortly before 1330) was apparently the first to use both northern and southern tunes in one and the same composition.[14] There is some doubt as to whether he did so in his plays as well as his non-dramatic *qu* works, but certainly the habit of doing so became fairly widespread during the last few decades of the Yuan, in both *zaju* and *nanxi*. In *Little Butcher Sun* one finds two such song-sets, as well as other northern tunes scattered elsewhere in the play. As is known to be the case with some later southern plays, the southern style of singing would probably dominate even the northern tunes used in a *nanxi*, so that the total musical effect of the play would not lose its homogeneity, or not drastically so.

The two mixed song-sets in *Little Butcher Sun* were sung by one person throughout in each case, but the habit in most other known *nanxi* plays was for two characters to alternate the singing, one in fairly close response to the other, frequently as little as a line at a time being sung by each. The singing was not restricted to the main roles, nor did one character usually sing through a whole act by himself or herself. One act was not limited to one song-set. The key and rhyme could be changed within the act, often in reflection of a change in the course of the plot. Thus there was not the same coincidence of musical and rhyming effects with the act unit that the Yuan *zaju* evinced. The alternation of the singing enabled some of the plays to have very long uninterrupted passages of singing, longer and more frequent than in the northern dramas.

Since we cannot be certain as to the nature of the speech parts in Yuan *zaju*, the possibilities of comparison in that direction are decidedly limited. *Top Graduate Zhang Xie* is a very full text, and has much more verse than plain speech, as do both *Little Butcher Sun* and *In the wrong career*, which are however very brief texts as they survive and quite possibly unrepresentative of the whole performance. Passages of speech in the early southern plays are very extensive, and ably handled, in *Moon prayer* by shop-keeper Shi Hui, for instance, often far surpassing in their deft coherence and nimble humour anything to be found in the Yuan editions of Yuan *zaju*. In contrast to the predominantly prose speech of the northern dramas, the *nanxi* speech often, even in the 'vulgar' earlier plays, contains a great deal of verse, sometimes quite ornate and intricate. Most probably that reflects some general prevalence of verse as a medium of speech in the *nanxi* rather than a superior level of formal education or more highbrow literary aspirations on the part of the southern dramatists.

It may be that, in the absence of firm central government during these decades, censorship and other restrictions on the subject-matter and language of drama were unusually lax or ineffective. The *nanxi* also seems to have been more nearly a folk or popular product than the Yuan *zaju*, and to have been held in less general esteem by the scholar gentry. Some of those who wrote northern songs and plays at that time were well known even in other notable fields of endeavour, such as government and painting, but we know hardly any of the authors of the early southern plays, and it is probable that they were for the most part obscure or anonymous writers even in their own day. Some of the few names of authors attached to these plays were seemingly those of men working for *shuhui*, and some seem to have adopted the names of more famous northerners. Not only was the authorship of the plays obscure, but their topics and treatment of topics were often vulgar or unashamedly direct. This 'naturalness' was displeasing to some late Ming critics, and such displeasure may have been another reason why *nanxi* drama was largely consigned to oblivion.

Killing a dog, sometimes attributed to a certain Xu Zhen, the anonymous *White rabbit*, *Moon prayer* attributed to Shi Hui and *Thorn hairpin* by Ke Danqiu or a Top Graduate Wang, were vigorous and often rumbustious.[15] Some Ming and later critics specifically objected to these plays for their lusty vulgarity and frequent use of slang, one remarking that they were all unbearably coarse in their poetry, particularly *Killing a dog*. It is sometimes difficult to be sure whether the critics objected most to the language or to the content of the plays, and perhaps the two aspects were often not clearly separated in their own minds. One of the few Ming scholars whom we know to have championed *nanxi* remarked, however, that while apart from a certain few plays, 'the rest are all vulgarisms and slang, yet they have one outstanding merit, which is that their language is natural and unadorned [*bense*] every word of it, with none of the literary airs of modern writers'.[16] This, too, is a sweeping generalisation, but serves to balance some of the sweeping condemnations.

Some of the *nanxi* used the same themes and titles as Yuan *zaju*. In some cases this may simply have been that both styles drew from similar or identical sources. In other cases it is clear beyond doubt that the southern dramas directly adapted, or were influenced by, northern plays of the same theme that were already popular. Imitation was most likely a major means of emulation in the late Yuan. Shi Hui's *Moon prayer*, for instance, closely followed the plot of Guan Hanqing's *Moon prayer pavilion*, and actually took a considerable amount word for word from Guan Hanqing. Nonetheless, it was a fuller play of very different form and style, and remains a sparkling example of the attractions of the southern drama.

The freshness, roughness, bawdy mischief and free humour of the plays were no doubt important in ensuring the early southern drama's hold upon its audiences, and many of the early Yuan *zaju* had appealed through similar qualities, but it was a play of a rather different kind which, perhaps as a result of suddenly altered political circumstances, was to have the most influence on a national scale and in later ages. The play was *Lute* by Gao Ming (c. 1301–c. 1370).

In 1368 rebel armies, united under the command of the ex-mendicant-bonze Zhu Yuanzhang, swept northwards, took Khanbalik, and drove the Mongol rulers from China. Zhu Yuanzhang thus became the first emperor of the Ming dynasty, which lasted from 1368 until 1644. A man of humble origins, as were many of the rebel leaders, he came from a line of farmers, sericulturists and gold-panners, and was well aware of the delights and power of popular drama. When he ascended the throne, he and his imperial clan showed enormous active interest in both northern and southern drama. The various princes were obliged to send him seventeen hundred volumes of 'songs', which almost certainly included a large number of plays.[17] A number of the imperial clan became leading playwrights themselves. Emperor Chengzu (r. 1402–24) ordered the compilation of a gigantic collection of literature which included many story-tellers' tales, over a hundred Yuan and Ming *zaju*, and thirty-four *nanxi*.[18] Emperor Xianzong (r. 1465–87) was said by a near-contemporary to have been so fond of listening to plays and songs that his quest for them 'almost exhausted the world of their editions'.[19] Emperor Wuzong (r. 1506–21) shared the same inclinations in this respect and would generously reward people who presented such editions to him. Three gentlemen together presented him with several thousand volumes of plays, songs and stories.[20] There is an account of his obtaining a copy of a rare novel for fifty pieces of gold, which is some measure of the ardour of his hunt for popular literature.[21] The interest in drama remained strong at court for the rest of the dynasty. There were huge acting establishments in the imperial courts, and the emperors were mostly very drama-conscious. Emperor Xizong (r. 1621–7) even acted in a play – playing the part of an emperor![22]

There was the usual duality of attitude, however. While the emperors were fully aware of the entertainment and educative values of the drama for themselves and their clans and court, they were equally anxious to curb and supervise drama among the ordinary populace. In 1369 the ban on actors and their families taking part in the imperial examinations was reinforced.[23] In 1389 officers and soldiers stationed in the capital were forbidden to learn 'singing' on pain of having their tongues cut out.

Chess, 'double sixes' (backgammon) and *cuju*-football were also banned. Officers and men caught playing board games were to have a hand cut off, and those playing football to have a foot cut off. Such penalties and worse were actually carried out, to the horror of later commentators. Actors were permitted to perform plays about saintly immortals, chaste women, filial sons, obedient grandsons, and other themes conducive to morality and to the upholding of peace and social order, but were subject to arrest and punishment for performing anything offensively familiar towards or blasphemous about emperors and kings or virtuous sages and saints such as Confucius. The punishment for actors and for persons who permitted such performances was a hundred strokes of the heavy rod. The seditious and rebellious dangers of drama were quite obvious to the emperors. This ban on the performance of 'throne plays' (*jiatou zaju*) was repeated, and punishments ferociously specified, in 1411. People who dared to maintain in their possession, perform, print, sell or otherwise propagate such plays were to be at once arrested and duly punished. Five days' grace after the promulgation of the edict was allowed for people to take the plays to the authorities for burning and destruction, after which those who kept them were to be executed along with all their family. Appreciation of the drama by the Ming emperors was evidently coupled with an acute apprehension of its social and political possibilities, and there is no denying that both their pleasure and their fears had considerable influence on the shape and course of Ming drama.

During the last years of the Yuan dynasty, while taking refuge from the military disturbances, the literatus and government official Gao Ming – a man of Yongjia – wrote his *nanxi* entitled *Lute*. He felt that the scholar hero of *Zhao Chaste Maid* had been slandered and unjustly treated in that play, so produced another play on the same theme to rectify matters. In *Lute* the scholar is not struck dead by thunder and lightning but is reunited with his wife, morally redeemed, and rewarded with lofty rank and title. We are told by the leading Ming source on *nanxi* drama that Gao's lofty, exquisite poetry swept aside the 'vulgarities' of the earlier *nanxi* drama.[24] In fact, although his poetry is indeed fine and shows much evidence of a markedly literary education, it still retains many qualities of the earlier 'naturalness'. Gao Ming is said to have lived in a little tower for three years before completing the play, and where his feet tapped out the rhythms of the songs the boards were said to be all worn through.[25]

In the following extract from *Lute*, we can see some of the attempts to justify the scholar, and some of the intricate linking of dialogue, the subtlety of sentiment, and the quiet humour that have helped to earn the play so much admiration. The scholar, Cai Boxie, has left his wife, Zhao Fifth Maiden, and parents, and gone to the capital, where, after coming out Top Graduate in the imperial examinations, he is coerced into marrying the Prime Minister's daughter, Miss Niu. Meanwhile, there is famine in the home region, and, in spite of all Fifth Maiden's loving care and toil, Boxie's parents pass away. He writes home and sends money, but neither his words nor his money are delivered by the villain to whom he entrusts the task. His second wife, Miss Niu, learns of Boxie's longings for Fifth Maiden, and persuades her father, the Prime Minister, to send one of his retainers, the somewhat comical Li Wang (played by a *chou* – which role category is discussed later in the present chapter), to fetch Fifth Maiden and Boxie's parents to the capital. Fifth Maiden has, however, already set out for the capital, leaving her home in the hands of an elderly neighbour called Zhang Guangcai. He is a noble soul, and at the beginning of this extract is sweeping the Cai family graveyard, which is where Li Wang encounters him.[26]

Lute by Gao Ming: Act Thirty-seven, 'Sweeping the pines'

(*Enter Zhang Guangcai.*)
ZHANG GUANGCAI.
      (*Sings*) Always, always these green hillocks . . .
             When was it not? when shall it cease?
             How many men have fallen their prey,
             snatched from the world of the living!
             Lonely tombs, mounds of solitude,
             who sweeps away your rank-weed moss?
             From neighbouring graves the gloom winds blow
             paper sacrificial money, the litter of offerings to others.

(*Says*) Dark, dark, eternal night, that knows no morning,
　　　　lorn, lorn, hollow mounds, so many passing autumns.
　　　　Did any sleeper ever wake from the doze of afterlife?
　　　　Lamenting winds rise soughing from the pines and the catalpas.
Some while ago, Zhao Fifth Maiden entrusted me with the task of looking after this graveyard. I have been rushed off my feet these last few days with other jobs, so I haven't found time to come and look around the place. Huh, goodness me – !
　　　　(*Sings*) All I see is withered leaves
　　　　　　　　floating, scuffling,
　　　　　　　　blanketing the tombs.

(*Performs motions of chasing.*)

　　　　(*Sings*) Foxes and rabbits playing chase-me eve ʾwhere.
(*Gazes*) Why, I do believe some rascals have been hacking wᴏ   from the trees!
　　　　(*Sings*) The grove of pine trees and catalpas
　　　　　　　　grows steadily more sparse.
(*Slips.*) Ugh, what the devil was that, tripped me up like that?
　　　　(*Sings*) Why, moss has sealed the bricks
　　　　　　　　and bamboo-shoots have split the muddied path.
No good, give up, give up!
　　　　　　　　I fear your tomb will not outlast
　　　　　　　　this hundred years,
　　　　　　　　For who is there now still to come
　　　　　　　　and watch your little patch of earth?
Hm, I can see some fellow over there in the far distance. And he's coming this way. Wonder who it can be?

(*Enter Li Wang.*)

LI WANG. (*Sings*) Across the rivers and over the hills,
　　　　　　　　much toil and weary trudging,
　　　　　　　　and now I reach this deserted hamlet.
　　　　　　　　Gazing afar, all I see is one old man,
　　　　　　　　I must ask him where they live and what's their dwelling.
　　　　　　　　With rapid strides I press ahead towards him,
　　　　　　　　and, why, it's just one graveyard wilderness.
ZHANG GUANGCAI.　And where do you come from, brother?
LI WANG.　From the capital.
ZHANG GUANGCAI.　And what business brings you to these hollow mounds of ours?
LI WANG.　I wanted to ask you where I could find the manor hall of the Cai family?
ZHANG GUANGCAI.　Oh, we're just a little backwater here. You won't find any such manor hall. But there is a farmstead belonging to a family called Cai.
LI WANG.　Since there's a Cai farmstead, it must be Lord Cai's, I imagine?
ZHANG GUANGCAI.　What's the personal name of the lord you're looking for?
LI WANG.　Why, a mere nobody like me, I wouldn't dare for a moment to say it out loud!*

*Because of the taboos on personal names, especially those of the high and mighty.

ZHANG GUANGCAI.   Come now, friend, what harm can there be in telling me?

LI WANG.   This old fellow must be a dried-fish seller – life and death are all one to him! Look here, if I so much as mentioned Lord Cai's personal name in the capital (*makes gesture*), it would be my head for the chop-chop.

ZHANG GUANGCAI.   All right, so you can't mention it in the capital. But here in this out-of-the-way hole with no one to be seen for miles around, what on earth is to stop you telling me!

LI WANG.   If I tell you, promise you won't shout it about the place!

ZHANG GUANGCAI.   Out with it, now. What's the gentleman's name?

LI WANG.   He's called Cai Boxie.

ZHANG GUANGCAI.   Shut your mouth!
  (*In a fury, sings*) Don't you mention Cai Boxie!
                     Talking of such a heartless rogue!

LI WANG.   What's he done wrong! Mind your manners, old geezer!

ZHANG GUANGCAI.
            (*Sings*) Top Graduate in the imperial exams,
                     a minister these six or seven years past,
                     but he leaves his parents in the lurch,
                     casts off his own true wife,
                     ignores her altogether.

LI WANG.   So the old squire and his old lady have both died. Would you by any chance know how they passed away?

ZHANG GUANGCAI.
            (*Sings*) After he went away and left them,
                     famine and disaster struck this land.
                     There was no one here any more
                     for them to depend on in their plight.

LI WANG.   But someone must have looked after them both. Who did?

ZHANG GUANGCAI.
            (*Sings*) Lucky for them, their daughter-in-law
                     looked after them with tender care,
                     Pawned her clothes and combs and pins.

LI WANG.   But pawning things doesn't get you far. There must have been a limit to what she could do?

ZHANG GUANGCAI.   Exactly. The young lady bought rice for her parents-in-law with the money she got from the pawn-shops,
            (*Sings*) While she herself all unbeknown to them
                     managed somehow on meals of chaff and husks.
                     Yet, for all her pains, her parents-in-law
                     looked on her with dark suspicions.

LI WANG.   I suppose her parents-in-law must have thought she was eating good stuff on the sly?

ZHANG GUANGCAI.   That's just what happened.
            (*Sings*) Till her parents-in-law both realised,
                     before the two of them died.
                     No money for their funeral,
                     so she cut her own hair
                     and sold it to buy their coffins.

LI WANG.   But if she had no money, how did she manage to build a tomb for them?

ZHANG GUANGCAI.

      (*Sings*) She went among the hollow mounds,
               bearing earth in her apron,
               her fingers streaming blood.
               She awoke divine compassion,
               and by its aid she had a tomb created.

LI WANG.   Where is the young lady now?

ZHANG GUANGCAI.

      (*Sings*) Departed to the emperor's capital.

LI WANG.   And how is she meeting the expenses for her journey?

ZHANG GUANGCAI.

      (*Sings*) By playing the lute and acting the beggar.

LI WANG.   A wretched business! His Excellency Cai sent me here specially to fetch them all to him. But now the old squire and his lady are both dead and the young lady has departed, I've had my journey all for nothing.

ZHANG GUANGCAI.   (*Shouts*) Old squire! My good lady! Your son has become a great man in government, and has sent someone to fetch you! . . . Ah, what a sadness.

      (*Sings*) No answer comes to my calls,
               Where have their souls gone wandering?
               Useless tears in pearls of grief
               flood o'er these aged cheeks of mine.

LI WANG.   Well, I had better be on my way back now. And I'll tell His Excellency to show more willing and provide some requiem services for the good of their souls.

ZHANG GUANGCAI.   (*Laughs*) When they lived, he could not serve them. When they died, he could not bury them. Now they are buried, he cannot manage sacrifices for them.

      (*Sings*) Thus thrice lacking in love
               for the parents that gave him life,
               His crime is mighty sin against Heaven itself.
               What use now will be
               his memorial masses and pious fasts!

Where is your lord and master now?

LI WANG.   Nowadays he lives in with his parents-in-law, at the residence of Prime Minister Niu.

ZHANG GUANGCAI.

      (*Sings*) Take yourself back where you came from,
               and say Old Zhang tells Cai Boxie . . .

LI WANG.   Tells him what?

ZHANG GUANGCAI.

      (*Sings*) Splendid the way you now worship
               the parents of someone else,
               when your own father and mother lie dead
               and you deem them not worth a single prayer!

LI WANG.   Come now, sir. Don't blame people unfairly. He wanted to resign his post, but the emperor would not allow him to. He wanted to back out of the marriage, but Prime Minister Niu refused to let him. He is still desperate to return to his home here, but just can't manage it.

ZHANG GUANGCAI.   Ah, so that's how it was. In that case,
       (*Sings*) After all he had no choice,
                   it looks as if the gods and demons
                   pulled all the strings.
Even in the old days he wanted to stay at home and refused to go and take the imperial
examinations, but his father would not let him have his way.
       (*Sings*) It was their insistence that wrought their destruction,
                   He lacked no love, he committed no crime.
LI WANG.   Yes, my good sir, you almost fell into the error of condemning a man who
never deserved it.
ZHANG GUANGCAI.
       (*Sings*) It was nothing more than his parents' ill fate,
                   their meagre destiny,
                   In human life it's Providence that calls the tune.
LI WANG.   What is your name, by the way, venerable sir?
ZHANG GUANGCAI.   I'm Zhang Guangcai, none other. When Cai Boxie was on the eve
of his departure, he consigned his parents and wife to my care. If on your journey you see
a woman dressed in Taoist fashion, holding a lute and carrying on her back a portrait of
the dead, that will be Cai Boxie's wife. Give her some money for her travel, and see her
carefully to her destination. And convey this message to His Excellency. Tell him Zhang
the Butler says:
                   Lorn of their son's support
                   your father and mother have passed away,
                   And your return would be far too late
                   even if you came today.
LI WANG.   I seek no meal of fish to eat
                   on the chilly river, this dead of night,
                   Emptily homeward sails my boat
                   laden but with moonlight bright.

Before ascending the throne Zhu Yuanzhang had already seen *Lute* and greatly
admired it. When he became emperor, he tried to employ Gao Ming, but Gao
escaped by feigning madness, much to the emperor's disappointment. Someone
presented the play to the emperor, who smiled and remarked, 'The Five Classics
and Four Books are cloth, silk, pulse and millet – something that every household
has. Gao Ming's *Lute* is like some splendid delicious delicacy, and no truly noble
household should be without it.'[27] He commanded daily performances of the play
by his actors, but soon afterwards, troubled by the lack of accompaniment by
stringed instruments, he ordered officials of the Music Academy to devise music
for it, northern tunes for the southern songs, so that it could be accompanied by
the *pipa*-lute and the *zheng*-zither. Nevertheless, the singing still retained its
sinuous, mellifluous, 'free and randomly wandering' qualities and did not
become 'clashing and strident' like northern music. *Lute* remained a favourite
play for centuries, and greatly affected the development of southern drama,
which during the Ming dynasty came to be referred to as *chuanqi*, 'marvel tale'.
The word *chuanqi*, we note, is also that used for the Tang novellas. Yuan writers

also applied it to *zaju*, only later rationalisations reserving it for the southern drama of the Ming.

The organisation and structure of *nanxi* were very different from those of Yuan *zaju*. The number of acts was not fixed and could be very many, forty or more. The acts were of varying length, sometimes as short as one stanza, and sometimes as long as or longer than the main acts of Yuan *zaju*. A very distinctive, and dramatically very interesting, feature of these southern plays, which, as far as we know, was absent in the Yuan *zaju*, was the prologue. As far as can be seen, this prologue had two *raisons d'être*. First, it seems to have been a historical development from earlier multiple bill performances when other, short forms of entertainment provided a prelude to the main play. Although the multiple bills continued and plays sometimes had other shows as curtain-raisers, some of the prelude entertainment seems to have become an inextricable part of the actual play, as a first-act prologue. Secondly, the dramatic value of the prologue in providing an immediate framework for audience comprehension and in creating anticipatory suspense and excitement is obvious. The prologue of *Top Graduate Zhang Xie*, translated in chapter two above, provides an astoundingly flexible, richly theatrical and highly imaginative introduction to the play. The main content of it is the departure of Zhang and his encounter with the brigand, told in *zhugongdiao* ballad form. This is only a very small glimpse of one scene of the main play to come. The prologue is followed by the *sheng*'s comic dance-introduction, which ends with the *sheng* subtly merging into his stage role as Zhang Xie.

The prologues of the other two early *nanxi* are decidedly different, although we cannot be certain that the written texts represent even nearly the full performances. *Little Butcher Sun* has a complete, if tantalisingly mysterious, summary of the play to come.[28] The summary is preceded by the universal theatrical exhortation to enjoy life while one can. *In the wrong career* has only a brief, one-verse summary of the plot.[29] These two prologues are rendered below in continuous prose, although in the original they consist of recited *ci* poems:

Little Butcher Sun: Prologue

PROLOGUE.   White hair urges time on, and youth's spring never blooms anew. I urge you, sirs, not to use too much mental energy. Be merry and have fun, and when you feel inspired to joy, take the chance – don't be a stick-in-the-mud and let joy slip you by. In this drifting, shifting world, the falling petals flow with the stream, and truly, like them, we meet rarely and part often. You must realise that the happy dream is gone in the turning of a head, and which of us lives a hundred years?

When this leisurely music and recitation is over, let us search back among ancient tales and past events, and in casual reliance on our imaginations, perform for you in the manner and style of the Pear Orchard, composing for you new sounds of music's treasury. Now still your noise and hubbub, fix your gaze upon the merriment, and benignly greet our rhapsodies of spring.

You, actors to the rear, I wonder if you know what play we're performing?

ALL.   *The vicissitudes of Little Butcher Sun who undergoes hanging.*
PROLOGUE.   Once upon a time, one fine day, a certain Sun, whose two-syllable personal name was Bida, was making merry in the spring-breeze season of love. A certain Jewel Plum-blossom, Miss Li by her family name, was selling wine in her pavilion, and they chanced to meet, and subsequently were betrothed as man and wife. Sun's brother advised him there would be trouble, but they took no notice of him, and he went off elsewhere. Jewel Plum-blossom was as fickle and inconstant as stream water, and renewed with ardour an old love affair. She and her lover secretly removed her maidservant's head, and stealthily slipped off to some other place. Her husband fell into the trap, and his brother Bigui was hanged outside the city. By good fortune, Heaven caused him to be restored to life, and they encountered his sister-in-law, who revealed the truth concerning her insane deeds. Three ghosts appeared, and together the men and the maidservant made an arrest, and judgement was passed in Kaifeng.

(*Exit Prologue. Enter Sun Bida.*)

SUN BIDA.   (*Sings*) [. . .]

In the wrong career: Prologue

PROLOGUE.   Wanyan Shouma dwells in the Western Capital, a dashing, ardent blade, and rapier wit, and there he meets the vaudeville actress Wang Golden Notice, which leads to his father's driving him from his door. He becomes a strolling player, all for the love of a beautiful woman, using all his gold and jewels until he has not a farthing left. Noble sirs, I bid you hush to watch us perform this *Grandee's son takes the wrong career.*
WANYAN SHOUMA.   (*Sings*) [. . .]

The prologues of other surviving *nanxi* and later *chuanqi* were generally on a similar pattern to that of *Little Butcher Sun*, containing a complete summary of the play. The later term for this one-act prologue was *jiamen*, which means literally something like 'pedigree', 'credentials', 'background'. A variety of other terms were also used: *kaichang shimo*, 'opening run-through', *jiamen shizhong*, 'background run-through', *biaomu*, 'points and purposes', *jiamen yinzi*, 'background introduction', *xiansheng*, 'harbinger', *kaizong*, 'basic purpose', *kaichang*, 'opening of performance', *tonglue*, 'summary', *fumo kaichang*, 'assistant male-role opening of performance', and so on. Usually it consisted of only one or two stanzas, which briefly greet the audience, acquaint the audience with the playwright's motives and the spirit in which he hopes the play will be taken, and give a summary of the plot. There were later attempts to restore some of the theatrical liveliness to the prologue, but a glance at the prologue of *Lute* indicates how far removed could be the Ming literary man's prologue from that of the stage-conscious, red-blooded prologue of *Top Graduate Zhang Xie*:[30]

Lute by Gao Ming: Prologue

PROLOGUE.   The autumn lamp burns bright in her emerald-curtained boudoir, and at the night-time desk he reads his 'rue-compilations'.* . . . In modern times and throughout antiquity, how many stories there have been, with no lack of beautiful ladies and brilliant young men, and tales of gods and angels, supernatural mystery and uncanny beings, so petty and trifling and unworthy of one's attention. Yes, truly, matter that pays no heed to edification, however attractive it may be, is still a waste of time. If we look at plays, why, how facile a task it is to amuse people, and how fine and complex a one to stir their emotions. Gentlemen whose spirits are attuned to mine regard this present play in another light. Do not judge it on its witty gestures nor on its comic patter, neither scrutinise its prosody and musical patterns, but look solely at how loving a son is the son, and how noble a wife is the wife. When a Pegasus† steps forth, does any horse in the world dare strive for the lead?

Miss Zhao is a lady of comely looks, Cai Boxie matches her in his literary polish, and they have been married man and wife for two months when the imperial court issues its decree, calling for the services of gentlemen of noble ability throughout the land. What else can he do! His sublime genetrix and sire sternly command him, and he is obliged against his will to go to the Spring Portals.‡ At his first endeavour, it is 'the head of the sea-turtle',§ and he marries a second time, to a Miss Niu, and, bound by career advantage and drawn by fame, he does not return home after all. There is famine and starvation, and both his parents die, and at this juncture the situation is truly lamentable. Poor Miss Zhao struggles on, and cuts off her 'fragrant clouds'¶ to pay for the funeral of her parents-in-law. In her silken skirts she bears the earth to build the mound of their tomb, and, describing her bitter grief upon her lute, she at last makes her way to the metropolis. Ah, a loving son is Boxie! Ah, a noble woman is Miss Niu! And when they all meet in his study, what cruel sorrow there is. They restore the thatch tomb-vigil hut, and the one husband and his two wives are by imperial decree awarded a plaque of honour for their virtue, to glorify their portals.

The *nanxi* had four main role categories: *sheng, dan, jing*, and *chou*. *Chou* and *jing* may be regarded as more or less the same. Both embraced the roles of farcical butt, slapstick clown, dolt, sly villain, and so forth. In *Lute* the *chou* at one point refers to himself as *fujing*.[31] One explanation of the etymology of *chou* is that it means 'ugly', since the *chou* roles did indeed daub their faces with soot and powder and aim to look grotesque, and since the Chinese character used is a common abbreviation for the character *chou* which commonly means 'ugly'.[32]

---

*i.e. his books. This kind of rue, *ruta graveolens*, was used as a book fumigant. These phrases depict the beautiful lady and her counterpart the brilliant scholar as they might be found at the beginning of many a romantic tale.

†Literally a 'Hualiu', Hualiu being the name of a famous horse of an ancient king. It could gallop a thousand *li* in one day. Is Gao Ming referring to the virtue of his protagonists here, or to his play, or to both? Probably to their virtue, as he later uses the term Hualiu of Cai Boxie's ability, in the opening lines of Act Two.

‡The imperial civil service examinations held in the capital during the spring.

§i.e. in his first attempt at the examinations, he comes out Top Graduate. The 'sea-turtle' was a commonplace term for great success of such kind.

¶Term for a lady's hair.

This seems a disconcertingly facile popular-style etymology, however, and another very plausible eighteenth-century suggestion is that *chou* may be an abbreviated writing of one of the words for *zaban*.[33] Thus the *chou* may quite likely have been in origin the *zaban* clown. There were, then, really three main role categories in *nanxi*: *sheng*, *dan*, and *jing/chou*. *Sheng* may have been a role category which first arose with the *nanxi*, and, apart from a few exceptions which may be errors of editing, it remained a peculiarity of southern dramas, *nanxi* and, later, *chuanqi*. The *sheng* in *nanxi* was the main male role. It was not, however, quite the same as the *zhengmo* of the Yuan *zaju*, being more exclusively limited to Confucian scholars and young students and not covering such martial roles as those of a Zhang Fei or Guan Yu. Originally it may simply have meant 'young man'. The *dan* was the leading female role category, as in Yuan *zaju*. In addition there were other, secondary role categories. *Mo* was a secondary male category. *Wai* was usually male, but in *Top Graduate Zhang Xie* is also found as a secondary female role. *Tie* was a secondary female role category. Some of these and others are much the same as the role categories and type characters of Yuan *zaju*.

A number of other features distinguish *nanxi* from Yuan *zaju*. Themes of romantic love were much more common, with very little of the warlike drama seen so often in the northern plays. A northerner could perhaps have complained of the southern drama, as Westerners often do of Chinese stories, that it was 'always' about scholars and beautiful ladies, but that would have been as unfair and pointless as complaining that too much European drama is about warriors and merchants. All these and other differences made *nanxi* a very distinctive form. The conflict of northern and southern styles was beneficial to the life and development of Chinese drama as a whole, as far as one can tell, and similar north-south divisions and their interinfluence play an important part in the Chinese theatre of later ages.

The northern *zaju* by no means disappeared on the advent of the Ming. On the contrary, it seems for a while to have enjoyed something of a revival.[34] Some of this revival was certainly due to imperial patronage and participation. Most of the *zaju* playwrights of the first few decades of the Ming had been born during the Yuan, and in some cases had served in the Mongol régime. A few of them were medical men. Most of them came from Chekiang and Kiangsu provinces in the south. Several of the leading dramatists were closely associated with the Ming imperial court. Perhaps it was partly a nostalgic respect for the defunct dynasty or an attempt to emulate the Yuan that caused the Ming emperors to foster *zaju*. No doubt their taste in entertainments, and the general vigour of the genre and the esteem in which it was held, were also important reasons for its continued flourishing. The emperors, who, as we have seen, were avid collectors of drama editions and manuscripts, maintained large acting establishments, and cultivated the close cooperation of playwrights.

Yang Ne, a Mongol from the Yuan, was a fine *pipa*-lutanist, joker and deviser of riddles.[35] Around 1403 he was summoned to serve as adviser in the Ming palace. He wrote eighteen *zaju*. Among them was *Pilgrimage to the west*, which had six sections and a total of twenty-four acts. It concerns the pilgrimage of the Buddhist devout Xuanzang and his legendary disciples, principally the trouble-making Monkey, Sun Wukong, describing how Xuanzang acquires his disciples, the various encounters they have with demons and supernatural monsters, and the final accomplishment of Xuanzang's goal, the obtaining of the holy scriptures and his own immortalisation. It is a feast of combat and weird adventures.

Jia Zhongming (1343–post 1422) from Shantung is our most important source of information on late Yuan and early Ming drama.[36] He was a friend of most of the leading playwrights and celebrated literati of his time. Some while before 1402 he served in close attendance upon the prince who was later to become the Emperor Chengzu, and the prince treated him with great favour and affection, we are told, commanding him to compose something for every feast that took place and never failing to praise all his verse. We are also told that he was a handsome man of splendid upright bearing, immaculately elegant in his attire, and vastly magnanimous and generous by nature – although since he himself may well have written the biography from which these details derive, we must perhaps take all this with at least a small pinch of salt. He wrote about fourteen plays and many non-dramatic *qu*, and published other literary works of his own, all of which earned him 'the respectful submission of his contemporaries'. Without doubt he was well versed in the Yuan *zaju* and a close heir to its traditions. He seems to have had access to the vast *zaju* libraries of the Ming imperial clan.[37]

Jia Zhongming's own drama seems to have made bold innovations. Already during the Yuan the *zaju* had been influenced by southern music. Jia Zhongming went a step further and in his play *Dream of immortality*, for instance, not only used both northern and southern songs, but also created an alternation of singing between leading male and female roles, rather in the manner of southern plays, the man singing the northern songs and the lady responding with the southern ones.

Tang Shi, a close friend of Jia Zhongming's for a long time, held a humble post in local government, probably towards the end of the Yuan. Disappointed with this, he drifted into the world of itinerant entertainers. Later, around 1380, he too came into the service of the future Emperor Chengzu, and when Chengzu ascended the throne in 1402 he treated Tang with unceasing favours and fre-quently bestowed gifts upon him. Tang was still alive around 1422. Author of two popular plays, he composed a huge number of non-dramatic *qu* songs which still survive. He was a great humorist, and his wit is very much in evidence in these surviving works.

Two imperial princes were fine and prolific dramatists. Zhu Quan (d. 1448) was the sixteenth son of the founder of the dynasty. With a passion for learning, vast knowledge and overweening curiosity, he wrote books on a wide range of subjects, such as divination, the *qin*-dulcimer, chess, and Taoistic yoga. Above all he excelled in the songs of drama. He wrote twelve *zaju* plays and also wrote the fullest early work on the prosody of Yuan *qu*.[38] Zhu Youdun (1379–1439), Prince of Zhou and eldest son of the fifth son of the founding emperor, wrote no less than thirty-one *zaju*, all of which survive. Most of them were written after 1425 when he became Prince of Zhou. He was studious, with a fondness for ancient things, a connoisseur of calligraphy and an expert on music. His many non-dramatic songs were very popular, and remained so for centuries.

Resembling Guan Hanqing not solely in his prolificity, Zhu Youdun liked to make women the protagonists of his plays. A third of his plays revolve around singing girls, whores or female musicians, whom he describes with great sympathy. Others concern lady saints. His plays about brigands and warriors are action-packed and exciting. In his play *Peach spring scenes* he includes a few Mongol characters and some Mongol speech and songs. Technically he went even further than Jia Zhongming, often allowing other than the leading roles to take part in the singing, and sometimes introducing choral song. Consciously – of that there can be little doubt – he adopted features of southern drama and music, while still retaining much of the vigour and simplicity of the north.

In the later parts of the fifteenth century the northern drama seems to have gone into decline, while the southern drama entered a new phase by gaining a number of highbrow scholar-playwrights. Carrying the literary tendencies of *Lute* to excess, Shao Can, who was born some time during the years 1436–56, is considered the founder of the 'extravagantly euphuistic' school of *chuanqi* drama. Ming critics accused him of flaunting his pedantry, stuffing his writing with high-flown literary devices, and forever using the language of the Tang poet Du Fu and the ancient *Book of odes*.[39] The justification of these criticisms was clearly displayed in his play *Perfume sachet*, where the bombastic, ornate language was often quite inappropriate to the characters to whom it was assigned.[40]

In contrast to the general run of Yuan *zaju* playwrights, a number of the early *chuanqi* playwrights were orthodox scholars of high standing like Shao Can, respected literati and high-ranking officials. Their works often promoted established ethics and loyalty to the state in a very overt manner. Qiu Jun (1421–95), a major source of inspiration to Shao Can, is a conspicuous example. Nearly all these playwrights came from Kiangsu or Chekiang, but he was an exception in that he came from Canton in the deep south. He enjoyed a brilliant career, holding several high-ranking offices, attaining one of the most eminent ministerial positions, and becoming Grand Protector of the Crown Prince and also a Grand Academician. Profoundly versed in ancient and Neo-Confucian philosophy, he wrote several learned volumes on such subjects; he also had considerable knowledge of other branches of learning, ancient and modern, from poetry and prose to medicine, Taoism and Buddhism. Legend has it that when young he wrote a novel called *Beautiful loves*, embodying his own remarkable adventures in the realm of illicit love, and that he wrote the play *Five moral relationships* to try to repair the damage this did to his reputation. Whatever the excuse, the play was a patent piece of moral propaganda, and he was criticised for 'showing off his learning and writing stinking rotten pedantry'.[41]

Certain other playwrights of this period to some extent followed the manner of Qiu Jun and Shao Can, although their language was generally less obtrusively ornate and their plays more suited to stage performance. On the other hand there were plays such as *Three origins* by Shen Shouxian (fl. c. 1475), which was said to contain much market slang.[42] In early southern drama one very often finds the two extremes of style side by side, and sometimes not as well integrated as in Yuan *zaju*. The salient vulgarity may have been an obstacle to popularity with a more politically ascendant orthodox scholardom, and thus to popularity on a nation-wide scale at all levels of society. Shao Can and Qiu Jun, as erudite orthodox scholars, may by their involvement in *chuanqi* drama have afforded it a useful aura of respectability, but the harmful effects of their pedantic example continued to appear in the work of many, even some of the best, later Ming dramatists.

Two playwrights, Kang Hai (1475–1540) and Wang Jiusi (1468–1551), wrote plays called *Wolf of Mount Zhong* on the subject of the philosopher who rescues a wolf from huntsmen, is then himself menaced by the wolf, and seeks three arbiters to decide whether he should be eaten or not. This was already an old tale, and very similar stories have been told in ancient times in Korea, Siberia and Norway, and elsewhere in Europe and Asia. Both plays were vehicles for the satirical expression of a grudge against a government official. Kang's was a standard four-act *zaju*, but Wang's, written in about 1510, was a short one-act play calling itself a *yuanben*. For all its brevity, Wang's play was more akin in form and spirit to the Yuan-Ming *zaju* and *chuanqi*. From the early 1500s quite a number of such short plays were produced, and we may perhaps refer to them as 'brief *zaju*' or 'one-act *zaju*'.

The number of plays termed *zaju* that continued to be written is somewhat deceptive. Apart from the brief *zaju* there were many that were at least superficially more akin to the Yuan *zaju* in form. But the latter were in fact strongly influenced by southern drama and losing their distinctive identity. They included a heavy admixture of southern songs, and the language of the songs and speech was often southern. The number of acts became less strictly observed, and '*zaju*' came to designate short plays with anything from one to seven main acts. Many dramatists wrote both such *zaju* and *chuanqi*, but it is clear that the southern drama was in the ascendancy. The majority of playwrights of both *zaju* and *chuanqi* for whom domiciles are known came from the south, principally Kiangsu and Chekiang provinces, and very few from the old heartland of Yuan *zaju* in Hopeh province. Playwrights and critics who lived in the sixteenth century tell us that the northern *qu* music had more or less died out and that the northern drama had largely ceased to be performed.[43] Even songs northern in name and prosody came to be played and sung with essentially southern tunes, or at least in a style that no longer retained any purely northern character.

Yet matters were more complicated than that. While the northern form faded as a living entertainment, so the interest of literary men and dramatists in its literature and poetry seems to have revived. Such interest becomes increasingly evident during the sixteenth century, and in turn influenced the drama through literary channels.[44]

Li Kaixian (1501–68) wrote both *zaju* and *chuanqi*, and in many ways typifies the synthesis of northern and southern, of old and new. He came from Shantung, and by the age of thirty-nine had risen to a very responsible government post. He then retired to his native village, where he gathered musicians and entertainers around him and devoted himself to singing, composing and playing stringed instruments. An avid collector of folk-songs and popular songs, he himself composed with a free disregard for convention, and could dash off prose and verse with great ease. His collection of books was enormous, unequalled in the Shantung region, and must have included many Yuan plays, since he revised a large number of Yuan *zaju* and songs. He wrote about six *zaju* himself, which were probably all in the nature of Jin and Yuan *yuanben*. Better known were his three *chuanqi* plays, in particular *Precious sword*, first printed in 1549. This, too, is supposed to have been a political satire, against the villainous, tyrannical Prime Minister Yan Song. On the subject of brigand adventures, it constituted a departure in theme for the *chuanqi*. It contained a fair amount of euphuism, but it was also greatly admired for its stylistic forcefulness.

Singing and music have played a much greater part in Chinese drama than in general in Western drama, and increasingly after about 1500 the history of drama in China becomes a history of types of music rather than genres of play, or, more accurately perhaps, the music tends more wholly to characterise the genre. Music was, of course, a vital element in the Yuan *zaju*, but its role in the *chuanqi* and later regional dramas was even more important in typifying these dramas. In the Yuan, regional pronunciations had been a strong characterising feature of the northern and southern dramas, but in later ages different types of drama spread more freely and rapidly all over the country, and overall musical features were a stronger defining characteristic in many cases than pronunciation and the form of the play alone.

The kind of accompaniment provided on imperial command for *Lute* subsequently became common for other plays and was known as Xiansuo Guan-*qiang*, 'official stringed music'. We cannot ascertain its nature. What is clear, however, is that it was gradually ousted by various local kinds of music, in particular Haiyan-*qiang*, Yuyao-*qiang* and Yiyang-*qiang* music.

The identification of the origins of the kinds of music which played a part in the history of Chinese drama, and the rediscovery of their precise musical features, their dissemination, and their subsequent course of development, are problems fraught with immense complexity and hotly disputed by scholars of many divergent opinions.[45] All that can be done here is to suggest some conceivable general answers. The roots of Haiyan-*qiang* music seem to go well down into the Sông dynasty. Haiyan, in north-eastern Chekiang province, was near to Hangzhou. Zhang Zi (1153– ?) seems to have instigated changes in the then current music which led to a distinctive kind of Haiyan music. More certainly, the sinicised Uighur named Guan Yunshi (1286–1324) and Xianyu Biren (early fourteenth century), both of them Yuan *qu* poets of renown, together with their friends the general and playwright Yang Zi of Haiyan and Yang's sons, were responsible for creating a new kind of music which was seemingly northern *qu* music with the admixture of some of the southern music already current in Haiyan, perhaps that of the *nanxi*. In the Ming dynasty, Haiyan-*qiang* music was accompanied by the *pipa*-lute, and such stringed instruments as the *yueqin*-guitar and the *zheng*-zither, clearly a northern influence. The *xiangban*-clapper was also used. Early in the sixteenth century this kind of music was fairly widespread, but exclusively sung only in Wenzhou, Jiaxing, Huzhou and Taizhou. Elsewhere in Chekiang and Kiangsu provinces Yuyao-*qiang* music was prevalent. Yuyao is also near Hangzhou; the vigour and independent diversity of local styles of music in these regions is a source of never-ending astonishment. The singing in this kind of music seems to have been only rhythmically punctuated by percussive instruments. The style may have originated from *nanxi* music, and it may have included some *bangqiang*, 'choral backing'. Neither Haiyan-*qiang* nor Yuyao-*qiang* seems to have survived the seventeenth century as a flourishing independent form, although some say that Yuyao-*qiang* may have persisted in a kind of local drama.[46]

Yiyang-*qiang* music originated from Yiyang in Kiangsi province. It used drums and cymbals for the rhythm, had *bangqiang* choral backing in the final lines of the songs, and was brisk, vigorous and loud in delivery, 'bellowing' or 'making an angry hubbub', as one Ming critic complained. It differed from Yuyao-*qiang* music in its melodies and the enunciation of words, among other things, and soon attained a far wider dispersal, becoming popular in Kiangsi itself, Peking, Nanking, and Hunan, Fukien, and Canton provinces. Yiyang-*qiang* music, and the styles of music developed from it, were to have an enduring effect on Chinese drama.

By the latter decades of the fifteenth and the first couple of decades of the sixteenth century all these three kinds of music were in strong circulation, often altering and being altered by the music, pronunciations, rhyming patterns and singing fashions of other regions. Then came what was perhaps the most important and enduring innovation of all, the creation of Kunshan-*qiang* music. This event is closely datable and attributed with certainty to particular persons, principally Wei Liangfu (born some time after 1522), who was assisted first by the efforts of two old music masters named Yuan the Beard and You the Camel-hump, and later by the singer Zhang Yetang and others. The music masters were versed in the music of a form of play local to Kunshan in Kiangsu province, that music too being sometimes referred to as Kunshan-*qiang*, while Zhang Yetang was the leading exponent of northern *qu* song in Kiangsu in his time.[47] Over some period during the years 1540–66, utilising their knowledge of northern *qu* singing, Haiyan-*qiang* music, Yiyang-*qiang* music and the music of local plays, Wei (himself originally a public singer of northern *qu*) and his friends devised what was known as Kunshan-*qiang* music.[48] It was also called Shuimodiao music, 'water-polished music', this name referring to the painstaking care taken by its creators. Essentially southern in character, but utilising both southern and northern *qu* tunes for its basis, it was accompanied by strings and various pipes and flutes. The cool, plaintive note of the bamboo flute became the most characteristic accompaniment of Kunshan-*qiang* singing.

Initially used for amateur and non-dramatic singing, Kunshan-*qiang* music rapidly became very popular. In about 1579 the dramatist Liang Chenyu (1520–80 or later) established it in the theatrical world by writing his *chuanqi* play *Washing silk* to suit it.[49] Rapturously received, the play earned him universal adulation. It concerns the love affair of merchant-politician Fan Li and China's 'Helen of Troy', Xishi, telling how they assisted the King of Yue to avenge himself against the King of Wu, then both eloped into the wilds. Indirectly at least, it derived much from the pretty language and elegant literary manner of *Lute* and created a fashion for such styles of writing among a number of dramatists who came to be regarded as constituting a Kunshan school of drama. At first Kunshan-*qiang* music seems to have appealed on a broad popular level, but partly because of its inherent qualities, partly because of the language of the playwrights who used it, and partly because of the patronage it received, it tended more and more to be associated with lofty, highbrow modes of expression and was accordingly designated 'refined music'.

Washing silk was performed all over the country, and old *zaju* and *chuanqi* were adapted and new ones written for performance with Kunshan-*qiang* music, which in time came to dominate other kinds of 'refined music' and even hastened the demise of the old *qu* music in the north. Taking over the tunes and keys of the old northern and southern *qu* music, it altered them to its own rules, so radically in some cases as to make it impossible to assume that a tune was a survival from an earlier similarly or identically named kind of music. This music spread throughout China, influencing, altering and often dominating local kinds of music for many ages to come. Since the lyrics of Kunshan-*qiang* music were composed to the prosody of northern and southern *qu* with their uneven line length, dramas principally performed to it came to be referred to by the abbreviated term Kunqu ('Kun *qu*'). Kunqu dramas are performed to this day. Kunshan-*qiang* singing is typically southern in its melismatic manner of delivery.[50]

Two outstanding playwrights who further ensured the reputation of Kunshan-*qiang* music were Tang Xianzu (1550–1617) and Shen Jing (1553–1610). A fiercely independent and most generous spirit, Tang destroyed his civil service career by his frank criticisms of the government in 1590.[51] Banished to remote Kwangtung province, he was later appointed a county magistrate in Chekiang, but in 1598 contrived his own dismissal from government service. He was a fine writer of prose and poetry. His four *chuanqi* plays, all completed after his retirement, were greatly admired in his day, and all reflect his own views of life and career experiences. His intricate style is often the manifestation of the subtlety and minuteness of his thought. Contemporaries, however, sharply criticised him for musical shortcomings,[52] among other things for failing to match his prosody with the music, but these 'shortcomings' were probably a conscious attempt at certain musical innovations. Most celebrated of his plays was *Peony pavilion*. In this play a young lady, Du Fair Maiden, dreams of an ideal lover, then pines to death with longing for him. Later, a young student named Liu Mengmei sees her portrait when staying at her home, falls in love with her and communicates with her in a dream. She is miraculously resuscitated from the grave. Going to the capital to take the imperial examinations, he subsequently encounters the girl's father, an important official, who, hearing his story, takes it to be a fraud, and in fury prepares to punish him. The news of the student's success in the examinations and Fair Maiden's explanations combine to save Mengmei from castigation, and all are happily united at last. The following extract from the play shows something of the elaborate style, intricate description and sensuous finesse of Tang Xianzu's play. First the heady lushness of spring is evoked, as the heroine, Du Fair Maiden, walks through the garden with her maid, Spring Fragrance, and this slow elaboration is a startlingly effective foil to the sudden action of her subsequent dream, in which the young student, Liu Mengmei, makes love to her.[53]

Peony pavilion by Tang Xianzu: Act Ten, 'Startled from a dream'

(*Enter Du Fair Maiden.*)

FAIR MAIDEN.
      (*Sings*) Called back from my dreams by orioles' warbling,
            back to this season's scenes, that everywhere
            distract my soul with frenzied longings,
            I stand by the little, lost and lonely courtyard.

(*Enter Spring Fragrance.*)

SPRING FRAGRANCE.
      (*Sings*) Aquilaria incense burned to ashes
            through long-night waking,
            Embroidery threads cast aside and torn
            in all your fretting.
            It seems this spring perturbs you more
            than springs of other years gone by.
FAIR MAIDEN.
      (*Speaks*)Dawn comes, and I gaze through Plum-Blossom Pass,*
            my last-night's adornment in sorry array.

---

*A range of mountains some way to the south of where Fair Maiden lives.

SPRING FRAGRANCE.
>Your 'springtime-becoming'* tresses loll awry,
>as this moment you lean against the balustrade.

FAIR MAIDEN.
>'I cannot scissor in twain, and tidying but tangles more'†
>these endless threads of moody caprice.

SPRING FRAGRANCE.
>But I have urged the blossoms, the orioles and the swallows
>to lend us spring, that we may view its charms.

FAIR MAIDEN.   And have you given instructions yet for the paths between the flower-beds to be swept, Spring Fragrance?

SPRING FRAGRANCE.   Yes, I have told someone to do that.

FAIR MAIDEN.   Then bring me my mirror and my clothes.

SPRING FRAGRANCE.   (*Approaching with mirror and clothes*)
>(*Speaks*) After you have combed your cloudy tresses,
>towards your mirror turn your face,
>'Before you change your silken dresses,
>add yet perfume to your grace.'‡

Here are your mirror and clothes.

FAIR MAIDEN.   What a lovely season and what lovely weather!
>(*Sings*) Wafting silks by waking insects spun§
>drift through speckless skies
>to our courtyard and its still seclusion,
>fluttering, rippling their strands of spring.
>I spend an age here fingering
>my flowered hair-clasps into place;
>Sly mirror,
>now you've stolen half my face
>and lured my locks lopsided!¶
>(*Walks*) But then, pacing in this maidenly boudoir,
>I can never be seen to the full!

SPRING FRAGRANCE.   You're dressed up so prettily today!

FAIR MAIDEN.
>(*Sings*) Yes, don't you think
>the scarlet of my skirt and smock stands out
>so fresh and vividly,
>the jewels in my flowered clasps are set
>like gorgeous sparkling crystal!

---

*It is generally said that this refers to an ancient custom whereby at the onset of spring women would adorn their hair with silk cut-outs of swallows, above which they would stick the two characters meaning 'spring-becoming', but it is possible that here the words are meant in a more general sense.

†This line comes from the poetry of Li the Latter Monarch (Li Houzhu, Li Yu, 937–78).

‡This comes from the poetry of Xue Feng (fl. c. 853).

§Chinese poetry in general makes considerable mention of the threads which caterpillars, spiders and other insects spin, and which, drifting through the clear spring air and gleaming in the spring sunshine, seem indeed a prominent characteristic of the season.

¶This is sometimes taken to mean that she is so coy that she only ventures shy sideways glances at the mirror.

> – You can tell how all my life
> a taste for beauteous adornment
> has come naturally to me.
> But here I am in the very bloom of springtide,
> and none to see me!
> Why, at the sudden sight of my fair looks
> 'fish would dart down and swans alight',*
> and birds amazed all clamour;
> Surely, at my comeliness,
> 'the bashful moon would hide her light,
> and blossoms in their shame'† all tremble!

SPRING FRAGRANCE.   It's time for breakfast now. Let us go, if you please. (*They walk.*)
Just look:

> (*Speaks*) The ornamental porticos
> half-strewn with golden paint,
> The pool-side summer-houses
> with unbroken stretch of verdant moss.
> As you tread across the turf take care
> lest mud splash your new embroidered stockings,
> And if you cherish the blossoms there
> make the tiny bells of gold ache bitterly.‡

FAIR MAIDEN.   Unless you wander in gardens and groves, you can never know what
spring is really like!

> (*Sings*) You see all the maidenly purple and dimpling carmine everywhere
>   around in bloom,
> thus cast upon the mercies
> of derelict broken wells and crumbled walls.
> Hopeless Heaven,
> sending such 'splendid days and wondrous sights'!
> Worthless garden,
> flaunting such 'merriness and pleasure to the heart'!§

Never let my mother and father ever mention such pretty scenery in praise to me again!
FAIR MAIDEN AND SPRING FRAGRANCE.

> (*Sing together*) Winged ornamental rafters,
>   curled portal drapes of pearls,¶
>   emerald halls, cloud-coroneted;
>   Gay-carved pleasure-boats mid misty ripples,
>   silk-strand rain and gossamer-slivered breezes.

---

*This phrase derives from the work of the philosopher Zhuang-zi (third century BC).
†This phrase is a commonplace, usually used in conjunction with the phrase concerning fish and swans.
‡The usual explanation of this conceit is a reference to the Prince of Ning during the Tang dynasty (in the
period 742–56), who was so fond of flowers that he had golden bells closely strung on red silk, and
attached to the branches of blossom, so that whenever birds gathered, he could tell the gardeners to ring
the bells and scare off the birds to prevent them from damaging the blossoms. Tang Xianzu hyperboli-
cally extends this to give the bells feelings.
§The quotations in these lines are the words of the poet Xie Lingyun (385–433); 'In this world splendid
days, wondrous sights, merriness and pleasure to the heart are four things rarely found in combination.'
¶These two lines derive from the poet Wang Bo (648–75).

> – We maidens behind our damask screens
> hitherto little imagined
> such spring magnificence!

SPRING FRAGRANCE.   All the flowers are out, but those peonies are early, though.

FAIR MAIDEN.

> (*Sings*) All over the hillocks of spring
> azaleas weep their blood,*
> Behind the briar roses
> the misty silks hang drunken soft.

Oh, my Spring Fragrance,

> It is true, the prettiness of peonies!
> But when they reign supreme, 'tis time
> to say farewell to parting spring.

SPRING FRAGRANCE.   You swallows and you orioles, in your lovers' pairs, all two by two,

> (*Sings with*   Idly gawping, idly glancing,
> *Fair Maiden*)   chatter chatter swallows talking,
> bright sharp sounds like scissors shearing;
> warble warble orioles singing,
> lilting rounded music gliding.

FAIR MAIDEN.   Let us go, shall we.

SPRING FRAGRANCE.   There's no end of things to look at in this garden. You could never see enough of it!

FAIR MAIDEN.   Do you need to tell me that! (*They walk on.*)

> (*Sings*) Ensnared by its charms
> my eyes are never sated,
> But were I to roam throughout
> its dozen summer-houses and bowers,
> nought would it avail me.
> Better to have done with this fascination,
> and go indoors to while away my time
> in pointless pastimes.

(*They arrive back.*)

SPRING FRAGRANCE.

> 'Throw wide the doors of our western chamber,
> open forth the couch of our eastern chamber!'†
> Place purple azaleas in the vases,
> and fill incense-burners with garu-wood.

Now rest yourself for a little while, my lady. I am going to take a look at your mother. (*Exit.*)

FAIR MAIDEN.   (*Sighs*) [. . .] Oh dear, this kind of weather makes one feel so sleepy. Where are you, Spring Fragrance? (*Looks all around, then lowers her head, and muses to*

---

*In the Chinese this plays on the connection between the word for azalea, *dujuan* (*hua*), and the word for 'goatsucker or nightjar', *dujuan* (*niao*), the latter legendarily being supposed to weep blood.
†These lines closely follow lines in a 'Poem of Mulan' written during the Tang dynasty.

herself.) Oh Heavens, now I can really believe that springtime vexes people! I've often read poems and songs in which girls of olden times are moved to love by the spring and become terribly miserable when autumn comes. That's so true. I'm fifteen now, but I still haven't met a 'cassia-plucking'* man to be my husband. These spring yearnings suddenly come over me, but where am I to find my 'Toad Palace wanderer'?† In the olden days, Madam Han managed to meet Master Yu,‡ and Scholar Zhang by chance encountered Mistress Cui,§ and people wrote those two books *Poem written on the red leaf*¶ and *Legend of Cui Hui*,** and in all these cases there was a beautiful lady and a gay genius who first arranged secret trysts of love, then later managed to become man and wife. (*Gives a deep sigh.*) I was born of a patrician lineage and grew up in the halls of a celebrated family, but I now wear my hair pinned up and am of a marriageable age, and if I don't manage to find some eligible match, I shall be condemned to a useless frittering away of my youth's green springtime, with time simply flashing by. (*Weeps.*) Poor me, as pretty as the flowers, and to think my destiny should be as meagre as a flimsy leaf!††

[. . .] Oh, this lassitude! I think I'll just lean on the table and have a sleep. (*Goes to sleep, and dreams of the scholar Liu Mengmei. Enter Liu Mengmei, holding a sprig of willow.*)

LIU MENGMEI.   When orioles meet with sunny days
their gracious carols glide,
When a man encounters warm romance
his lips in laughter open wide!
All the way there were fallen flowers
as along the river I wended,
Today, Ruan Zhao's wanderings abroad
in paradise have ended.‡‡

I have been following Mistress Du back here along the paths, but where on earth is she now? (*Turns round and sees her.*) Ah, young lady, Mistress Du!

(*Fair Maiden gives a start, and rises to her feet. She and Mengmei acknowledge each other.*)

LIU MENGMEI.   I have been searching for you everywhere in vain, and why, here you are!

(*Fair Maiden glances shyly sideways, and does not say anything.*)

LIU MENGMEI.   By chance I have plucked this small twig from a weeping willow here in the garden just now. Mistress Du, since you are so deeply versed in the classics of literature, could you compose me a poem in praise of this sprig of willow?

---

*To pass the imperial examinations was called 'to pluck the cassia'.
†Similarly, meaning 'scholar hero'. There was said to be a cassia tree on the moon, and the moon was sometimes called 'Toad Palace'.
‡A famous love story in which a Master Yu You and the palace lady Madam Han used maple leaves with poems on them as their *billets-doux*.
§The story which was used for the play *West wing*.
¶Tang Xianzu's friend Wang Jide wrote a play of this name on the theme of the love affair of Madam Han and Master Yu You.
**A story of the love affair of the courtesan Cui Hui and a certain Pei Jing.
††These two similes come from the poetry of Yuan Haowen (1190–1257).
‡‡This refers to the ancient story of Liu Chen and Ruan Zhao who wandered into paradise and found angelic lady loves there.

FAIR MAIDEN. (*Surprised and delighted by the request, she is about to speak but stops herself. Aside*) I have never met this young man, and we are not in any way acquainted. What can have brought him here?

LIU MENGMEI. (*Laughs*) Mistress Du, I could die of love for you!

(*Sings*) Only for your flower-like beauty,
for what seems like fleeting years
I everywhere have sought in vain.
You cherished yourself within your secluded bower.

Young lady, let's go and have a word together somewhere.

(*Fair Maiden smiles, but does not go. Mengmei tries to pull her by her sleeve.*)

FAIR MAIDEN. (*In a whisper*) Where shall we go?

LIU MENGMEI.

(*Sings*) Round this trellis of peonies,
and close beside the Great Lake rockery.*

FAIR MAIDEN.(*Softly*) What for, sir scholar?

LIU MENGMEI.(*Softly replies, in song*)

Now let me loosen the button of your collar,
and undo the girdle of your dress;
Let the tips of your sleeves kiss your teeth,
those 'unmarred slips',†
and you shall now patiently forbear
as tenderly caressing we sleep a little while.

(*Fair Maiden looks bashful. Mengmei goes closer and puts his arms round her. Fair Maiden pushes him away. [. . .] Mengmei carries Fair Maiden off in his arms by force. Exeunt.*
(*Enter Flower God, wearing 'hair-binding' hat and red robes, and with flowers stuck over him.*)

FLOWER GOD. [. . .] I am the Flower God in charge of the flower gardens to the rear of the Prefect of Nanan's residence. Prefect Du's daughter, young Mistress Fair Maiden, and the scholar Liu Mengmei are destined some day to be married to one another. Mistress Du has been strolling mid the spring scenery, which has stirred her heart with melancholy emotions, and Scholar Liu has been sent into her dreams. We flower gods have special care over love's jewelled and fragrant delights, so I have come here in person to render them my protection, and to ensure that they attain blessed ecstasy in their sweet loving. [. . .] Now, scholar, you are still only half-way through the dream. When the dream comes to its end, gently escort Mistress Du back to her fragrant boudoir, for now I shall leave you. (*Exit.*)

(*Enter Mengmei and Fair Maiden, hand in hand.*)

LIU MENGMEI.

(*Sings*) Thus for a brief moment

*An ornamental display of the rocks from the Great Lake in Kiangsu and Chekiang, which were full of holes, rather like some kinds of surrealist sculpture.
†Possibly referring to clay-whitened slips of bamboo used by children for writing practice.

Heaven smoothed the path for mortals,
and Green Nature loaned her blossoms for our bed.
Are you all right, dear young lady? (*Fair Maiden only bows her head.*) [. . .] Dear lady, your
limbs are weary, so rest and recover. Go and rest now. (*He sees her back, and she goes off to
sleep as before. He lightly pats her.*) Young lady, I am going now. (*Glances back at her as he
goes.*) Young lady mine, rest well and plentifully, and I shall come again to see you! [. . .]
(*Exit.*)
FAIR MAIDEN. (*Waking with a start, calls softly.*) Sir scholar, sir scholar, oh you've left me!
(*Then she slumps blurredly off to sleep again. Enter Madam Du.*)
MADAM DU. [. . .] Daughter, daughter, why are you dozing here?

(*Fair Maiden wakes up calling the scholar still.*) [. . .]

Tang Xianzu came from Linchuan in Kiangsi province, and a number of Ming
dramatists who respected and imitated his literary style came to be known as the
Linchuan school. They included Wu Bing, a Ming loyalist who starved himself to
death in 1650 after capture by the Qing forces; Meng Chengshun (fl. c. 1644),
editor of two famous collections of Yuan *zaju*; and Ruan Dacheng (c. 1587–1646),
who after an exciting career met his death during a campaign against the
remnants of the Ming in 1646.

Shen Jing from Wujiang in Kiangsu province was one of the sharpest critics of
Tang Xianzu's supposed musical failings, and even wrote a *qu* song-set voicing
his scorn. He was a leading dramatic and musical theorist. An infant prodigy and
very handsome, he rose to some eminence in government service before retiring
through illness in 1588 at the age of thirty-five to throw himself into the composition of plays and *qu* poetry. He revised *Lute* and some of Tang Xianzu's plays,
adapted northern *qu* to southern tunes, produced a number of treatises including
the only comprehensive work on the poetic and musical form of southern *qu*, and
wrote many plays. Among his plays were two collections of *zaju*. His *chuanqi* plays
were a contrast to those of Tang Xianzu, being characterized by a fine correspondence of prosody to music, and, in the later plays, by natural, easy, unornate
vigour of language. He was in fact criticised himself for being over-fussy in his
concern for musical precision.[54] Ming playwrights who followed him in his
attitudes to music and language formed the Wujiang school of dramatists. Many
were men of great note. His nephew Shen Zijin (fl. c. 1628) was also a musical
theorist and poet, as was Wang Jide (d. 1623/4), who had a private collection of
several hundred 'Yuan' *zaju*.* Yuan Yuling (c. 1600–74) was a roguish wag who
twice ruined his career, once through his love for a whore and once through his
sharp humour. Feng Menglong (1574–1646) was one of China's greatest, most
versatile and most prolific literary figures, reviser of numerous plays, superb
novelist, poet, commentator on the classics, and collector of anecdotes, jokes and
bawdy folk-songs.

The playwrights of the various above-mentioned schools were dominant in the
late Ming, and although the schools represent in some respects slightly arbitrary

*They probably included many Ming plays.

groupings, very few major dramatists had no connection with any of them. Some, such as Ye Xianzu (1566–1641), seem to fall between the Linchuan and Wujiang schools. Most of the famous playwrights wrote both *zaju* and *chuanqi* during this period, and the distinction between the two kinds of play becomes less and less relevant to major developments. Some playwrights, such as Xu Wei (1521–93), still wrote only *zaju*. Xu Wei was a vivid character who led a wilder life than he no doubt wished. When a patron of his was jailed, Xu went insane with anxiety as to his own fate and several times tried to commit suicide. He also spent several years in prison. Released through the intervention of a friend, he returned to his home in the country, thereafter devoting his life to painting and literary activities. He was famed for his calligraphy, painting and poetry, and in all these media expressed his delight in the wonders of both Nature and the man-made world. His five *zaju* were immensely admired, and four of them appeared in a large number of early editions. He wrote, too, on the theoretical aspects of drama and music, his works including the most important treatise on *nanxi* drama. An incorrigible eccentric, he broke as many rules as he observed in his own plays, varying the number of acts and freely mixing northern and southern *qu*. His free style with its unrestrained panache sets him apart from the three schools.[55] Others tried to imitate him, but he stood alone with his ebullient genius, rhyming and versifying in the spirit of the Yuan, akin in versatility and vigour to the best playwrights of that classical period.

It must not be imagined that in actual performance Kunshan-*qiang* music reigned unchallenged. That is a biased impression all too easily gained from surviving plays and from our knowledge of the playwrights of the time. Certainly the more respected literary men about whom we have detailed knowledge tended to favour the 'refined music'. In some respects, however, the importance of the playwright may have lessened somewhat. A great number of fine and famous plays existed by the late Ming, so performers had less and less absolutely to depend on new creation. The coming together of northern and southern drama, and the rediscovery of ancient drama texts that was taking place, meant that there was a vast choice available even without any new plays. From the earliest times there must in fact have been revision and adaptation of older plays and dramas, and a great deal of it by the late Yuan no doubt, but from this period onwards there seems to be greatly increasing evidence of such revision and adaptation. Of course, great new plays continued to be written, but, in the absence of radical political or social reorientation or other cause for a fundamental change in tastes, the performers could have gone a long way without new plays. More and more during the next couple of centuries the history of drama seems to concern performers and performance rather than new playwrights. Yet we must be careful. The distinction between revision and creation is very often a fine one, and a contributory cause of the apparently lessening importance of the playwright may have been that during the late Ming and afterwards, as perhaps earlier with *nanxi*, the revisers were not given the fame and immortality their contributions to drama should have won them. Or perhaps many of them,

1 *Above Yuanben* or Sông-style *zaju* performance depicted on a thirteenth-century tomb sculpture (modern sketch)

2 *Below left* The Emperor dreams of Lady Yang. Scene from *Rain on the Paulownia tree* by Bai Pu (from 1633 edition)

3 *Below right* Wang Lady Splendour contemplates the River Amur as she is led away to become the bride of the Hunnish Khan in *Autumn in the Han palace* by Ma Zhiyuan (from 1663 edition of 1615–16)

4   Yuan troupe on stage; from a Yuan dynasty mural

元
明
戯
曲
人
物
扮
相
（
采
自
明
刊
本
「
忠
義
水
滸
傳
」
插
圖
）

明
代
戯
曲
人
物
扮
相
王
夭
（
鼻
人
圖
）
（
采
自
明
刊
本
「
荷
花
蕩
」
傳
奇
戯
中
戯
插
圖
）

元
明
清
戲
曲
人
物
形
象

元明戲曲人物扮相（部分圖）
（采自明刊本「忠義水滸傳」插圖）

清初崑曲人物扮相「醉打山門」
（采自「唐土名勝圖繪」北京查樓演劇圖）

明代戲曲脚色敗扮圖（局部）
（采自明刊本「荷花蕩」傳奇戯中戯插圖）

5　Actors in their roles, as depicted in Ming and Qing works

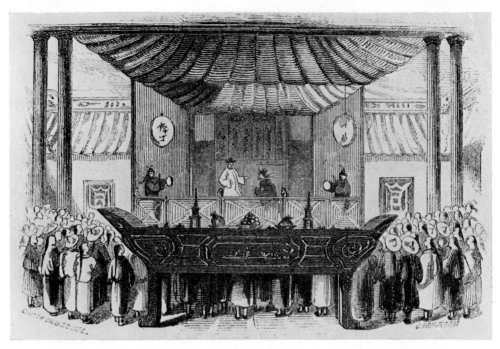

6 Theatrical performance at a marriage (mid-nineteenth-century drawing)

7 Officials feasting to the accompaniment of a play (early nineteenth-century engraving)

because of the social, moral and legal climate, preferred anonymity. But we may suppose that actor-playwrighting and the prevalence of adaptations of old plays also played a part in producing our picture of performance in the ascendancy.

By the late sixteenth and early seventeenth centuries numerous dramas were performed with Yiyang-*qiang* music and regional variants of it, and other kinds of 'vulgar singing' or 'miscellaneous music'. Although they did not enjoy the same high literary esteem as plays using the 'refined music', these plays were sometimes printed or circulated round the acting world in manuscript form. It was no doubt the lack of respect accorded to them by the higher levels of society that discouraged people from proclaiming their authorship of such plays, and the identities of the playwrights are no longer known. Not attaining, and perhaps not even aiming at, the same literary polish as the plays of the great orthodox literary figures, they excelled rather in their lusty energy and unaffected charm.

Many dramas, including those originally intended for performance with Kunshan-*qiang* music, were adapted for performance with other kinds of music. Only *Washing silk* seems to have remained unamenable to this treatment. One of the most effective ways in which adaptation was done was by what was called *jia-gun*, 'adding roll', or *gun-diao*, 'roll music', which involved the addition of speech and verse between the lines of the original songs.[56] This had three main effects in performance, some of them very similar to the effects of *chenzi*, but more marked. First, elaborations and the use of more explicit or more colloquial language could render the meaning of the original wording clearer, and more lively and directly comprehensible to the audience. Secondly, stretching out the proportion of words to that of the meaning to be expressed could counterbalance the difficulties which the noisy percussive styles of music posed for comprehension. Thirdly, the opportunity could be used to improve upon the sense and dramatic validity of the original, which not infrequently had been written by a literary man little acquainted with stage conditions.

One of the variants of Yiyang-*qiang* music that was used for plays with *jia-gun* was the Qingyang-*qiang* music which arose in Anhwei province.[57] Already during the late Ming many distinctive kinds of local music had developed and gained wide popularity, often spreading along the main routes of commercial expansion. During the early Yuan the situation had, as far as we can tell, been relatively simple: one kind of written drama was performed with one kind of music common to a particular region. By the late Ming the situation was quite different. Singing, the most important element in most traditional Chinese dramas, had come more than ever to be the main feature characterising a dramatic genre. Local and national forms of music merged, adapted to new conditions, and borrowed and appropriated from each other. New forms appeared, to persist and flourish, or sink and die. Some combined with local kinds of play to produce new distinct genres of drama. Often the new separate kinds of music retained the mark of their sources. The total result was a dazzling kaleidoscope, we can be sure. Vogues for a local kind of drama or music could rapidly have nationwide consequences, and the tracing of the origins and courses of these vogues poses many problems.

6
The Theatre World during the Ming Dynasty

And what of the players and their playing? By and large there were two kinds of acting company during the Ming: the private troupes kept by wealthy merchants or aristocratic households and clans for prestige and private entertainment, and sometimes for profit, and the 'independent' troupes, often financed by joint capital, and acting in public for their professional livelihood. The actors of the private troupes were 'family musicians' or 'household servants', sometimes specially engaged with a view to forming a troupe, sometimes recruited and trained from among servants already in household employ. Often their status was fairly low, and they had frequently to perform household duties as well as act. They acted at feasts, religious festivals and other grand occasions and were sometimes loaned for performances outside the household. The fashion for keeping private troupes flourished very strongly in the late Ming. The playwright and politician Ruan Dacheng personally trained his troupe, and it often gave outside performances of his own plays.[1] Zhang Dai (1597–1689?) of Chekiang, author and wealthy landowner, grew up in a household that maintained several troupes of actresses, with such names as Feastworthy Troupe, Luxuriant Park Troupe and others.[2] Prime Minister Shen Shixing (1535–1614) kept a private troupe, from which came the famous actor Zhou Tiedun.[3] There was a vast number of independent troupes, many of them drawing their members from Haiyan, Yuyao, Yongjia and other towns and areas in Chekiang that were famed as cradles of the acting profession.[4] Some of the troupes stayed in one locality to perform when called upon, while others wandered from place to place by land and water.

The chuanqi and zaju generally speaking retained the system of role categories of the nanxi and Yuan zaju, but partly because casts of plays tended to become bigger and bigger, especially in the longer chuanqi, there were some additions and differences. In zaju, for instance, a chongmo ('rush-on mo') was added. This role very often opened the play, with an introductory or scene-setting passage, perhaps in emulation of the introductory act of the southern plays. The fumo also performed this function on occasions – often in chuanqi – but was now simply a secondary male role without necessarily any special connection with the jing. All the role categories could have major and minor divisions, such as xiaodan, 'little dan' and xiaochou, 'little chou', the multiplicity of characters in some dramas requiring greater diversity of nomenclature and a greater number of acting personnel. The larger troupes would have two or more actors specialising in each of the main role categories, and could thus spare separate personnel for the sub-categories when required by a play, but the ordinary run of troupes might have only one or two actors for each main category, so would require greater flexibility from the actors or even the doubling of parts.

Costume and stage properties were often elaborate in Ming performances.[5] Some editions of plays specify such matters in great detail, in many cases indicating changes of costume for different acts. Studies of Ming editions of fifteen Yuan *zaju* reveal forty-six kinds of hat, forty-seven kinds of dress, five kinds of shoes and stockings and six kinds of girdle or belt worn by male roles, with slightly less but still considerable variation in the female attire.[6] In one play the heroine had to appear in a smock sprinkled with gold. In another the scholar fop of one act had to appear in rags in the next. Chinese soldiers wore 'red-bowl helmets', and Mongol soldiers wore 'Uighur hats'. Ordinary ranks sometimes wore 'black-cloth nail armour', while the high-ranking general would wear a flowing full-length battle robe. Poor women wore patched quilted jackets. There were some attempts to provide historically accurate costume, but that depended naturally on such things as the availability of finance and the requisite knowledge. In troupes run on a shoestring there would be only the most generalised costumery and only the vaguest period distinctions. Make-up was commonly used, as were false beards of various kinds. Swords, pikes, fans, dolls used as babies, sticks, cudgels, flags, bows, arrows, lanterns, whips, baskets and other objects were carried on stage, and a hobby-horse, head in front and tail behind, was still sometimes used by mounted characters, as in the Yuan. Various sound effects from backstage included cockcrows, the call of wild geese and parrots, whistles, watch-drums, battle-cries, thunder, dogs barking, and so on.

Raised stages were sometimes used in the Ming, but private troupes generally performed on flat ground in a courtyard or hall, with a space marked out and covered with a red felt carpet to serve as a stage, the musicians being located at the back of the carpet. Actors would enter from the audience's left side, and exit by the right. Since it used no big drums or big gongs and so often depicted intimate and relatively tranquil love scenes, and since its singing was so delicately drawn out and its acting so attentive to finesse of movements, Kunqu drama was particularly suited to such small-scale, intimate performances. 'On the red carpet' came eventually actually to mean 'on stage', and the stage could be referred to simply as 'the carpet'. Some bigger residences did have slightly raised permanent stages but a red carpet would still be placed on the stage to serve as a central acting space.

There were also temple stages and village stages, and some larger guildhalls or meeting halls and ancestral halls had stages as well. Village stages were temporary platforms set up in grain-drying yards or some other open space against a hill or by a river. Ming copies of the famous Northern Sông panoramic painting 'Going to the river on the Festival of Pure Light' by Zhang Zeduan add a picture of such a stage. Some such later copies show the red carpet on the stage. Both temple and village stages were about man-height or higher, and immediately overlooked a thoroughfare or food-stalls. For all their height from the ground, such stages were left open on three sides, and these were bounded only by a low railing, very much like the railing of the Globe stage. Perhaps the railing was some vestige of the *goulan*, 'balustrade', which had given its name to the theatres of earlier dynasties. Kunshan-*qiang* music could be performed on such stages, but clearly they were much more suited to Yiyang-*qiang* and other vigorous and loud styles of music with heavy percussion and brisk manner of singing, which were more likely to be audible and to attract attention from a high, open-sided stage situated in a large open space, with an audience that could easily consist of a thousand by no means breathlessly hushed people. In 1933 when Bernard Shaw chatted with the famous actor Mei Lanfang, he expressed himself mystified at the noise of gongs and drums which accompanied Chinese drama. Mei explained that some Chinese drama such as Kunqu did require silence from the audience.[7] Japanese critics also complained about such noise. Answering this common criticism on a later occasion, Mei pointed out that the heavy percussion should really be heard in the countryside on rough stages for its origin, point and merits properly to be appreciated.

It was possible to adapt Kunshan-*qiang* music to such conditions to a certain degree. Some percussion could be added and the more active and exciting Kunqu plays could be chosen, but there were decided limits to the adaptation possible. Kunshan-*qiang* was more suited to the intimacy, enclosure and refinement of the private stages. On the other hand Yiyang-*qiang* and similar kinds of music could scarcely fail to sound somewhat coarse and cacophonous to gentry connoisseurs accustomed to Kunshan-*qiang* music. To this extent did differing stage conditions govern the social realms and physical environments in which the two main divisions of music tended to find their greatest popularity.

In the late Ming, when 'refined music' had established itself as such, it could be taken as a discourtesy or insult for a host to entertain his guest with a troupe specialising in Yiyang-*qiang* or similar kinds of music. Guests would protest at such treatment or even leave the feast outright. Yet while the distinction of 'vulgar' and 'refined' may have a certain validity in this case, it can be a misleading over-simplification. To understand Ming drama as a whole, and also to appreciate later developments in both 'refined' and 'vulgar' spheres, it will not do to adopt the prejudices of highbrow connoisseurs. Competition developed Kunqu drama in certain respects. Kunshan-*qiang* music could not allow of such vulgarising devices as *jia-gun*, could not, given its essential qualities of lofty literary elegance, permit so much tampering with the words. Denied *jia-gun* as a means of making a play more comprehensible and appreciable to the audience, it seems that Kunqu found other means: the placing of greater stress on bodily movements and facial expressions to emphasise the meaning of the words and to highlight the melody was probably one of the means used. Thus the finesse of later Kunqu and Peking Opera acting no doubt owed a great deal to competition between the different kinds of music and drama.

The role categories of Kunqu drama as it evolved became very numerous and fine in their distinctions. The four main categories, *sheng, dan, jing* and *chou*, subdivided into many others, broadly as follows:

1. *sheng*: the more serious male roles, with unpainted faces, but very often wearing beards.

   (a) *laosheng*, 'old *sheng*', also known as *zhengsheng*, 'main *sheng*', dignified middle-aged or elderly roles, imposing patriots, etc. Bearded.

   (b) *wai*, also called *laowai*, 'old *wai*', similar to (a) but secondary roles. Bearded.

   (c) *mo*, also called *fumo*, similar secondary roles to (b), also elderly household stewards, presenters of prologue. Bearded.

   (d) *guansheng*, 'hat *sheng*', leading roles of young lovers or young scholars, such as the hero of *Lute* and Emperor Minghuang in *Palace of Eternal Life*.

   (e) *jinsheng*, 'cloth-cap *sheng*', young scholars, sometimes main male romantic roles, but sometimes secondary undesirable characters.

   (f) *jimaosheng*, 'chicken-feather *sheng*', also called *zhiweisheng*, 'pheasant-tail *sheng*', young princes or warriors, youthful military roles.

   (g) *xiepisheng*, 'shoe-leather *sheng*', also called *kusheng*, 'suffering *sheng*', and *qiongsheng* , 'poor *sheng*', poverty-stricken young scholars.

2. *dan*: female roles.

   (a) *laodan*, 'old *dan*', secondary roles, middle-aged or elderly women.

   (b) *zhengdan*, 'main *dan*', popularly known as *cidamian*, 'female big-face', principal young women roles.

   (c) *zuodan*, 'action *dan*', variety of young women roles, sometimes substituting for the *zhengdan, cishadan* or *tiedan* but not the *guimendan*.

   (d) *cishadan*, 'stabbing-and-killing *dan*', vigorous, courageous and fighting young women.

   (e) *guimendan*, 'harem or lady's bower *dan*', also called *wudan*, 'fifth *dan*', refined aristocratic young ladies.

   (f) *tiedan*, 'assistant *dan*', also called *liudan*, 'sixth *dan*', and *xiaodan*, 'little *dan*', maidservants, etc.

3. *jing*: forceful male roles, sometimes generals, warriors or powerful villains. Painted faces.

   (a) *damian*, 'big face', also simply called *jing*, or *zhengjing*, 'main *jing*', imposing, resolute, ferocious characters, mighty generals, etc.

   (b) *baimian*, 'white face', sometimes also simply referred to as *jing*, also called *fujing*, 'assistant *jing*', violent or powerfully villainous characters.

4. *chou*:* comic characters. Painted faces, but with less elaborate make-up than the *jing* roles.

   (a) *fu*, 'assistant', also called *ermian*, 'second face', generally sly, sinisterly or villainously comic characters.

*See pages 85–86 above on the difficulty of providing a translation of this term.

(b) *xiaomian*, 'little face', generally agreeably, nobly or admirably comic characters.

There are variations and exceptions to this scheme, one list giving as many as twenty-five separate categories,[8] and the roles were further distinguished by acting, costume and more detailed make-up differences. The *jing* had complex facial make-up in various colours and patterns. The *chou* had a whitened nose, the *fu* more white across the eyes. There were considerable variations for individual characters. The villain known as Rat Lou in the modern Kunqu version of *Fifteen strings of cash*, for instance, had a decidedly rat-like make-up, with whiskers, and a rat's sharp features deftly drawn in black or another dark colour. He was played by a *chou*, an exception to the above scheme. The exceptions were many, and we cannot be certain how far the situation in the late Ming corresponded to that of the Kunqu of later times.

In later ages Kunqu divided into northern and southern schools, with some distinct regional variations in style. The southern is more minute in the finesse and detail of its acting, and more gentle and lilting in its singing, while the northern has a somewhat more powerful manner of delivery, but both are characterised by the flute-accompanied, mellifluous singing and by meticulous attention to the gestures, postures and movements of acting. A recent book of analysis and reminiscence by a famous *chou* actor, for instance, gives twenty-seven major kinds of set foot movement, standing, walking and so forth, and thirty-seven kinds of special finger, hand and sleeve movements, as well as a host of other intricate knacks and techniques.[9] The hundred different ways in which Rat Lou contrives to convey visually the rattishness of his sly soul have to be seen to be believed, and are an astonishingly impressive example of the power of Kunqu acting.

Government surveillance of drama and play-acting continued in the late Ming, and there is also increasing evidence of moralistic disapproval. Fan Lian (1540–?) describes how at spring festivals in the country markets and fairs round Songjiang in Kiangsu province, after a period of Japanese piratical invasions local louts and trouble-makers made a habit of assembling crowds for the purpose of performing plays taken from fiction and legend, plays that were 'ludicrously coarse and vulgar'. At first they would dress up in the normal way of professional actors, but in 1590 two or three hundred horses were hired in each place, and the performers were all clad in gaudy robes, leather boots and shoes and jewel-enclustered hats and silk caps. It was, Fan said, like some triumphal procession of a top graduate in the imperial examinations. They used three jewelled or pearled whips each worth over a hundred taels. Thirty or forty singing girls were brought in extra, and the former rustic, action-packed plays were replaced by more lascivious items with female leading roles, everything being most sumptuous. There were coloured pavilions, flags, drums and weapons, all with rare and marvellous qualities 'too numerous to describe'. All the streets and bridges were decked with

cloth awnings to guard against the eventuality of bad weather. Gentry and commoners of the region vied to take their families to the spectacle, so that boats and
carriages blocked the waterways and highways, and it was 'as if the whole nation
had gone mad'. The performances could last four or five days at each place, at a
daily expenditure of a thousand *taels*. Fan found such unrestrained extravagance
in those years of famine and starvation quite incomprehensible, and applauded
the severe ban which a certain government commissioner imposed upon the plays
in 1592.[10]

Such laws and prohibitions had the blessing of puritans, guardians of moral
fibre and others. Guan Zhidao (1537–1608) was scandalised by the 'vile dissi-
pated habits' prevalent in Kiangsu and Chekiang provinces. Young gentlemen
students were involving themselves in acting, 'ignoring noble friends and celebrated scholars to join the ranks of players and such riff-raff, carousing in gangs,
singing, and turning day into night'.[11] To his further indignation the literati and
officials, their seniors, were quite unperturbed, indulgently regarding such things
as no different from the risqué poetry and songs of antiquity, failing to realise that
if vagabond habits were cultivated by the menfolk outside the home, 'lewd
breezes would fan' among the womenfolk in the home, leading inevitably to dis-
graceful immorality on their part. He urged an end to the widespread habit of
entertaining with plays at feasts. In a typically puritan manner he condemned the
lewd plays not only because of the desires they excited in their audiences but also
because they stimulated that purportedly negative emotion called sadness.

Huang Zuo (1490–1566), eminent literatus and debater, listed the performing
of plays, along with chess, polo, horse-riding, gambling, curio-hunting, listening
to ballads, collecting patterned stones, hunting, hawking, and other such sports
and pastimes, as an idle, unprofitable pursuit which distracted people from the
serious purposes of career and family. Earlier, Lu Rong (1436–94), the poet and
minister famed for having persuaded the emperor not to permit a state welcome
for lions sent as tribute or as presents from another state, had put matters even
more strongly. Noting that Haiyan, Yuyao, Cixi, Huangyan and Yongjia, all in
Chekiang province, produced many actors, and that even young gentlemen from
respectable families were not ashamed to take up acting, he declared that the
plays they acted were concerned at every twist and turn with women and with
weeping, inducing in the audience a strong propensity towards melancholy and
gloom, being 'truly the music of ruin of the Southern Sông state'! 'Those who
impersonate women,' he said, 'are called *zhuangdan*, and in the gentleness of their
voices and the slow grace of their deportment, in their postures as they bob and
curtsy, they are often most realistic, so that literati who aspire to maintain their
households in the path of virtue should wholly and utterly exclude them and
avoid them.'[11]

Yuan Huang of the late sixteenth and early seventeenth centuries, leading
strategist in campaigns in Korea against the Japanese, and expert in music, hyd-
raulics, the calendar, logistics, geomancy, astrology and astronomy, carried his
bent for scientific classifications into the realm of morality, and awarded merits

for good deeds and black marks for bad deeds. Destroying the blocks of a lewd book earned one three hundred merits, producing a book condemning lewdness only one hundred. Keeping actors, singing girls or handsome footmen in one's household was the thin end of the wedge of vice and iniquity and earned ten black marks per day. Letting one's wives or daughters listen to lewd ballads was thirty black marks a time.

There was a great deal of complaint in the period about the immorality presented by plays. Tao Shiling (d. 1640) complained:

> Most of the recent plays written are about illicit and indecent sex affairs between men and women, every one of the vast mass produced being utterly loathsome without exception. Yet people still frequently put on such plays in their homes, fathers, sons and brothers in the same room as their womenfolk, watching together the fulsome comedy and disgusting filth with its whole range of scandalous postures and gestures, quite shamelessly without turning a hair. No different from when the ancients used to have their women gambol about naked! A whole hall of people is scarcely more than beasts. How lamentable.[12]

He further remarked:

> This is a common occurrence and once bitten people cannot call a halt. Have they never reflected that sexual desires are like oozing, seeping water, and that cases of moral collapse and sin constantly occur even if one takes precautions immediately or in good time, let alone when such desires are actually channelled by the presentation of concupiscence! Imagine how the audience must feel on such occasions, how not only young and wanton people's lusts must be aroused. If they have hitherto been neglectful of the state of their decorum and moral code, then they will now unconsciously find their appetites whetted, and it needs only a little relaxation of self-control and they enter the gate of bestiality. They must beware.[13]

It was Tao Shiling, too, who conceived the ingenious notion of classifying all plays into four categories on the basis of the four section headings of the ancient classic of poetry, the *Book of odes*. Some of the stuffier plays, such as those of Shao Can and Qiu Jun, he deemed suitable for weddings, celebrations and ordinary performances in private residences or at banquets. Some of the lightly romantic plays such as *Moon prayer*, which he equated with the decidedly back-to-nature and robustly spicy section of the *Book of odes* known as *feng*, 'folk-songs' or 'songs of customs', he grudgingly allowed to be performed in private courtyards and secluded apartments at small gatherings of a few male friends. The many plays with some sort of religious or supernatural theme of which he did not disapprove but which did not fit into his strained and creaking classifications were to be termed 'remnants' and could be performed in temples and monasteries, in place of various rituals and religious services. As for salacious plays like *West wing* and *Thorn hairpin*, they were to be absolutely excluded both from honourable classification and from performance. He would have liked to forbid bookshops to sell them, or actors to learn them, on pain of sharpest punishment. This, he believed, would of itself greatly help to reform social habits as a whole and to set men on the right track.

Some eminent men simply disapproved of plays without apparently any reservations. Others at least had enough wit to realise the potential of drama for promoting their own notions of good. The epoch-making philosopher Wang Shouren (Wang Yangming, 1472–1528) acutely perceived the uses to which ancient rulers had put drama-like musical performances, and suggested that plays should be utilised for the purposes of moral propaganda, removing all the licentious ones or any lecherous wording, and leaving only the dramas of loyal subjects and filial sons to do their subliminal advertising of virtue for the improvement of society. Tao Shiling was also aware of the educational possibilities of drama. Remarking on the 'supernatural' immediacy of drama's effect on the audience's emotions, he considered the drama twice as efficient as aged pedagogues in their dry-as-dust classes expounding the classics or doddering priests mounting the pulpit to preach the laws of Buddhism. He praised such plays as *Converting the ant* and *Returning the belt* as examples of the way in which drama could reform people's morals and make them aware of the theories of divine retribution without their being conscious of any sermonising, inducing in them a spontaneous and full delight in virtue.

Tao's views were quoted with approving comments by Li Zongzhou (1578–1645), a giant of a moral stickler and, to his own cost, frequently the self-appointed conscience of the government. He was thrice degraded to the status of a commoner for his stern advice, once for opposing the emperor's employment of the Jesuit Adam Schall. On the fall of the dynasty he refused food for twenty-three days in noble despair and loyalty until he starved himself to death. Observing the prevalence of popular drama, Li realised that one could scarcely abolish such a social phenomenon, but felt that it might well be a medium for general moral reform if properly used.

Ming plays were performed by both men and women, but it is arguable that towards the end of the dynasty the age-old moral prejudices, present at least as early as the Tang, against actresses and mixed troupes were strongly favouring all-male troupes. Certainly we hear much more of male performers. Early in the dynasty Zhu Youdun's play *Falling back into whoredom* describes the career of a singing girl-cum-actress very similar to the stars of the Yuan. In the late Ming there were also singing girls who acted, and they included performers of all kinds of role and singers of all kinds of music. One, for instance, excelled in both Kunshan-*qiang* and Yiyang-*qiang* singing. Her name was Chen Yuanyuan. Mao Xiang (1611–93), poet, painter, calligrapher, expert on tea and orchids, free spirit and mighty *bon viveur*, probably a descendant of Yuan dynasty Mongols who had remained in China, saw her performing in a Yiyang-*qiang* play and enthused: 'The tunes of the popular music of Yan [i.e. Hopeh province] are the hullabaloo of children and the squawking fracas of birds, but set to Lady Chen's movements and issuing from her lips they become like clouds drifting from some lofty peak, make one almost die, almost pass into immortality mid the heavenly delight of it.'[14] Yu Huai (1616–96), poet, avid collector of inkstones and another expert on tea, was in addition a keen student of women. Besides a treatise on women's shoes and stockings, he also wrote a book of reminiscences of Nanking singing girls and actresses during the Ming. Once, describing the actress Zheng Comely Maiden (Zheng Ruying) and the famous instrumentalist Dun Ren, he said, 'Dun's *pipa*-lute music and Comely Maiden's songs should really only be heard in paradise, for when otherwise do you hear such things in this mortal world!'[15]

Actors of this period would strive for perfection in their arts. The erudite Zheng Fujiao (1596–1675) said in praise of the actor Zhou Tiedun that even a superb falcon or a hawk in flight could not surpass the deft verve and agility of his acting.[16] Around the middle of the Ming there was an actor called Yan Rong, whose courtesy name was Keguan, meaning 'Worth Seeing' or 'Admirable'. He had a fine resonant voice, and was a virtuoso in the postures and gestures and facial expressions of acting. On one occasion, when playing the highly emotional part of Gongsun Chujiu, elderly former minister who protects an orphan baby, last surviving heir of an annihilated noble clan, in the play *Sole heir of the Zhao clan*, Yan Rong failed to obtain any audience reaction whatsoever. Returning home, he seized his beard in his left hand and slapped his face with his right, by way of self-punishment for his ineffectual performance. Then he faced a mirror and, clasping in his arms an orphan carved from wood and weeping as he sang and recited, practised the part without rest for a very long time. Later he performed the part on stage again, and when he rendered the crucial emotional section, all the thousands of people in the audience wailed and wept so vociferously that eventually they lost their voices with crying. After this performance he went home, looked into the mirror, bowed to his image, and said, 'Yan Rong, you really are Worth Seeing now!'[17]

Another actor, Ma Jin, came from one of China's Islamic minorities, and was dubbed Mohammedan Ma. The theatre fan, poet and master of prose Hou Fangyu (1618–55), who kept a troupe of boy actors and who himself, along with his mistress Li Lady Perfume, was immortalised in the famous play *Peach blossom fan*, mentions Ma Jin as once playing the *jing* role of the tyrannical early Ming Prime Minister Yan Song in a drama performed in Nanking. There was competition from another troupe presenting the same play in the same city at the same time, with an actor named Li playing Yan Song. Mohammedan Ma learned that the public preferred Li's version, and immediately fled incognito to Peking. There he took up service as a footman in the household of some high-ranking minister, devoting all his time and concentration to observing the deportment, airs and mannerisms of his master and learning to imitate his way of speaking (reminding one of the story of how the Zhou dynasty jester Meng once impersonated the Prime Minister Sunshu Ao). After three years in Peking, he at last returned to Nanking. This time when he performed Yan Song, he was watched by his rival and Li had no choice but to concede the superiority of Mohammedan Ma's performance.[18]

For all kinds of music, prime importance was accorded to singing ability, the distinct pronunciation of words and strict adherence to the beat of the music. Kunshan-*qiang* stressed mellifluous, extenuated, rounded tone, and Yiyang-*qiang* stressed cadence and rhythm more, but both alike required intense training. One mid-Ming teacher used a novel method of teaching his pupils. He would sit facing them in the dark, and conduct them with a lighted stick of incense to indicate the correct rhythms and pitches.[19]

The most famous and well loved of Chinese dramas are mostly about love. This is generally true, as far as we can tell, even of the plays of Yiyang-*qiang* and similar styles of music, though the vigorous and noisy percussion and the high, open stages which they used favoured the enacting of battle or fighting interludes. Fighting was often represented by acrobatic displays, sometimes very symbolically, at other times closely reflecting actual fighting. There was a long and intimate connection between drama and acrobatics in China. Athletic and acrobatic contests such as the Horn Butting Games, as we have seen, probably helped to mould the early drama consciousness, and all early genres of play included acrobatics on occasions.

As mentioned earlier, the Northern Sông *zaju Maudgalyāyana saves his mother* was performed for seven or eight days on end. A Ming performance of *Maudgalyāyana saves his mother* took three days and three nights.[20] It was organised by a certain Yu Yunshu, who set up a big stage on a military parade ground. There were a hundred *loges* for women round the stage. He had selected thirty or forty actors from Zhengde and Qingyang in Huizhou, Anhwei province, all energetic and agile fellows, skilled at fighting and tumbling. Among the many skills they displayed were tightrope-walking, rope-climbing, somersaulting, jumping the hoop, doing handstands, leaping through fire and through swords. In a most extravagant production, the scenes of the supernatural were represented as vividly, we are told, as the Tang master Wu Daozi's painting 'Various scenes from Hell'. Thousands of pieces of paper sacrificial money were burnt – presumably by the audience in dread and fear of the hell which suddenly seemed so real and near to them? All the faces beneath the lamplight took on a ghostly hue. During a couple of the more gripping scenes the acting would call forth fierce shouts from over ten thousand voices in unison. The regional governor took it for the sound of pirates or sea-borne invaders making an incursion inland and sent his constables to investigate. Yu Yunshu had to go in person to reassure him and prevent serious repercussions.

It is not quite clear how the acrobatic interludes were inserted into the play, but beyond doubt they were a considerable part of it. It is of great interest that the actors came from Anhwei province. Just as the Anhwei developments of Yiyang-

qiang music were to have a profound influence on later Chinese drama, so the actors of Anhwei were to be famed for their acrobatic skills in drama. Peking Opera, internationally admired for its displays of acrobatics in military plays, owes a great deal to the Anhwei tradition. There used to be a saying current in the Yangtse regions, 'Kunshan singing and Anhwei fighting', epitomising the fame of the Anhwei acrobats. The private troupe of Mi Wanzhong (d. 1628), eminent politician, painter, calligrapher, seal-carver, landscape gardener and collector of ornamental rocks, used real swords and spears in their fighting scenes[21]– a measure of their skill rather than of their imprudence no doubt.

There may have been scenery or painted backcloths in the production of *Maudgalyāyana saves his mother* described above. Although the widespread use of scenery has been a twentieth-century development in China, we have details of an experiment with scenery in the late Ming. The actress Liu Sunlight Fortune conceived ingenious uses of it for the play *Resplendent Emperor of the Tang travels to the moon*. At first the back of the stage was shut off by a black curtain, then, when the Taoist magician responsible for organising the space travel came on stage, he gave a flourish of his sword, a noise rang forth, and the black curtain was withdrawn to reveal a moon, a round shape cut out with curling clouds painted all round it. In the middle of this moon sat the Moon Fairy. The immortal Wu Gang, whose Sisyphean task it was eternally to fell a cassia tree, was there also, and the White Rabbit pounding medicines, both customary denizens of the moon. Over the front of the moon hung gossamer silk, behind which were lit several lamps to give an effect of moonlight, producing an opaque, greenish light rather like that of the new dawn. Another piece of cloth was then spread out to serve as a bridge, along which the Taoist slowly led the Emperor Minghuang up to the moon. All this apparently created a wondrous atmosphere, making the audience quite forget that it was only a play that they were watching. The absence of scenery in old Chinese drama was certainly not due to lack of inventiveness; we must seek other reasons, inherent features of Chinese drama and society, for its absence.

The late Ming period was a golden age of Chinese literature, a fascinating age when many forms of Chinese literature and scholarship came into being or established themselves securely. The genius of Feng Menglong (1574–1646) and Ling Mengchu (1580–1644) ushered in the vernacular short story as a literary genre, while the novel, the folk-song anthology, humorous writing and the compilation of humorous works, woodcut art, and many philosophical ideas received vital impetus. The theatre was firmly established: huge audiences from the ordinary populace attended it regularly; there was a strong army of élite connoisseurs and wealthy patrons; there were many playwrights and many and varying kinds of drama and dramatic music; drama movements had nationwide implications; the acting profession was an accomplished and complex one. It was an era of unique literary consciousness in which old, half-forgotten genres were re-examined and restored, when men looked with a fresh, inquisitive and confident eye at China's literary past and attempted to synthesise it into meaningful modern expositions and to channel it back into the living world of literature and performance. One major consequence was the rescue of Yuan *zaju* from what might easily have been virtual oblivion for eternity, and another was the writing of some excellent theoretical works on poetry, music and drama.

Those now still extant Yuan *zaju* actually printed during the Yuan may well have survived through being in the collection of Li Kaixian, who was also responsible for producing an edition of revised Yuan plays some time during the years 1526–67. Around 1588 a certain Xu published a collection of Yuan and Ming *zaju*, probably based on versions from the palace libraries.[22] Xi Jizi in 1598 and an anonymous editor (possibly Wang Jide, d. 1623) during the period 1573–1620 both produced such collections, also based on palace versions. During the years 1614–17 Zhao Qimei (1563–1624) copied some borrowed palace versions, and collated a large number of palace versions and other privately owned editions, printed and manuscript. These and other editors and bibliophile collectors, including playwrights such as Tang Xianzu and Shen Jing, all played a notable role in the preservation of Yuan *zaju*, but the greatest service of all was performed by Zang Maoxun (d. 1621). During the years 1615 and 1616 he published the collection *Hundred Yuan songs*, more commonly known as *Selection of Yuan songs*, which contains *zaju* mainly from the Yuan. Until fairly recently this was the sole current representative collection of Yuan *zaju*. Zang, to be sure, blurred our picture of the original Yuan plays by heavy alterations of their wording and by large-scale additions of speech and action.[23] Many of the editions he worked upon no doubt contained little or no more than the songs. Nevertheless, he did make them into whole pieces of dramatic literature. Without the activities of Zang and the other late Ming editors our present knowledge of Yuan *zaju* might have been very sparse indeed, and later Chinese drama would have been deprived of a source of considerable inspiration. Meng Chengshun published two collections of Yuan and Ming *zaju* in 1633, lifting an enormous amount directly from Zang. Both Zang's and Meng's collections were illustrated by some of the finest woodcut specialists of their day.

Many constructively critical and theoretical works were written during the late Ming, which scraped together some of what could still be gleaned about Yuan *zaju* and analysed old and contemporary drama, song and music. Many of the authors of these works were also playwrights of note, such as Li Kaixian, Xu Wei, Shen Jing, Wang Jide, Wang Shizhen (1526–90), Ling Mengchu, and others. Tables of prosody and musical rules, and a wealth of treatises, provided early Chinese drama with a solid body of acute and searching written theory.

7

A Diversity of Dramatic Styles during the Early Qing

Grouping the phenomena of Chinese literature and entertainment under dynastic headings is often artificial and inappropriate, as indeed any other less-than-whole treatments, any other categorisations, are likely to be. Literary and social developments overlap and sometimes seem largely independent of the major political changes. Yet there is often some purpose in using the dynastic divisions. Change of dynasty very often did entail cataclysmic change for much of society, or constitute a major cause of the initiation of such change, altering élites and being a dominant factor in changing intellectual, literary and entertainment trends. Early in the Qing dynasty drama reveals a continuity, personal and spiritual, from the Ming and thus opposes the dynastic divisions, but soon the influence of the ruler on drama becomes so marked as to indicate the use of them.

The Qing dynasty (1644–1911) was founded by the Manchus, a tribe of the same ancestry as the Jurcheds who founded the Jin dynasty. They dwelt in Heilungkiang, Kirin and Ningkuta to the north-east of China and, at a time when China was torn by maladministration and internal dispute, their conquest was achieved with the help of many renegade Chinese literati, officials and generals. Unlike the Mongols, the Manchus fostered certain aspects of Chinese culture with great enthusiasm, and, once they had conquered China, obtained the cooperation of many wealthy and influential people and a large section of the intelligentsia. Under strong, astute rule there ensued a period of relative peace, during which there was a certain reflorescence of drama. Peking, the 'northern capital' of the Ming, was established as the Qing capital throughout the dynasty and increasingly became the centre of new developments in the theatre.

Kunshan-*qiang* music originated in Kiangsu province and it was from there that most of the actors and writers of Kunqu drama continued to come during the early Qing. Some of the playwrights were Ming loyalists turning their backs on service with the Qing and venting their indignation, or simply finding self-expression, in the world of theatre. A number who came from Suzhou, or nearby, were outstanding, and among them the most prolific and well-known was Li Yù (c. 1590–c.1660; the Yù is the character meaning 'jade'). He was attached to the household of Shen Shixing in some capacity, and career frustrations, partly due to Shen's son's obstructions, drove him to vent his resentment in writing four of

114

his most popular plays. It was after 1644 that he finally abandoned all thoughts of a government career, and the early years of the Qing were perhaps his most active as a playwright. He wrote at least thirty-two plays, and a further two jointly with other dramatists. In addition Li wrote what is to this day the most comprehensive analysis of Yuan *qu* prosody.[2] Many of his plays had a love theme, while a number concerned very recent historical events. One of these latter plays dramatised a rising against government officials in an attempt to save a righteous man, and another dealt with a protest strike and rising by weavers. Something of the power of Chinese drama and its close relevance at times to burning social and political issues can be seen from such plays.

Zhu Zuochao (fl. c. 1644) wrote some thirty plays, one of them in cooperation with other playwrights including Zhu Hao (sometimes pronounced Zhu Que; better known as Zhu Suchen, fl. c. 1644), who himself wrote the *Fifteen strings of cash* which in various adaptations and re-creations has remained so popular, and which has produced splendid modern stage and cinema versions. Ye Zhifei (fl. c. 1644) wrote eight plays, one of which touched upon the virtues of a pirate. This subversive note incurred the wrath of the authorities and they threw Ye into jail, where he almost died. Qiu Yuan (fl. c. 1644) was a wild, unconventional man, poet, tippler, author of eight plays and painter of landscapes, especially snow scenes.[3] By contrast, Zhang Dafu (fl. c. 1653) lived in a Buddhist monastery, a plain, simple-hearted man, well versed in the scriptures of Buddhism and indifferent to material wealth. But his unworldliness seems to have been no impediment to his writing of dramas, for he was the author of no less than twenty-three. The 'Suzhou playwrights' often expressed themselves in a pedantic manner, but they kept the stage in mind and generally wrote performable plays, sometimes even using refreshingly direct and unadorned language. Posterity made widespread use of their plays.

There were a number of other important dramatists during the early Qing, chief of whom was Li Yú (1611–85), Yú meaning 'fisherman'.[4] To avoid confusion with the playwright Li Yù, he will here be referred to by his other name of Li Liweng, Liweng meaning 'old man with the bamboo rain-hat'. He is one of the eternally shining stars of Chinese literature, and was a most colourful personality. During the Ming he had several times failed to pass the provincial examinations, and on the fall of that dynasty he resorted to writing in order to provide for himself and forty wives, concubines and children. He maintained a troupe of singing-girl actresses, and, travelling for fifteen years over a large part of China with them, he attempted to earn his living by writing and producing plays which they performed in the residences of high-ranking officials where he was received as a guest. He made acquaintance with many famous men, but materially his life knew extreme vicissitudes. Poverty forced him to sell his home and beautifully landscaped gardens more than once. One of these, in Nanking, was called Mustard Seed Garden, and he also ran a book-shop of the same name. The most famous Chinese encyclopaedia of painting, compiled by his son-in-law and others, was named after this garden retreat.

Li Liweng was playwright, novelist, drama theorist, poet, and expert on the sexual arts, feminine charm, architecture, travel, recreation, diet, hygiene, and household equipment and furnishings. He enjoyed a great reputation in both China and Japan for his literary versatility and astounding catholicity of interest, although the more strait-laced Chinese literati frowned upon him. Such was his popularity in Japan that a Japanese author wrote a book and attributed it to him.

One of Li Liweng's miscellaneous anthologies of his own writings, his *Random expression of idle feelings*, includes valuable and incisive expositions of his views on drama and the playwright. He believed that the playwright should write such clear and straightforward speech and poetry that educated and uneducated, women and children, are all alike able to comprehend his words. He felt that the dramatist needed to be closely conversant with the stage, and to put himself in the place of both actor and audience. When writing dramas himself, 'his hand grasped the writing-brush but his mouth mounted the stage.'[5] His plays, mostly on the subject of romantic love, are demonstrations of his theory. He was vigorously attacked by some of his contemporaries for the colloquiality and unpretentiousness of his language, but these qualities were actually among his most attractive.[6] In his great respect for dialogue, too, he shames some other dramatists who considered that only the songs were of any real importance.[7]

By contrast, You Tong (1618–1704) used drama to flaunt his erudition and fine literary style.[8] Noted early in life for his learning, he met with career frustrations and disillusionment, which determined the subject-matter of some of his plays. From 1652 to 1656 he was a police magistrate. In 1657 there was a public scandal connected with the discovery of malpractices in the imperial examinations, implicating a large number of people. That autumn, while on a journey, he was forced by military troubles to tarry at an inn. There he wrote a play satirising corruption in the exams. On its première in Suzhou the local authorities arrested and flogged the entire cast, demanding that they reveal the names of the author and the promoter of the production. By this time already in Peking, You was able through an intermediary to reach some compromise, and the matter was hushed up.[9] In 1679 he was at last successful in the examinations. He obtained a post in the Hanlin Academy and played a part in the writing of the official history of the Ming dynasty before resigning in 1683. He also wrote a massive bibliography of works written during the Ming dynasty.

Previously, You's poems and essays had attracted the favourable notice of the Emperor Shizu (r. 1644–61), who praised his genius. On his entry into the Hanlin Academy he was honoured by the Emperor Shengzu (r. 1662–1722) with the title of Elder Celebrated Scholar. People paralleled the relationship of Shengzu and You Tong with that of the Tang dynasty Emperor Minghuang and the mighty poet Li Bai. When Shengzu made a tour south, You composed odes in his praise, which earned him a plaque of honour and a scroll both inscribed by the emperor himself.

Another man whose plays were redolent with poetic talent and literary elegance was Wu Weiye (1609–71), better known as Wu Meicun.[10] Active in Ming politics and administration, he refused to serve the new dynasty for nine years. When finally pressurised into doing so he never forgot his resentment, although he subsequently rose to high office, and on his death-bed he willed that he should be buried in the garb of a bonze and have carved before his tomb the words, 'Tomb of Wu Meicun the poet'. It was as a poet that he wished to be known to posterity. His plays, all permeated with grief at the fall of various states, reflected his nostalgia for the Ming.

Some have considered Wan Shu (fl. c. 1692) the best playwright of those times.[11] Besides twenty-two or more plays, he also wrote a large manual on music and prosody. The wedding of words and music was his dramatic forte. Employed by a governor-general of Kwangtung province, he wrote plays in his spare time. As soon as the draft of a play was ready, the governor-general would order his private troupe to perform it. Wan eventually died of melancholy, feeling that his ability had never earned its due reward in life.

The Suzhou and other playwrights made a certain amount of use of Kunshan-*qiang* music, but outside Chekiang and Kiangsu provinces Yiyang-*qiang* and related forms of music were gradually replacing it. This happened in the north especially, to such an extent that some came to regard the Yiyang-*qiang* as the typical music of popular drama in Hopeh province. In Peking the form of Yiyang-*qiang* music that had adopted the local pronunciation and features from the music of local kinds of play became known as Jing-*qiang* music, 'capital music'.

Few early Qing playwrights of fame came from the north, but one of the paragons of Chinese literature, Pu Songling (1640–1715) from Shantung province, made an interesting contribution to drama.[12] Descended from Mongol or Turkic ancestors who had held responsible posts under the Yuan dynasty, he himself is chiefly famed for a collection of 431 short stories, ingenious tales about ghosts, sprites, supernatural happenings and the oddities of the mortal world. He collected some of them by setting out tea before his gate for twenty years and forcibly inviting passers-by to tell him any strange tales they knew. He also wrote a very long novel, three plays and many poems, songs and ballads. His songs used popular tunes current in the north, and also used the Shantung dialect. The plays, alas, do not survive, but among the ballads is a 'Spell to tame the shrew' in thirty-three sections which are strongly akin to the acts of a play.[13] Its wording is racily colloquial, and its tunes seem to include popular folk-songs such as were certainly not used by Kunshan-*qiang*, nor, as far as is known, by the main kinds of Yiyang-*qiang* music. Possibly, if his non-extant plays were in similar form, Pu Songling may have been the pioneer of a mature use of local drama music, and have created a drama quite distinct in its musical qualities from the mainstreams of Kunshan-*qiang* and Yiyang-*qiang*.

Many kinds of dramatic music and drama competed with each other in the early Qing. Some were local offshoots of Yiyang-*qiang* which had acquired an identity and competitive force of their own, while others were more purely local forms of music, extending their range and attaining popularity away from their home area. Even though many regarded Kunshan-*qiang* as the orthodox music, it was not only succumbing nationally to the Yiyang-*qiang* kinds of music but was losing ground to other kinds, too. Liu Tingji (fl. c. 1676), for instance, mentioned, with some distaste, Siping-*qiang*, Jing-*qiang* and Wei-*qiang*, and the 'much inferior' Bangzi-*qiang*, Luantan-*qiang*, Wuniang-*qiang*, Suona-*qiang* and Luoluo-*qiang* varieties of music, while claiming that Kunshan-*qiang* was still the orthodox or standard music.[14] The music used by Pu Songling may have been the Liuzi-*qiang* of later ages, or have had some connections with it.[15] There was clearly some danger that Kunshan-*qiang* would become the interest solely of an esoteric minority if such tendencies continued to gain ground, but at that juncture there appeared two masterly dramas which, by using it and gaining immediate and enormous acclaim, served to revive its flagging fortunes, and to establish it more firmly as the 'orthodox' music. These plays were Hong Sheng's *Palace of Eternal Life* and Kong Shangren's *Peach blossom fan*.

Hong Sheng (1645–1704) from Chekiang province was eminently connected through his wife, who was the grand-daughter of a Grand Secretary (Prime Minister).[16] She was an expert on music, and some of his passion for songs and plays was due to her influence. Hong was an accomplished *shi* poet, and pupil of some of the leading scholars and poets of the age, but because of his unfashionable poetic theories was often at loggerheads with his teacher Wang Shizhen (1634–1711), sometimes considered the foremost *shi* poet of the age. Hong was also a fine essayist, and in addition wrote ten or more plays. As a student of the Imperial Academy or 'National University' he spent some years in Peking. There, in 1687 or 1688, he completed *Palace of Eternal Life*, begun in Hangzhou in 1679. It was staged at once. A troupe which specialised in Kunshan-*qiang* and was suffering from the lull in the fortunes of that music performed the play, and one performance shot it to fame. It came to the notice of Emperor Shengzu, who praised it highly and awarded the performers twenty taels of silver. The grateful actors invited Hong to a special performance of one of the acts in the summer of 1689, but unfortunately he had incurred the wrath of a certain Mr Huang whom he had neglected to invite. Huang discovered that it was a period of national mourning, perhaps for an empress, when such entertainments were forbidden. He addressed a memorial to the throne, urging the impeachment of those concerned. All the guests at the performance were dismissed from office, including the merry eccentric poet Zhao Zhixin (1662–1744), a friend of Hong's who had newly won his doctorate. Hong himself was marched out of Peking under escort. A sad poem commemorates this event. Left in desperate circumstances by this blow, Hong died a few years later. One day when travelling drunk by a stream, he lost his footing, fell in, and drowned.

Another version of the story claims that Zhao Zhixin brought about the action against himself and Hong by snubbing a Censorial Minister. Whatever the details of the scandal it no doubt served to boost the fortunes of the play. In consequence of its fame in Peking and elsewhere, Kunshan-*qiang* music became favoured for many more plays.

Palace of Eternal Life, like many earlier plays and other writings, concerned the love affair of Emperor Minghuang of the Tang and his favourite wife Lady Yang Yuhuan (Yang Gui-fei). It was much longer and more elaborate than any earlier drama on the same theme, and had fifty acts. Unlike *Rain on the paulownia tree* it does not limit itself to Lady Yang's death and the emperor's sorrowful memories of her. From Act Twenty-six onwards she frequently reappears as a spirit. She sees her intriguing relatives carried off to Hell. The grieving emperor has a lifesize image of her carved in precious wood. Meanwhile in the capital, after an unsuccessful assassination attempt by a loyalist musician, the adopted son of the rebel An Lushan murders Lushan. Tang armies restore the empire, and the emperor returns to the capital. On his way he reaches the spot where Lady Yang lies buried, and orders her exhumation for reburial. The grave is empty but for her perfume sachet. A woman brings one of Lady Yang's silk stockings to him, and these two mementos renew his sorrow. Back in the capital, he engages a Taoist necromancer to try and contact Lady Yang's spirit. With the collusion of the sympathetic gods, and the help of the Taoist, the two lovers meet once more. The Taoist conjures up a bridge, and the emperor journeys to the moon to rejoin Lady Yang. Already deities in a previous existence, they are now restored to heaven and reunited in their love for ever more.

The play is superbly free in its imagination, and much of it is one ornate lyric poem to love. Hong Sheng took immense care in polishing it and in expunging some of the more spicy love scenes to shift the emphasis to a dancing scene. Later, feeling that this weakened the love element, he revised it once more. Only after a third major revision did he settle its form and title. A music master added his expertise to Hong's vast knowledge of music for the songs.

Although the play has a happy ending in the Chinese tradition, the element of personal and political tragedy looms large in the workings of the plot. The following extract from the play, as well as showing how Hong Sheng could handle the vigour of a martial character, is a key one in anticipating the tragedy that will later overtake both Lady Yang and the Tang empire. Heavier than usual annotation is provided, partly to avoid the too great departure from the original Chinese that would otherwise be necessary for considerable passages of the translation, and partly to indicate the literary concentration and denseness of allusion in much of Hong's writing.[17] The protagonist in the act translated is Guo Ziyi, a military man, famous in history both for his military achievements and for his friendship with the poet Li Bai. It is he who later plays the major part in the military restoration of Tang power.[18]

Palace of Eternal Life by Hong Sheng: Act Eleven, 'The writing on the wall'

(*Enter Guo Ziyi, wearing warrior's hat, and with a sword at his waist.*)

GUO ZIYI.   The world remains oblivious of my mighty aspirations,
                   one sword to guard me, I drift for a while with idle inclinations,

> But when comes the hour of crisis, and the world has woes to settle,
> then shall the age find its saviour in need, its man of honest mettle!

I am surnamed Guo, and my personal name is Ziyi, and I hail from Zheng county in Hua subprefecture. I have studied all the arts and stratagems of warfare, and rendered myself replete with political acumen and the skills of leadership, for I have it in mind one day to become the mightiest hero of this world, and to fulfil some enterprise that will bring peace to my land, and security to my nation. Now, having passed the military examinations, I have come here to the capital for the selection interview to decide my appointment. These days, with Yang Guozhong having usurped the reins of power,* and An Lushan wallowing in lavish imperial favours, the whole central government seems to be going to the dogs. I wonder when, or if, someone like myself, like Guo Ziyi without even any post or rank of any sort to his name, will ever get the chance to do the imperial court a good turn!

> (*Sings*) A man who claims to be a man
> must himself find his vent for his bold aspirations,
> – He is not inclined to raise his voice
> in vain appeals to the Heaven over Qi!†
> I laugh at those who act like 'swallows perching on top of the hall',‡
> none of them 'looking up to see the ravens on the roof'!§
> No precautions are taken against captive tigers and caged bears,¶
> and freedom to rampage is granted 'altar-rats and city-wall foxes'.**
> No news ever of a cockcrow-riser brandishing his sword
> alone before the night is fled.††

*Yang Guozhong was the paternal first cousin of Lady Yang, and made himself Prime Minister. It was said to have been his jealousy of An Lushan that sparked off the latter's rebellion.

†The term 'Heaven over Qi' seems to derive from the philosophical work *Lie-zi*, written some time before about 300 AD, in which there is mention of a man of the state of Qi who was so afraid that the heavens might collapse and fall on him that he could no longer sleep or eat. Here Guo Ziyi seems to be saying that he has no intention of passively relying on a heaven wrongly reputed to listen to one's prayers.

‡The *Kong-cong-zi* of the first or second century BC has the words 'Swallows and sparrows dwelling on top of the hall[. . .] think themselves secure, and when the stove suddenly flares up and sets fire to the beams and house, they do not realise that the disaster will affect them, too.' Guo mocks those passive onlookers who think the fate of the court will not affect them.

§In the *Book of odes* the lines 'Gaze up at the raven alighting, Onto whose house' take the raven as an il omen. Another tradition takes the ravens' alighting as referring to peoples' giving their allegiance in time: of strife to an inferior leader. In the latter case, Guo is referring to the growing number of adherents to the causes of such rogues as An Lushan and Yang Guozhong.

¶'Tigers and bears' anciently meant 'bold generals', but here must mean 'bold *bad* generals', i.e. A Lushan and his ilk.

**In the Zhou dynasty or early Han work *Yan-zi-qiu* 'altar-rats, is used as an image for the hangers-on o evil men. 'Altar-rats and city-wall foxes' is found in the Tang *History of the Tsin*, meaning evil hangers-o whom it is desirable to remove, but whose removal would mean disaster for the political personalit whom they 'infest'. The idea seems to be that the destruction of such vermin would entail the destructio of the very 'altars' and 'city-walls' wherein they dwell. Here it must mean the evil hangers-on of A Lushan, the Yangs, and so on.

††Zu Ti (266–321), hearing a cock crow in the middle of the night, would rise and practise his swordplay Later he became the military saviour of his decaying nation.

Ah, history is full of fame's vicissitudes,*
but if you can bequeath the world a name for noble deeds,
what matter if your glory grow old mid woodcutters and
fishermen!†

Well, I think I'll go to Changan market, and buy myself a little liquid merriness!
(*Walks and sings*) I slowly stride the 'celestial streets',‡
and, to melt my cares a while, seek a little ease within some tavern.
All that meets the eye is milling crowds in teeming confusion,
a jumbling tumult, like rowdy drunkards hard to prop upright.
– Where now walks any Minister of Chu, lone and sober weaving his
verse!§

And me, Guo Ziyi,
(*Sings*) Were I to seek a soul-mate, I fear the Angler of Fishes is gone,¶
the Shooter of Tigers is far away,** and the Butcher of Dogs is no
more.††

(*Exit.*)

(*Enter pub-keeper.*)

PUB-KEEPER.   We're a very special public-house, with a high-class line of wine,
I swore there'd be no booze on tick when I put up my sign,
So if you have the money, you can drink and never stop,
without, you won't get water, not a single drip or drop!

I'm the taverner of this New Feng Restaurant and Grand Wine Emporium here in the centre of Changan. This public-house of ours is situated between the eastern and western markets of the city, and there's always a mass of traffic here, crowds bustling to and fro. Without exception, all the lords, princes, government nobs, business people, and the ordinary soldiers and farmers from in and around the capital call here for a couple of pots in our establishment. Some come just for a drink, some have snacks with their wine, some buy liquor to carry out, and some make party bookings for drinking on the premises. It's one never-ending job serving them all. There, the words are hardly out of my mouth, and here comes another gent with a thirst!

---

*Seemingly a phrase from the poet Han Yu (768–824).
†It was a commonplace remark that the last word on the 'great men' of history was always had by the ordinary woodcutters and fishermen, who still plied their trades when the mighty empires lay in ruin and oblivion.
‡i.e. the streets of the capital. The term is found at least as early as in the poetry of Han Yu.
§The Minister of Chu is Qu Yuan, China's earliest nameable poet. A conscientious minister, his advice went unheeded and he eventually drowned himself. Perhaps because he drowned himself in water, rather than his sorrows in wine – as is sometimes pointed out in later Chinese literature – he is often associated with sobriety, as well as being regarded as an archetypal loyal minister.
¶Possibly Lü Shang, bastion of the Zhou dynasty, and first discovered by King Wen as he was angling. More likely Han Xin, a general who helped found the Han dynasty.
**Perhaps Li Guang (d. 119 BC), a doughty defender of the Han empire, or, anachronistically, the Five Dynasties general Li Cunxiao, a famous tiger-shooter.
††Perhaps Fan Kuai, but there were many other famous dog-butcher heroes. Possibly in all three cases, of Angler, Shooter, and Butcher, Hong simply intends to convey the generalised notion of 'hero bastions of the nation'.

(*Enter Guo Ziyi, walking.*)

GUO ZIYI. (*Sings*) I see afar a willow green, that leans at the
                corner of a gaily painted hostel,
         and the fluttering flapping vintner's sign,
         one blue cloth strip dancing before the breeze.
         Ah, could I but find a tippler from Yan Market*
         to join me in a round of wine!
(*Shouts*) Are you there, mine host?

PUB–KEEPER. (*Coming out to welcome him*) Please take a seat upstairs, sir. (*Guo Ziyi goes upstairs.*)

GUO ZIYI. What a splendid drinking-house!
        (*Sings*) Broad-bayed windows, bright, sunlit, and airy,
          and all around I see whitewashed walls covered with
            paintings of drunken gods.

PUB-KEEPER. Are you drinking alone, sir, or waiting for some other guests?

GUO ZIYI. I'll just drink a couple of pots on my own. Bring me top-quality wine, if you have any.

PUB-KEEPER. We do indeed. (*Brings wine*) Here you are.

VOICE BACKSTAGE. Barman, here!

(*Pub-keeper replies, and hurries away. Exit.*)

GUO ZIYI. (*Drinks wine and sings*)
        No wine-loving sideline-sitter Governor Tao am I,†
        nor yet a disciple of toping, roaring, Ruffian Guan,‡
        steady, hard drinking to rouse bold bile.
        Who will heed me, with my eyes so sober?
        Wonder if the Land of Booze is big enough to hold me?
        I hear such clamour down there in the streets,
        yet they 'leave out in the cold' this Guzzler of Gaoyang.§

(*He rises to his feet to look out of the window. Enter eunuchs,¶ and officials in sumptuous festive attire, with a retinue of attendants bearing gifts of gold, and leading sheep and carrying wine for a feast. They make a processional tour round the stage. Exeunt. Enter pub-keeper bearing wine.*)

---

*i.e. Jing Ke, the famous would-be assassin of the fearsome First Emperor of the Qin dynasty. Guo Ziyi thus likens himself to this tippling hero.

†i.e. Tao Yuanming (365–427), the famous poet, who retired from his magistracy, and became a boozy hermit.

‡Guan Fu was a swashbuckling warrior who lived in the early Han dynasty, and was for a while governor of Huaiyang. He was an inveterate drinker, and forthright in his cups. Once, drunk at a Prime Minister's party, he berated the company for their corrupt sycophancy, and was subsequently impeached, and executed along with the rest of his family.

§Li Shiqi from Gaoyang. Once, during the Qin dynasty, a man called on the Duke of Pei (later the first emperor of the Han), and was announced as looking like a Confucian scholar. A notorious anti-intellectual, the duke sent back the message: 'Tell him I am busy conquering the world, and have no time for meeting scholars.' On receipt of this message, the visitor, Li Shiqi, placed his hand on his sword, and railed at the messenger in a fury, 'Be off with you. Go back in, and tell the Duke of Pei that I am the Guzzler of Gaoyang! No scholar I!' He subsequently became an important counsellor and diplomat of the duke's. Guo is likening himself to Li, as someone who drinks and who could be of momentous service.

¶Played by *laodan*.

PUB-KEEPER.   Here is some nicely heated wine, sir!

GUO ZIYI.   Might I ask you something, taverner? Where are those government officials beneath our window going to?

PUB-KEEPER.   I'll tell you while you're drinking your wine, sir, shall I? It's all to do with the Imperial Uncle, Yang Guozhong, and the three ladies, the Dame of Han, the Dame of Guo, and the Dame of Qin.* Our emperor, may he live for ever,† has granted each of them the right to have a new residence built here in this part of the city, the Xunyang quarter. Their mansion-gates are all next to each other, all four in a row, and all four mansions are built in the same fashion as the emperor's Inner Palace itself. First one tried to outdo the other, then the next tried to surpass that one, and so it went on. If one saw that the other's was more grandly built, he would demolish his own, and build a new one from scratch, insisting that it be exactly the same, and not resting content till he'd made sure it was. One of their main halls alone cost a good billion taels of silver to build. Now today they've finished all the work, and that's why all the officials of the central government, whatever their rank, have provided themselves with sheep to eat, and wine and presents, and are making their way past here towards the mansions, to offer their congratulations and best wishes at each.

GUO ZIYI.   (*Horrified*) Hah, so that's what's happening!

PUB-KEEPER.   Just a minute, I'll go and get you some more wine. (*Exit.*)

GUO ZIYI.(*Sighing*) So, the relatives of Lady Yang are enjoying such lavish favours! What will come of it!

> (*Sings*) Strange that commoners should usurp such power and rank,
> outdoing each other in luxury, and flaunting splendid architecture.
> And all the lords are content to bob and bow to their wishes,
> jostling towards those Halls of Power as if flocking to some fair.

And now there's no one left to

> (*Sings*) Tell his Celestial Majesty the grievances of the world,
> that their scarlet ridge-tiles and emerald bricks
> are painted with commonfolks' blood and fat!

(*Rises to his feet.*) You get worked up and indignant, and all of a sudden the wine rushes to your head. Let's have a look round the room for a bit, just for a stroll. (*Peers closely.*) Hm, there are a few lines of writing on this wall over here. Someone's written a poem. Let's have a look now. (*Looks at it, and reads it aloud.*)

> 'The people of Yan market have all gone,
> No horses return from Box Valley Pass;
> If you meet a ghost at the foot of the hill,
> upon the ring is tied the silken dress.'‡

Hm, very odd this poem, very odd indeed.

---

*Three sisters of Lady Yang Yuhuan, who obtained their titles through her influence.

†Literally, 'Ten thousand [years] father', a term for the emperor.

‡This cryptic poem comes from the *Unofficial biography of Yang Taizhen* (Lady Yang) by Le Shi (930–1007). The first line is a prediction of An Lushan's rebellion, the second of the defeat of the Tang general Geshu Han on the frontier, the third and fourth of Lady Yang's death at Mawei Slope. The 'ring' refers to her, since her personal name includes the word for 'ring', and the silken dress means the silken cloth with which she hung herself. Thus the poem as a whole foretells the national disaster of the Tang, and the personal disaster of Lady Yang.

(*Sings*) I fix my eyes upon it, and read it right through,
                perusing line by line from start to end,
                and, on reflection, this poem bears little omen of joy!
Who wrote it up? Let's have a look. (*Looks again, and reads out loud.*) 'Written by Li
Xiazhou' . . . (*Looks pensive.*) Li Xiazhou . . . hm, that name sounds very familiar. Oh,
yes, I've heard there's a fortune-teller called Li Xiazhou, who's very skilled at analysing
the past and foretelling the future. It must be him.
                (*Sings*) It must conceal some prophecy of doom
                that cannot openly be expressed,
                – Ah, where are those experts at riddle-poems!*
                But don't they say:
                'When drunk, with heedless random brush,
                he daubed the wall in crazy-crow characters'!

(*Sounds of hubbub from backstage.*)

GUO ZIYI.(*Shouts*) Are you there, mine host?
PUB-KEEPER.   What's the matter, sir?
GUO ZIYI.   What's all that row outside this time?
PUB-KEEPER.   Come over to the window, sir, and look down. You'll see what it is.

(*Guo Ziyi looks. Enter An Lushan, wearing the robes of a prince, riding a horse, and preceded by royal
sceptres and insignia as his officers lead the way. They make a processional tour round the stage.
Exeunt.*)

GUO ZIYI.   Who's that?
PUB-KEEPER.   (*Laughs, and points.*) Why sir, can't you see his great big belly? That
man's called An Lushan. Our Sovereign Lord treats him with every favour under the
sun, and has even granted him the privilege of sitting within the Golden Cock Screen†
before the imperial throne. And now, into the bargain, he's conferred the title of Prince
of Dongping Shire upon him. An Lushan has just left court. Been to thank the emperor
for that kindness. The emperor's granted him leave to return to his new residence outside Eastern Hua Gate, and his route runs past here.
GUO ZIYI.(*Horrified. Says, in anger*) So . . . so that's An Lushan? What great deeds has he
done for the country to suddenly earn himself the title of prince? Huh, that knave has the
face of a rebel, and if anyone is going to set the world in a turmoil, it'll be him!
                (*Sings*) When you see such a pretentious mongrel shepherd-slave,‡
                his hornet-eyes and hyena-voice§ tell you: there's a rogue
                for sure!

---

*Riddle-poems were a popular game, and there were often societies of expert devotees of such games. Guo
is wistfully wishing that he had someone so expert to help him unravel the mystery of the poem.
†A screen bearing designs of golden cockerels which was placed around the emperor's divan. He allowed
An Lushan to sit at his feet, and both of them would watch performances of the Hundred Games (*baixi*)
together.
‡An Lushan was half Chinese, half Sogdian. Non-Chinese people of central and northern Asia often
being pastoral nomads, the term 'shepherd-slave' could be used as a term of abuse for such foreigners.
§This term derives ultimately from the *Zuo-zhuan* of the Zhou dynasty. 'Hornet'- or 'bee'-like eyes means
big, bulging eyes. The 'hyena' is actually a ferocious wolf-like animal.

How could you make a lodger of such a savage wolf!
I fear he may fulfil the poem written on the wall,
when he joins those power-mongering Yangs
in their goblin sorcery.

PUB-KEEPER.   What's got you so upset now, sir?

GUO ZIYI.   Agh!

(*Sings*) I find my hair a-bristling, the chill of rage across my scalp,
While fury blazing hot almost explodes my breast,
Again and again I eye the sword that clangs impatient at my waist.

PUB-KEEPER.   Please calm down, sir. Why not allow me to sell you another bottle of wine?

GUO ZIYI.   Tcha!

(*Sings*) Were I to down a thousand cups and drain a hundred bottles,
how could it swill away this leaden load of sorrow!

(*Starts to depart.*)

I won't drink any more now. Clear away these wine-cups.

PUB-KEEPER.

(*Clearing up*) Others come and, for a couple of pence, out grief goes,
but, one upset, and this customer fills the world with his woes.
(*Exit.*)

GUO ZIYI.   (*Descends the stairs, turns, and walks*) I think I'll go back to my lodgings.

(*Sings*) Seeing such wretched happenings, shock after shock,
and coming across that cryptic poem, ill omen every line,
I fear that Heaven's will and men's intentions are alike impalpable,
and it plunges me into useless brooding, distorts my brow with
gloomy foreboding.
Now look –
the slanting sun gilds all the ground, and dusk comes on,
as I return to my cheerless inn, still faltering with doubt.

(*Reaches lodgings, enters, sits down. Enter military retainer.*)

MILITARY RETAINER.(*Presents himself before him.*) Beg to report, sir, that a communiqué has arrived from the imperial government.

GUO ZIYI.   (*Reading it*) 'Issued by the Ministry of War, and concerning the promotion and appointment of officers: In accordance with the decree of His Holy Imperial Majesty, Guo Ziyi is hereby appointed Commissioner of the Tiande Army. Such is the Emperor's command.' So, an edict has already been issued. I must quickly pack my luggage, and I'll leave today to take up my post at once!

(*Military retainer assents to this order.*)

GUO ZIYI.   Well, Guo Ziyi, your rank may be low and your responsibilities small, but this will now enable you to repay your debt to the imperial court in deeds.

(*Sings*) Now it is just as if I have found
a foot of water wherein to spread my fins,
a thorn-shrub wherein to flutter my feathers!

Let's rejoice in this chance to ascend Celestial Roads and soar to the
    Empyrean!
I shall persevere till I re-aright the world,
and work the noblest deeds of a hundred thousand years.
Though I be beset by witching miasmas and venomed ills,
yet shall I shoulder the sun and moon, and raise the Mighty Tang
    once more.
(*Says*) For useless years my horse hooved the lowly dust,
the mighty always held the keys to power and trust.
Far as from the welkin stands the man of lowly station,
but what sort of man is he, who cares nought for his nation!*

A Shantung man, Kong Shangren (1648–1718) was a sixty-fourth generation descendant of Confucius and very much preoccupied with his illustrious forbears.[19] In 1684 he finished a voluminous genealogy of his family, and re-edited a history of the locality where Confucius was born. He was an eminent teacher of rites and music, and when Emperor Shengzu passed through Shantung, also in 1684, he commanded Kong to lecture to him on the ancient classics, and in recognition made him a doctor in the Imperial Academy. Subsequently Kong held various important posts in Yellow River conservancy in Honan province, and at the Board of Revenue in Peking. He was a collector of antiques, bronzes and paintings, and of examples of epigraphy and calligraphy. A small Tang musical instrument, a *hulei*-mandolin, that fell into his possession partly inspired the theme of his first play, written jointly with a playwright friend in 1694. He may in fact have begun *Peach blossom fan* even earlier, perhaps in 1689. He asked the music master Wang Shouxi to check every word of its songs, and revised it again and again very radically before, after probably about ten years, he finally completed it in the spring of 1699. The play was performed in the imperial palace that autumn, and by the following spring was already widely popular. People bracketed him and Hong Sheng together in fame, and the saying went, 'Hong in the south and Kong in the north'.[20] Peking, where he wrote his plays, was already making itself strongly felt throughout the world of Chinese drama.

Peach blossom fan was a long play of forty acts, with a very involved plot. To those Westerners who think of all Chinese art and literature as whimsical vehicles

---

*Each of these four lines is taken from a Tang or Sông poet: Hu Su (996–1067), Sikong Tu (837–908 Wang Jian (fl. c. 751–835), and Lü Wen (772–811) respectively. It was a common habit in the *chuan* plays to end an act with a verse composed in such a fashion, and the device is referred to as *ji*-Tang, 'Tar assemblage'. It cannot, as it might easily tend to be, be dismissed as mere flaunting of pedantry. T quotation of such lines would have among its various effects that of providing a ring of venerable antiqui such as may endear even some of Shakespeare's most ordinary lines to an English-speaking audienc The ingenuity displayed in the compilation of such a poem, for all that it sometimes involved obvio strain, would often give the play extra value as literature, and would sometimes provide the requis strong, resounding end to the act in stage performance.

of distant disconnected antiquity and gossamer fantasy it might be surprising to realise how politically and socially immediate many Chinese plays are. Much of his material Kong obtained from relatives who had close and contemporary acquaintance with the events involved. The leading characters in the play were all real historical characters: scholar-politician Hou Fangyu, singing girl Li Lady Perfume, and Ruan Dacheng, politician and playwright. After 1644, as the Ming dynasty struggles to hang on in Nanking, the reins of power come into the hands of the unscrupulous Ma Shiying and his crony Ruan Dacheng. Ruan tries to win Hou Fangyu over to his cause, but turns to thoughts of vengeance when he receives a snub. Fabricating charges, he contrives an order for Fangyu's arrest. Fangyu flees. While he is away, a minister tries to force Fangyu's mistress Li Lady Perfume into marriage. She attempts to commit suicide by dashing her head against the ground, her blood splashing across a fan given to her as a token of betrothal by Fangyu. The marriage is avoided by the substitution of her foster-mother. Later, in the title-act, Act Twenty-three, the famous painter Yang Wen-cong (1597–1646), a friend of Fangyu's, sees the fan and paints the blood-spots into a picture of peach blossoms. When eventually Fangyu returns to Nanking, Li Lady Perfume has been forced to become an entertainer in the palace. They fail to meet, and this time Ruan Dacheng succeeds in having him thrown into jail. When Qing forces effect the disintegration of the Ming court, Fangyu and others find freedom. Li Lady Perfume also escapes from the palace. Fangyu, who is bearing the fan, meets her in a temple, but a Taoist priest tears the fan to shreds, and converts them both to a life of meditation and reclusion. The two lovers part for ever, freed from the folly of mortal love and sex.

The love affair is the central theme of the play, but much of the background and atmosphere is concerned with the struggle between the survivors of the 'eunuch party' and the Revival Party (heir to the Donglin Party) who were so prominent in the internecine politics of the dying Ming dynasty. In a way the play is a dirge for the Ming, and an analysis of the self-destructive quarrels which drove it to its doom. The historical events had occurred only fifty years before the play appeared, and their consequences were still of enduringly vital contemporaneity. One can well imagine how gripping the portrayal of these events must have been for audiences in those times. The following excerpt shows how essential was the historical setting to the emotional appeal of the play. The reader should bear in mind that it deals with a great historical moment for the Chinese: the end of a dynasty that had ruled China for nearly three hundred years, and which in defeat was giving way to another dynasty, a dynasty of foreign conquerors, that would, incidentally, rule China for the next two and a half centuries, until 1911. This momentous event is dramatised through the mouths of central participants in the fall of the Ming. At the same time, one can conceive that the stress on loyalty to the dynasty, although not the particular directions of that loyalty, must strongly have appealed to the Qing authorities. In the following excerpt, Shi Kefa, commander of a very small Ming force in Yangzhou, has seen the city fall and is fleeing to Nanking.[21]

Peach blossom fan by Kong Shangren: Act Thirty-eight, 'Drowned in the Yangtse'

(*Enter Shi Kefa in haste; wearing a felt helmet. He turns his head, and gazes behind him.*)

SHI KEFA.   (*Sings*)   I see the beacons and smoke-signals afar,
                          and the vapours of war hang their heavy pall,
                          as Yangzhou seethes with tumult.
                          All those living souls rolled up in the mat of death,
                          that massacre all the fault of my foolish unswerving loyalty!
                          Officers and men alike,
                          strength gone, breath gasping,
                          all become a mere heap of limp corpses.

Yes . . . I, Shi Kefa, led three thousand young men to the do-or-die defence of Yangzhou, little foreseeing that we should reach the end of our resources and provisions without receiving any relief from elsewhere. Tonight the northern forces* attacked and took the northern walls of the city, and I was fully resolved to put an end to my life. Then suddenly I recalled how the Ming dynasty's altars of state, which have stood these last three hundred years, were now left with none but me to prop them up. How could I, by my pointless death, abandon my sovereign monarch in his present isolation? With such thoughts in mind, I lowered myself by means of a rope over the southern wall of the city, and fled straight for Yizhen, where by good fortune I encountered a courier boat, which has carried me across the Yangtse to this spot (*Points.*) Those city walls and look-out towers that I can vaguely discern in the distance are Nanking. But, curse it, my old legs are aching, and buckling under me. I can't move another inch on foot. What on earth can I do now? (*In surprise*) Hey, where the dickens has this white mule come from! Well, let's mount it, and ride off full-speed along the banks of the Yangtse. (*Mounts mule, and plucks a switch of willow to serve him as a whip.*)
                          (*Sings*)   I straddle a white mule's saddle-blanket,
                          and emptily wend through the riverside wilds,
                          with the sound of my weeping rocking the world.
                          Nearer lies the sun than far 'Changan',†
                          but, plying the whip, I head for the palaces mid the clouds.

(*Enter, running, old Ritual Precentor, carrying a bundle on his back.*)

RITUAL PRECENTOR.   In my twilight years, still fleeing from turmoil,
                          and at sunset, too, still longing for home.

(*Shi Kefa rides into the Ritual Precentor, and bowls him over.*)

RITUAL PRECENTOR.   Agh, hey, ah! I almost tumbled into the River Yangtse. (*Looks at Shi Kefa*) Why don't you look where you're going, old general!
SHI KEFA.   (*Alighting from the mule to help him to his feet*) I must apologise. Please forgive me. Might I ask where you have just come from?

*i.e. the Qing forces.
†i.e. the capital, Nanking, is very far away, or very hard to reach. 'Changan' was the capital of more ancient dynasties, and this whole line is an allusion to a famous question asked by the Tsin dynasty Emperor Ming-di (323–66) of his father: 'Which is nearer to us, the sun or Changan?'

RITUAL PRECENTOR.   From Nanking.

SHI KEFA.   How are things going in Nanking?

RITUAL PRECENTOR.   Don't you know yet? The old emperor has fled the city two or three days ago, and at this very moment the northern forces are crossing the Yangtse, and the whole city is in chaos, with all the city gates locked.

SHI KEFA.   Ah, curse it! – Nothing good will come of his leaving like that. (*Weeps brokenly*) High Heaven and Sovereign Earth! And oh, both you imperial progenitors of this dynasty, and all the imperial ancestors! Why cannot we preserve even the half of our domains!

RITUAL PRECENTOR.   (*Astounded*) When I hear him weeping like that, it sounds just like Minister Shi. (*Asks him*) Are you His Excellency Shi?

SHI KEFA.   Yes, I am. How did you recognise me?

RITUAL PRECENTOR.   I am one of the old Ritual Precentors in the Office of the Grand Constancy,* and I once stood in attendance upon Your Excellency outside the Great Peace Gate.

SHI KEFA.   Ah yes, you were the one who wailed and lamented so bitterly over the previous emperor that day, old friend.

RITUAL PRECENTOR.   Your compliment is too kind. But might I ask you, Your Excellency, why you yourself are now so distracted?

SHI KEFA.   Yangzhou fell this evening, and I left immediately afterwards by letting myself down on a rope over the city walls.

RITUAL PRECENTOR.   And where are you going now?

SHI KEFA.   I had intended going to Nanking to defend the emperor, little imagining that His Holy Majesty would have fled, too. (*Stamps his foot, and weeps.*)

> (*Sings*) I, this boat with tattered sail, am now cast adrift,
>   I, this homeless dog, am left in the lurch,
>   to cry my thousand vain appeals to Heaven and Earth.
>   No path back,
>   no way forward.

(*Climbs to a prominence, and gazes out.*)

> (*Sings*) Those rolling tumbling waves that slap the very sky
>   could never wash away the grief of this 'victim of the River Xiang'.†

(*Points*) I know . . . now I know – there, that is my burial ground!

> (*Sings*) Better by far than ten feet of brown soil,
>   to stretch out in the maws of Yangtse fish.

(*Looks at himself*) I, Shi Kefa, am a sinful servant of a state that has ceased to exist – it is unthinkable that I should go clad in all my robes of lofty rank! (*He snatches off his hat, and pulls off his robes and boots.*)

> (*Sings*) So I pluck off my robes, my boots, my hat of rank.

RITUAL PRECENTOR.   Why, it looks to me as if His Excellency is preparing to commit suicide! (*Pulls him back.*) Your Excellency, think well, think again! You must not destroy your own life in the chagrin of the moment.

---

*The organisation in charge of imperial court ceremonies, etc.

†The poet Qu Yuan, Minister of Chu, was guiltless of any crime, yet felt obliged to drown himself in the River Xiang. Shi Kefa feels similarly deserted by his monarch.

SHI KEFA.   See all this vast vast world – but if I, Shi Kefa, were to try and stay, there is
no room to put me.
        (*Sings*) By this day, the bold hero is weary unto death,
               and, seeing these hills and streams change their lord,
               has nothing to linger on for.

(*Jumps into Yangtse. Exit by rolling off.*)

(*Ritual Precentor stands gazing in stupefaction for a long while, then, clasping the robes, boots and hat
in his arms, weeps, and calls out*) My lord Shi! My lord Shi! Truly you were a loyal minister
to the end, a flawless martyr, for had you not encountered me, none would have known
how you drowned yourself in the Yangtse!
(*Weeps copiously*) [. . .]

Kong Shangren's approach of *cent fois sur le métier remettez votre ouvrage* left a
strong mark on the play. The studied ingenuity of his language is so concentrated
and sustained that it must at times have strained audience comprehension, but it
has compensatory literary value, and is furthermore balanced by the liveliness of
much of the action.

Wealthy men provided astonishingly lavish productions of *Palace of Eternal Life*
and *Peach blossom fan*. A salt merchant in Yangzhou who had his own private
troupe is said to have paid four hundred thousand taels of silver for the costumes
and stage properties of a production of the former. A prominent official had his
private troupe perform the tearful act where the emperor weeps over the wooden
statue of his beloved Lady Yang, and for this he commissioned a statue carved out
of the extravagantly expensive, hard, perfumed garu-wood (*Aquilaria agallocha*).[22]
Another Yangzhou salt merchant spent 160,000 taels of silver on a presentation of
Peach blossom fan.[23] The lavishness of these magnates is some indication of the
widespread fervour which the plays evoked. As both plays used Kunshan-*qiang*
music, Kunqu enjoyed a brief period of great revival. From the advent of the
Emperor Gaozong in 1736, however, a new era for drama and dramatic music
began. The rise of various kinds of music in Peking, and changes elsewhere, combined greatly to alter the face of Chinese drama.

The Manchus were familiar with Yiyang-*qiang* styles of singing and drama
before their conquest of China, although not apparently with Kunqu,[24] and from
the beginning their emperors took a close interest in drama. From the beginning,
too, they used drama for imperial entertainments. Even puppets featured in such
entertainments as those given by Emperor Shizu, according to old European
accounts:

The father of the emperor Kang-hi deemed this kind of exhibition not unworthy of the
  gravity of the grand Lama himself.
    This prince, when encamped in the plains of Tartary, was visited by several Kalkas or

Tartar princes, who came to pay him homage. Among these was the grand Lama, the most important personage of all. The emperor gave them a grand entertainment, during which various performances by puppets were exhibited. The strangers, having never seen anything of the kind before, were so struck, that most of them forgot to eat. The Lama alone preserved his gravity; for he not only abstained from touching the dishes, but paid very little attention to the spectacle; and as if he considered such amusements unworthy of his profession, he sat almost the whole time with downcast eyes and a very grave look.[25]

The hostile interpretation is open to doubt, but the facts are interesting. Already in 1658 Emperor Shizu, who was very interested in Chinese plays and novels, had commanded the dramatist Wu Qi (1619–94) to compose a play, significantly entitled *Loyal griefs*, which was performed in the palace and earned its author high promotion in government office.[26] In 1659 or 1660 the same emperor was quoting passages from the critical edition of *West wing* with a commentary by that cynosure of literary critics Jin Renrui (d. 1661), better known as Jin Shengtan, which was published in 1656.[27] He praised the critic as 'highly talented but of eccentric, unconventional views'. It was perhaps partly Jin's unconventionality which led to his execution in 1661, six months after Emperor Shizu's death.

The next emperor, Shengzu, a vigorous ruler, who consolidated China's frontiers and central government, acquired a reputation as a giant of Chinese culture. The reputation was hardly deserved for his personal creations, but he was a great patron of certain aspects of scholarship, painting, literature and other arts. He welcomed, and generously rewarded, performances of drama in the palace. He kept his own palace troupe and in 1683 spent the sum of one thousand taels of gold on the performance of a Maudgalyāyana play in which live tigers, elephants and horses took part. For the celebrations of his sixtieth birthday in 1713 he progressed from a park outside Peking to the palace in Peking. All along the lengthy route were set up entertainments commanded by a royal decree of the previous year. There was an astonishing abundance of stages interspersed among the natural scenery, houses, crowds and celebratory arches, and dramatic presentations dominated the entertainment provisions. The stages bore notices indicating who the promoters were, and the plays came from all over China. Various officials and military officers also contributed stages and plays. Drama played a similarly important part in many other imperial festivities.

Emperor Gaozong, born in 1711, reigned from 1736 nominally until 1795 when he dutifully abdicated so as not to outstrip the length of his grandfather Shengzu's reign. Effectively he remained in control until his death in 1799, which made a reign of over sixty-three years, the longest of any Chinese emperor. A forceful ruler of remarkable energy, he directed an era that was militarily expansive, and to all surface appearances one of glory and prosperity. Some have seen him as an unparalleled patron of culture. He himself was a prolific writer and painter, and over forty-two thousand poems are attributed to him. At some periods at least, he gave over his afternoons as a daily routine to reading, painting or verse composition. He employed large armies of scholars in the compilation of enormous encyc-lopaedias and collectaneas, one of them over thirty-six thousand volumes in length. His patronage of drama was a salient feature of his cultural and govern-mental activities. In Peking he fostered actors and playwrights with enthusiasm and lavish favours, and on his extravagant tours south of the Yangtse valley in the years 1751, 1757, 1762, 1765, 1780 and 1784 a major part of the welcoming entertainments consisted of dramas. His birthday celebrations likewise included dramas, and dramas were a central and regular aspect of the welcome to foreign envoys. Lord Macartney notes in his diary for the day Wednesday, 18 September, during the British embassy to Gaozong's court in 1793:

> We went this morning to Court, in consequence of an invitation from the Emperor, to see the Chinese comedy and other diversions given on the occasion of his birthday. The comedy began at eight o'clock a.m. and lasted till noon. He was seated on a throne opposite the stage, which projects a good deal into the pit; the boxes are on each side without seats or divisions. The women are placed above, behind the lattices, so that they can enjoy the amusement of the theatre without being observed. Soon after we came in the Emperor sent for me and Sir George Staunton to attend him, and told us, with great condescension of manner, that we should not be surprised to see a man of his age at the theatre, for that he seldom came thither, except upon a very particular occasion like the present; for that, considering the extent of his dominions and the number of his subjects, he could spare but little time for such amusements. I endeavoured in the turn of my answer to lead him towards the subject of my Embassy, but he seemed not disposed to enter into it farther than by delivering me a little box of old japan[. . .] and a small book, written and painted by his own hand[. . .]
>
> The theatrical entertainments consisted of great variety, both tragical and comical; several distinct pieces were acted in succession, though without any apparent connec-tion with one another. Some of them were historical, and others of pure fantasy, partly in recitative, partly in singing, and partly in plain speaking, without any accompaniment of instrumental music, but abounding in love-scenes, battles, murders, and all the usual incidents of the drama.
>
> Last of all was the grand pantomime, which, from the approbation it met with, is, I presume, considered as a first-rate effort of invention and ingenuity. [. . .][28]

Most of the officials present were, according to Macartney, Manchus, but there were also some 'Mussulmen', 'chiefs of those hordes of Kalmucks'. There was an interval for the embassy from one p.m. until four p.m., when they returned to the court to see the evening's entertainments, on a lawn in front of the great imperial tent. Macartney gives a vivid, if perturbed and occasionally supercilious, account of the wrestling, dancing, tumbling, acrobatics, balancing acts, 'posture-making' and juggling, feeling a duty to observe, 'I saw none at all comparable to the tumbling, rope-dancing, wire-walking, and straw-balancing of Sadler's Wells; neither did I observe any feats of equitation in the style of Hughes's and Astley's amphitheatres, although I had always been told that the Tartars were remark-ably skilful in the instruction and discipline of their horses.' These remarks at least serve as a healthy reminder to us of how prevalent the multiple-bill entertainments still were in England, too. Above all Macartney admired the fireworks display. With some air of reluctance he observes:

> However meanly we must think of the taste and delicacy of the Court of China, whose most refined amusements seem to be chiefly such as I have now described, together with the wretched dramas of the morning, yet it must be confessed there was something grand and imposing in the general effect that resulted from the whole spectacle, the Emperor himself being seated in front upon his throne, and all his great men and officers attending in their robes of ceremony, and stationed on each side of him, some standing, some sitting, some kneeling, and the guards and standard-bearers behind them in incalculable numbers. A dead silence was rigidly observed, not a syllable articulated nor even a laugh exploded during the whole performance [. . .][29]

On 19 December the embassy was entertained in a theatre in Kwangtung province by a company of comedians 'who are reckoned capital performers' and who had been sent down from Nanking specially for the purpose. The following day Macartney observes:

> The theatre, which is a very elegant building with the stage open to the garden, being just opposite my pavilion, I was surprised when I rose this morning to see the comedy already begun and the actors performing in full dress, for it seems this was not a rehearsal, but one of their regular formal pieces. I understand that whenever the Chinese mean to entertain their friends with particular distinction, an indispensable article is a comedy, or rather a string of comedies which are acted one after the other without intermission for several hours together. The actors now here have, I find, received directions to amuse us constantly in this way during our time of residence. But as soon as I see our conductors I shall endeavour to have them relieved, if I can do it without giving offence to the taste of the nation or having my own called in question.
>   In case His Imperial Majesty Ch'ien-lung should send Ambassadors to the Court of Great Britain, there should be something comical, according to our manners, if my Lord Chamberlain Salisbury were to issue an order to Messrs. Harris and Sheridan, the King's patentees, to exhibit Messrs. Lewis and Kemble, Mrs. Siddons, and Miss Farren during several days, or rather nights together, for the entertainment of their Chinese Excellencies. I am afraid they would at first feel the powers of the great buttresses of Drury Lane and Covent Garden as little affecting to them as the exertions of these capital actors from Nankin have been to us.[30]

It might be hoped that the Chinese Excellencies would have acquainted themselves well beforehand with the language and cultural traditions of their hosts, but Macartney's comparisons are thought-provoking and vivid. In fact, during the early years of his reign the emperor had been very interested in European music, employing two Jesuits, Jean Walter and Florian Bahr, as musical instructors at court. These Jesuits trained Chinese pupils to put on a comic opera, *Cecchina*, which was then fashionable in Rome. The emperor enjoyed the performance and ordered the formation of a Western-style orchestra, for which eighteen young Chinese pages were trained as musicians, probably learning the European violin among other instruments.[31]

Empress Xiaoyi (1737–75), wife of Gaozong, was according to some accounts originally an actress from Suzhou, bought or employed by the office which was in charge of theatrical entertainments in the imperial palace. She was the mother of the Emperor Renzong (r. 1796–1820). One of Gaozong's wives (possibly the same lady?) seems to have been banished to the isolation of the 'Cold Palace' and deprived of her honours and titles on charges of 'wild extravagance, love of the theatre and insubordination to the Emperor's mother'.[32]

Undoubtedly the interest shown by these rulers and their families encouraged drama in some ways, but predictably there was another side to the coin.

Statutes prohibiting and controlling drama, plays and players abound during the Qing dynasty. The government was from the beginning acutely aware of the dangers and possibilities of popular entertainment and literature. As early as 1635 the Manchus had banned the translation of popular fiction from Chinese.[33] Later, Manchus were forbidden to enter theatres. Measures were reaffirmed against night performances, the stage depiction of Confucius, sages, or other worthy persons, and 'lewd songs'. In 1652 there was a ban on the printing of 'fictional songs and lewd tales'. In 1671 the setting up of theatres in the Inner City of Peking was banned in perpetuity (further bans on this were required in 1781, 1799, 1802 and 1811), and those outside the city were subjected to stricter surveillance. Among other statutes of Shengzu's reign were those against itinerant actresses who came into the cities and financially ruined officials and others by their harlotry.

Emperor Shizong (r. 1723–36), who probably murdered his father, Shengzu, was particularly sensitive about popular literature and entertainments, and maintained a spy system throughout China. He complained that Manchus were haunting the theatres, and that officials and soldiers were neglecting their duties by spending all their time in such pursuits, and by forbidding them to attend the theatre he sought to restore the pure, pristine customs of the Manchus such as archery, equestrianism, and the fighting arts. He also inveighed against the habit prevalent among officials of keeping private troupes of actors, pointing out the corruption and waste this entailed, and that, for instance, to keep a troupe of twenty or thirty actors must cost over several thousand taels a year. One military commander circumvented this latter problem by enrolling his actors in the forces so that they might obtain free subsistence. Shizong ordered an investigation and stern action against persistent offenders. Because of the financial extravagance, corruption and other dangers they involved, he also attempted to suppress various plays performed by the people of Suzhou and Songjiang in Kiangsu on the pretext of being thanksgivings to himself, dismissing the attendant religious activities as mere white-washing. He also banned such things as the performance (often lasting for days on end) of plays at funerals, and the stage depiction of

Guan Yu. He ordered action against specific persons, as for instance in 1728, when he commanded an investigation into the affairs of a general in Tibet who had been buying Tibetan women and using his soldiers to perform plays at parties.

The apparent duality of attitude towards drama is nowhere better illustrated than in the person of Emperor Gaozong, often referred to by his reign-title as Qianlong. Utilising his massive patronage of compilatory projects, he conducted the most deliberate and thorough literary inquisition. Between 1774 and 1782 thousands of books were destroyed, and many more totally banned or partially altered, in the attempt to suppress writings deemed subversive to Manchu rule or otherwise immoral.[34] At the same time, savage punishments were meted out to various offending writers, and sometimes to their families and descendants. Of the profusion of edicts against vernacular literature and drama, we may, briefly, mention but a few. In 1735 the translation and printing of the novel *Fenlands* and the play *West wing* were banned in the homeland of the Manchus. A more general ban of 1736 aimed to suppress *Fenlands*, or more especially the plays based on this novel, which was often, with certain justification, viewed as a source of rebellious ideas. An edict of 1762 forbade the performance of plays by monks and nuns in the Peking area at 'charitable gatherings' for which the audience, mostly women, paid an entrance fee. In various other edicts he condemned Bannermen* who frequented theatres, night performances, officials who kept actors and singing boys, and the keeping of actresses in private homes. Among the latter were mentioned the folk-singers known as *yangge*, 'rice-seedling song', women – though such performers did actually take part in palace entertainments on occasions.

The subtle care with which Gaozong conducted his inquisition is seen from the following edict of 6 December 1780, sent to his Grand Ministers of the Privy Council and others:

[. . .] Previously I have commanded all provincial authorities to make rigorous investigations, and to obtain the surrender of all literature which contains contrary and obstructive phraseology, and to send it under escort to the capital for expunging and destruction. Now, since governors-general and others have steadily been forwarding many such pieces of literature, it has occurred to me upon reflection that the editions of plays now performed may likewise not be free of contrary and obstructive passages. Those which enact tales of the Ming dynasty and the early part of this dynasty, and which contain wording relating to the present dynasty, should of course without exception be subjected to examination. Even the provincial printings of such plays which treat of the Southern Sông and Jin dynasties frequently contain improper presentations, giving rise to the falsification of realities, and, since they have been passed down for a very long time, ignorant people may even mistake such editions of plays for the truth. This is a matter of the utmost concern, and must be thoroughly looked into.

Such editions of plays are for the most part probably concentrated in places such as Suzhou and Yangzhou. My command is to be transmitted to Ilinga and Quan De, that

*The Manchu army was organised into eight 'banners'.

they may proceed to investigate with circumspection, and apply their efforts to the careful consideration and treatment of those requiring expurgation. They are further to send the original editions of the plays, along with the expurgated passages and pasted tally-slips, to the capital to be proffered for inspection. They must, however, make no hue and cry about it, and must avoid causing the slightest panic or alarm. Quan De has never been very conversant with the written Chinese language, and I fear that if he alone is put in charge of proceedings, he will be unable to act with balanced discretion. For all cases requiring investigation and prohibition in the Suzhou region, Ilinga is to assist him in his transactions.[35]

Ilinga and Quan De were both Manchus, Ilinga being something of a poet and painter. Their mission obtained the zealous cooperation of regional officials. Hao Shuo (sentenced to public execution for extortion, but allowed by the emperor to commit suicide, in 1784) was from 1777 to 1784 governor of Kiangsi province, and was probably the most efficient of all the book inquisitors. That province was not among the greatest centres of literary activity or scholarship in those times, but because of Hao's efforts only one other province, Kiangsu, had as many authors whose works were burned during the latter part of Gaozong's reign. In 1781 he submitted a memorial which went into detail about his endeavours in the realm of drama. The document also attempts a summary of some aspects of popular drama:

[. . .] Apart from investigating Kun[shan]-*qiang*, I note that there are also Shibei-*qiang*, Qin-*qiang*, Yiyang-*qiang* and Chu-*qiang*, which are very popular in Kiangsi, Kiangsu, Fukien, Chekiang, Szechwan, Yunnan, and Kweichow provinces.[. . .] On receipt of the letter I made investigations, and discovered that there is very little Kun[shan]-*qiang* in Kiangsi province, and popular kinds of performance there go under such names as Gao-*qiang*, Bangzi-*qiang* and Luantan-*qiang*. This Gao-*qiang* is also called Yiyang-*qiang*. Examining the old gazetteers of Yiyang county, I found the term Yiyang-*qiang* in them, and, fearing that some play editions might have been passed down there, I ordered the county magistrate to investigate with circumspection, and I accordingly report that it is not known when the name Yiyang-*qiang* originated, that there are no leads to further elucidation of its origin, and that what is nowadays sung is in fact the same as Gao-*qiang*, and does not have any separate, distinct plays whatsoever.

Further to this, acting upon a report from Nanchang prefecture, which is attached to this province, and following the transmission of the decree to all play troupes that play editions which treated of the Ming dynasty or touched upon matters of the Southern Sông and Jin dynasties in an unsuitable manner were to be rigorously suppressed and eliminated, I despatched officials to examine all the plays that were handed in. Among them were two plays, *Happiness of the whole family* and *Heaven and Earth quiver*, of which some of the wording is contrary and obstructive, and also a *Red Gate Monastery*, which is performed in the costumes of this dynasty.[. . .] The conclusions of my investigations are identical with those of the Provincial Treasurer and Provincial Judge.

We have ascertained that there are Gao-*qiang* and other troupes in the south, of which the plays are all in dialect, being vulgar and coarse without any literary refinement, and mostly off-the-cuff renderings by country yokels who alter them just as and when they think fit. They are in no way similar to the Kun[shan]-*qiang* plays, which stem from the hand of the literary man, are printed in whole editions and are circulated all over the country. That is why there are not many editions of these plays and those that have been handed in are tattered, incomplete manuscripts.

Of the three plays picked out by our investigations, *Red Gate Monastery*, being set in this dynasty, and *Heaven and Earth quiver*, being a story of the Sông and Jin, should be suppressed. *Happiness of the whole family* is extravagant in both its titular designation and its wording, and on examination of this play we concluded that it was not worth expunging parts or revising it, and that it should be wholly destroyed. [. . .]

As for the prefectures of Ruizhou, Linjiang and Nankang, they are mountainous, out-of-the-way regions, having no local actors and only rarely being reached by troupes from elsewhere. But in the prefectures of Jiujiang, Guangxin, Raozhou, Ganzhou and Nanan, whose confines are contiguous with those of Kiangsu, Kwangtung, Fukien and Chekiang provinces, there is a frequent coming and going of Shibei-*qiang*, Qin-*qiang* and Chu-*qiang*. I have commanded those in charge of these prefectures to keep a constant look-out, and, if the play troupes come to their borders, to elucidate to them one and all that they should do their utmost to observe the prohibitions and mend their ways, so as to bring further glory to Your Imperial Majesty's perfect reign that seeks to restore fundamental moralities and reform social customs. [. . .][36]

Gaozong had been hunting down and destroying plays even before he issued his rescript. In 1777 or 1778 he established a temporary bureau of drama censorship in Yangzhou under the directorship of a certain Huang Wenyang (1736–?). In its four years of existence this bureau carried out its task of compiling an immense catalogue of dramas, entitled *Ocean of plays*. One living playwright had his play destroyed, and doubtless many others suffered for their dramas. While in many of its features Gaozong's inquisition was by no means new, but had antecedents and precedents in previous reigns and previous dynasties, including a number of savage executions for literary offences under Shengzu and Shizong, it was more sustained, more minute, more comprehensive, and more destructive, and incredibly slight-sounding offences were visited with incredibly harsh punishments. As late as 1742 Gaozong averred that he had never punished anyone for their writings or utterances, but from the late seventies there were a number of executions for literary offences. In 1777 the compiler of a dictionary was executed, although conceivably for some deeper motive, on the charge of criticising a dictionary sponsored by Shengzu, and of unsuspectingly using the taboo names of Confucius and the Qing emperors. Twenty-one of his family were arrested, one son and one grandson executed, and other sons banished into distant slavery. Three high-ranking officials were dismissed for their handling of the case, and another for having written a poem in praise of the dictionary.

Xu Shukui, a prolific writer and a dramatist, had already died by 1778 when the Board of Censorship, established in Nanking in 1774, submitted his case to the emperor. The authorities saw, or somehow imagined, rebellious innuendoes in his writings, and had his and his son's corpses exhumed and dismembered, one grandson executed and another sent into slavery among the far northern aborigines, and two of his students condemned to death. The prefect of Yangzhou and the local magistrate were flogged and banished, and the financial commissioner of Kiangsu, who died in prison, was, along with one of his secretaries, sentenced to death, all for negligent and tardy handling of the case. Curiously enough, the only work of this writer to survive was a drama. For all his apparent literary eminence and prolificity, the authorities so efficiently blotted out the written records of him that very little is known about him. In 1781 another writer irritated the emperor by pestering him for a title for his late father. Gaozong had his work examined, and seditious and disrespectful comments were duly found in them. The man was sentenced to death by strangulation, and his works and even something his wife had written were destroyed for ever. These and many other cases of punishment for writings, for tenuous personal connections with literary offenders, or for failure to persecute such offenders or to expunge with sufficient vigour are no doubt only the iceberg-tip of suffering and fear occasioned by the inquisition. It is easy to feel that they must have been a considerable inhibition to playwrights and the theatre world in general.

Qing provincial and regional statutes often echo the pronouncements of the central government, and of earlier documents, but at other times are elaborated with great feeling and embroidered with much local colour.[37] The plays performed at festivals and fairs were a constant source of anxiety, and, although bans were imposed, the authorities generally seem to have felt that they could only hope to contain what was clearly a powerful and fundamental feature of ordinary life. Again and again there appear the old complaints of the attendant dangers to the moral, physical and financial well-being of society, of public mingling of the sexes, violence, murder, gambling, harlotry, seduction, illicit love, abduction, street-blocking, and the neglect of agriculture and other basic professions.

Tang Bin (1627–87) took action against play-acting, as intendant of a circuit in Shensi from 1656, and as governor of Kiangsu from 1684. In the latter post, he claimed to have suppressed many immoral activities, to have excluded women from monasteries, and the music of pipes from the riversides, and to have stopped religious carnivals and processions and the composition of pornographic songs. Kiangsu was one of the main centres of printing, and one of Tang Bin's prohibitions affords a glimpse of the way in which some plays were printed:

[. . .] The book-merchants of Kiangsu are conscious only of their quest for gain, and specially engage worthless, ignorant, profit-seeking, unscrupulous fellows to write novels and plays, which propagate lewdness, preach trickery, and are filled with the utmost eye-sullying, ear-sullying filth and pornography. These they produce in *de luxe* editions most intricately designed with the finest of workmanship. When such books come into the hands of people who lack firm standards of conduct or of youngsters who have not yet acquired any settled moral direction in life, it rouses their animal desires, they daily conceive ever more dissolute longings, habits of treachery and falsity are copiously nourished, and social customs crumble irremediably into decadence. These books are utterly deplorable and should be rigorously suppressed.[38]

The close connection between religious activities and drama, especially rural drama, can scarcely be overstressed.[39] Religious festivals and institutions were major fosterers of drama. The modern mind tends to pose the question whether the religion was there for the drama, or the drama for the religion. The question is misleading in that religious sentiment and festive merry-making were very often inextricably associated in those times. On the other hand, it is clear that very often the religion was merely the veneer, the pretext, for the plays, as is explicitly stated in such documents as one of 1718 which launched measures against plays, puppetry and other shows in Kiangsu that were performed at festivals on religious pretexts. Tian Wenjing (1662–1732), governor-general of Honan province from 1724, was noted as a stern administrator, and was favoured by the emperor, who even commanded that his documents should be published as a model for others. In 1725 Tian prohibited all religious processions and carnivals, which he viewed as the root of all social evils and disorders. It must be emphasised that his objections were not based merely on moral abstractions: he and many others in authority feared the festival drama as a breeding ground for the dreaded and explosive secret societies, which were indeed a major force of opposition to the Qing government in later years. His ban lucidly gives expression to this fear:

Frequently, when they are idle after autumn harvests, and also in the second and third months of spring, certain ordinary people join together for a religious festival, going from door to door to collect money, sometimes lashing together high stages and performing Luoxi plays, sometimes enacting stories, celebrating the festival with music, enticing young men and women, and gathering gangsters from far and near. Initially they falsely assume such group designations as 'Three Emperors', 'Buddhist', and 'Pure Tea' to delude the ignorant populace, but as the weeks turn into months, making no move to disperse their gatherings, they form illicit societies, burning incense, taking oaths and disseminating false rumours, and, as time goes on, the names of such societies as the 'Massed Swords' and 'Iron Maces' appear. These are virtually impregnable. This is a source of heretical doctrines. If we want to block heretical doctrines, we must first be strict about religious festivals. Examining a rescript received during the ninth month of the year [. . .(1723)], I see that the performance of plays during religious festivals was prohibited in Hopeh, Shantung and Honan provinces [. . .] but, as time has gone by, laxity has set in, and the same path is now being trodden once more. [. . .] Henceforth, let the men go to their ploughing, and the women to their weaving, all keeping to their basic vocations, and let them not heed the beguilements of treacherous villains who feign charitable activites and willingly embrace heterodox doctrines. With the exception of the common people's autumn and winter harvest-prayers and harvest-thanksgivings, in all cases where it is required to hold sacrifices to the gods, the matter must be reported to the local headmen, who in turn are to petition the local authorities for permission. It is only permitted to perform plays and hold sacrifices and prayer-sessions during the daytime, and these must not extend into the night, nor must they continue for more than three days. [. . .][40]

There is also a close association in these documents of sinisterly subversive rebellion with common gangsterism, an association that sometimes seems mysteriously facile. It may be partly the customary official propagandistic habit of denigrating rebels or invaders as mere bandits, but, on the other hand, it was an undoubted fact that the violence of gangsterism could easily merge into the violence of rebellion. Both for the latter reason, and because of the common dangers that gangsterism posed for ordinary society, the documents were often preoccupied with the violent crime that they claimed was encouraged by the performance of plays. Tian Wenjing declared in a prohibition of 1728:

> Any fortune-tellers, medical men, necromancers, or itinerant preachers or priests, as well as any such as sell medicaments, play board-games for a living [. . .], sing with puppets, give shows with performing monkeys, mountebanks, [. . .] story-tellers, and balladeers, if they have come from afar, are of uncertain identity, or arouse suspicion by the difficulty of tracing their movements, should all be examined with the utmost rigour and immediately driven away, so as to ensure the peace of the area. [. . .] As for the setting up of stages and performing plays among the ordinary populace, it tends most readily to attract gangsters, who by their deceits damage the people's livelihoods. [. . .][41]

The same ban points out the criminal activities connected with the Luoxi plays:

> [. . .] I have recently also ascertained that there is a type of play-acting known as Luoxi, which bears no relation whatsoever to the normal skills of the acting profession, that always uses boy actors [?], but is merely performed by vagabonds and idlers from all over the place, who randomly mouth a few lines of what might or might not be a song to what might or might not be a tune. Taking their wives and children along with them as decoys, they travel through the towns and villages. There they find a certain kind of villainous local tyrant and local government beadles, who lust to commit fornication with the wives, and who also harbour the husbands as a means of accumulating money when the latter set up their stages and perform their Luoxi plays. Their backing and protection mostly come from corrupt gentry, while their food and sustenance chiefly come from the local chiefs and village heads, and their costumes and properties are largely provided by the beadles. For this reason they are unafraid of the authorities, and have no dread of the law, but openly flout the prohibitions, and commit reckless acts without any qualms.
>
> When these vagabonds who sing Luoxi have a play to perform, they gather together to do so, but otherwise they scatter in every direction to commit thefts, or may even go as far as to form gangs and conspire in robberies and murders, sometimes entering the houses of the wealthy and committing violence, and sometimes lying by the roadside in ambush to accomplish murder. [. . .] Although their wives are not registered entertainers, they are really no different from local harlots, selling their smiles, flaunting their seductions, and ably succeeding in beguiling men out of their wits, so that they vie to commit fornication with them, even frequently resorting to armed combat over them. [. . .]

The problems posed to the administration by popular play-acting constantly recurred, as we see from the documents of Chen Hongmou (1696–1771), philosopher, moralist, leading statesman and one of the most persistent holders of high provincial posts in his time. We find him attempting to curb the same crimes attendant upon festivals, fairs and play-acting as governor of Kiangsi, Shensi and Kiangsu provinces during the 1740s, 1750s and 1760s. In 1759 he announced measures against Kiangsu monks and nuns. Bonzes were, he complained, adapting sutras into plays and performing them as imposingly as professional actors, while nuns were dressing up and enticing men exactly as ordinary harlots.

Among the practices that Chen Hongmou and others tried, in vain, to suppress were performances, sometimes 'shockingly' realistic, of Maudgalyāyana plays. A common means of exorcising locust plagues was to erect a stage and hire actors to perform the Maudgalyāyana *chuanqi* play. This was apparently effective locally. Perhaps because of the noise it created? The habit snatches us uncannily back to the shamanism of the Shang and Zhou dynasties, and reminds us how close some kinds of Chinese play remained throughout the centuries to their religious and superstitious cradle. One bold Qing scholar suggested that the success of the plays against locusts was a good reason for lifting bans on them.[42]

Many officials zealously attempted to suppress popular play-acting, but it is clear that this and the festivals were such a deeply ingrained part of ordinary people's life that there was little or no possibility of effecting total prohibitions. As Tian Wenjing said in his prohibition of 1728: '[. . .] But autumn and winter thanksgiving festivals, when the ordinary people express their gratitude to the gods for having answered their prayers, are not in themselves improper, and are indeed quite reasonable. Therefore we shall merely prohibit night performances of plays, and disallow their protraction for days on end. [. . .]' When one official closed the theatres of Suzhou, the 'streets were filled with the noise of resentment',[43] and in the countryside drama was even less eradicable. Quite apart from the spiritual and administrative reasons for this, there was the undeniable fact that the theatre provided employment for a huge number of people, as was sometimes consciously recognised in those days. In Suzhou alone there were scores of theatres that performed every day, and that directly and indirectly employed thousands of people. The sudden closure of the theatres would have had severe social consequences. One mid-Qing scholar declared that the theatres, along with the monasteries, gambling dens, singing-girl houses, cricket-fighting booths and quail-cock-pits, were a great charitable institute for the poor, and asserted that the alternative, if people were suddenly thrown out of employment in such institutions, would be to drift into vagabondage, thuggery, beggardom and thievery.[44] It seems that the entertainment complex centred on the theatre was so much part of society that, even economically, the suppression of the theatre would have entailed grave and possibly perilous disruptions, even had it been philosophically or administratively feasible.

Emperor Gaozong commissioned a number of plays for his actors, with their costumes of Suzhou silk and pure gold,[45] most famous being those composed and adapted by Zhang Zhao (1691–1745),[46] aided sometimes by Yinlu, Prince Zhuang (1695–1767), sixteenth son of Emperor Shengzu.[47]

Coming from Kiangsu province, Zhang Zhao embarked upon a government career early in life, which quickly rewarded him with a succession of high-ranking posts. By 1733 he attained the lofty heights of President of the Board of Punishments. In 1735 there was a rebellion by Miao tribesmen in Kweichow province. He volunteered to quell it, was appointed Grand Minister for the Pacification of the Miao, but failed in his mission. Sentenced to death for the failure, he obtained a pardon because he was a fine calligrapher and the emperor was very interested in calligraphy. By 1742 he was back in his presidency of the Board of Punishments, and concurrently in charge of the Office of State Music. He died while hastening home for his father's funeral. Gaozong showed him many favours. His calligraphy was very similar to Gaozong's own, and it is very likely that many of the examples of calligraphy attributed to the emperor actually came from Zhang's hand. He was an erudite musicologist and a respected painter, excelling particularly in the painting of plum blossoms. He wrote and compiled five 'bumper' plays. The standard length for the bumper plays was ten parts, each part containing twenty-four acts, thus amounting to a total of 240 acts.

Golden statutes for promoting virtue was based on an earlier Maudgalyāyana play, probably that of the Ming playwright Zheng Zhizhen, or the one performed in Shengzu's court, which may both have been one and the same, but it retained only two to three tenths of it, and more than doubled the number of acts.[48] Zhang Zhao added material from other plays, including Yuan *zaju*, and other stories, aiming both to 'correct' the musical arrangements and to improve the moral tone of the earlier play. A stated aim of his version was to 'discuss loyalty and filiality'. *Precious raft for a pacific era* derived its substance from the sixteenth-century novel *Journey to the west* concerning the pilgrimage of the Tang Buddhist Xuanzang to India. Its copious quotations from the Buddhist scriptures and the theme of Buddhist morality were in accord with the tenets of the Qing court, which had embraced the Lamaist form of Buddhism, and with Zhang Zhao's personal strong leanings towards Buddhism.

Various other palace dramas attributed to other authors were probably at least edited by Zhang. *Annals of the tripod division*, largely based on earlier plays, dramatised the adventures of the great military heroes of the Three Kingdoms period (220–65), the general theme being in harmony with the Qing rulers' claims to dynastic legitimacy. The play may also have been making a more recent reference to the suppression of three rebel princes under Shengzu, and may have served the further political function of complimenting the Mongols, who were important allies of the Manchus. *Jade picture of loyalty* strung together earlier plays and stories of the *Fenlands* cycle, providing a conclusion in which the bandit heroes of the novel are reformed and give their loyal allegiance to the emperor.

The themes of the court plays suited the propaganda, self-confirmatory and entertainment purposes of the emperor. A whole bumper play would take ten days to perform, but with some of the more rarely acted bumper plays just one part or act would be selected for performance. The plays were performed for various festivals and each at a particular time of the year. In this way they fulfilled some of the functions of the court music of antiquity. *Golden statutes for promoting virtue*, for instance, would mostly be performed at the end of the year, parts of it serving as a substitute for or equivalent of the ancient rites of *qunuo*, 'demon-exorcising'.

The palace productions used lavish costumes and stage properties, and the specially designed stages of the various palaces were no less remarkable. The three biggest stages have survived into modern times. All consist of three levels or storeys, with five big 'wells' (i.e. cellars or *dessous*) under the lowest, making in effect a total of four storeys. The various levels could represent the range from Heaven above to Hell below in plays like *Golden statutes for promoting virtue*, the top being the abode of Buddha, the next down for ordinary gods, the next for mortals, and the cellars for demons and devils. This sequence could vary to suit the play. The cellars also had a special function in the matter of stage furniture. In one act a five-storey pagoda was winched up from them by means of iron wheels. In another, five huge golden lotus flowers were winched up, and as they reached the stage their petals opened to reveal five icons of Buddha sitting there. In another, *arhats* (original, saintly disciples of Buddha) had to cross the ocean. This act used as one of its properties an enormous fish which carried a couple of score of people. It was installed with a mechanical pump which sucked water up from the cellars and spurted it out through the fish's mouth. This was possibly the whale witnessed by Lord Macartney.

Last of all was the grand pantomime, which from the approbation it met with, is, I presume, considered as a first rate effort of invention and ingenuity. It seemed to me, as far as I could comprehend it, to represent the marriage of the Ocean and the Earth. The latter exhibited her various riches and productions, dragons and elephants and tigers and eagles and ostriches; oaks and pines, and other trees of different kinds. The Ocean was not behindhand, but poured forth on the stage the wealth of his dominions under the figures of whales and dolphins, porpoises and leviathans, and other sea-monsters, besides ships, rocks, shells, sponges and corals, all performed by concealed actors who were quite perfect in their parts, and performed their characters to admiration.

These two marine and land regiments, after separately parading in a circular procession for a considerable time, at last joined together, and forming one body, came to the front of the stage, when, after a few evolutions, they opened to the right and left to give room for the whale, who seemed to be the commanding officer, to waddle forward, and who, taking his station exactly opposite to the Emperor's box, spouted out of his mouth into the pit several tons of water, which quickly disappeared through the perforations of the floor. This ejaculation was received with the highest applause, and two or three of the great men at my elbow desired me to take particular notice of it, repeating at the same time '*Hoha, hung hoha*' ('Charming, delightful').[49]

This account provides a further view of the power of the theatrical spectacles in the court. An eminent poet and historian who lived in that period left a description of a performance of *Precious raft for a pacific era* that he witnessed in the Jehol palace:

> The greatest number of actors was found in the palace troupe, and their robes, official's writing tablets, armour, helmets, costumes and properties were the like of which the world has never seen. I once saw them in the Jehol Travel Palace [. . .] on a stage that was nine feast-mats wide, and altogether three storeys. Some of the sprites came down from above, while others would suddenly shoot up from below, the two wing buildings serving as the dwelling of Bodhisattvas, and the whole central area was filled with people astride camels and prancing horses. Sometimes all the deities and demons would assemble together, wearing hundreds of thousands of masks and not one the same as the other. [. . .] On the day when the bonze Xuanzang collected the sutras at Thunder Voice Monastery, the Buddha(Tat'agata) appeared in the temple, and the Kāshyapas, the Arhats, the Pratyekas and the personal disciples sat divided into nine tiers from top to bottom, several thousand of them in serried rows, and yet there was still plenty of space left on the stage.[50]

Most of the court actors were palace eunuchs, over seven hundred of them at any one time. They came, from about 1740 onwards, under an organisation known as the Southern Treasury. There were also actors from the ordinary populace. For instance, in 1751 the emperor made a tour south and so enjoyed Kunqu drama in the Kiangsu-Anhwei region that he took many actors of the style back with him to Peking. The outside actors came to constitute a separate body of court actors. The lavish scale of productions in the palace inevitably exercised a considerable influence on the world of Chinese drama in general. Naturally there were limits to emulation, but the wealthy merchants and officials of Kiangsu and Chekiang provinces provided gargantuan entertainments to welcome the emperor on his southern tours, particularly in Yangzhou, where the salt-merchants of Kiangsu and Anhwei provinces, who derived great wealth from the government-licensed salt monopoly, put on stupendous dramatic receptions.[51]

Palace plays at this time used basically only Kunshan-*qiang* and Yiyang-*qiang* (or Jing-*qiang*) styles of music, the former for romantic and delicate scenes and the latter for noisy battles, vigorous action, or when large casts were on stage. The two kinds of music co-existed, and to some extent interacted. In welcoming the emperor, however, the Yangzhou merchants and officials presented a variety of troupes specialising in different kinds of music, including some of the many other kinds that flourished in the ordinary society of that age. When the emperor's boat entered the Yangzhou area, there were booths lining both banks of the River Cao for several miles, the river being divided into thirty sections. Each section had a make-shift stage upon which a drama was performed. There were ten to twenty or more separate troupes. In addition there were in Yangzhou permanent stages which showed bumper plays, or portions of them. The emperor's six southern tours all passed through Yangzhou, and as a consequence a number of troupes settled there permanently, kept jointly by several salt-merchants, or as private troupes of individual salt-merchants, to provide for the welcome of the emperor. Yangzhou in general was a major centre of drama. The plays presented by the Yangzhou salt commission and the Suzhou and Hangzhou silk manufactories for the tours of 1780 and 1784 all came from the hand of Shen Qifeng (1741–post 1784). Author of no less than thirty or forty plays, Shen was very popular in the Yangtse basin region: a continuous stream of actors would call at his house to ask for plays, 'the toes of the ones behind pressing on the heels of the ones in front'.

It must by and large have been a brave man, a very foolish man, someone very well placed, or at least a superb literary tight-rope-walker, who ventured to write plays and circulate them in public under his own name during the reign of the intellectual inquisition. That is no doubt one, though only one, of the reasons why known playwrights of the period are relatively few and why collectively their role in the theatre world does not seem so great as at other periods. They seem further from the actors. Many others, who may have been more intimately involved with the stage, and have had a more decisive influence by their writings and adaptations, left no name. There are, all the same, a number of whom we do know and who merit attention here for one reason or another. Often they were officials closely connected with the imperial court.

Zhang Jian (1681–1771) wrote his first play at the age of eighteen. When young he had read *West wing* and *Moon prayer* behind his teacher's back, and they inspired him to write his own play, just as a game. Afraid, however, of rebukes, he hid it at the bottom of his trunk for ten years before showing it to anyone and making it public. It was such a success that his second play was bought by Nanking actors immediately he had finished the draft, and won great acclaim from audiences. He wrote altogether four plays. In 1771, lodging in a tavern one evening, he saw an old woman sewing clothes. He noticed that she was using for her needlework notebook a manuscript copy of his first play, decorated with countless margin comments and annotations. He learned that the seamstress's employer had had a little daughter who was highly accomplished in poetry, and who had been very fond of reciting the play. At the age of fifteen the girl had died of consumption, leaving the book to the woman. Glancing through the pages, he found a poem the girl had written expressing love for him and his genius. Unable to obtain her name from the old seamstress, he nonetheless managed to buy the book for a tael.[52]

In 1751 Dong Rong (1711–60) produced a much admired play about two famous women generals, historical personalities from the end of the Ming dynasty. His friend Tang Ying (pre 1713–post 1752), also a friend of Zhang Jian's, is best known to posterity for porcelain products made under his direction and referred to as Tang-*yao*, 'Tang kiln'. He wrote many articles on the porcelain industry, and also thirteen plays, all completed before 1749. Some of these plays seem to be adaptations of local village dramas into Kunqu.

Yang Chaoguan (1712–91) became a prefect in Szechwan province. There he sought out the ruins of the place where the famous heroine of a Han dynasty love story had lived, and built himself a mansion called Singing Wind Pavilion on the spot. He wrote plays and had actors perform them to celebrate the completion of the building. His thirty-two one-act plays, published as a collection in 1774, reflected the influence of the palace bumper plays. One of them, *Stopping the feast*, was a highly moving play. The eminent minister and man of letters Ruan Yuan (1764–1849) once held a performance of it. Like the hero of the play Ruan had been poor as a child, and his mother had undertaken his education. By the time he achieved eminence, she had already died, and the play now filled him with such grief that he wept bitterly and, again like the hero of the play, abandoned all feasting and carousing.[53]

Perhaps the most famous dramatist of the period was Jiang Shiquan (1725–85), one of the great orthodox literary figures of the age, whom the emperor openly admired for his scholarship.[54] He came from a fairly poor family, and it was his mother who taught him to read and write, when he was three, by splitting up bamboo splints into the shapes of the various fundamental strokes of the written characters, and then reconstructing the characters from them. In later life he held fairly high government posts, and was manifestly grateful for imperial favours shown to him. A tall, handsome man, he was reputedly of upright morality and had the air of the ancient sage doyens of Chinese scholarship. He was one of the two or three most respected poets of his era, and wrote sixteen plays, four of them for the occasion of the empress dowager's birthday.[55] The earliest plays he wrote in 1741 and the last in 1780, the date of two being unknown. One of his plays dramatised the life of the playwright Tang Xianzu, but depicted him as the righteous government official rather than as the wild character he more probably, and more dramatically, was.

Jiang stood very high in some mid-Qing scholars' estimation. One declared; 'His plays are the best of modern times. With a deeply ingrained knowledge of the classics of poetry and history he is able to pluck forth poesy at will. Always graceful and cultivated poetry. Not like Li Liweng and the others, whose language is nothing but actors' wisecrack chatter.'[56] That only one of his plays seems to have been performed at all commonly in those times offers a different yardstick by which to judge them. They concerned such themes as the wise concubine of a rebel prince, the tragic life of another concubine, the heroism of a patriot statesman, the valour of a loyal minister, an official's salvation, by means of a letter, from literary inquisition and the annihilation of his family. The play on the latter theme enacted real-life events of the early Qing dynasty.

However, playwrights' freedom of expression was generally tightly bridled, and as the imperial tours and other, commercial factors facilitated the regional interchange and mobility of different forms of drama, the spotlight shifted more and more away from playwrights and onto performers and techniques and styles of performance. The battle between the various kinds of music and their associated dramas and styles of presentation intensified, and the change of vogues for particular kinds of music accelerated, particularly, it would seem, in Peking.

Northern audiences did not generally take to Kunshan-*qiang* music, and ordinary audiences seem, according to some writers, to have positively disliked it.[57] In Peking, after its temporary comeback, it had by the early years of Gaozong's reign more or less yielded its position as the standard or 'orthodox' music to Jing-*qiang* music, a variety of Yiyang-*qiang*. Yiyang-*qiang* music had been current in Peking as early as the sixteenth century, and taking on distinct local colouring acquired the name Jing-*qiang* during the late seventeenth century, probably first in 1684. The Six Great Famous Troupes of Jing-*qiang* and its celebrated actors, who went by such names as Sixth Huo, Baldy Third Wang, Big-head Huan, Tiger Zhang, Old Lu, Continuous Delight and Ugly Chen, came to dominate the theatrical world in the capital. During the years 1778–9 one of the troupes, called the Princely Palaces New Troupe, was riding a high crest of popularity and was called upon to entertain at most important banquets and public occasions. The situation altered radically in 1779, however, with the arrival in Peking of an actor named Wei Changsheng (1744?–1802) from Szechwan.

Seventeen seventy-nine was the year before the emperor's seventieth birthday, his sixty-ninth by the Western system. The governors and governors-general of the provinces were already busy preparing their contributions to the birthday celebrations, which besides costly presents also included the sending of troupes of the most celebrated actors to Peking. It is possible that Wei Changsheng was the leading actor of a Szechwanese troupe sent for the celebrations. In any case he arrived in Peking from Szechwan in the year 1779, and, specialising in *dan* roles, he dominated the Peking world of theatre and gay society for the next six years, ensuring the fortunes of the kind of music which he sang, Qin-*qiang*.

Qin-*qiang* music in some form or other was not new to Peking. Originating in Shensi province, it had been used by companies known as Shansi-Shensi Troupes, which had already visited the capital frequently during the period 1622–1722. Some came to settle there permanently, and with the support of Shensi and Shansi provincials, and more vitally of the Shansi merchants, who were a powerful body in the economic life of the capital, these troupes had established a firm foothold. Wei Changsheng's form of Qin-*qiang* shared some basic characteristics with that of the Shansi-Shensi Troupes. The chief instrument was the *huqin*-fiddle, assisted by the *yueqin*-guitar. The *sheng*-mouth-organ and *di*-flute were not used, but rhythm was punctuated by the *bangzi*-clapper of jujube wood. 'Its music,' declares an eighteenth-century critic, 'clucks away like everyday chatter, and *dan* actors who have no real singing voice always avail themselves of it to conceal their inadequacies.'[58] The Shansi-Shensi Troupes had, in the matter of music, paved the way for Wei Changsheng's success in Peking. Another thing to his advantage was the sudden fall from favour of the Princely Palaces New Troupe. An actor of that troupe arrived late for a play at a public banquet. A censor dealt him a clout, and a few days later lost his job for 'blemishing the code of a government official'. This sign of intimidatingly excessive influence put the troupe in malodour with playgoers and patrons, and damaged the popularity of the Six Great Famous Troupes and Jing-*qiang* music.[59]

At this juncture Wei Changsheng, with some of his fellow Szechwanese, joined one of the Six that was out of favour, promising to improve things for them within two months or gladly suffer punishment. By the performance of one play he took the city by storm, drawing daily audiences of over a thousand, and immediately eclipsing the other troupes of the Six. Even the Shansi-Shensi Troupes suffered. Princes, dukes and other noblemen and high-ranking officials hired him for vast sums of money, and for a while anyone who was not personally acquainted with him was considered of no account in Peking high society. Even the all-powerful minister Heshen (1750-99) was captivated by him, and showed him great favours and esteem. Once, acting in Yangzhou, Wei earned a thousand taels for one one-act performance.

Wei Changsheng's Qin-*qiang* music appealed because of its variety and the urgency of its rhythms, while his plays appealed because of their colloquiality and the sexual suggestiveness of their language, but perhaps his greatest attraction was his acting technique. In performing his *dan* roles his vivid portrayal of the female sex captivated audiences. Since the sixteenth century there had been a very strong fashion for young male actors, and copious literature attests to the yet greater rage for them during Gaozong's reign.[60] Their artistry on stage and their private sexual attractions were intimately interconnected in the emotions of many of their admirers. This gave great prominence to male-acted *dan* roles.[61] Wei revolutionised the make-up and coiffure of the *dan*, using false hair-pieces to enhance the latter. To accord with the current particularly fervent delight taken by men in small female feet, he popularised the habit of wearing small clogs or false feet. These gave the impression of tiny feet and obliged or encouraged the actor to walk in a seductively feminine manner, wiggling alluringly at the waist and hips. Standards of theatrical connoisseurship were high, however, and, although one writer claimed that Wei's success was due to his 'obscene acting and jesting which inspire lubricity',[62] his reputation also depended on the finesse of his acting and his acrobatic ability. His personal charms and generous character also played their part in his popularity.

In the wake of Wei's success, other Szechwan actors established themselves in Peking, and actors of the Six Great Famous Troupes found themselves obliged to join Qin-*qiang* troupes, or to change over to Qin-*qiang* styles. There was a certain marrying of Jing-*qiang* and Qin-*qiang*, but the old Jing-*qiang* plays seem to have gone out of circulation. Wei Changsheng and his disciples ruled the roost for a number of years. Sex appeal continued to be their forte. One of Wei's leading followers, Chen Yinguan (1763?–?), would present a mime of naked lovemaking as a prelude to one of his plays. Such flaunting of sex was no doubt a major cause or pretext for bans on Qin-*qiang* music in Peking. A ban of 1782 specially directed against Wei Changsheng was easily circumvented, but a more general ban of 1785 had a telling effect. Whether the pretext was moralistic or aesthetic, the political potential of Qin-*qiang*, with its capacity for immediate and powerful expression of ideas, may well in fact have been a more fundamental reason for the government's wariness. It was a blow to Wei Changsheng while still in the days of his stardom, and no doubt damaged his career. Perhaps it was the reason why he went to Yangzhou in 1788, where he greatly influenced drama. An actor in Yangzhou who imitated his manner earned a great reputation and the nickname 'Femme Fatale'. In 1786 Chen Yinguan was arrested on some charge and expelled from Peking. He returned to Szechwan, and so, in 1792, did Wei Changsheng. In 1800 or 1801 Wei was to make a brief comeback in the capital, but in 1802 he fell ill during a performance, and died shortly afterwards. But another event had already occurred in Peking to alter the course of theatrical history.

Seventeen ninety was the year of Gaozong's eightieth birthday. Outstanding among the troupes that came from the provinces for the celebrations were the Anhwei Troupes, which from 1790 to 1798 were the chief vogue in Peking drama. Their basic music was Erhuang-*diao*, and one of their most important achievements was to establish it in the capital. As early as 1780 they had already made their mark in Yangzhou with this kind of music, but versatility was one of their strongest points and they were also able performers of Kunshan-*qiang*, Qin-*qiang* and many other kinds of music. In addition they won admiration for their high standard of stage acrobatics, leaving their permanent mark on Chinese drama by raising the general importance of acrobatics, and by bequeathing various plays that were inextricably associated with an acrobatic presentation. They also impressed by their fine costumes and stage properties, and neatly ordered and comprehensive provision of role categories.

A number of Anhwei Troupes arrived in Peking in succession over a period of several years, following the first successes. Since they were already masters of all or much that Qin-*qiang* troupes could offer – the 1785 ban, like so many others, had clearly been neither absolute nor totally enduring in its effects – they rapidly overcame their competition. The star of the earliest Anhwei Troupe to enter the capital was a certain Gao Langting (1774?–?). He came originally from Kiangsu, and it is worth noting that many, quite probably the majority, of the actors in the Anhwei Troupes actually came from Kiangsu province, mainly from Yangzhou and Suzhou. Acting *dan* roles, he replaced Wei Changsheng as the darling of the Peking theatre-goers. But their styles were very different. Their contemporaries typed Wei as excelling in 'romantic and naughty gaiety' and Gao as excelling in 'spiritual expressiveness and grace'.[63] Perhaps he was more subtly or loftily sexy than Wei had been. With their versatility and their numerically large acting strength, the Anhwei Troupes were advantageously situated to compete, adopting the popular plays, absorbing the actors and the music, imitating the costume and other features of other troupes.

One *dan* play that was performed in the middle and late eighteenth century and that has remained popular into the twentieth century is *Longing for laity*. As may be seen from the following translation it was in the main a simple but saucy sung monologue, about a young nun who detests her celibate existence and yearns for a lover and love in the lay world. The play offers ample scope for suggestive and comical intonations and gestures, and enables the actor to give full play to his interpretative genius. The lines concerning the Arhats would be accompanied by vivid miming, for instance. A large part of the play, as found in the collection *Sewing the white fur* compiled by Qian Decang during the years 1764–7, is identical with act nine of part five of *Golden statutes for promoting virtue*, and is either an adaptation from that play or comes from some unknown mutual earlier source. Some later acting and other editions omit the entry of the acrobatic Arhats, and of Avalokhitesvara and her divine attendants.[64] The pompous intrusion of the goddess certainly seems to clash with the pert naturalness of the little nun, and the appearance of the Arhats as flesh-and-blood actors would seem to diminish the nun's scope for miming, and the audience's scope for imagination, but it may well be that the acrobatics, the sudden action, and the ethereal presence of the gods were sometimes a welcome break for the audience, and for the nun-part, from the sustained singing. Alternatively, the presence of the deities, and Avalokhitesvara's disturbing mood-break at the end, may well have served as a prudent apology for the freedom with which the nun expresses her sentiments. In order that the reader may judge for himself, the following translation is of the version given in *Sewing the white fur.*[65]

Longing for laity

(*Enter Zhao Materiality Void.*)

MATERIALITY VOID.
        (*Sings*) In olden times there was a Buddhist bonze
                Maudgalyāyana, so I've heard tell,
                who, so that he could save his mother's soul,
                turned up in person at the gates of Hell.
                But excuse me, how far is the road to Holy Mount
                where the saints and sacred Buddhas dwell?
                – One hundred and eight or so thousand miles,
                plus a couple more miles as well!
                Namo-amitabhaya! Praise be to the name of Buddha!
        (*Says*) I shaved my hair and became a nun,
                poor me, it makes you weep,
                And one *dhyana*-lamp in my cell
                is my only bed-mate when I sleep.
                Time flits easy, and time slips sly,
                time hurries you old, the years scurry by,
                I neglect my youth, fail to give it its due,
                while my beautiful springtide's green and new.
My name is Miss Zhao, and my *dharma*-name is Materiality Void. I entered the Doctrine of Vacuity, became a Buddhist that is, when I was only a little girl, and years and years

ago I wrapped the black robes round myself and had my hair cut off, and was made a nun. Oh dear! I'm worshipping and performing devotions day and night, chanting the name of Buddha, and reading the sutras – have I got to carry on doing that for ever and ever! The convent cell's so bleak and lonely, you know, with no man to share it with me. And the birds are calling and the blossoms falling, but no one knows or cares about me. Oh, it makes me feel so utterly miserable!

> (*Sings*) I'm a little nun, just sweet seventeen,
> in my tender prime, in life's morning fair,
> And along comes the abbess, snip snap snip,
> and shears off all my pretty hair.
> I light the incense and change the water
> in the Hall of Buddhas, day in day out,
> And sometimes outside the convent portals
> I spy young gentlemen larking about.
> They eye me up, and eye me down,
> and I eye them in return,
> They for me, and me for them,
> both sides we burn and yearn.
> Oh, bitterly beloved, surely it's our destiny,
> if only I could yours for ever be!
> Even if it meant that when I died,
> I'd have to go to Hell, even though
> it meant I'd have to suffer there below,
> go to Yama Raja's Palace to be tried,
> I swear I wouldn't care if there
> they pounded me with their pestles,
> and sawed my limbs and bones,
> and ground me with their stones,
> and popped me in their pot of oil
> and left me there to boil and broil.
> Let them!
> And anyway, all I see is the living
> getting punished with worldly pains,
> I've never seen a single ghost
> in pillory and chains!
> Blow them!
> – If your eyebrows catch on fire, it's still most wise
> to bother about the here and now that lies before your eyes!

You know, it was never *my* idea to come into a nunnery, like this.

> (*Sings*) It was all their fault:
> my father so fond of studying the scriptures,
> and mum always mouthing a chant or a prayer,
> at worship day and night in the Hall of Buddhas,
> burning incense, and making offerings there.
> I was born a poorly, sickly one,
> so they chucked me out to the Buddhists,
> to spend the rest of my life as a nun,
> in prating prayers for dead folk, all of them strangers to me,

so that I could mutter 'Amita' 'Amita', Buddha's name,
     indefinitely!
All I hear is booming bells and *dharma*-drums,
non-stop tapping tympanums and tinkling tintinnabulums;
Cymbals clashing, ringers rattling,
drumheads dinning, trumpets tootling.
Unasked for and unpaid, we busy convent maids
are simply doing jobs for the King of the Shades!
I've read till I know by heart the *Scripture of the heart*,
the *Peacock scripture* makes no sense to me,
but the knottiest of all is the seven volumes long
Scripture of the lotus – still a perfect mystery.
Our abbess, even in her sleep and dreams at night,
has told me again and again to recite
a few *Namo-amitabhas*,* a couple of *tathātas*,†
and some *Bôdhisattva-maha prajñā-pāramitās*.‡
But for every few *Amitas* I recite,
I pop in a 'procuress!' for spite;
for every few *Svāhas*§ I intone,
I utter a loud despairing moan;
and for each few *tathātas* I chant to the skies,
little does she know, I spill a dozen sighs.

Pooh! I'll have to take a stroll through the cloisters for a bit, just so as to cheer me up a little, and so that I don't feel so pent-up. (*Exit.*)

(*Sounds of drums and gongs, with smoke and fire, on stage. Enter Arhats,¶ doing somersaults. Exeunt, doing somersaults.*)

   (*Light, stringed music from backstage. Enter Avalokhitesvara, Goddess of Mercy; Treasure Begetter;* ** *Dragon Princess;*†† *and Wei Tuo.*‡‡)

AVALOKHITESVARA.
          (*Sings*) On a solitary cloud from mid the peaks
                    I descend from Jade Heaven on High,
                    Smiling I pluck the petals of blossoms
                    and flutter their myriads through the sky.
                    With Golden Ropes is lined the road,
                    the path to realisation,
                    With the Precious Raft you can ferry over

---

*'I put my trust in Amita Buddha' or 'Hail Amita'.
†'Thusness', 'Buddha nature', or some incantation.
‡'Oh great Enlightened One, give me wisdom for crossing to the other shore.'
§*Svāha* being a Buddhist equivalent for 'Amen'.
¶Arhats are the five hundred original disciples of Buddha. Here the eighteen deified personal disciples whose images appear in temples are referred to. They are usually depicted as very emaciated and gloomy-looking.
**Treasure Begetter is a Buddhist boy deity, usually depicted on the Goddess of Mercy's lef-hand side.
††This particular Dragon Princess was one said in one sutra precociously to have attained Buddhahood.
‡‡Wei Tuo, also known as Wei Kun, and as General Wei, was another popular Buddhist deity, and one of the 'guards of the *dharma*'.

the stream of deluded imagination.*
Boundless is the power of the *dharma*,
Boundless is the power of Buddha's way;
With compassion I come to ferry over
all those in the Slough of Error gone astray.

(*Says*) I am strong in the power of the *dharma*,
in compassion to save man from pain and dismay;
Mid bamboo groves where parrots flit,
my reedy flute I play.
I have only to glance with my All-seeing Eyes
and all of the universe I can contemplate,
Between my eyebrows the hairs of Buddhahood
their white light of glory radiate.

I am Avalokhitesvara Bodhisattva from Mount Luoqie in the Southern Ocean. Today I shall ascend my throne, and expound the Law. See, all the Arhats come to add their encouragements to my inspiration!

(*She sits on her lotus throne. Treasure Begetter and Dragon Princess stand on either side of her, and Wei Tuo stands exactly in the middle. All the Arhats leap on stage;† each pays his respects to the goddess, then sits in solemn and stern posture. Enter Materiality Void.*)

MATERIALITY VOID.
(*Sings*) In and out of the cloisters I wind
to blow the glum cobwebs from my mind.

Hey now, look at those Arhats on either side of me. What terribly stern and poker-faced sculptures they are!

(*Sings*) But, on second looks, whoever made those models
sculpted both rows of Arhats as spoony noddy-noddles:
That one hugging his knees at ease
is murmuring moonstruck all for me,
and him, silent as sin, cupping dainty chin,
he's willing me his so ardently,
and him, with dull eyes and a look of surprise,
he's ogling me lovesick and languorously.
But . . . Calico Sack, this Arhat here,‡
is only guffawing loud and clear,
mocking me in such a state,
'cos time's flashing by and it's getting late,
and who would want to, who would think to. . . ?

---

*The Precious Raft is the doctrines of Buddhism. These lines are here translated as they are found in a poem by Li Bai. The play actually has 'spade' instead of 'rope', an easy visual error, but perhaps intentional and somehow humorous, 'With a golden spade is opened the road[. . .]'. One sutra mentions a land where the ground is of glazed tiles and the roads are bounded by golden ropes. Presumably the Golden Ropes also refer to the doctrines of Buddhism here.
†The text says 'leap off'. That might mean that they leap down from their niches. But it seems more consistent with the rest of the text if we consider 'leap off' as a printing error.
‡Maitreya, the Laughing Buddha, the Buddhist messiah, a popular figure, usually depicted as very jolly and with Falstaffian paunch, and carrying a calico sack into which he can pop countless evil-doers, etc. Commonly known as Monk with the Calico Sack, or just Calico Sack.

no one's going to marry somebody like me,
already an old granny, and as ancient as can be!
That Dragon Master* over there is giving such a grumpy stare,
That Tiger Tamer† over there is shooting me an angry glare,
And the Mighty God, Long Eyebrows,‡ speeds sad sympathy my
    way,
All worrying what will become of me when I'm old and grey!
Ah, the lamps that burn at Buddha's feet
would be no good as candles in a bridal suite;
the convent refectory could not cater to the call
for a swell wedding reception in some posh dining hall;
nor would the belfry be right as a look-out tower
to gaze for my loved one's coming to our nuptial bower;
and my prayer-mat of rushes would never never do,
as a lotus-twined and downy mattress made for two!
Oh but I'm a delicate and dainty damsel,
not some spartan, he-man tough,
Why should I wear the brown sash round my waist
and the rigid cassock coarse and rough!
When I see other people, man and wife together free as air,
couple after couple, pair after pair, all clad in silk and brocade
    attire,

(*Exclaims*) Oh, Heaven! Oh, Heaven!
    (*Sings*) It makes me go all hot inside . . . can't help it,
          can't help it, feel all ablaze like fire!
Pooh, I've had enough! Today, while the abbess and most of the other nuns are away, I must make the best of their absence, and escape down the mountain into the ordinary world. And perhaps I'll be lucky. You never can tell. That's right, that's what I'll do.
    (*Sings*) I'll rip my murky camlet habit into shreds,
          and bury all the scriptures safe and sound,
          I'll chuck away my Wooden Fish chanting-clapper
          and throw my pot-lid cymbals to the ground.
          For I could never learn to quell demons,
          as did the virtuous Rakshas' Daughter,§
          Nor could I grace a Southern Ocean throne,
          like the Goddess of Mercy Moon-musing Mid the Water.¶
          When, deep at night, I sleep in solitude,
          when I get up, to sit alone and brood,

---

*Seng She, a monk of the Former Qin dynasty (351–94) was able by means of secret incantations to bring down dragons into his begging-bowl.
†The monk Seng Zhou of the Northern Qi dynasty (550–77) and the monk Tan Xun of the Sui were both able to part fighting tigers with their rattle-staffs, and make tigers lower their heads and obey commands. Probably only one of them is the icon here.
‡Unidentified as yet.
§Rakshas is a spirit or genie of Indian mythology. This must refer to some Buddhist tale.
¶Avalokhitesvara is often depicted upon a lotus throne, rising from the waters, or gazing at the moon reflected in the water. Originally she was a male Indian deity, so the Chinese always referred to her as being 'of the Southern Ocean', i.e. of southern, tropical climes. 'Moon and water' is also used as a metaphor for lofty virtue and moral purity.

is there anyone else as lonesome?
anyone anywhere quite so on-their-ownsome?
What's the point if that's how I fare, of bothering to shave my hair?
How I hate, how heartily abominate;
those priests and laity, with their lies and prating piety!
– There's no such thing as the Buddha of Groves and Trees!
There's no such thing as a Glorious Buddha of every twig and leaf!
There's no such thing as the Buddha of River Shores and Sands!
All those eighty-four thousand Buddhas are quite beyond belief!
From now on, I'm leaving these bell-towers behind,
leaving the Halls of Buddhas, and going far away,
I'm going down the mountain to find me a young lover,
and with him forever I shall stay.
They can curse me, they can whack me,
they can scold me, they can mock me,
I shall never become a Buddha, with all my heart I sha'n't!
and *Amita* and *Prajñā-pāramitā* I never more shall chant!
Enough of that stuff – let's just look forward to escaping into the real world!
(*Sings*) All I pray for's a little baby, my own, ah, if I could,
I'd die of gladness, go merrily mad outright I would!

(*Exit, laughing.*)

AVALOKHITESVARA.   Excellent! Excellent! Sister Zhao has suddenly been affected by
cravings for the mundane world, and fled down into ordinary society. When will the
retribution for her sins ever be accomplished to the full! Now, Arhats all, recompose
yourselves once more in solemn severity. (*Exit.*)

(*Exeunt all, leaping.*)

Both in Peking and elsewhere, even in Suzhou, the area where Kunshan-*qiang*
was born, the 'non-refined', popular kinds of music and drama were flourishing
during the 1790s.[66] This situation prompted an imperial edict in 1798, based on
the ban of 1785:

Not only is the music of Luantan, Bangzi, Xiansuo, Qin-*qiang* and such plays of a nature
which incites to lewd immorality, but the subjects of their performances are invariably
sordid, depraved, indecent and profane stories, or weird, monstrous, seditious and
rebellious tales, which have a considerable effect on social customs and individual
attitudes. Although these kinds of music arose in Shensi and Anhwei, they have spread
all over the country. Even in Suzhou and Yangzhou, where Kunshan-*qiang* has always
been the custom, there has recently been a sated boredom with old things, and an
infatuation with novelty, so that everyone has come to regard Luantan and the other
kinds of music as delightfully novel, turning to them and deserting the old familiar
Kunshan-*qiang*. Since the latter is daily diminishing in public esteem, it is vitally necessary for a strict prohibition to be enforced. Hereafter, apart from the Kunshan-*qiang* and

Yiyang-*qiang* forms of music, which are still permitted, plays using Luantan, Bangzi, Xiansuo, and Qin-*qiang* music are one and all no longer allowed to be performed. All areas of the capital are to be assigned to Heshen for him to enforce the prohibition with all rigour. The edict is also to be sent to the governors of Kiangsu and Anhwei provinces, the superintendent of silk manufacture in Suzhou and the salt commission in the Two Huais [i.e. the region between the Yellow River and Yangtse in Anhwei and Kiangsu], so that they shall uniformly, and in concert, carry out investigation and enforce the prohibition with all severity.[67]

Thus even in its home, Kunshan-*qiang* was on the wane and giving way to other kinds of music and drama. Clearly the edict was concerned to protect it, and to revive its fortunes by legal action. Why? Aesthetic reasons certainly played a part. Some people at higher levels of society preferred it as being a more 'high-brow' or elevated medium. Yet aesthetic, moral and political attitudes were sometimes inextricable from each other, and Kunshan-*qiang* was also less intrinsically suited for the conveying of ideas inimical to the predominant polit-ical and moral order. This was no doubt another reason why it was preferred to more word-meaning-dominant, impromptu and popular-level kinds of music and drama. The prohibition was aimed chiefly at the Anhwei Troupes, both in the capital and in their Anhwei and Kiangsu homelands, giving no less a minister than Grand Secretary Heshen himself the prime task of curbing them in the capital.

The prohibitions of 1785 and 1798, although not absolutely effective or enduring in either case, did, along with government patronage and other forces at work, assist the struggle of Kunqu. Before Wei Changsheng arrived in Peking, there was only one prominent Kunqu troupe there, but during the years 1785–1810, roughly speaking, there was a certain revival of Kunshan-*qiang*. Offi-cial approval encouraged wealthy and powerful men to keep their own private troupes. Government officials in Peking often took their private troupes with them when they were appointed to provincial posts. When certain officials fell from grace, their troupes, either by splitting up or by otherwise being left to fend for themselves, spread Kunqu styles of acting and music in various regions with lasting effects. In the capital itself a number of successful Kunqu troupes appeared.

Yet the 1798 prohibition did not devastate the Anhwei Troupes. They already had a grounding in Kunshan-*qiang* and some of them specialised in it. Tending even to favour their versatility, the prohibition did not anyway remain effective in Peking for more than ten years, if for that. In 1810 we find Qin-*qiang*, often referred to as Bangzi-*qiang*, and Erhuang-*diao* still there, sharing the scene with Kunshan-*qiang*. Increasingly the actors were coming from Anhwei rather than Kiangsu province. The major Anhwei Troupes went from strength to strength in the early decades of the nineteenth century, and, as leaders of the Peking theat-rical world, played a decisive role in the creation of one of the most powerful kinds of Chinese drama.

8

The Nineteenth Century and the Emergence of Peking Opera

The imperial household's involvement in theatre, and the government's concern about drama, were maintained until the late years of the Qing dynasty. Gaozong's successor, Emperor Renzong, was by nature a very different sort of man, and was faced with very different situations. Maladministration, much of it directly fostered by Heshen, and the White Lotus Rebellion (1795–1804) originating in Hupeh, both severely disturbed Chinese society, and many of Renzong's efforts were directed against financial extravagance, governmental decay, and the decline of the Manchus' military morale, in all of which the theatre played a part. Manchu patronage of drama became increasingly important, and proved to be of no mean consequence to the dynasty.

Renzong's third son, Miankai, Prince Dun (1795–1839), was very familiar with a eunuch in the office that controlled the palace drama, the Ascendant Peace Bureau.[1] In 1827 the emperor tried to reform him by degrading him, but to no avail, as the prince continued to harbour actors. In 1832, the empress dowager ordered him to remove two actors from his residence, but he soon smuggled them back again. Further measures were taken against him in 1838, and the actors were sent back to Suzhou.

Encouraged in part by the official approval of Kunqu, many officials, even governors-general, were keeping troupes, often maintaining them from public monies supplied by local authorities who taxed the ordinary people. Renzong referred to this as 'extorting the ordinary people's fat and grease to provide the pleasures and entertainments of important officials, and misdirecting unauthorised taxes to the detriment of my common people'.[2] Only too wisely he suggested that the financial burden might be encouraging the White Lotus Rebels. In the capital, the Manchu élite was a leading force in the establishment of illegal theatres, having used its connections to set up theatres in the Inner City. In 1799 Renzong banned theatres once more from the Inner City, but clearly the tide was gaining, and his ban now explicitly permitted them in the Outer City. He blamed theatregoing for much of the decadence of the Manchus, their ignorance of the military arts and Manchu language, their foppish silk attire, and their general dissipation. To circumvent social and governmental disapproval, officials even frequented the theatres incognito. A measure of 1803 tried to curb this, but in

157

1806 a considerable scandal occurred over such a matter. A Censor, Heshun, accused six Manchu Bannermen of performing plays in a theatre. The Manchu Lukang and others countered the charge by alleging that the Censor himself was a regular theatregoer. The usher of a theatre substantiated their charge by identifying the Censor as someone who had once fought for the best seat. Another Manchu official was discovered to be running a business hiring out stage properties and costumes. A member of the imperial clan was found guilty of fraternising with actors in the theatres. Many of these offenders were demoted, dismissed, or stripped of rank, and some were exiled to Mukden, Kirin, or Ili in Sinkiang, to reacquaint themselves with pristine Manchu 'virtues'. In 1808 a high-ranking Manchu was given forty strokes and sent to hard labour in Ili for watching plays while in mufti, and for having hauled another official from his carriage while drunk.

The difficulty of finding any final solution to such problems is illustrated by the fact that an edict of 1808 sought to stamp out the moral decay resulting from officials' patronage of drama and maintenance of actors at Ili, one of the places to which offenders were being exiled! 'This is a military camp – what need is there of play-acting?' the emperor asks plaintively. His task was not easy. He was constantly under pressure, principally from Manchus, to allow theatres in the Inner City, and his bans were far from rigidly accepted. Renzong again complained, in 1811. 'Egged on by others, Lukang has many times memorialised the throne requesting permission for the establishing of theatres there [in the Inner City], but I have refuted his arguments, and rejected all his requests.' Deep rifts underlay the dispute. In that same year Lukang lost his post as commandant of the Peking Gendarmerie for failing to check gambling in his own and in other officials' households. In 1813, troops under his command joined rebels who attacked the imperial palace in Peking. He died in banishment in 1816.

Renzong also kept an anxious watch on popular drama. An edict of 1813 reinforced measures against fighting plays, and he also imposed several bans on drama that used Qin-*qiang* music, popularly known as Bangzi-*qiang*. This may have assisted other, less vigorous and direct forms of drama and music, but does not seem to have affected the popularity of Qin-*qiang* to any great degree. More than previous rulers, however, Renzong acknowledged that the theatre was the legitimate rice-bowl of many. In 1807, when banning the performance of plays during the purification fasts for rain, he modfied the more extreme restrictions proposed, because 'I fear that those of the people who make their livelihood by acting would become unemployed, and thus be unfairly picked out for suffering.' Again, in 1811, an edict declared, 'The capital is the hub where the spokes converge, the hub of concourse for the whole country, and the play-acting and entertainments of the tea-houses, wine-houses, streets and byways are a means of livelihood for the poor people, so we can scarcely put a stop to such things. Provided that they do not use them as a pretext for stirring up trouble, we can allow things just to take their natural course.'[3] How far this was simply a sage recognition of the inevitable is difficult to say.

Under Emperor Xuanzong (r. 1821–50) China suffered severe political and military reverses. The opium trade which Britain imposed upon China was draining it of silver, and further depleting the country's financial resources. Attempts to stop this trade led to the First Opium War (1840–42), after which Britain obliged China to accept the trade and pay a large indemnity. Xuanzong, even more than Renzong, was concerned to promote economies (he would even wear old patched clothes) and to restore military and administrative moral fibre among the Manchus, and, for all his own passionate fondness for drama, this concern permeates his measures concerning the theatre. Yet, like the general political situation, the problem of drama seemed to be growing steadily beyond his control, as far as the nobility and officialdom were concerned. There were repeated bans on the patronising of actors, with the threat of summary arrest, a ban on eunuch officials' frequenting of theatres, and repeated threats to Bannermen that if they engaged in play-acting, they and their descendants would lose their élite status, but the number of recorded punishments for such offences proclaims the ineffectuality of the bans. An assistant military governor was dismissed and banished to Urumchi for performing shadow shows in his headquarters while clad in his state robes; another official was dismissed for watching market shadow shows and for scuffling with soldiers; a Bannerman was dismissed for performing plays in his home and seducing young Mongols into acting plays; in 1838 officials were proceeded against for having attended plays in a temple, a prince and duke for opium-smoking in the same temple, and another duke for taking singing girls to the temple to sing or act there; at about the same time various officials including an assistant military governor were punished for showing plays and encouraging soldiers to perform and sing in them; and even in the final year of his reign, 1850, Xuanzong sent a general to hard labour in Sinkiang for various offences, prominent among them fondness for play-acting and inducing young gentlemen under his command to indulge in play-acting. Most of the offenders in these and other cases were Manchu Bannermen.

Xuanzong also occupied himself with the problems of the palace and popular theatres of Peking. In 1824 he banned the further establishment of theatres (*xiyuan* and *xizhuang*) in the Outer City, where there were by now about ten, and also banned actresses and feasts from the playhouses there. In 1827 he dismissed the outside actors from the palace, and placed the by now greatly reduced number of court actors under the control of the Ascendant Peace Bureau. He took further stern action against certain kinds of popular entertainer and two kinds of popular play. In 1835, in purported reaction to widespread thefts, horse- and mule-stealing, and the disappearance of small children, he ordered the expulsion from Peking of swindlers, quacks, pedlars and vagabonds, including gangs of three or four female fortune-tellers, female acrobats, pole-climbers, tightrope dancers, and performers of the kind of play known as Gaoqiao, 'high-stilts'. Another kind of play, known as Taipinggu, 'great peace drums', was also suppressed in Peking during his reign. Large crowds of these players, as many as a hundred and fifty or so, clad in sheepskin coats, would enter Peking and perform, clashing long-handled tambourines of all sizes as they wandered. They were accused of using the noise of their music and the attendant hullabaloo as cover for the abduction and rape of beautiful women. Several of the ringleaders were executed, and the vogue for these plays came to an end. How far the abduction was a major part of the activities of the Taipinggu players is hard to tell, but this case is a good example of the explosive vitality of such popular Chinese play forms, and the threat to settled society which they sometimes entailed, or seemed to entail.

Xuanzong's successor, Emperor Wenzong (r. 1851–61) came to the throne at the age of nineteen, and within a few months had the massive Taiping Rebellion to face. By 1853 the rebels had captured Nanking, not far from the northern heartland. The rebellion nearly overthrew, and extensively shattered, the Manchu empire, and was not quelled until 1866. In 1855 there were massive flood disasters when the Yellow River changed its course. From 1857 to 1860 the Second Opium War was fought. French and British forces marched on Peking, pillaged the Summer Palace, and imposed humiliating treaty conditions. Again, the decline of the régime had its echoes in measures concerning the theatre. In 1852 a decree attempted yet again to curb the Peking theatres, although expressing acceptance of them as an inevitable phenomenon, even referring with nostalgia to a better and more respectable theatrical past. The decree complained that there were now(!) night performances, women in the audiences, feasts, and daily more extravagance, with theatres vying in luxury, and that the old morally edifying plays had been replaced by 'slushy' music, ferocious fighting acrobatics, and plays that encouraged treachery and banditry. In the same year, the emperor ordered action against play-actor 'rogues' calling themselves *zouhui*, 'walking congregations', who performed each autumn and summer in a temple east of Peking.

After 1860, as European envoys became permanently established in Peking, Western influence in China steadily increased, and Chinese independence, central cohesion and governmental confidence greatly decreased. The next emperor was only five years old when he ascended the throne in 1861, and from 1860 onwards his mother Yehonala (1835–1908), later and usually known as Cixi Taihou or Old Buddha, increasingly tightened her hold on the reins of national power, and maintained that hold until her death in 1908. Much of her energy was occupied with ruthless palace intrigues. Administrative decline, imperial extravagance beyond imperial means, eunuch power, military humiliations at the hands of Oriental and Occidental foreigners, the mounting influx of Western ideas and the growing internal demand for political reform all made this a typical era of dynastic twilight. The edicts concerning drama continued, but surviving examples are rarer – perhaps in part this reflected the steady crumbling of the dam. In 1862 an edict ordered castigation for a prefect who celebrated his sixtieth birthday with plays, and for his son, and for a magistrate who celebrated his mother's recovery from illness with plays, these crimes being the more serious in a period of national military crisis. As late as 1905 the old prohibition was reiterated forbidding Bannermen to watch plays in the theatres, with a penalty of a hundred strokes. Much of the action against the theatre throughout this period, however, consisted of specific control rather than generalised directives. The problems of eunuch and Manchu involvement in the theatre loomed ever larger.

In spite of the dismissals of 1827, outside actors had returned to the court in small numbers, and for Wenzong's birthday in July 1860 even some of the big outside troupes were brought in. In September 1863 the Grand Secretariat petitioned for the removal of outside actors, and was apparently successful, but eunuchs were now acting and producing plays on a lavish scale again. Also in 1863, a well-meaning but perhaps naively hopeful Censor named Jia Duo memorialised the throne about a rumour that tribute silk from the imperial treasuries had been used to make play costumes, and that the eunuchs were daily receiving largesse to the amount of almost a thousand taels for their efforts in drama. The 1864 edict of reply to Jia Duo was in the name of Yehonala and her co-regent, and expressed hurt indignation that the Censor should suggest such inflammatory and improper things at a time of national exigency, and so soon after the death of the previous emperor. But righteously, if reluctantly, it ordered an investigation.[4]

All Peking knew that Yehonala was an ardent devotee of drama, and greatly under the influence of eunuchs. Early on, she had as one of her favourites and confidants the eunuch An Dehai (1844–69), a handsome and capable actor, who did much to organise the court pageants and theatricals of which she was so fond. One of the most famous photographs of her, even in much later years, was of her dressed in the role of Goddess of Mercy and in the company of her eunuch favourite, former cobbler's apprentice Li Lianying, nicknamed 'Cobbler's Wax Li', he in the guise of a Bodhisattva. While she publicly feigned agreement with her Censors' condemnation of eunuch extravagance, it was common gossip in the tea-houses that Li's slightest whims were law in the palace, that he and Yehonala, dressed in fancy costumes from historical plays, would make frequent extravagant excursions on the palace lake, and that he was behind many of the orgies and sinister happenings in the palace. Even in 1864, all knew her decree to be so much 'fine writing on waste paper'. The extravagance continued, and in 1884 the empress dowager reintroduced outside troupes into the palace for her birthday celebrations. The eunuchs in no way abandoned acting. Again, in 1872, a Censor complained of eunuchs' running a troupe of actors known as the Splendid Spring Culture Stars, which performed in the public theatres. Within the palace the eunuchs continued their plays.

The hold of the theatre upon the nobility became stronger than ever. Although action was announced in 1870 to reinforce bans on theatres in the Inner City, in 1881 another edict ordered stern proceedings to stop play-acting at two locations within the Inner City. One of the major offenders was Prince Zaicheng, heir of a son of the Emperor Xuanzong, who was having plays performed to win the approval of his mistress. Irreverently, he set up a play-house only a hundred days after the decease of the empress who had been Yehonala's co-regent. Furthermore he sinned by allowing the mixing of the sexes in the audience. Five or six other Inner City theatres followed his lead in this latter respect. Daily he went in disguise with his mistress to watch lavishly produced plays. A prince yet closer to the throne was going to have him arrested, so Zaicheng's father instructed a Censor to complain openly of Zaicheng's conduct, and that same day destroyed the theatre. Another theatre which Zaicheng had opened only one day previously in the Outer City was closed at the same time.

The age-old problem of women's endangering their morals by watching plays remained. Monasteries and convents in Peking, according to a counter-measure of 1869, were luring women to watch plays as a means of acquiring donations, and officials and their families were also attending these plays.

The empress dowager often, and not infrequently in moments of great crisis, deserted the government of the country to occupy herself with drama. In June 1900, as Boxer activities were becoming more frenzied, she watched plays in the Summer Palace for four days on end. Later, in flight during the Boxer Rebellion, her Summer Palace having just been despoiled by the Allied troops, she settled down in exile to enjoy some plays, which seemed to give her as much pleasure as those in Peking. The heir apparent at that time, Pujun, shared her taste for the theatre, as a confidential document of the time reveals:

The Heir Apparent is fifteen years of age; fat, coarse-featured, and of rude manners. He favours military habits of deportment and dress, and to see him when he goes to the play, wearing a felt cap with gold braid, a leather jerkin, and a red military overcoat, one would take him for a prize-fighter. He knows all the young actors and rowdies and associates generally with the very lowest classes. He is a good rider, however, and a fair musician. If, at the play-houses, the music goes wrong, he will frequently get up in his place and rebuke the performer, and at times he even jumps on to the stage, possesses himself of the instrument, and plays the piece himself. [. . .] On the 18th of the 10th Moon, accompanied by his brother and by his uncle, the Boxer Duke Lan, and followed by a crowd of eunuchs, he got mixed up in a fight with some Kansu braves at a theatre in the temple of the City God. The eunuchs got the worst of it, and some minor officials who were in the audience were mauled by the crowd. The trouble arose, in the first instance, because of the eunuchs attempting to claim the best seats in the house. [. . .] The eunuchs were afraid to seek revenge on the Kansu troops direct, but they attained their end by denouncing the manager of the theatre to Governor Ts'en, and by inducing him to close every theatre in Hsi-an. Besides which, the theatre manager was put in a wooden collar, and thus ignominiously paraded through the streets of the city. The Governor was induced to take this action on the ground that Her Majesty, sore distressed at the famine in Shansi and the calamities which have overtaken China, was offended at these exhibitions of unseemly gaiety; and the proclamation which closed the play-houses ordered also that restaurants and other places of public entertainment should suspend business. Everybody in the city knew that this was the work of the eunuchs. Eventually Chi Lu, Chamberlain of the Household, was able to induce the chief eunuch to ask the Old Buddha to give orders that the theatres be reopened. This was accordingly done, but of course the real reason was not given, and the Proclamation stated that, since the recent fall of snow justified hopes of a prosperous year and good harvests, as a mark of the people's gratitude to Providence, the theatres would be reopened as usual, 'but no more disturbances must occur'.[5]

As in the case of the early Manchu emperors, the empress dowager made magnificent theatrical entertainments the core of her birthday celebrations. For her seventy-third and last birthday on 3 November 1908, for instance, the main streets of Peking were decorated, and in the palace five days of theatricals were ordered. On her birthday she and the concubines amused themselves with a masquerade, she appearing in the costume of the Goddess of Mercy. That evening she caught a chill which was probably largely the cause of her death later in the month. Her interest in drama had always been a very active one. She had not only performed, but also selected the plays to be performed each day on theatrical occasions and was very free with her advice to players. Manchus of the imperial house continued to be prominent in the world of drama even after the proclamation of the Republic in 1911.

   The general official attitudes of provincial authorities towards drama, and the steps they took concerning it, continued much the same during the latter half of the Qing dynasty.[6] The Mongol noble Yuqian (Yukien, 1793–1841), a notoriously severe administrator, was provincial judge of Kiangsu in the late 1830s and was very active against popular printing and entertainments, warning against the Kiangsu custom of hiring priests to perform plays at funerals, and threatening dire action, including the confiscation of costumes, against troupes that performed obscene or bandit-lauding plays. The many surviving prohibitions and lists of banned plays, novels and songs, especially from the Kiangsu region, show that during the nineteenth century officials were still busily hunting, banning and burning. Ding Richang (1823–82), a one-time colleague of General Charles Gordon's and an enthusiastic advocate of Western technology, was from 1867 to 1870 governor of Kiangsu, and seems to have been outstanding for his inquisitory zeal. He culled for destruction 'hundreds and thousands' of 'lewd' books, some of them with very staid titles, and many of them probably plays. He once noted with disapproval that almost every household had a copy of *Fenlands* and *West wing*, and that almost everyone carried them around in their breast-pockets. One prefect in Hunan lost his post through his zeal in trying to prevent women from watching plays in the temples. His method was to raid a performance and order each monk to carry a woman from the premises on his back. The gentry to whom many of the ladies were related created such an uproar over this that the prefect was dismissed. Some time during the period 1821–50, another official similarly raided a theatre. He forced all the young ladies present to write a firm undertaking never to attend plays any more before allowing them to leave the building. He, it seems, was more successful in his attempt to uphold the prohibitions.
   Various provincial forms of play-acting were suppressed. At some time during the Qing a kind of show known as *lianhualuo*, 'Lotus flowers falling', which had an

influence on some kinds of local drama, was banned in the north of China. Also called *luozi*, it was viewed as the same as the rustic *huagu-xi* plays of the south,* and condemned as mere stage harlotry. After one ban, it continued to be performed under the name of *taiping geci*, 'Great Peace Songs'. Ningpo in Chekiang was a centre of theatre, and surviving warnings against play-acting there indicate a tolerance of the religious uses of drama, but an attempt during the years 1851–61 and after to suppress that clandestine form of acting known as *chuan-ke*, 'string-together acting'. This seems to have been a casual banding together, especially in isolated villages beyond the easy reach of the authorities, of a number of relatives or friends to form troupes, but its critics claimed that its main purpose was the fostering of gambling, that it was plotless, amoral, and fulsome, and that it was sometimes performed at nights or for days on end. The authorities offered rewards of five thousand copper cash to informers.

Fenlands plays and Maudgalyāyana plays still caused official concern. One mandarin complained: '[. . .] Nowadays when we see people go on stage and perform *Fenlands*, we only see brigands running wild with their villainy and achieving their aims. [. . .] It can only serve to foster the climate of violence, and encourage villainy and murder.'[7] One ban on Maudgalyāyana plays, which had been popular since the tenth or eleventh century, announced:

[. . .] There have for a long time been prohibitions on the performance of Maudgalyāyana. For dressing up in the parts of gods and demons and brandishing swords and spears to entertain the deities cannot call forth their blessings, and to try to exorcise evil by such means will only invoke ill fortune. [. . .] In the performance of plays for the entertainment of the gods, no matter which ones you perform, you are not permitted to perform Maudgalyāyana. If you venture to persist in doing so, I shall immediately have chiefs, village heads and troupe managers arrested and punished without mercy. [. . .][8]

Yet, amid all the official anxieties, legal action, punishments, suppressions, book-confiscations and book-burnings, and the wars and rebellions of the nineteenth century, Chinese drama was passing through one of its finest periods, and fashioning one of its finest and most intricate styles.

The two most notable events in the history of Chinese drama during the nineteenth century were the appearance of what is internationally known as Peking Opera† and the decline once more, and more drastically, of Kunqu. The Anhwei Troupes were closely involved in both. The first of the Anhwei Troupes had arrived in Peking in 1790. By the 1810s four of them, the Four Great Anhwei Troupes, had established a hegemony of the Peking theatrical world. These Four were the Three Celebrations, the Four Delights, the Spring Stage, and the Gentle Spring. The Anhwei Troupes were used in all the bigger theatres and on impor-

*See page 220 below.
†Although, but for this convention, we would prefer to call it 'Peking Drama'.

tant occasions for the main entertainment. Each of the Four Great Anhwei Troupes was reputed to excel in a particular aspect of performance.

The Four Delights Troupe was noted for its Kunqu, and either established or enhanced its reputation by a new full-length production of *Peach blossom fan*. The Gentle Spring (i.e. Springtime) Troupe was noted for its acrobatics, for the stunts, sword-play and other kinds of weapon-handling in the military plays. Anhwei actors had a long tradition of excellence in this aspect of acting. The popularity of acrobatics at this period may partly be traceable to actual social conditions. The profession of bodyguard or escort for the transport of currency and valuable goods and for the guarding of residences flourished around Peking and elsewhere, as banditry increased. Popular literature and entertainment during the nineteenth century seem strongly to reflect this social situation, with many tales of criminal investigation, and of heroes skilled in the fighting arts. Conflicts with foreign powers and dynastic decline were all no doubt likewise contributory causes. Far from being mere stage gymnastics, the actors' weapon-handling frequently reflected real fighting skills and techniques.

The Spring Stage Troupe based its public reputation upon its 'children' or 'boys'. Most troupes probably had a large proportion of young actors, but perhaps this troupe's were unusually young, or combined unusual youth with unusual ability. One account tells us that the career of boy actors in the early nineteenth century was always very brief.[9] They would start at the age of twelve or thirteen, and end at the age of sixteen or seventeen, being considered 'grannies' by the age of nineteen. The old actors would buy them and teach them to sing and dance to entice people, 'with more seductive looks and sexy garb than you would find in the brothels'. Another early nineteenth-century account tells us that whereas during Gaozong's reign most of the actors had come from the north-east, some had been stars in their late twenties, most were around nineteen, and there were relatively few young boys – now the boys, all coming from Suzhou, Yangzhou and Anqing (in Anhwei), would be hired by their master from their parents at the age of seven or eight for a fixed number of years, taken to the capital, taught to sing and act, dressed up in glamorous clothes, and put into service at feasts, their masters running them as a profit-making investment.[10] If wealthy men bought them before the contract expired this could shoot their purchase price up two or three thousand taels, depending on the boy's age. By the time a boy was nineteen, nobody was interested in him any more. These accounts refer to a general situation, from which the Spring Stage Troupe must have profited, and which it no doubt fostered. It would seem to be the extreme, and chronologically fairly logical, conclusion of the rage for young male entertainers that had flourished in the previous century.

The Three Celebrations Troupe was noted for its performance of whole plays.[11] During the Sông and Yuan dynasties, as far as we know, plays were generally or always performed straight through from beginning to end, although, of course, some of the longer southern plays and *West wing* would require separate sessions, matinée and evening, or performances on separate days in succession.

The four-act Yuan *zaju* were anyway so short that there could have been little point in performing only portions of them; indeed they were often supported by extra acts and plays. The Ming *chuanqi* were very long, but early in the dynasty it must still have been the habit to perform whole plays without abbreviations. From the late Ming onwards, however, when there were plays the length of Zhang Zhizhen's *Maudgalyāyana* and the Qing bumper plays, attitudes towards abbreviation, adaptation and supplementation became much freer. Sometimes extra acts containing episodes not strictly necessary to the plot would even be added to fill out a play. A play would sometimes be abridged by reducing it to the acts vital for the plot, or to the dramatic essence, or to the few acts around the dramatic high-point. In *Lute*, for instance, those acts in which the leading female and male roles predominate would suffice to provide a connected story, and the rest could be omitted. Or a couple of acts from two or three plays could be performed on one bill with some unifying feature to link them, such as their all being *dan* acts. What became by far the most common practice in Chinese drama into modern times, except with Western-style dramas or plays of a few of the more localised Chinese genres, was the performance of a single act from a play not linked to others on the bill, or of a play the length of a single act. From the late Ming onwards a number of such one-act selections were published in anthologies. There were also, from the late Ming onwards, many short plays written as such, of one or two acts, which were referred to as *zaju*, the longer plays still generally being termed *chuanqi*. But the one-act selections were more common in performance.

The one-act selections were the general rule by the early nineteenth century, in the more national forms of drama, but perhaps they were most suited to esoteric audiences. Such was the wealth of dramas by now that audiences certainly could not always know the background story of every play available. The one-act selections were most suitable for only the best known stories and plays. It was probably by performing whole plays lasting for days on end, with new arrangements, and topical subjects presented in a racy, colloquial fashion, that the Three Celebrations Troupe achieved its distinctive éclat.

After about 1810, Kunqu seems to have gone into general decline, gradually at first, and with occasional partial comebacks, but on the whole steadily yielding to other kinds of music and drama. Some old music masters from the Three Celebrations Troupe formed their own troupe to perform pure Kunqu and revive its popularity, but it had disbanded by 1828 after auspicious beginnings, after only six months or so of life. The elderly Kunqu performers of the Four Delights Troupe went against the tide and continued to perform Kunqu for many years. Even in the homeland of Kunqu, the Suzhou area, the leading Kunqu troupe disbanded itself in 1827. Plays such as *Lute* came to be regarded by the public as fusty and old-fashioned, and people demanded more elaborate, noisy plays than the Kunqu, ones with more costumery and facial masks. Putting on an old play was apparently enough to disperse an audience in Suzhou.[12] In Peking the Four Delights Troupe, by sticking loyally to Kunqu, became like a 'famous park grown wild, overgrown with tangled weeds', but in 1837 it enjoyed a revival, largely because of its new star singer, a man called Xiao-tian-xi, 'Little Heavenly Delight'.[13] In general, however, the stage had been reached where it could be regarded as ridiculous to prefer Kunqu. A novel of the period contained the remark, 'How ludicrous, those people only appreciate Kunshan-*qiang*, and have no taste for Erhuang.'[14]

A devastating blow to Kunqu in its decrepitude was the Taiping Rebellion of the early 1850s. The rebels occupied the region that included Suzhou and Kun-shan, and for a number of years Peking was more or less deprived of new Kunqu recruits from Kiangsu. From the 1870s onwards, after the end of the rebellion in 1866, there was another revival in the Suzhou area, but by the end of the Qing dynasty in 1911 Kunqu was seemingly doomed to virtual extinction. In about 1921, however, a group of wealthy enthusiasts in Suzhou established an Institute for the Teaching of Kunqu, using old actors to teach new generations of Kunqu performers. Later, a northern Kunqu troupe was also established in Peking, chiefly composed of Kunqu performers from other mixed music troupes. In this way the arts of Kunqu were preserved as an independent living tradition.

The key development in the birth of Peking Opera was the coming together of two styles of music, the Erhuang-*diao* and the Xipi-*diao*. Peking Opera is often referred to as Pihuangju, a name combining the core syllables of the names of these two kinds of music, although the repertoire of Peking Opera companies in fact embraces other kinds of music too.

When they first entered Peking in 1790 the Anhwei Troupes were already masters of Erhuang-*diao* music. Arguments abound as to its origins. Most probably it originated in Yihuang county in Kiangsi province, its name being a phonetic error for 'Yihuang'. Its formation into a proper system of polished dramatic music, however, occurred after it had spread to Anhwei province, and it came to be regarded by early writers as originating from Anhwei. It first used the *di*-flute, but after reaching Peking adopted the *huqin*-fiddle as well.

The earliest known use of the term 'Xipi' was in 1828, but the phenomenon certainly arose before that. Essentially it seems to have been much the same thing as Qin-*qiang*. The Anhwei Troupes were playing both Erhuang-*diao* and Qin-*qiang* music as early as 1790. A similar situation also occurred, perhaps in the 1820s, in the province of Hupeh. There, a form of Qin-*qiang* music acquired the name Xipi-*qiang*. Erhuang-*diao* had already reached that province from Anhwei, so the two forms of music came habitually to be played together. Some time during the years 1828–32 Hupeh actors went to Peking and earned a reputation for their performances with the 'new music'. There is some doubt as to whether this means the two kinds of music played together, or just Xipi-*qiang*, but either way the Hupeh actors reinforced the situation already prevailing in Peking, where Qin-*qiang* and Erhuang-*diao* had for decades coexisted in the theatre world and often within the same one Anhwei Troupe.

The Anhwei Troupes espoused Xipi-*qiang* and Erhuang-*diao* jointly as their chief form of drama music. If we may perhaps view this espousal as the birth of Peking Opera, it was, nonetheless, many years before Peking Opera was truly established as an independent form.[15] The very strength of the Anhwei Troupes, and indeed of Peking Opera, lay in their comprehensiveness and ability to utilise heterogeneous styles of music and acting. For a long while the other kinds of music continued to play a large part, with separate plays and so forth, in the repertoire of the Anhwei Troupes. Kunqu, for instance, continued for many years to figure prominently in the Anhwei Troupes' performances. Its well-known actors and plays, its exquisitely fine acting, and its mellifluous, refined manner of singing retained the nostalgic affections of some fair portion of the audiences. The early Pihuang music was sung high and loud with relatively little variation, and its actors had nothing like the same finesse as the Kunqu actors. The full transition to Peking Opera was not accomplished until decades after the arrival of the Hupeh actors.

We know of a number of outstanding Kunqu actors who performed in the Anhwei Troupes. Yang Mingyu, for instance, who came to Peking some time during the 1850s or 1860s, speaking nothing but Suzhou dialect, established himself as the only Kunqu *chou* clown, and a superb one at that. Various performances of *Fifteen strings of cash* were very popular in China a decade or two ago, including the 1956 revised version by the Chekiang Kunqu Opera Company and a magnificent colour film. In these the actor who played the criminal Rat Lou displayed a miraculous agility in the scene where the official disguised as a fortune-teller prises a confession of his crimes from him.* At one point where the official frightens him and he 'falls' off a bench where he is sitting, the actor performed a back-flip and came up on the other side from under the bench. Yang Mingyu's rendering would have outshone even this. In the same scene the actor playing Rat Lou held a tube of fortune-telling lots, and as he performed the back-flip he threw the tube in the air, emphasising his panic by that visual device. Then he popped up again on the other side in time to catch the tube so deftly that not one of the lots fell out. In another play he managed, while holding a military signal-flag constantly unfurled behind his back, to perform all manner of somersaults, tumbling and turning, but never curling the flag or wrapping it round himself. As a Buddhist monk in another play, he made his way to the stage exit flattening himself step by step until at last it seemed as if he were lying on the ground.

In the 1840s and 1850s the momentum towards a cohesive Peking Opera as a distinct, complex theatrical form and institution increased. One of the most significant changes which took place during this period was that the fashion for *dan* roles yielded considerably to one for *laosheng*, older male roles. The transition can be traced back to earlier decades, and was possibly encouraged by the national military crises and the in some senses tougher, more 'male' times. The gradual

*See the translation of this scene beginning on page 239 below, from the modern revised version.

change was accelerated by the skills and innovations of three actors, Cheng Changgeng (1812–1879/80) of the Three Celebrations Troupe, Yu Sansheng (fl. 1845–57) of the Spring Stage Troupe, and Zhang Erkui (d. 1860?) of the Four Delights Troupe, who created three schools or styles of *laosheng* singing and acting. A poem that was current around 1845 associates two of them together in fame:

> The rage is for Erhuang that bellows like thunder,
> none promotes the Kun and the Yi of yesterday,
> Yu Sansheng is nowadays the fashion
> and youth vies to learn from Zhang Erkui.[16]

Yu Sansheng reached Peking during the period 1821–50. He came from Hupeh province, and excelled particularly in Xipi-*diao* singing, but he also sang Erhuang-*diao* and other kinds of music, blending them in a novel manner. A number of incidents illustrate his stage presence and aplomb. Once when an actor was late putting in an appearance on stage, Yu was able to extend his own singing faultlessly for a few score lines to fill in time. Asked afterwards what would have happened if the actor had never appeared, he calmly replied that he would have continued with a passage of speaking once he had run out of song and, if need be, have finished off the play by himself. Another time, he acted in a play with Zhang Erkui and Cheng Changgeng. His role was one generally considered insignificant, but by impromptu additions of elaborate arguments, based on his knowledge of the novel of the same theme, he was able to transform the part so much that the audience broke into applause.[17]

Zhang Erkui was probably a Peking man, although some said he came from Anhwei and others that he came from Chekiang. He achieved fame by playing monarchs and emperors, acting with a very imposing royal or imperial bearing. Singing *laosheng*, his main music was Xipi-*diao*. In his singing he was said to have been 'clear and resounding of voice, not fond of decorative flourishes and turns to the melody' (in contrast it seems to Yu Sansheng), but with every word firm and full, 'unbreakably strong and resilient'.[18] How long he lived is uncertain, probably till the early 1870s, but it is clear his fame had faded by the early 1860s. A poem published in 1864 goes as follows:

> Now Erkui has sunk to perdition
> and Sansheng's fortunes wavered long,
> Who reigns in the world of song, you may ask,
> – Why, all yield place to Cheng Changgeng.[19]

The third of the three great *laosheng* actors, Cheng Changgeng, came from Anhwei. At first his singing was very poor, and people were always slighting him because of it. Spurred on by shame, he polished his singing furiously for three years. Then one day at a banquet in Peking, at which some wealthy and influential person was feasting high dignitaries, those present took it into their heads to test the actors with a certain play that required considerable singing skills. None dared to volunteer at first. Then Changgeng stepped forward, earning piqued looks from the others. As they heard him, however, it became obvious that he was master of all the arts of singing, his voice 'like the wind in the heavens and billows on the ocean, golden carillons and mighty bells'.[20] All present were utterly astonished by his vocal perfection, and the occasion gave a great boost to his reputation. Perhaps in that instance he was singing Xipi-*diao*? He also became highly proficient in Kunqu, which gave his singing in general its great clarity of enunciation and its exquisite pitch and cadence. When singing certain Xipi-*diao* tunes, his voice would 'soar through the clouds and split rocks, its reverberations trailing deliciously round the rafters, but amidst the superb, soaring clarity of it conveying another deeper and more powerful note'.[21] A Peking poem of 1853 goes:

> The Titan of Luantan, hand it to Changgeng,
> and flawless in his Kunqu, perfect every word,
> So capturing those fine young peacock players
> that they all revere him as teacher and as lord.[22]

Luantan here means the kinds of music other than Kunqu, Erhuang-*diao* being his main music.

During the period 1845–1879/80 Changgeng was leader of the Three Celebrations Troupe. When the Emperor Xuanzong, as he often did, summoned that troupe, the Spring Stage Troupe and the Four Delights Troupe to perform in the palace, Changgeng would act as director of all three. He was a uniquely able organiser of actors and acting, and was known in affection and respect as 'the Big Boss'.[23] Kindness, loyalty and firmness to his actors were the key to his success. When the troupe hit difficult times, he would use his acting ability and fame to assist it financially. There was a custom whereby the best actors from various troupes would be asked to sing at private banquets. Cheng Changgeng would never consent to do such external acting on his own, and insisted that if anyone wished to hear him at such an occasion they would have to invite the whole troupe. Many people later regarded Cheng Changgeng as the father of Peking Opera, and in the twentieth century the acting world revered him almost as a god of the theatre. Certainly it was he and the other two great actors who firmly established the fashion for *laosheng*, creating a new era for the Peking theatre, and providing the foundations for a golden age of Peking Opera and Pihuang music in the last three or so decades of the nineteenth century.

There were other consummate *laosheng* actors in the early days of Peking Opera, and fine performers in the other role categories were not lacking. Some came from the ranks of the amateur actors, who played such a large part in the world of Peking Opera; some were masters of Kunqu, as well as other kinds of music; one famous *chou* was a Manchu, a hereditary cavalry captain, and a master of the racy Peking dialect in its purest form. Mei Qiaoling (1842–81), grandfather of the most famous Peking Opera actor of the twentieth century, Mei Lanfang (1894–1961), came from Yangzhou, but was adopted by a Suzhou man at the age of eight, and later sold as a young apprentice to a Peking troupe. During the 1850s and 1860s he was manager of the Four Delights Troupe, and noted for his generous treatment of his actors. Very amply built, he was nicknamed Chubby, and specialised in *dan* roles, being greatly admired for his stately portrayal of a certain empress. His two sons, Zhufen and Yutian, were also famous performers. Mei Zhufen, father of Mei Lanfang, was furthermore a virtuoso of the *huqin*-fiddle, but he died too early for the full realisation of his ability. The elder son, Mei Yutian, was a still greater *huqin*-player, the best of his age, and highly esteemed as the accompanist of the great Tan Xinpei. He was also an expert on the *di*-flute, and could play no less than three hundred Kunqu plays. In addition, his abilities extended to the *suona*-clarion, drums and clappers.

The relative peace in Peking after the end of the Taiping Rebellion until 1900, when the Boxer Rebellion shattered the life of the capital, fostered conditions in which Peking Opera could and did flourish as an independent and widely popular form. It was once more a number of oustanding actors who constituted the most prominent manifestations of the success of Peking Opera, and were its leading inspiration. Most celebrated of these was undoubtedly Tan Xinpei (1847–1917).

Tan Xinpei came from Hupeh province. His father was an actor, nicknamed Skylark, which name was also applied to Cheng Changgeng at one time, and Xinpei was also known as Little Skylark. His basic grounding seems to have been in the fighting skills, and at one time he actually served as a bodyguard. He went to Peking where he initially performed as a *laosheng*. For a while he was obliged to tour with the 'porridge troupes', so called because of the meagre returns they obtained, in the country towns and farming villages near Peking. This was a hard but excellent training for his later acting. He was just in time to be a pupil of Cheng Changgeng's, and in 1875 joined the Three Celebrations Troupe. Cheng sagely predicted that after his own death Tan would achieve great fame. In 1879 Tan furthered his reputation by performances in Shanghai. Later, he damaged his voice, and had to play *wusheng*, for which his experience of weapon-handling stood him in good stead. In 1887, his voice having recovered, he joined the Four Delights Troupe and sang *laosheng* roles again. By the end of the century he was so celebrated that when the Allied Forces attacked Peking and Tientsin in 1900 a poem appeared with the lines, 'Who cares about the fate of the nation! The whole city competes to talk of Little Skylark.'[24] The statesman Liang Qichao (1873–1927) once inscribed a painting by Tan with the words, 'Unique in the universe, Tan Xinpei, whose fame these thirty years has shouted with the sound of thunder.'[25] In 1917, obliged to perform some plays against his will, he suffered a depression and died.[26]

Equally outstanding in Kunqu and the other kinds of music and drama, as at home in scholar as in warrior parts, Tan was master of three or four hundred plays. His singing was celebrated for its airy deftness and vivacity, its natural ease of pitch, and more than anything for its unpredictability and excitingly wide range of possibilities. Gramophone records of his voice still survive. In acting and singing he derived something from Cheng Changgeng, Yu Sansheng and other famous predecessors, but while culling the best of others he also created his own individual and integrally unified art. He was a genius at putting life into old, half-forgotten plays, but could always add polish and novelty even to established favourites. His technical accomplishments alone were remarkable. To mention but one small example, during a riotous scene in one play he was able to kick one of his shoes up into the air so that it landed fair and square on his own head. One of his sons was a first-rate actor, and a grandson of his also became an idol of the Peking theatre.[27]

There were two other *laosheng* actors of particular note performing in Peking at the same time as Tan: Wang Guifen (1860–1908) and Sun Juxian (1841–1931). Thus, as in the previous generation, three traditions of *laosheng* acting were created. Sun Juxian came from a merchant family in Tientsin, and the people of that city came to refer to him by the affectionate name of 'Old Fellow-townsman'.[28] He had a fine voice, and took up amateur acting. He spent his youth, however, pursuing a military career, joined up at the age of twenty, served under the notoriously blood-thirsty and bellicose general Chen Guorui (1837–83), and was twice wounded in action. Later he rose to the very high rank of lieutenant-major in Kwangtung and Kiangsi provinces. Not until he went to Shanghai at the age of twenty-nine did he take up the theatre as a profession. He and some friends opened a tea-house theatre, which soon had to close because of debts. Afterwards he went to Peking and joined the Four Delights Troupe. Surprisingly, he played *laosheng* and not *wusheng* roles. His singing showed borrowings from all three early *laosheng* schools, and his voice, which had a wide range, was capable of great volume. Always sounding very natural and easy, he enunciated his words with vigour, 'like chopped nails and sliced iron'.[29] He sang in a straightforward manner without many fancy turns to the melody, and when he reached the last line of a song would open his throat and let the sound pour out in an endless rumbling like thunder going into the ground, which earned him the nickname Sun One Rumble. He lived to a ripe old age, and in his later years, when he rarely acted, was forever doing charitable deeds to help the needy.

Wang Guifen from Hupeh province was nicknamed Wang Big Head.[30] Originally he sang *dan* roles, but he also sang some *laosheng* roles. Losing his voice for a while, he went over to playing the *huqin*-fiddle for Cheng Changgeng. In 1881, after his voice had mended, he returned to acting. Familiar as he was with Cheng's manner, his *laosheng* singing earned him the reputation of being 'a reincarnation of Cheng Changgeng', but he also had his own distinct style. His voice was famed for its amplitude and penetration, and for its rich variety of mood and expression. Some described Tan Xinpei's voice as a 'cloud-veiled moon', not very clear or ringing as he started to sing, but gradually becoming louder and more distinct. Wang Guifen's voice was a 'back-of-the-head sound', ringing forth loudly as soon as he opened his mouth and still leaving lingering echoes in the head after he had stopped singing. While it was difficult to attain the finesse of Tan, so people said, it was impossible without a full and ample voice even to try to imitate Wang's manner of delivery.

The appeal of the *laosheng* plays was natural to a China beset by military activities and dangers, internal and external, and a good example of the vigour of such plays is *Capture and release of Cao Cao.* This is a tense and violent Peking Opera. It was one of the favourite plays of Yu Sansheng and Sun Juxian. Cao Cao, arch-villain of Chinese legitimist history and more especially of Chinese literature and theatre, and later ruler of Wei, the most powerful kingdom in the divided China of the Three Kingdoms period, has just failed in an assassination attempt against the tyrannical Dong Zhuo, who has seized the reins of power in the tottering empire of the Han dynasty. As he flees, Cao Cao comes into the hands of the magistrate Chen Gong, a man renowned for his upright character and sense of honour. Instead of giving Cao Cao up to Dong Zhuo and claiming the reward, Chen allows Cao Cao to persuade him to join him in his flight, and his attempt to gather forces to overthrow Dong Zhuo. During their flight they meet with Lü Boshe, a sworn brother of Cao Cao's father, who insists that they stay a while in his house, and plans to entertain them with every generosity, first going down to the village to buy some good wine. While Lü is away, Cao Cao hears warlike cries from the back of the house, and with his hyper-suspicious mind presumes at once that Lü has betrayed him and is planning an attempt to capture and kill him. Chen Gong tries in vain to restrain him, but he rushes into the living quarters of the house, and kills every member of Lü's household. Then Chen Gong discovers in the kitchen proof that the warlike cries had simply been the sounds of some of the family slaughtering a pig for the feast. As Cao Cao and Chen Gong flee, they encounter Lü Boshe returning with the wine. There is a tense scene as they tear themselves away, Cao Cao in pent-up fury, and Chen Gong tearfully trying to beg forgiveness and exculpate himself without telling Lü what has happened. They start to ride off, at which point the following final scene takes place. The *laosheng* part is that of Chen Gong, while Cao Cao is played by a *jing* , Lü Boshe by a *wai*, and the innkeeper by a *chou*.[31]

Capture and release of Cao Cao: Scene Seven

(*Enter Cao Cao and Chen Gong.*)

CAO CAO. (*Sings*) Jerking the silken reins, I once more halt my horse.
CHEN GONG.
          (*Sings*) Something is amiss, that he halts his flight mid-course.
Why have you reined in your horse again so soon, illustrious lord?

CAO CAO.   I forgot something very important that I was going to tell the old cur.
CHEN GONG.   Oh, spare his old life!
CAO CAO.   Mind your own business!
CHEN GONG.   For the love of Heaven and the sake of humanity!
CAO CAO.   Hey, uncle, turn back will you please.

(*Cao Cao and Chen Gong dismount.*)

LÜ BOSHE. (*Backstage*) Coming! (*Enters.*)
           (*Sings*) We had no time for heart-to-heart talk, as we met just now,
                but here's another chance for me to chat with my dear Cao Cao.
Well, noble nephew, am I justified in my hope that you are thinking of turning back after all?
CAO CAO. That's it. I thought I would come back . . . Why, who's that there behind you?
LÜ BOSHE.   Where?
CAO CAO.   Taste my sword! (*Kills Lü Boshe.*)
CHEN GONG
           (*Sings*) The sight chokes my throat at once with speechless horror,
                as this old white-haired patriarch dyes the ochre sand.
                Oh, most venerable, aged man,
                all your family, too, both young and old, have fallen to the
                    swordsman's hand.
CAO CAO.   (*Laughs*) Ha, ha, ha!
CHEN GONG.   Agh, come now!
           (*Sings*) Let me talk to Cao Cao again, to try and clarify what I cannot
                understand.
Illustrious lord, not content with massacring his whole family, for which you have shown no remorse, as we leave his farmstead you now hack down the old gentleman himself at the side of the road with your sword. How can you explain it!
CAO CAO.   I killed the old cur to prevent his causing any trouble for me in the future.
CHENG GONG.   Aren't you afraid that killing on mere suspicion like that may earn you the vilification of the whole world!
CAO CAO.   Eh? I . . . Chen, old chap, all my life, whatever I have done, I've always preferred to wrong the world than let myself be wronged by anyone in the world!
CHEN GONG.   (*With the dawn of sudden great enlightenment*) Ah . . . I see!
CAO CAO.   (*In anger*) Tcha! (*Draws his sword. Chen Gong steps back out of the way.*)
CHEN GONG.
           (*Sings*) To hear his words shakes my soul with dread and alarm,
                I turn aside and condemn my error, but all too late.
                Once I took him for a big-hearted hero,
                now I see him, a rogue without honour, a walking sack of hate.
                My horse hooves a narrow path, no room for turning,
                yes, now 'petals follow the stream, for the stream never stays',
                At such a stage, I must endure him for a while,
                Since we share a mighty aim, I must try to mend his ways.
CAO CAO.   What's all that nonsensical long-winded muttering about?

CHEN CHONG.

> (*Sings*) Do not accuse me of muddled, long-winded chatter,
> You play the man of honour, and belie it by your dealings,
> – Lü Boshe was your own father's faithful friend,
> how could you slay his family for your mere suspicious feelings!
> And if there were some justification for slaughtering all his kith and
>   kin,
> why, when we were on our way, did you need to kill the old
>   gentleman?

CAO CAO. (*Sings*) Cease your bitter rebuke, Chen Gong, and let us mount our steeds.

(*Cao Cao and Chen Gong both mount their horses.*)

> As we sit in our ornate saddles, let Cao Cao now explain his deeds.
> Lü Boshe was a faultless friend to my father, what you say is true,
> but I mistook him for an enemy, a threat to me and you,
> and when I rage, let mighty Mount Tai go crash and tumble!
> and when I weed, I yank the roots, to stop them sprouting new!

CHEN GONG.

> (*Sings*) Good words cannot reform a blockhead ox, a wooden horse,
> This rogue's as narrow-visioned as a well-bottom toad.

CAO CAO. (*Sings*) Ply the whip and speed our swift and superb steeds,

> in the dim dusk and heavy mist a house lies ahead on our road.

Chen, old chap, it's getting late. Let's you and me turn in here and find some lodging for the night, shall we?

CHEN GONG.   Just as you wish.

CAO CAO.   Innkeeper?

INNKEEPER.   (*Backstage*) Aye, coming! (*Enters.*)

> Buy my wine, three cups will make you merry,
> I open my vats, and they scent ten miles around.

Might you two gents be wanting to stay in the inn?

CAO CAO.   Yes, of course! Take the horses through.

CHEN GONG.   But don't unsaddle them.

INNKEEPER.   No, all right.

(*Innkeeper takes horses. Cao Cao and Chen Gong enter the inn.*)

INNKEEPER.   What would you two gentlemen like me to bring you?

CHEN GONG.   One bright lamp, and one bottle of the best wine!

INNKEEPER.   Certainly, sir. One bright lamp and one bottle of the best wine. (*Fetches wine and lamp.*) Here's the lamp, and here's the wine.

CHEN GONG.   We'll call you if we want you again.

INNKEEPER.   Right. (*Exit.*)

CAO CAO.   Chen, old fellow, please help yourself to some wine.

CHEN GONG.   I'm worn out with all the riding. I couldn't swallow any.

CAO CAO.   Couldn't swallow any? Come off it! It's quite obvious you're still peeved at seeing me kill those few members of the Lü family by mistake, eh?

CHEN GONG.   Eh?! You and I are planning great things together – where do words like 'peeved' come into it! You're too suspicious.
CAO CAO.   Yes, old Cao Cao's always been too suspicious all his life.
            (*Sings*) Anyone I meet I tell but a third of what I think,
                        I'm used to pulling teeth from the tiger's jaw.
                        I'll drink a cup or two alone then go to sleep,
                        and in one brief dream return to my old home once more.

(*Sound of the first watch. Chen Gong takes the lamp in his hand, and goes outside to patrol and check that all is well, after which he comes back into the room.*)

CHEN GONG.   (*Shouting to see if Cao Cao is still awake*) Illustrious lord! Illustrious lord! – Hah! he's gone to sleep. Ah me, how bitterly I regret what I've done.
            (*Sings*) The moon's bright wheel shines at the window,
                        and Chen Gong's mind is tangled as gale-blown straw;
                        How I repent that I conceived such wild ambitions,
                        that I followed him, that I darkened Lü Boshe's door.
                        Lü Boshe, there was a chivalrous man of honour,
                        – he slaughtered swine and purchased wine to entertain his brother's son,
                        But what happened? The wretch was over-suspicious,
                        drew his sword against Lü's family, and killed them every one.
                        A whole household was put to the sword, all slain,
                        its aged master lost his life and stained the yellow sand.
                        Wronged souls, victims of murder, bear me no grudge,
                        The truth only Heaven and the spirits may understand.

(*Sound of second watch.*)

                        Hear the watchtower drums die away as they beat the second watch,
                        The more I brood the more I'm sure I made a terrible mistake.
                        How I repent that I ever left my hearth and home,
                        and cast aside my black silk hat of office to follow in his wake.
                        I thought the rogue had princely schemes, was a man of magnanimity,
                        He's the very root of ruin, the house of Han's future calamity.

(*Sound of third watch.*)

                        See how the scoundrel sprawls in sleep, serene and unconcerned,
                        slumbering like some foolish frog, deep in its well, safe on its stone;
                        The blackguard is like some dragon as yet unarmed with scales and claws,
                        The bandit, he's like some savage tiger, its ferocious fangs not yet grown.
                        A tiger, but still caged, and if I do not strike while strike I may,
                        am I to loose it to its lair, to claw down other men some day?

(*Takes sword.*)

I draw a sword to lop a villain's head,

(*Cao Cao turns over.*)

And almost bungle things again instead!

(*Puts sword away again.*)

Yes, I really should despatch him, with one blow of my sword,
but I fear lest the world suspect that I and Dong Zhuo had some
    secret accord.
I must write a poem to shake the wretch from his complacency,
Yes, leave a verse upon the table, but what shall the topic be?

(*Sound of fourth watch.*)

Ah, yes .'. . I'll take the fourth watch as my topic line:
'As the fourth watch is drummed and the moon beams its brightest,
Endless bitter regrets assail my heart unceasingly,
When I saw him kill Lü Boshe and family, innocents all,
I realised that Cao Cao –'

(*Cao Cao turns over.*)

Illustrious lord! Illustrious lord! (*Cao Cao is still sleeping and makes no reply.*)
'I realised that Cao Cao is paramount in perfidy.
Written by Chen Gong . . .' Now, while the rogue is still asleep, I must seize the opportunity to look for my horse and escape from here.

(*Seeks horse, leads horse away, opens gate, goes out of gate, and mounts horse. Sound of fifth watch.*)

(*Sings*) Yes, Chen Gong, 'twas an error indeed
to flee so far in this scoundrel's company,
But by choice, the blossom drifts with the stream,
'tis not the unfeeling stream that loves the flower from its tree.

(*Exit Chen Gong.*)

CAO CAO.
(*Sings*) In one brief dream I returned to my old home once more.
Oho! . . .
(*Sings*) Chen Gong's disappeared, something's amiss for sure.
It's light now. Wonder why Chen Gong vanished. There's a poem written out on the
table. Let's have a look at it:
'As the fourth watch is drummed and the moon beams its brightest,
Endless bitter regrets assail my heart unceasingly,

> When I saw him kill Lü Boshe and family, innocents all,
> I realised that Cao Cao is paramount in perfidy.

Written by Chen Gong.'

Bah, pah, tcha! Oh, Chen Gong, oh Chen Gong, if some day I do not take your life, I swear to quit all human intercourse! – Hey, innkeeper! Here's my money for the room. I'm leaving now.

> (*Sings*) Damn you, Chen Gong, you did wrong to do that,
> to revile me with that verse, you shouldn't have dared:
> I shall gather all the princes and raise a mighty host,
> and when I catch Chen Gong, he'll not be spared!

(*Exit.*)

The ordinary populace of Peking would casually hum lines from the plays of Tan, Sun and Wang in the streets. There were also many other colourful and accomplished actors. The *chou* actor Liu Gansan excelled in deadpan wise-cracking, and was summoned to serve in the imperial palace. The Empress Dowager Cixi Taihou commanded him to play the part of an emperor in a certain play. At that period she was persecuting the Emperor Dezong (r. 1875–1908) and, risking his neck, perhaps through some strange confidence in Cixi's love of drama and her grim sense of humour, Liu at one point extemporised the comic lines: 'I'm only a make-believe emperor, and yet I have my throne, while he, the flesh-and-blood emperor, stands daily in attendance, and can't even sit down.'[32] Protected by the jester's privileges, or more likely by good luck, he survived immediate destruction. In one play he devised his own version of the one-man band, his hands playing the *huqin*-fiddle, cymbals tied to his knees and a baton held between the toes of his right foot, with which he struck a golden gong hung from his left foot, all these blending in perfect rhythm as he sat on a table and sang. He kept a donkey, which he rode round the city, and the sound of the bells round the donkey's neck advertised his coming, and made him a familiar figure to the general public. In one play he even came on stage leading the donkey, this being a major cause of his subsequent reputation. In 1895 an official was punished for a military defeat. Liu performed another piece of extempore satire in a court play. The official's brother-in-law, son of the mighty statesman Li Hong-zhang (1823–1901), was present in the audience, took it as a great insult, and had Liu arrested and cruelly flogged, as a result of which the actor fell ill and died.

The Empress Dowager Cixi Taihou was very fond of Pihuang drama. The palace eunuchs changed over from Kunshan-*qiang* and Yiyang-*qiang* music to Pihuang, but, like many an emperor before her, she preferred the outside actors of Peking Opera, and summoned many of the most famous, including Sun Juxian, Tan Xinpei and Wang Guifen, to serve in the palace.[33]

During the latter decades of the Qing dynasty, Peking Opera spread to other parts of China, in particular to Shanghai where it developed vigorously with its own local mood. Shanghai performances tended to be more lavish and showier, 'mongrel, impure, and extravagant', using more scenery. Whether this represented improvement or not, the Shanghai productions certainly had spirit and novelty, and also, moreover, contributed to the national impact of Peking Opera. Shanghai was in fact a major *entrepôt* for the export of Peking Opera to the middle and southern regions of China, and it was very often a Shanghai brand of Peking Opera that reached those regions. Shanghai in turn exercised an influence on Peking, and some talented Peking actors received their first polishing, or found their professional niches, in Shanghai, Wang Xiaonong (1858–1918) being a notable instance. A Manchu Bannerman, he became a county magistrate, but was dismissed on the grounds of his addiction to song. He became an amateur actor, and later expressed to Wang Guifen his desire to turn professional. 'Easier said than done!' replied Wang with a smile. So he called himself Wang Xiaonong, which means 'Wang Laughed at Me', and blithely turned professional.[34] It was not until he went to Shanghai in 1915, however, that his undoubted abilities received their due of public recognition. Wang Xiaonong is also of great interest as a playwright and dramatic innovator, and in this connection will be mentioned again.

There has been more discussion, in the West, about Peking Opera than about any other form of Chinese drama.[35] The very complexity of this drama, and the bulk of detail available about it, make any brief outline inevitably an over-simplification. There is for instance a manual of 260 packed pages devoted entirely to the *longtao*, 'dragon suite', the group of four minor actors which serves to represent armies.[36] Some Chinese, moreover, object to the very term 'Peking Opera', and it is true that besides Pihuang it also embraces other styles of music and acting, some of which still exist as largely independent kinds of drama in their own right. Yet geographical location, the passage of time and the unifying influence of various individuals' acting fashions have produced a certain homogeneity which to some extent justifies the use of the term. Some generalised observations may therefore be made about the nature of the main body of Peking Opera, understanding that these refer sweepingly to early twentieth-century features as well as to those of the nineteenth century.

It is strictly speaking unwise to contrast acting and singing with word-meaning in Peking Opera, since all are interdependent. The meaning of the words of Peking Opera is certainly a vital part of the impact of the play. Yet by and large the acting and the singing are the most striking features of it. Many *zaju* and *chuanqi*, as well as being eminently performable, make excellent reading. Most of them have full, lucid texts. A number of Peking Opera plays, however, taken in isolation as literature, are often sparse nearly to the point of incoherence, and quite unrepresentative of their excellence on stage. In length and in mood the Peking Opera play is more usually a quintessence of some much larger story, and it is the acting and the singing which give the quintessence its compensatory fulness. Recent estimates of the total number of Peking Opera plays claim a total of some 3,800 titles, of which some 1,400 are still available for the stage. Much research needs to be done on these as literature, but the literature must, more than with most kinds of drama, be understood in the light of actual stage conditions and performance.[37]

Peking Opera has four main role categories, and many of its subdivisions are similar to those of Kunqu:

1. *sheng*:
   (A) *wusheng*, 'military sheng':
       (a) *wulaosheng*, 'military old *sheng*', middle-aged or elderly dignified warriors. White-bearded.
       (b) *changkao*, 'long armour', high-ranking, dignified warriors in full stage armour with four flags attached to their shoulders.
       (c) *duanda*, 'short fighting', bandits, fighters from the ordinary populace, swordsmen, fist-fighters. Not required to sing. Close-fitting black costumes.
   (B) *wensheng*, 'civil or literary *sheng*':
       (a) *wenlaosheng*, 'literary old *sheng*':
           (i) *laosheng*, middle-aged or elderly dignified men, often of low social status.
           (ii) *xusheng*, 'bearded *sheng*', sometimes viewed as synonymous with the term *laosheng*, middle-aged or elderly officials, statesmen, scholars, literary men, etc.
           (iii) *wai*, as in Kunqu.
           (iv) *mo*, as in Kunqu.
       (b) *wenxiaosheng*, 'literary little *sheng*', using falsetto voice:
           (i) *shanzisheng*, 'fan *sheng*', young scholars, etc., characterised by the manipulation of the fan.
           (ii) *qiongsheng*, as in Kunqu.
       (c) *wuxiaosheng*, 'military little *sheng*', known generally as *zhiweisheng*, 'pheasant-tail *sheng*', although sometimes the two terms are slightly distinguished from each other, young military heroes.
       (d) *hongsheng*, 'red *sheng*', acts mainly Guan Yu roles.
2. *dan*:
   (a) *laodan*, as in Kunqu.
   (b) *qingyidan*, 'black-clothes *dan*', also known as *zhengdan* (although sometimes explained as being different), refined, graceful young women in love, virtuous young ladies, respectable young wives, etc.
   (c) *huadan*, 'flowery *dan*', term going back to the Yuan dynasty, coquettish, flighty, seductive young women, harlots, singing girls, etc.
   (d) *guimendan*, 'boudoir *dan*', young, unmarried, refined women, similar in some respects to the *qingyidan*.
   (e) *wudan*, 'warrior *dan*', young women, usually in short tunics, who fight, generally on foot.
   (f) *daomadan*, 'sword-and-horse *dan*', sometimes equated with the *wudan*, young women who fight, often on horseback.

    (g) *caidan*, 'coloured *dan*', villainous, scheming women, ugly women, maidservants, matchmakers, etc.

    (h) *tiedan*, as in Kunqu.

    (i) *gongnüdan*, 'palace women *dan*', female attendants, etc., who generally just stand in attendance.

3. *jing*, the vigorous, violent, powerful, swashbuckling or crafty characters, villainous or virtuous:

    (a) *zhengjing*, 'main *jing*', important, upright characters.

    (b) *fujing*, 'assistant *jing*', usually the powerful villains.

    (c) *wujing*, 'military *jing*', parts which emphasise military acrobatics and fighting as opposed to singing, acting, and speech.

4. *chou*:

    (a) *wenchou*, 'civil *chou*', the clown in non-military plays.

    (b) *wuchou*, 'military *chou*', the clown in military or fighting plays.

Again, it must be stressed that this is only a very rough guide. There are numerous variations, other kinds of nomenclature and diverse traditions and exceptions, as well as not a few conflicting opinions. There have, moreover, been constant shifts in the scopes of the various role categories. Some authorities make a number of *mo* roles into a fifth major category, for instance, and there are quite different terms in use for the *jing* and *chou* role designations.

Generally speaking, young women and young men parts use a falsetto voice. As in Kunqu, the *jing* roles have elaborately painted *lianpu*, 'face characterisations', partly symbolic indications of types and personalities, many making striking use of bright colour, but the sly villains generally using flat white all over with a few lines of black and grey. The *chou* has white make-up just around the eyes and nose. The *laosheng* wears hardly any make-up, and the *laodan* none at all. The other *dan* roles have heavy red or lobster pink round the eyes fading to pale pink on the cheeks and chin, reddened lips and black-pencilled eyes and eyebrows, the bridge of the nose and the forehead being left quite white. The beard of the *laosheng* can be white, black, red or grey, and fits round the ears, sometimes with long sideburns. There are many varieties of shape and length, and most rest on the upper lip rather than immediately beneath the nose.

There is a wide variety of costumes and headdresses, and some of them are immensely elaborate and richly decorated. They are usually generalised or symbolic rather than historically or individually accurate. Until recent times there was no naturalistic scenery, and the limited range of stage properties consists nearly always of fairly small objects that are light to handle. There are sometimes tables and chairs, however, which are put to ingenious and conventionally imaginative use. A chair or bench may serve to represent a loom, prison gates, the edge of a well, a precipice, a wall, a cloud, high ground and so forth, and placed on or by a table can help to construct a mountain, Heaven, or a steep slope. A wooden board painted with wavy lines indicates clouds; a wooden candle or lanterns on poles, darkness; a flag with green waves on it, the surging billows; strips of cloth painted with wheels, a chariot or carriage; a dark blue, brick-patterned cloth, a city wall; an embroidered curtain, a bed; black silk streamers, the wind or a storm; a piece of black gauze above the head, that the actor is dreaming; and a whip held in the hand, that he is riding a horse. Besides these and other such symbols, realistic writing-brushes, water-buckets, bows, weapons, cups and other objects are used. In the old days the property and effects men used to operate in full view on stage.

Stylised gestures and miming are a prominent feature of Peking Opera.[38] Certain gestures indicate the opening of a purely imaginary door; stepping over an imaginary threshold, entry into a room; lifting up the hem of a skirt, mounting stairs; raising the leg and certain other movements, mounting a horse; swaying the body, stepping on a boat; and so forth. There is an extensive variety of finely distinguished hand, foot, body and sleeve movements. Some of the properties and gestures are naturalistic or nearly so, but a large number are so symbolic as to demand that the audience be already familiar with their meaning. At a certain level the main conventions and symbols are readily picked up and the general gist of the story is readily gathered, but for a full understanding of the whole meaning and finesse of many Peking Opera plays, a vast amount of initiation is necessary. But the symbolisation and stylisation can have enormous advantages in respect of dramatic depth, distillation of artistry, stage flexibility and economy. Dispensing with the need for elaborate realistic scenery and properties on one plane facilitates rapid and smooth change of scene, location and time, on another plane draws the audience's imagination fully into the essential emotional and aesthetic realities by relieving the attention of the need to occupy itself with visual objects, and on yet another plane means that Peking Opera is not the monopoly of elaborately furnished and heavily finance-consuming stages. It is true that the upkeep of many of the leading traditional Peking Opera companies has always been astonishingly expensive, but at the same time much of the style readily adapts to impromptu performance in a limited space. The symbolisation and stylisation foster the imagination, as well as offering the undoubted pleasures of esoteric connoisseurship.

Various instruments are used to introduce, to accompany and to provide interlude or bridge passages between songs, lines of songs, and action. Generally the orchestra consists of no more than about eight musicians, seated to the actors' left-hand side on the stage. The principal instrument is the *huqin*-fiddle, or, more strictly speaking, that type of *huqin* known as the *jinghu*-fiddle. Another deeper and more mellow-sounding version, the *erhu*-fiddle, was introduced in the 1930s. The *jinghu* itself may only have replaced the *di*-flute in the 1870s or even later on in the nineteenth century. Other instruments are the *yueqin*-guitar, the *sanxian*-banjo, the *ban*-clapper, various gongs, cymbals and drums, the *suona*-clarion and the *di*-flute. The last two are used only on certain occasions. Military plays mostly use only percussion, and the loud noise of gongs and drums at entrances, exits and passages of exciting action are, along with the skirling note of the *jinghu*, the most characteristic music of Peking Opera. The orchestra is led by a musician who plays a smallish drum, and beats time with the clapper. Quite often one musician is in charge of more than one instrument. Great stress is placed on the relationship between the leading singing actors and their *jinghu*-player. The music, as also the acting and singing, is taught from master to pupil by example and personal instruction, not primarily through written media such as musical notation. This method has the advantages of conveying many features of excellence that cannot easily be embodied in writing alone, and of giving theatrical immediacy and coherence to the training.

In many ways Pihuang is much simpler than the music of earlier kinds of drama, but the relative lack of total variety makes it all the easier for actors and audience to familiarise themselves with the moods conventionally associated with certain tunes and rhythms. The alternations of rhythm are one of the most striking auditory features of it. The amount of song in printed texts of Pihuang plays often seems very small compared with those of earlier forms of drama, but in performance the effect of the singing is more noticeable, and extenuated syllables often greatly expand its proportional effect. Unlike Yuan *zaju, nanxi* and Kunqu, the lines of the lyrics are generally of even length, usually either ten or seven syllables, divisible in sense and rhythm into 3–3: 2–2 and 2–2:3 respectively. The music closely follows the rhythmic and semantic divisions of the lyrics. Sometimes *chenzi* are added, sung very casually with no alteration of the basic music, but they are less prominent than in *qu*. There are, however, also sometimes eight-syllable and nine-syllable lines and irregular lyrics which have what are called *duozi*, 'piled characters', and which do require adjustments of the music. The lines are usually organised in groups of two. Rhymes are divided into thirteen groups, and any one passage of singing must in general keep to the same rhyme sound. The dialect is a mixture containing elements of pronunciation from Anhwei, Hupeh and Szechwan provinces, as well as from Peking. The very mixture gives this drama yet another distinctive quality. The *chou* roles use Peking colloquial, probably because their wit is best kept immediate and familiar-sounding.

Even a vaguely adequate treatment of the lore of Peking Opera would fill a great many volumes, and besides the aspects of stage performance there are copious and elaborate conventions and superstitions affecting all aspects of back-stage and offstage life. The organisation of troupes and the complex ramifications of the theatre world make another immense topic in themselves. The wealth of information available and potentially available about Peking Opera must not, however, lead us into the common error of seeing all previous kinds of Chinese drama retrospectively as reflections of Peking Opera. Peking Opera is a relatively recent phenomenon, and the similarities in subject-matter and other respects between it and, for instance, Yuan *zaju* should not obscure awareness of the many obvious differences. It is likewise important to realise that Peking Opera has itself been undergoing constant changes in all directions, and by the 1940s was different in many ways from what it had been in the nineteenth century. Important actors, schools, fashions and the very eclecticism and flexibility of Peking Opera all encouraged rapid and thoroughgoing changes.

9

Theatres and Playwrights

Chinese traditional drama, as opposed to the Western-style and various other modern dramas of the twentieth century discussed in later chapters, has in general placed much greater emphasis on music, words and actors than on scenery, lighting and stage properties, although such matters have been far from neglected and there have been many notable exceptions. Yet perhaps much of the strength of Chinese drama has lain in the relative simplicity of its equipment, or in its amenability to performance with the simplest of equipment. Apart from some of the elaborate machinery and stages of the palace, mentioned above, most drama performances, from those of the huge theatres and princely mansions to those of the grainyard, river bed or street corner, have been closely united by this relative simplicity and the attendant informality of the stage.[1] It is in this sense a small step from the rough outdoor stage built of planks, bamboo poles and matting lashed together with ropes and sometimes raised on roughish tree-trunk piles, or from the sparsely furnished temple stage, to the red carpet of the private residence, the garden pavilion stage, or the restaurant stage among the tea tables. Here lies a great strength. It means that the drama of the rich and the drama of the poor have not been very rigidly divided, and have been more easily able to replenish and renew each other. As we have seen, from Sông times and earlier, the street, market and village actors and vulgar, popular plays readily moved into the palace and back again, while in turn palace taste and distaste could rapidly affect the grass roots drama.

In general, for intellectual or spiritual motives, as well no doubt as because of economic limitations and other reasons, Chinese traditional drama stresses the realism of ideas rather than the literal realism of stage sets and costume. To aim at complete reproduction of straightforward visual reality on the stage is probably, dramatically speaking, a dangerous enterprise, and, sometimes at least, an uncalled-for risk. A slight slip in such realness is sometimes enough to ruin the whole atmosphere of a play. The disillusionment may nag at the audience's mind, quite irrationally perhaps, but sufficiently to spoil the entire play. On the other hand, if meticulous visual reality is discarded from the outset by the sheer unreal sparseness of costume and scenery, by the obvious abandonment of visual historicity or literal detail, or by the use of extravagantly unreal costumes and make-up,[2] the audience does not search for literal visual reality, and its attention is freer to concentrate on other dramatically more important realities, those of the ideas and emotions conveyed by the words, actions and music of the play. One of the reasons why puppetry can often be exciting is that, by its very nature, it is free from many of the demands of literal visual reality.

The paucity of surviving information about the Chinese stage and theatres of the Sông, Jin, Yuan and Ming partly no doubt stems from the fact that the people who wrote records paid little attention to such things, either through indifference, or more probably through an over-familiarity that blinded them to the fascinations of the physical media of drama. The relative insolidity of Chinese architecture is another hindrance to research in this direction, and no builders' legal contracts have survived such as are available for studies of Elizabethan and Jacobean theatres.[3] Much more may still remain to be gleaned, however, and for the Qing dynasty there is a fair body of information, including many more surviving stages and theatres than for the earlier periods.

The matshed theatres and stages have always been by far the most numerous, the nature of the traditional drama and various objective economic and social conditions of performance making this necessarily so. The great bulk of the Chinese population has always lived in the countryside, often in not easily accessible villages. Thus the opportunities have been greatest for mobile troupes of actors that could wander at will, set up their stages rapidly, and move flexibly in quest of their livelihood, by small boat, by cart or on foot. Government oppression and the dangers of being arrested must also have encouraged easy mobility. Business used until recent decades to be particularly good at fairs and festivals. Very often it would be wealthier local people who would sponsor the plays, but at other times they were financed by collections of money or subscriptions levied door to door, and access to the watching area was usually open at the festival and fair plays. There were also matshed theatres where admission was charged, as observed by Archdeacon Gray in 1878:

> There are societies or companies [. . .] who hire actors and give theatrical representations both to amuse the masses and to make money. Each society must include one or two persons who have taken literary degrees, and each is held responsible for the peace and good order of the spectators. Stage plays are generally acted in large tents, as among the ancient Romans. These tents, made of bamboo frames covered with matting, are in the form of squares. Three sides of the square are occupied by rows of benches for the spectators. Behind these, immediately in front of the stage, there is a gallery for ladies. There are different classes of seats, and the prices of admission vary accordingly, some of the benches having a rest for the back, and others having none. As theatres are made of bamboo or matting, there is a great danger from the displays of firecrackers, which sometimes take place during a performance, as representations of thunder and lightning.[4]

Besides the grainyards and other wide-open spaces, dry beds of streams have also been favoured as sites for temporary stages and theatres. The intrepid plant-smuggler Robert Fortune bears witness to this in an account of a visit to a large town in the region of Huizhou in southern Anhui on 2 November 1848 during a harvest holiday:

> One of the rivers was nearly dry, and its bed was now used for the purpose of giving a grand fête. The bank where we were was probably about 150 or 200 feet above the bed of the river, so that we had a capital view of what was going on below us.
>
> The first and most prominent object which caught my eye was a fine seven-storied pagoda, forty or fifty feet high, standing on the dry bed of the river; near to it was a summer-house upon a small scale, gaudily got up, and supposed to be in a beautiful garden. Artificial figures of men and women appeared sitting in the verandahs and balconies, dressed in the richest costumes. Singing birds, such as the favourite wame and canaries, were whistling about the windows. Artificial lakes were formed in the bed of the river, and the favoured Nelumbium appeared floating on the water. Everything denoted that the place belonged to a person of high rank and wealth.
>
> At some little distance a theatre was erected, in front of which stood several thousands of the natives [. . .][5]

The same writer, in an account of 1857, describes the festive goodwill at a town in Chekiang, where 'people seemed delighted to see a foreigner among them, and were all perfectly civil and kind', and the whole scene reminded him of a fair in a county-town in England. He continues:

> In the afternoon the play began, and attracted its thousands of happy spectators. As already stated, the subscribers, or those who gave the play, had a raised platform, placed about twenty yards from the front of the stage, and to them the whole was free as their mountain-air – each man, however poor, had as good right to be there as his neighbour. And it is the same all over China – the actors are paid by the rich, and the poor are not excluded from participating in the enjoyments of the stage.
>
> The Chinese have a curious fancy for erecting these temporary theatres on the dry beds of streams. In travelling through the country I have frequently seen them in such places [. . .]
>
> I was content to take my place in the 'pit', [. . .] but the parties who had given the play were too polite to permit me to remain among the crowd. One of them – a respectable-looking man, dressed very gaily – came down and invited me to accompany him to the boxes. He led me up a narrow staircase and into a little room in which I found several of his friends amusing themselves by smoking, sipping tea, and eating seeds and fruits of various kinds. All made way for the stranger, and endeavoured to place me in the best position for getting a view of the stage. What a mass of human beings were below me! The place seemed full of heads, and one might suppose that the bodies were below, but it was impossible to see them, so densely were they packed together. Had it not been for the stage in the background with its actors dressed in the gay-coloured costumes of a former age, and the rude and noisy band, it would have reminded me more of the hustings at a contested election in England than anything else.[6]

Temple stages too, in existence since the Sông and Jin at least, have played a big part in the history of Chinese drama, as may be seen from the legal documents

concerning various prohibitions. They are of two kinds, temporary and permanent. A Japanese writer described his impressions of one example of the former
which he saw in 1795:

About 120 yards from the port [Zhapu, near Haiyan in Chekiang province] there was a
theatre in the northern monastery. The monastery was enclosed with awnings, with a
wooden palisade round the outside, in which there was a little gate. Inside the theatre
area there were set up fairly high watching-platforms on three sides, with the stage
erected against the main temple hall and the tiring house to the side of the main hall.
Performances were held in the monastery every thirty days. When we went to this
theatre, there would be a watching-platform about eighteen feet long on the southern
side and we would be invited to sit on a bench about one foot broad and twelve feet long,
fitted with high legs. All manner of dainties, sweetmeats, dough-breads, fritters and
candies and so on were, moreover, laid out on the dais to keep us supplied for the whole
day's recreation.[7]

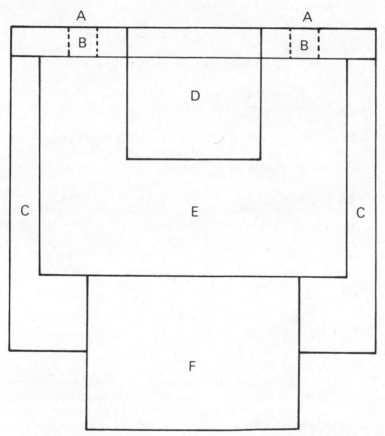

Plan of stage and surroundings in a City God Temple of Ningpo
A – gate; B – passage; C – storeyed building; D – stage; E – central courtyard; F – main
temple

Another Japanese recorded a similar impression of a temple stage in Kwangtung province in 1816.[8] In addition to the temporary stages, there have also been stages which were a fixed part of the temple buildings. It is difficult to ascertain how widespread these were before the Qing dynasty, and even such a big city and such a centre of drama as Yangzhou seems not to have acquired such fixed temple stages as the huge one of the Chongning Monastery till the eighteenth century. The two City God Temples in Ningpo also acquired massive fixed stages at about this time, one of them about nine feet off the ground and much more imposing in its proportions than those of the big Peking theatres of the Qing, with a building on either side of the stage serving as boxes for spectators. Certainly the permanent temple stages were a very common sight in Qing China and were sometimes very grand and colourful places, as Mrs Gordon Cummings confirms in her book published in 1888:

> I have been very much amused today by a great 'Sing-Song' at the Ningpo Joss-house, or, I should rather say, the great guild of the Ningpo merchants in Foo-Chow [i.e. Fuzhou], for the place is really their club; and in China, a temple, with its attendant theatre, forms a necessary feature in every well-regulated club [. . .] It is a strange sight to look down upon that densely packed yet ever-restless throng, almost all dressed in blue [. . .] The stage is always a separate building facing the temple – a sort of kiosque, open on three sides – its beautifully carved, curly roof being supported on carved pillars. The court is enclosed by open corridors with galleries, in which seats are provided for the mandarins and principal citizens.
>
> In the lower corridors many barbers ply their trade diligently, for skull-scraping and hair-plaiting is a business which must not be neglected, and which can be successfully combined with the enjoyment of the play. Vendors of refreshments find a good market for their wares [. . .]
>
> The kindly priests put us into a good place just in front of the great altar, whence of course we had a perfect view, and a stranger scene I never beheld – the temple, the theatre, and the side-courts one mass of richest carving in wood and stone, crimson and gold, with the grey, curiously carved roofs harmonising with the brilliant blue sky. The pillars supporting both the theatre and temple are powerfully sculpted stone dragons.
>
> The vivid sunlight gave intensity to the dark shadows, and brilliancy to the gorgeous dresses of the actors.[9]

The activities of the temple theatres have continued in the twentieth century. A well-known writer on the Chinese theatre describes a childhood visit to a temple early this century:

> When I was a child and went to my aunt's house at [. . .], I would always have to pass the Lord Guan Temple, and opposite the image of Lord Guan was the stage. The stage was rectangular in shape, with a pillar at all four corners, the southern side of it connecting with the backstage. The buildings on either side of the stage were the boxes from which the womenfolk watched the plays. Each and every one of them had to take their own stool along, and they would all squeeze together at the windows to try and watch the plays, only able to see them sideways. In front of the stage was the throng of male

spectators, but apart from Lord Guan himself none had any seat to sit on. And although to be sure there were stone steps in front of the door to the god's throne-room, they were all tiers for standing audience only and afforded us no opportunity whatsoever for watching in seated position.[10]

The same writer mentions that for most of his life he had never seen a performance on a red carpet, until once he saw one in Harbin, so this kind of performance, so intimately associated with Kunqu, may well have faded by the twentieth century or have become much rarer as Kunqu declined.

As has been mentioned in previous chapters, there were already in the Sông dynasty large theatres of a permanent or enduring kind, and subsequent dynasties also had their permanent or semi-permanent theatres, but it is not until the Qing dynasty that explicit and abundant information on the city theatres is available, in the form both of writings and of actual theatres. Some of the theatres, even some from the early Qing, have survived until very recently, and some still survive. The extensive use of wood in Chinese architecture has no doubt been a major factor in the paucity of architectural remains of many early theatres.

In the Qing dynasty there were broadly speaking two main kinds of fixed public theatre: the *xiyuan*, 'play garden', and the *xizhuang*, 'play establishment' or 'play emporium'. The latter were named such-and-such *tang*, 'hall', or such-and-such *huiguan*, 'meeting chamber', and were generally for selected groups of élite and wealthy customers, who held celebratory and other banquets there that were accompanied by plays (usually performed by the major troupes only), dancing, singing and music. The *xiyuan* were named such-and-such *yuan*, 'garden', such-and-such *lou*, 'storeyed building', 'tower' or 'bower', or such-and-such *xuan*, 'pavilion', and were also referred to as *xilou*, 'play bower', *chayuan*, 'tea garden', and *chalou*, 'tea bower'.[11] These were the main popular theatres, where tea was served but no wine or big meals, a place for casual tea parties and chats over tea, where the actors would mount the stage before large motley crowds, performing amid gongs, drums and thunderous clamour, and evoking applause that frequently sounded like 'the competing squawks of ten thousand crows'.[12] Various cities and towns, north and south, had such popular theatres; there were over twenty of them in Peking alone in the middle and later years of the dynasty. The major troupes would tend to monopolise the bigger theatres, and the lesser troupes to stick to the smaller, less savoury theatres, but the divisions were not rigid. Troupes would move round the various theatres. They would begin with morning performances and continue through the day, stopping – when they adhered to the laws – at dusk. Let us take a look at the lay-out of these theatres, making generalisations which must omit the many exceptions and variations.

Soaring up at either side of the door of the theatre were two big wooden pillars, painted black. Between them hung a big wooden signboard with the words 'such-and-such *chayuan*', or some like statement. The plays were announced by a poster stuck up at the door and in the markets and thoroughfares. This poster, known as the *baotiao*, 'announcement strip', was made of red paper, and on it, in big characters, was written that on a certain day at a certain date a certain troupe would be performing. It recalls the gaudy poster that caught the eyes of Du Renjie's gallivanting farmer in the early thirteenth century.

Inside there was the auditorium and, directly facing the main entrance at the far end, the stage, known as *qiantai*, 'front platform', *xitai*, 'play platform', or *wutai*, 'dancing platform'. The auditorium consisted of the main central space in front of the stage, called the *chizi*, 'pond', or *chixin*, 'pond heart', the spaces to either side of the stage, known as *xiao chizi*, 'little ponds', or *diaoyutai*, 'angling platforms', and the two-level accommodation round the sides, the second-floor accommodation consisting of verandahs accessible by stairs from the main entrance of the theatre. Upstairs on the verandahs to the right and left sides of the auditorium were the *guanzuo*, 'officials' seats', later popularly called *baoxiang*, 'enclosing or hired side-rooms', which consisted of three or four rooms, later as many as fourteen or fifteen, formed by screens or board partitions and situated at the end nearest to the stage. These were used as loges or boxes for the officials and wealthy people, and later on for women, when women were allowed into the theatres. The 'stage exit *guanzuo*' to the left-hand side of the performing actors were often the most sought after, for reasons summarised in the saying, 'fighting to sit at the stage exit', which was a euphemism for having or seeking immoral or intimate relations with the *dan* actors. The second of these left-hand side *guanzuo* was particularly prized by many, since it was located conveniently for ogling messages of love to the actors as they lifted the curtain to leave the stage. An early nineteenth-century poem contains the lines, 'Dazzling glances fly up to the gallery,/Fixing a rendez-vous for supper tonight'.[13] Each of these boxes could hold eleven or twelve people or in some cases fourteen or fifteen. At the front was a row of benches, for the tea things or for sitting on, behind which were high benches provided with blue cloth, cotton-waste-padded cushions upon which one could sit with greater comfort than down in the *chizi*. Further behind was accommodation for accompanying footmen. On the same side as the verandahs, beyond the *guanzuo*, were set out more benches called *zhuozi*, 'tables', in orderly fashion, 'like the scales of a fish', the prices for these diminishing the further they were from the stage.

The short verandahs at the back on either side of the stage were known as *daoguanzuo*, 'recessed officials' seats'. From there one could see little more than the actors' backs, and it was generally people like the actors' relatives who occupied such seats. The upstairs verandah facing the stage, the *zhenglou*, 'main upstairs', held no seats in the early days. Exactly why is not clear, but a possible reason is that it was kept free in case of the sudden appearance of an important dignitary to watch the play. Emperor Xuanzong once went in disguise to watch a play in a theatre called Yueminglou, 'Moonlight Bower', this event subsequently serving as the material for stories, plays, pictures, and the 'tales of women and little children'. Emperor Shengzu also visited the same theatre, and when he visited the Guanghelou, 'Wide Harmony Bower', theatre in disguise was apparently led to the *zhenglou*. In later times boxes were installed in the *zhenglou*, too.

Early nineteenth-century writers tell us that the *chizi* was provided with tables and benches, too, and that the audience was all made up of low market traders and brokers, servants and menials, grooms and lackeys.[14] The arrangement of these theatres was remarkably similar to that of the Globe and other early British theatres. Like the Globe, the central space of the auditorium may at one time have been unroofed and unprotected from the elements, which among other factors would naturally make it the area for the poorer spectators. The arrangement was anyway similar to that round the temple stages and other open-air stages, where the central space in front of the stage would be occupied by the ordinary people and would be the least likely area to have any covering. The same very often applied to innyard play-acting in mediaeval Europe.

Round the edges of the *chizi* and under the verandah were the *sanzuo*, 'non-official seats', where people sat shoulder to shoulder on long benches. Behind them were higher benches, the cheapest seats, where by sitting in a somewhat uncomfortable position one could manage a view of the stage. In later ages these were called *daqiang*, 'big wall', and were made of brick. You had to jump or clamber up onto them. The two *diaoyutai* each had a different prestige. The inveterate theatre fans valued them highly for their proximity to the stage, and in noisy conditions that was sometimes a vital consideration, but again the left-hand side near the stage exit was the preferred one, since the other side was right next to the gongs, music and loud noises that heralded the actors' entrances.[15] The two sides under the verandahs came to be referred to as the *lianglang*, 'two porticos'.

The audience paid *zuoerqian*, 'seat money', or bought a *chapiao*, 'tea ticket'. The *guanzuo* were by far the most expensive seats, and the *sanzuo* the cheapest. The *sanzuo* of the early nineteenth century at one time cost a hundred copper cash, or 192 for performances by the Anhwei Troupes, while a *chapiao* for a *guanzuo* seat cost seven times as much. A whole *guanzuo* box would in fact be hired en bloc. In many theatres, at least in later times, the payment was strictly speaking for the tea and not for the seat. Where there were tables in the *chizi*, they would have a bench on either side and be aligned not facing the stage but sideways on to it, so that the audiences were facing the *lianglang*. Oil lamps were used to light the theatre, which was often very hot and stuffy.[16]

The stage itself would be about three or four feet off the ground, roughly square with seventeen to twenty foot sides, with round black-lacquered pillars rearing up at the two front corners. Between them, about ten feet above the stage, stretched one or two horizontal bars, known as *zhougun*, 'axletree bars', which were used to assist in the fighting and acrobatics of the warrior plays. A low railing, one to two feet high, fenced the three open sides of the stage, just as in the Globe Playhouse.[17] The stage was roofed over with a very substantial, and sometimes elaborately architectured, roof. The actors' entry was on their right, and the exit to their left, both being doorways at the side of the rear partition and hung with curtains. The space in between was also hung with a big curtain, sometimes crimson and embroidered. The backstage, called *houtai* or *xifang*, was contiguous with the stage but oblong, being perhaps sixty to seventy feet in width, and about twenty feet in depth. The part immediately behind the stage was raised over two feet for more than six feet back, and this was where the actors awaited their cues. The rest of the backstage was on ground level, sometimes tiled, and usually had no upper storey.

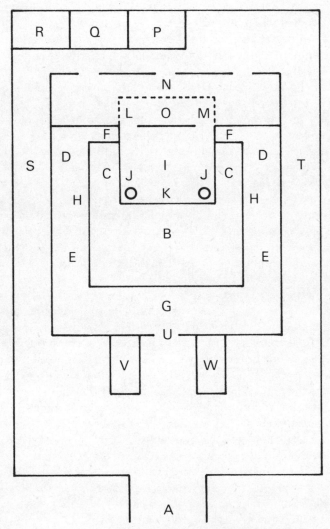

Plan of a Qing theatre

A – theatre door; B – *chizi*; C – *diaoyutai*; D – *guanzuo* (officials' seats upstairs); E – benches (upstairs); F – *daoguanzuo* (recessed officials' seats); G – *zhenglou* (upstairs); H — *sanzuo* (downstairs); I – stage; J – front pillars; K – *zhougun*; L – actors' entrance; M – actors' exit; N – backstage; O – waiting area; P – poster-writing room; Q – clothes and properties room; R – tea-rooms; S – passage; T – passage for actors, etc.; U – entrance to auditorium; V – counting-house; W – ticket-room

A number of very old theatres have survived into modern times, most illustrious of them being the Guanghelou,[18] dating from the early Qing (the late seventeenth or early eighteenth century). Their seating arrangements and other aspects have undergone radical alterations in later ages, but they have continued to operate alongside some bigger modern theatres.

The status of literary playwrights was probably lower in the nineteenth century than in previous centuries. Both in the quality of their work and in their public reputation, the playwrights of the period whom we know by name failed on the whole to match their predecessors. There are a number of reasons that may hesitantly be suggested for this state of affairs. Gaozong's literary inquisition had lasting inhibitory effects, and these were especially strong among the scholars. The widespread nurturing of analytical and compilatory scholastic pursuits, and the moral and penal crusades against various aspects of creative literary expression, must inevitably have reduced the available stock of lively genius among the literati, and intimidated most of them. The sheer brilliance of earlier playwrights and the abundance of great plays already in existence must also have been more than ever daunting to many, and must have readily encouraged wooden and pedantic imitations, as long as drama continued along largely traditional lines with regard to subject-matter and, with a few exceptions, did not in any great measure respond to the violently changing political and national conditions.

As important or more important than these matters, perhaps, although here cause and effect are far from entirely separable, were the fading of Kunqu, the rise of Pihuang and other 'vulgar' forms of drama, and the ever-increasing dominance of the actors, particularly in the metropolitan theatre world. Lacking the orthodox status of Kunqu, the more direct, colloquial and often truly more vulgar kinds of drama no doubt seemed to hold out less promise of contemporary literary reputation, and this may well have stopped many from writing these kinds of play, and stopped many others from attaching their names to their plays. On the other hand, with such well established theatrical traditions, such an abundance of well loved plays and stories, and such high quality players, conditions were very favourable to the actor-editor and the actor-playwright, and also favourable for the acting profession to take a strong hand or even the upper hand in any cooperation with scholarly writers. There was at various times a vogue for 'new' plays, but this did not lead to the emergence of any epoch-making literary playwrights of fame and name. In Peking Opera it was a very common thing for actors to adapt and devise their own plays. Not until the last decade or two of the Qing dynasty, when the dynasty was crumbling and China was faced with the unavoidable need to make rapid adjustments to Western notions and to intensified aggression from other nations, did the scholar-playwrights begin to come into their own once more. Nonetheless, there were during the nineteenth century a number of nameable playwrights of no mean achievements, of whom we may mention a few.

Shu Wei (1765–1816) belongs as much to the eighteenth century as to the nineteenth.[19] Born in Suzhou, in 1782 he went to Peking, his ancestral home, where he studied in his grandfather's huge library. In 1788 he passed the exams for the licentiate or second degree, but failed in nine attempts to obtain a doctorate. Occupying various government posts, he travelled widely in China. In 1797 he went to Kweichow province. A rising by the Miao people took place there, and, as adviser to the Manchu general dealing with it, he wrote a document urging the Miao to cease their rebellion. Some Miao could read Chinese and, 'moved to tears by his noble and persuasive words', the rebels disbanded. In 1809, when he was back in Peking, a friend introduced him to an imperial prince, Zhaolian (1780–1833). Shu wrote a number of plays, and the prince eagerly handed them to his private troupe to perform, paying a thousand taels to Shu and the friend who is said either to have helped compose, or to have composed, the music for the plays.[20] In fact Shu himself was a highly accomplished musician, master of the *di*-flute, drums, and *qin*-dulcimer, and such a fine song-composer that actors and musicians were able to perform straight from his drafts without any further rearrangements or annotation. He wrote six plays of the *zaju* kind, all based on ancient and often-used themes. He excelled in his wording rather than in his plots, but some of his plays were performed for a long while. In 1815, when his mother died, he was so grief-stricken that he abstained from food, and died himself seventy-three days later. Shu was a fine painter and calligrapher. Among his closest friends was the dramatist Jiang Shiquan.

Liang Tingnan (1796–1861) from Kwangtung province wrote four plays published in the 1820s, and a work on drama first printed in 1825.[21] Epigrapher, historian, expert on coastal defence and foreign diplomacy and biographer of the poet Su Shi, he also wrote works on foreign countries, Britain among them, and on the unsuitability of Christianity for the Chinese. Zhou Leqing (fl. 1829–52) from Chekiang province wrote his eight plays while on a journey northwards to Peking in 1829. All eight were on ancient themes of tragedy and grief, which he deliberately turned into comedies or plays with happy endings, sacrificing 'nobility in the face of sorrow' for a somewhat contrived and weak happy-ever-after treatment not easily or naturally suited to the themes. His friend Yan Tingzhong (fl. 1839–52), a rare instance of a known playwright from Yunnan province, also wrote three plays. These must have been very much a medium for a literary man's self-expression, for in his 1852 preface to them he remarked, 'If there is no one who will enjoy my music, I shall sing it for the cicadas and ancient trees to hear.' Huang Xieqing (d. c. 1862) from Haiyan in Chekiang province, on the other hand, was a more popular playwright. Unable, through illness, to take up an official post, he built himself garden retreats, where he spent his time cultivating flowers and bamboos, writing for his own pleasure and drinking and composing poetry with friends, until 1861 when the Taiping Rebellion forced him to flee. He wrote seven plays, mostly during the years 1830–47, but in his old age repented of it and destroyed the blocks. His son-in-law, however, later reprinted them. Some of them were on ancient themes, but others used material from the

Ming and Qing.

Many Chinese regard the novel *Red chamber dream* by Cao Zhan (d. 1763) as the greatest of Chinese novels. It inspired many adaptations and imitations in various kinds of literature and entertainment.[22] Playwrights wrote dramas on its themes, including three by Kiangsu dramatists around the first decade or two of the nineteenth century. Earliest and most successful of these was the one by an author known as Hongdou Cunqiao, a name meaning 'Love-seed Village Woodcutter'.

In the latter part of the nineteenth century notable playwrights of 'refined' plays were still fewer. Chen Lang (fl. 1885), a salt official, wrote eleven plays, but in general this was particularly the era of the actor-playwrights, the anonymous dramatists and Pihuang drama. From the late Ming onwards, Yiyang-*qiang* and related forms of music were able to utilise Kunqu texts to a large extent, but the other kinds of drama also frequently had their own plays written for them, often coming from the hand of actors, and often no doubt being so rough and ready or so crudely bawdy that it was not thought fit to print them. The general literary prejudice against them, whether justified or not, must have discouraged their printing. It was probably rare that a man of high orthodox literary standing spoke up in writing for the non-Kunqu plays. Jiao Xun (1763–1820), philosopher, mathematician, astronomer, expert on architecture and author of a book on drama and music, was one of the few to do so:

> The theatre world all esteems Kunqu, while the other forms of music have vulgar and yokelish lyrics and are collectively called Luantan, 'irregular playing'. But that is what I am fond of, all the same. Kunshan-*qiang* music is complex and, although its lyrics are harmonised to the utmost with the musical requirements, if the listener has not looked at the original text beforehand, he is bound always to be somewhat in the dark and unaware of what the words mean. Apart from the fifteen or so plays like *Lute, Killing a dog* [. . .] and so forth, they are mostly indecent sex, and such plays as [. . .] are just not worth watching. The other kinds of drama [lit. 'music'] are originally based on Yuan drama, and their stories concern loyalty, filiality and honour, and can have a strong effect on one's emotions. Their language is simple and straightforward, so that even women and little boys can understand it. Their music is spirited and stirring. For a long time they have been performed one after the other in the villages outside the city in the second and eighth months, old farmers and fishermen gathering together to enjoy them. But after Wei Changsheng from Szechwan sang his lewd, bawling, smutty-humoured songs, and such as [. . .] and [. . .] started imitating him in the towns, it infected the villages, and only in recent years have things been gradually reverting to what they were in the old days.[23]

Jiao Xun seems primarily to be supporting the virtues of rustic drama. For whatever reasons, very few plays of the various 'vulgar' kinds of music were printed during the eighteenth and early nineteenth centuries when Kunqu drama was still generally dominant. What survives is sufficient to justify some of Jiao Xun's claims for the liveliness of such drama. A number of these were taken up, and altered, by Peking Opera. Jing-*qiang* and other kinds of music were represented among the printed plays.

Many more non-Kunqu printed plays survive from the middle and latter parts of the nineteenth century. In 1840 an eighty-act Erhuang play by a certain Guan-ju Daoren, 'Play-watching Taoist', appeared in print. In 1862 Yu Zhi (1809–74) printed a collection of forty short Pihuang plays which he had written. Yu Zhi, a leading scourge of the evils attendant upon drama, was passionately fond of the Pihuang style of drama, and went into action against wickedness by touring the country with his own troupe and performing edifying plays with a view to encouraging people to adopt virtuous ways. His choice of themes in his plays reflected this mission. In that same year, 1860, a certain Li Shizhong published a collection of forty-six Pihuang plays, recently written but with no authorship specified. Towards the end of the century there were a number of playwrights for Peking Opera whose names have survived. Mostly they wrote only one or two plays of no great impact. A twentieth-century collection of Pihuang and Qin-*qiang* plays contained about five hundred plays, many of which must have come from the nineteenth century, and a few of them from even earlier. Hundreds more had been written and rediscovered by the 1920s, when three or four hundred of such plays were performed, over a hundred of them very often. Mostly they were single-act or very short plays, many deriving from Kunqu plays. It is not necessary, however, to assume that, because in many cases no full long play is now known from which such single acts could have been taken, hundreds of full-length plays have disappeared. Short plays were adapted beyond recognition from fuller plays, and were also created as original dramas from novels and other non-dramatic sources. Nonetheless, a few full plays for other kinds of play than Kunqu do survive from the nineteenth to the early twentieth centuries, but generally without any clear indication of authorship or date of writing.

In the years 1894–5 China's lowered national morale was further deeply shaken by defeat in the Sino-Japanese War, and movements within China for political reform and for revolution became stronger and more coordinated. In 1900 the Boxer Rebellion and foreign invasion intensified national humiliation. Drama and other forms of literature entered into a markedly new phase which in many ways reflected these political changes.

8   Stage-play during the early nineteenth century (engraving)

9   Water-side theatre, Tientsin (early nineteenth-century engraving)

10   Matshed theatre (late nineteenth-century drawing)

11   Temple theatre at the guild of Ningpo merchants, Fuzhou, Fukien province
(drawing by Mrs Gordon Cummings, 1888)

12
Street theatricals with rough stage,
late nineteenth century
(photograph)

13
Temple stage at Ningpo
(photograph)

14
Chinese students at St John's
University, Shanghai, dressed for
a performance of *The Merchant
of Venice*, c. 1902

15 Characters from *Fifteen strings of cash* (1956 edition); *see text, p. 238*

16 Informal singing of *geming xiandai jingju* (from a book cover, Peking, 1972)

10

The Appearance of Western-style Drama

Developments in twentieth-century Chinese drama have often closely reflected, and strongly influenced, national political and intellectual events and trends. Drama itself has undergone some immense changes, chiefly in the matter of the introduction on a large scale of spoken drama in the European style, and more latterly, in mainland China, of a wholesale rejection of the traditional themes of Chinese drama. At the same time, Peking Opera, while undergoing vicissitudes and suffering at times from a strong moral disrepute, has maintained a dominance over traditional kinds of drama, even extending its dominance, and has remained a major force in Chinese theatre. Both the spoken drama and Peking Opera have exercised an influence on the numerous regional and local kinds of drama, some of which themselves have become more and more part of the national theatre.

Defeat in the Sino-Japanese War in 1895 shook the Chinese all the more in that it was at the hands of an Oriental nation long associated with China in a traditionally subordinate role, who by her victories in battle strikingly demonstrated her success in adopting the weapons of Western science, technology and ideas. Among other things, it became abundantly clear to those Chinese prepared to face the facts that to defend herself China must, as Japan had already to a large extent done, appropriate large quantities of Western knowledge, and adjust her own political system to the needs of self-defence and national strength. For the purpose of promoting such a national reawakening, Kunqu, Peking Opera and various other dramatic and ballad forms were used among propaganda media.[1] A number of such propaganda plays appeared, especially after the Boxer Uprising and the occupation by foreign troops, and as foreign territorial rapacity rapidly intensified. Most of the early ones were in traditional *zaju* and *chuanqi* form,[2] but some of these took Western topics and occasional other Western features. Wang Xiaonong wrote a number of plays with a fresh note of patriotism and reform, including one written in 1904 which dramatised the events of a war between Poland and Turkey.[3]

Liang Qichao's *New Rome* is another example of the way in which playwrights attempted to wed the old with the new.[4] A principal disciple of Kang Yuwei (1858–1927), the leader of the reformists, Liang intended this drama as a Kunqu *chuanqi* in forty acts with a prologue. Seeing parallels between the plight of China and that of nineteenth-century Italy, he recommended solutions similar to those of the Risorgimento, of which his play was to be a sinicised dramatisation. The action was to last from the Congress of Vienna in 1814 to the entry into Rome of 1870, but he only published the prologue and the first six acts. The prologue is sung by Dante, as a bearded Taoist immortal with a crane for his steed. Shakespeare and Voltaire appear at the end of the prologue, riding on a cloud. The six acts go as far as Mazzini's founding of the Young Italy society. Metternich, the villain of the piece, is in the mould of Cao Cao, of the Three Kingdoms period, China's arch-villain of all ages, while Garibaldi is cast as a kind of Guan Yu. Mazzini, Cavour and Metternich quote Confucius, Mencius and ancient Chinese poets, not works from their own Italian or Austrian cultures, and the drama as it survives shows a marked imprint of Kong Shangren's *Peach blossom fan.*

The prologue of this play will serve as a brief illustration of the attempt to wed Western themes to traditional Chinese forms of drama, its significance being as a form of writing rather than living theatre. The prologue is particularly reminiscent of *Peach blossom fan,* and when we recall how powerfully and intimately that play was connected with only slightly earlier political events, it is not at all surprising that Liang Qichao should have been inspired by it for his own play which he intended to have a similar political urgency. The use of Dante, a *fumo* role, is particularly apt, since he was a literary figure and thus more likely to appeal to the Chinese literati, and since Dante was indeed an active politician whose literary works contributed considerably to an Italian sense of national unity. Perhaps, also, this brief excerpt may show something of the strong potential of this 'mongrel' form of drama, which, although seemingly doomed by history, was very capable of presenting universal ideas in a complex and forceful manner.[5]

New Rome by Liang Qichao: Wedge Act*

(*Enter Dante, dressed as an aged Taoist immortal.*)

DANTE. (*Sings*) Upon my far-winging crane I once again
                  after one thousand years have wended here,
                  and as splendidly made as some gorgeous brocade
                  this land's cities, dwellings and populace appear.
                  And simply because it is so, with tossing beard I laugh delighted,
                  for age-old lingering regrets are in these days requited.
                  Minutely to relate history's vicissitudes, in soliloquy I now shall
                      stand . . .
                  ah, how many heads and skulls were bartered for this proud
                      imposing land!

---

*Possibly Liang calls this a 'Wedge Act' to give an extra air of antiquity to the play.

> Spread the ground with gold, let song and dance commence,
> to celebrate the storm and stress of recent past events.
>
> (*Says*) The millennium of tears of a long-ruined nation
> yields to one single song of great peace and jubilation.
> Yes, the fewer heroes of letters arise
> the more there flourishes tribulation!

I am the soul of Dante, an Italian poet. I was born into life in a nation of renown, and, when still a youth, was a prodigy of genius. I always longed to be a statesman and set the world aright, and had some generalised ideal of freedom. But, alas, since the Roman Empire fell to pieces, all the powerful rebel nations have carved up its territory, chopped it up like chopping beans, sliced it up between them like slicing a melon. All the famous metropolises – Venice, Genoa, Milan, Florence and Pisa – mighty cities that blaze forth in history, they all became mere nostalgic memories of their former glory. The Ostrogoths, the Arabs, Spain, France and Austria preyed on us like wolves and tigers, invading and encroaching upon us one after the other with their greedy eyes and voracious appetites.

I was born several hundred years ago, and I was full of hot-blooded indignation at such things, and, like the captives of Chu who wept with one another in helpless desperation, I was moved to bitter sobs and fierce sighs.* Bearing in mind that the fundamental requirement in establishing a nation is to rouse the spirit of its people, I wrote a few novels and plays, complementing these with numerous poems and songs, which I hoped might catch on in the streets and markets of the popular quarters, and, if women and children came to know them, might serve in the future gradually to stir the spirit of the people and perhaps enable the national shame to be erased. I raise my thanks to Heaven on High for its blessings and loving concern, that in later ages men did arise, that the Three Mighty Men sprang forth together, and that One King suddenly towered over the land.

(*Laughs*) Ha, ha! And today my Italy has become once more as of old a powerful, completely sovereign, first-rank European state. See its one hundred and ten thousand square *li* of territory, and its united nation populated by thirty million brethren, with a government and parliament of its own. How magnificent and awe-inspiring! It has over five hundred thousand highly trained troops and over two hundred stout and incisive warships, which it can use for the waging of war and the maintenance of peace. A handsome sight indeed! And all this has been won by my compatriots and fellow citizens through a thousand hardships and ten thousand sufferings, in exchange for the blood of their tears, the blood of their hearts, and the blood of their necks.

As I wander at lofty leisure around the celestial realms above, I look down below to the dust-bound mortal universe, and, observing such things come to pass, I have wept with the utmost emotion. For all the foul unvented indignation that filled my belly during my lifetime may now be deemed well and truly dispelled. Today, having idle time upon my hands and nothing special to do, I am going to take a trip to China in the Orient, for a little recreation.

VOICE BACKSTAGE.   China is just a sick Oriental nation. Why do you want to go there, mighty immortal?

DANTE.   You are not cognisant of all the facts. I have heard that in China there is a

---

*In the *Zuo-zhuan* of the Zhou dynasty there is an account of how Chu captives wept thus when stirred by the sight of fine days and festivals that reminded them of home.

young man called Master of the Ice-drinking Studio* or some such name, who has written a play entitled *New Rome*, which is now being performed in the patriotic theatres of Shanghai. And that play treats of no less a matter than the founding of our Italy, describing the events stage by stage in a painting of sound and imagery that moves one to tears and to song. Every word of its forty acts of lyrics and dialogue is a jewel or pearl of literary lustre, and every syllable of its treatment of these past fifty years of political failures and successes is good medicine† for human behaviour. And I thought I would take along with me two friends of mine, such friends as between us the gaps in age are forgotten and create no awkward feeling whatsoever, one being Shakespeare from Britain, and the other being Voltaire from France, so that we might together watch and listen to the play.

VOICE BACKSTAGE.   Why did this young man suddenly compose such a drama out of the blue?

DANTE.   How can one remain indifferent to things! Every scholar gentleman has his ideals in life. The Jingwei Pheasant tries to fill the ocean‡ and the Foot Quail mocks it for its overweening folly.§ The nightjar cries from its bough, and the traveller passing by spills tears as he hears it.¶ I imagine that this young man, having drifted aimlessly in strange and foreign lands, came to turn his glance upon his old homeland, and felt a burning grief for his country, which grief, since he lacked any practical means of restoring the country's might and prestige, he sought, through the trifling skills of the writer, to express in subtle and weighty words that would serve as a stimulus, a bell to call others forward. He is merely someone afflicted by the same 'malady' as I myself was of yore, a man of like mind and sympathies.

VOICE BACKSTAGE.   If that's the case then, why don't you, as an old Roman harbinger of enlightenment, and as a famous personality of history, give us a preview of the matters treated in his play, so that we can obtain some kind of a general outline of it?

DANTE.   Let me tell you then.

      (*Sings*) Thousand-year Rome by its bullying neighbours
              was carved up, rent, annexed, and sundered,
              by the despot hands of peerless Kings of Treachery
              to the Austrian minister Metternich rendered.
              But the spirit of nationalism and principles of liberty
              blazed all Europe with their fire,
              The cries sped, the wails spread fast,
              ah, how much blood streamed forth in that sole hour!
              Then there came one king of wisdom and valour,
              and three mighty prodigies with moon-splendid patriotic hearts,
              who now worked alliances, now played diplomacy,
              sometimes waged war, and sometimes plied the orator's arts.

*Liang Qichao's pen-name.
†Lit., 'medicine and acupuncture', i.e. sound corrective advice.
‡In ancient mythology the Jingwei Pheasant was a reincarnation of an emperor's daughter who was drowned in the Eastern Ocean, which was why it carried trees and rocks in its beak in an attempt to fill in the Eastern Ocean. The Jingwei was also called the Wronged Bird.
§The Foot Quail was so-called either because it was only a foot long, or, more reasonably, because it was only able to fly one foot. Probably Dante is here saying that when fine, great people embark upon mighty enterprises, the mean-minded petty people mock them, and consider their task impossible and a waste of effort.
¶The call of the nightjar was said to evoke sad longings for one's own land. Referring to Liang's journeys abroad, which rendered his love for his homeland more acute.

> Before revolution came about,
> the states all united, suddenly,
> and the shame borne by our Italy
> was thenceforth cancelled out.
> Boundless are the ups and downs of every nation,
> and heroes are needed when it's sink or salvation!

VOICE BACKSTAGE.   Yes, very interesting indeed. But we're not very well up in history, and can't quite grasp it all, so might we ask you, mighty immortal, just to summarise the gist of everything for us once more?

DANTE.   Very well then:

> Metternich wildly wields despotic power,
> Mazzini organises the Party of Youth;
> General Garibaldi thrice leads forth his citizen army,
> Cavour brings unity to the whole of Italy.

(*Points*) Look, there are Shakespeare and Voltaire softly floating along, riding their clouds, and coming to meet me as arranged. I must advance to welcome them, and join them, so that we may together go to enjoy the music of the play.

(*Exit, airily floating.*)

Other plays dealt with Cuba's rebellion against the Spanish, Poland's loss of national sovereignty, an Italian heroine, Queen Victoria, the Russian occupation of Heilongkiang, Chinese emigrants in the United States, Napoleon in captivity, Japanese heroes, Greek revolution, the Sino-Japanese War (with the Japanese as the heroes), and the loss of Annam to the French.[6] Some plays were bitter attacks on the Qing court and régime, one of them depicting the Empress Dowager Cixi Taihou in the *chou* clown role; others advocated or attacked the reformist movements, or recommended revolution. A theme of many plays was female emancipation. Many concerned heroines such as the revolutionary Qiu Jin, executed in 1907, who was the main subject of a number of dramas. Other plays condemned foot-binding, promoted women's rights and sang of female warriors. There were plays on the Boxer Uprising and Allied occupation, plays condemning Chinese traitors, and plays extolling all manner of patriotic heroes, recent and ancient, the latter including the military men and officials of various Chinese dynasties, who resisted the Jurcheds of the Jin, the Mongols of the Yuan and the Manchus who founded the Qing. There were other topics of vital interest to that period, among them that of opposition to opium.

Some of the reformist or revolutionary (*xinxi, xinju*) plays written in the first decade or so after 1895 used Western topics. Initially most were traditional forms of drama, but some were translations from Western or modern Western-style Japanese plays, and others were Chinese plays in Western style. These the Chinese now usually include under the general heading of *huaju*, 'speech drama', the term originally having been used as a translation for the English word 'drama'. The *huaju* came to replace the classical Chinese of traditional drama by a written form of Chinese as spoken. It was perhaps not that the Chinese dramatic tradition as a whole lacked the resources demanded by an age of acute political crisis, but rather that, besides the inherent strong points of *huaju* as a form, the state of the Chinese theatre and the nature of other historical conditions at that particular period favoured the introduction of *huaju*. The very foreignness and novelty of *huaju* drama were to its advantage in an era when certain kinds of foreignness and newness were being widely viewed as the best or only way to defend and renovate China. These and other factors, including various predominant structural features of the *huaju*, such perhaps as the baldness of ordinary speech as opposed to the intricacies of much of traditional song and poetry, recommended the *huaju* to many. As important a reason as any, no doubt, was that the Japanese, who had so forcefully shown what could be done in the way of military and political renovation, had for a long time previously been busy adopting Western ideas, skills and institutions, and had also adopted Western-style drama. Much of the impetus for the Chinese *huaju* movement came directly from Japan.[7]

As early as 1810 a Japanese adaptation of *Romeo and Juliet* was performed in Japan. In the last three or so decades of the nineteenth century numerous Western dramas were translated into Japanese, especially the works of Shakespeare but also some by Molière, Calderón, Schiller, and others. In the first ten years or so of the twentieth century many translations of modern European playwrights were added, among them works by Ibsen, Sudermann, Hauptmann, Chekhov and Pinero. Particularly after Japan's defeat of Russia in 1904, there was a vast amount of translation of modern Western dramas, writings about Western theatre and creation of Western-style plays.[8] Viewed from the contracting perspectives of today, this was not much earlier than such developments began to take place in China, but the movement undoubtedly had much deeper roots in Japan, and it was largely from there that the initiative and early inspiration came to China. The Chinese *huaju* movement was also reformist or revolutionary in many of its expressions and features, and Japan was in the early years of this century a haven and inspiration for many advocates of political and cultural change. A number of early Chinese performers of Western and spoken drama were fostered by Japanese institutions and actors.

In China itself, Shanghai was from the start a nursery for Western-style plays and experiments in drama. A number of colleges and societies there, including missionary colleges, made bold ventures in such directions from 1889.[9] But the most decisive event for Chinese *huaju* theatre occurrred in Japan. In 1907 in Tokyo some Chinese fine arts students organised a drama society called the Spring Willow Society.[10] Assisted by a Japanese actor Fujisawa Asajirō (1866–1917), they performed an act from *La Dame aux camélias* by Dumas *fils*. The cast was all male. Lin Shu (1852–1924) had translated the play as a novel in classical Chinese in 1899, and a translation of the play into Japanese had appeared as early as 1903.[11] The Spring Willow Society followed this up in the same year by a more truly public performance, this time of a full five-act play, *Black slave's cry to Heaven*, which was the students' adaptation from Lin Shu's translation (1901) of the novel *Uncle Tom's Cabin* by Harriet Beecher Stowe. It can probably be regarded as the first real creative Chinese *huaju*, since it radically altered the material from the novel to suit its own dramatic purposes.[12] Its note of protest against 'white' oppression struck responsive notes in many Oriental hearts, and both the Japanese who saw the play and the Chinese overseas students in Japan greeted the performance with warm enthusiasm. One of the actors was Ouyang Yuqian (1889–1963), who was to be a powerful force in Chinese drama in later years.

The Spring Willow Society performed a couple more one-act plays in the winter of 1907. A year later some of its members formed a branch drama-club called the Shenyou Society. They performed three one-act plays,[13] and then, in 1909, the four-act play *Hot blood*, adapted from a Japanese translation of *La Tosca* by the French playwright Vitorien Sardou. Another branch club called the Remarkable Life Society was formed around the same time.

Black slave's cry to Heaven was such a success in Japan that it inspired developments in China, principally in Shanghai. An amateur drama society performed the play there in the same year. In subsequent years many organisations were formed to promote the new drama movement and to perform its plays. In 1910, for instance, Ren Tianzhi and others organised its first professional troupe, the Evolution Troupe (collapsed in 1912), which presented many plays advocating revolution.[14]

The Revolution of 1911 led by Sun Yat-sen (Sun Wen, 1866–1925) managed with the consent of the military commander-in-chief Yuan Shikai (1859–1916) to overthrow the Qing dynasty, but with Yuan then dominating the scene as President of the Republic the majority of changes sought by the revolutionaries remained unaccomplished. The new drama entered upon a period of feverish activity for a few years, with many new troupes appearing, mostly ephemerally. In 1912 Lu Jingruo and others, some of whom had been members of the Spring Willow Society, formed a new drama company, which performed under the label Spring Willow Theatre and felt itself to be the main direct heir of the Spring Willow Society. During the three years or so of its existence it had a repertoire of some eighty-one plays. All but three or four were full plays with a number of acts. Twenty or thirty were based on ancient and modern Chinese tales, and eight or nine on translations of foreign novels, while eight or nine others were adaptations of foreign plays, and only three were straight translations. One was a completely original creation, and between ten and twenty were improvisations roughly sketched but never written out as full plays called *mubiaoxi*, 'act-outline plays'.[15] In 1912 a literary organisation named the Enlightenment Society was set up in Shanghai, from which the new plays of the early decades came to be known as *kaimingxi*, 'enlightened plays', or *wenming xinxi*, 'civilised new plays'. More generally the early plays of this kind are referred to by the term *wenmingxi*, 'civilised plays'.[16]

Japanese influence on *huaju* remained paramount for the first twenty years of this century. Japanese styles of acting and modern Japanese plays and stage production all left a strong mark on the early *huaju* movement. Even the European influences were often derived second-hand through Japanese translations. All this was clearly inadequate of itself to provide the movement with sufficient energy. Doubtless, moreover, increasingly predatory moves on the part of the Japanese towards China and growing tensions between the two nations served to a considerable extent to negate the power of Japanese theatrical influences and to lessen their appeal to many.

After a few years the new drama, still centred on Shanghai, underwent a lull.[17] The Spring Willow Theatre company collapsed in 1915 after the death of Lu Jingruo, and by about 1917, as the number of performances declined and other troupes disbanded, the new drama movement was becoming more and more feeble. Yet various historical events and circumstances were at that time about to grant it a new lease of life. The number of Chinese with direct experience of Europe and America and profound knowledge of European languages was rapidly increasing. Thousands of Chinese went to Europe during the First World War, and the number of students travelling to Europe and America was vastly greater than in the early years of the century. The impetus for literary and political change given by the May the Fourth Movement, which began in 1919 as a reaction to the terms of the Paris Peace Treaty, and the general movement towards colloquial, analytical, Western-modern literature also boded well for *huaju*.[18] The cinema increasingly provided competition but also helped to accustom the public to purely spoken and Western-style performances, and to create a taste for them.[19]

What the early performances of *huaju*, or *wenmingxi*, had achieved was not wasted. It was vital to the success of the *huaju* in the long run. The early performances had to some extent familiarised the Chinese with purely spoken plays, the extensive use of scenery, the occasional use of modern Western styles of clothing and other foreign and historically more precise kinds of costume, the division of a production into acts terminated by the closing of the curtain,[20] and various other features either absent from the traditional drama or not stressed in it. They had to some degree revived the habit of performing full-length plays with whole integral stories contained within them. Perhaps more important still, they had established acting institutions, tradition, experience and personnel. Yet there clearly remained some large-scale needs. The amount of direct translation was minimal, as was the amount of new, polished plays. Many of the plays performed were never wholly written down, let alone published. This, coupled with the dominantly commercial basis of the leading troupes, tended to limit the possibilities for expansion and innovation. In short, artistic quality and high aesthetic principles were difficult to maintain in the absence of strong creative and literary backing and the constant reinfusion of new spiritual life and zest. Creative dramatic literature in China seems to have needed, if it was not to succumb to the weight of native tradition and long established attitudes, the large-scale translation of foreign material.

A healthy world of grass-roots amateur drama is perhaps always a necessary complement to commercial drama, if drama is not to degenerate into cheap spectacularity or to become the preserve of stiflingly small intellectual circles. Through the efforts of men such as the playwright Chen Dabei, who had experience in *wenmingxi*, amateur dramatic societies began to flourish. *Aimeiju* was the term used for this amateur drama, *aimei* being a phonetic rendering of the English word 'amateur'. Translations of European and American playwrights, Wilde, Björnson, Strindberg, Ibsen, Pinski, Chekhov, Shaw, and many others, became rapidly more abundant, and were of a higher quality than earlier translations.[21] In the early years of the May the Fourth Movement the bulk of *huaju* plays performed were translations of European and American plays, and there were very few native *huaju*. At the same time, however, a number of people who were later to become leading and often prolific *huaju* playwrights were already in the late 1910s and in some cases even earlier engaged in activities to promote *huaju*.

With the May the Fourth Movement and accompanying developments, the supporters of *huaju* drama very often became openly and violently scornful of traditional Chinese drama.[22] The reasons for this hostility are complex, but among them were certainly the ostentatious, self-establishing defiance of the newcomer seeking to proclaim his superiority by downing his rivals, and the general political and literary attack on many aspects of the past. The attitudes of some may be seen from the manifesto of the Popular Drama Society founded in 1921:

> Bernard Shaw once said: 'The theatre is a place for propagating ideas'. This is not necessarily so, but at least we can say this much: the time is past when people took theatre-going as [mere] recreation. The theatre occupies an important place in modern society. It is a wheel rolling society forward. It is an X-ray searching out the root of society's maladies. It is also a just and impartial mirror, and the standards of everybody in the nation are stripped stark naked when reflected in this great mirror, that allows no slightest thing to remain invisible [. . .] This kind of theatre is precisely what does not exist in China at present, but it is what we, feeble though we are, want to strive to create.[23]

This statement neatly captures the spirit of many of the pioneers of *huaju*. It must be remembered that *huaju* was quantitatively only a drop in the ocean at this time. The traditional dramas were still the most popular among the majority of the populace and with large numbers of the wealthy and ruling strata. The advocates of *huaju* tended very much to be young intellectuals, and often young intellectuals strongly influenced by Western education. They were also people self-consciously concerned with promoting bold ideas for social change. The loftiness of their mission no doubt seemed to them to contrast with the often earthy and sensual entertainments of the then current traditional drama, and with the bawdy and homosexual atmospheres of the old theatre world. Since, moreover, they were often people who had undergone their advanced education and obtained their major qualifications and much of their theatrical experience in Europe, America or Japan, their writings sometimes strike one as more foreign than Chinese, or at least as having their more peculiarly national characteristics of expression watered down, in contrast with the writings of many of those who specialised in traditional forms of literature. By background, by aspiration and by the nature of predominant literary and political trends it was fairly natural for many of these young intellectuals to oppose traditional drama. The ideas they wished to advocate were, furthermore, often in direct conflict with basic attitudes and ideas embodied in much of the traditional drama. In traditional drama, for instance, even in plays which lauded rebellion against parental tyranny, the basic ideology of the family had rarely been subjected to frontal attacks (although some plays on Buddhist topics advocated the virtues of abandoning family life). Many of the plays of the Spring Willow Theatre had been concerned with domestic situations, and during the 1920s and afterwards opposition to the old family system, the keystone of traditional society, became a very common theme of dramas.

Many of the leading figures of the new literary and political movements, and indeed of twentieth-century Chinese literature as a whole, wrote *huaju* plays in the early 1920s. Dramatists of the period included Chen Dabei, Xiong Foxi (1900–65), Ouyang Yuqian, Ding Xilin (1893–), Guo Moruo (1892–), Hou Yao, Tian Han (1898–), Hong Shen (1894–1955), and many other prominent writers. Various drama societies and institutions sprang into being to assist the new upsurge of *huaju*, such as the Popular Drama Society of Chen Dabei, Ouyang Yuqian, Xiong Foxi, Mao Dun (1896–), Zheng Zhenduo (1897–1958) and others, the Life Art Drama Technical School founded by Pu Boying in 1922, the drama section set up in 1925 at the Peking Fine Arts Technical School and run by the famous poet Wen Yiduo (1899–1946) among others, and the South China Society founded as an extension of a film company by Tian Han in 1927.[24] At the same time there was a great deal of writing in journals and books, and of translation, to further the *huaju* movement.[25] There was also a conscious movement during the early 1920s to dissociate *huaju* from the *wenmingxi*, and the new *huaju* were sometimes referred to as *zhen xinju*, 'truly new drama'.[26] There were still many problems to be faced in actual performance, apart from the constant ones of audience taste, moralistic opposition, and government interference and suppression. One key problem faced Hong Shen in his early days as a playwright. Returning in 1922 from six years' study of engineering, literature and drama in the United States, he turned to writing a play for the stage. Thoroughly loathing the custom of having female roles played by male actors, 'perhaps because I had read too much of Freud on sexual abnormality', he wrote a play called *Zhao King of Hell*, based on the formula of *The Emperor Jones* by the American playwright O'Neill, and having no female parts. The public reaction was 'unanimously that I was mentally deranged' to want to avoid having male actors play women. On the recommendation of Ouyang Yuqian, he the same year joined the Shanghai Drama Association, which had been founded in 1921 and lasted until 1933, which is the longest survival time of any *huaju* company. In that society, to demonstrate his point, he put on two plays, the first with actresses playing the female roles and the second with male actors playing them. Perhaps he loaded his dice, but anyway it had the desired effect. The audience for the most part found the mincing affectations and falsettos of the actors utterly ludicrous after witnessing the actresses' display of natural femininity, and, following that, the habit of impersonating females 'died a natural death' in the company.[27] Hong Shen also set up new standards for the arts of stage performance with his production of a version of Oscar Wilde's *Lady Windermere's fan*, as a result of which, incidentally, he became involved in film-making. His adaptations of Ibsen's *A doll's house* and Shakespeare's *Merchant of Venice* were also well received by theatre audiences.

Since 1911, warlords and their followers had controlled the north and other parts of China, and the revolutionary organisations had been largely based in the south. In 1927 Nationalist Party leaders turned against their Communist collaborators, and in the following year Nationalist-led armies marched northwards, and took Peking and most of northern China. The capital was moved to Nanking. These events, with the hopes and indignations they engendered, and by creating a geographically and administratively more united nation, contributed to the greater energy and wider operative range of the *huaju* in the late 1920s. In other ways, too, the activities of journalists, performers, translators, playwrights and scholars made the time ripe for an expansion and intensification of the *huaju* movement. There were in the late 1920s a good number of vigorous *huaju* companies and societies in existence, and for a couple of years the South China Society was particularly flourishing. Consciously, the supporters of *huaju* began to extend its scope of popularity, attempting now to establish it more solidly both in the nation's attentions and in a commercial sense. With Shanghai still very much the centre of activities, partly because of the influence and protection afforded by the foreign presence there, *huaju* companies now toured widely, sometimes under rough and trying conditions. Peking, Nanking and other cities also had their own drama societies and troupes for *huaju*. Plays were performed in factories, villages and small towns as well as the big cities, and a campaign of promotion that was fully under way in 1930 greatly increased the interest in *huaju* in the universities, many of which acquired their own lively *huaju* drama societies.

In autumn 1929, Zheng Boqi and a number of others formed the Shanghai Art Drama Society, which the following year performed several successful plays. Although by now the number of *huaju* written by Chinese was considerable, and the total rapidly mounting, most of the plays which this society performed were French, German or American. In April 1930 government action terminated the society. In the autumn of the same year, the government also suppressed the South China Society. *Huaju*, as one of the spearheads of change, was increasingly subject to suppressions, and actors and playwrights were even arrested, as in the case of Tian Han and a number of other dramatists in 1932.

The process of popularising *huaju* continued during the early 1930s. Japanese aggressive and acquisitive moves against China, and the increasing conflict and ideological distance between Communists and Nationalists, found their reflections in the drama of the period. Various anti-Japanese, patriotic dramas appeared. In the Communist bases *huaju* obtained grass-roots experience of performance in some of the same conditions which had helped to mould, toughen and polish traditional kinds of Chinese drama. A number of troupes did propaganda work in the villages and among the soldiers, and a number of plays were written on anti-Nationalist and other political themes. In Nanking a National Drama School was set up in 1935, under Luo Jialun (1896–) and Zhang Daofan (1897–).

In Chinese society in general, *huaju* continued to rely very heavily on translations from foreign playwrights. One of them, Bernard Shaw, came to Shanghai in February 1933. He was entertained to lunch by the Shanghai Pen Club, and his hosts included some of the most eminent literary figures in China and also the great Peking Opera actor Mei Lanfang. A short Chinese book was subsequently written, entitled *Bernard Shaw in China*.

The persistent inspiration provided by European and American playwrights manifested itself most strikingly in Cao Yu (1910–) from Hupeh province, who is generally acclaimed as the greatest of all Chinese *huaju* playwrights. A university student of English in Peking, he delved deeply into the drama of Aeschylus, Euripides, Shakespeare, Chekhov, Ibsen, O'Neill and other Western playwrights, who profoundly influenced the writing of his own plays.[28] In 1933, before graduation, he completed his play *Thunderstorm*. A wealthy mine-director Zhou Puyuan has two sons in his household, one called Ping, aged twenty-eight, by a woman called Shiping whom he drove away with their younger son Dahai twenty-seven years ago and whom he believes drowned, and the other called Chong, by his second wife Fanyi. Fanyi has had a love affair with Ping. The Zhous' servants Lu Gui and Lu Gui's daughter Fourth Phoenix are Shiping's second husband and Shiping's daughter respectively. Dahai is now a mineworkers' representative and works in Zhou's mines. None is initially aware of the connection of the two families through Zhou Puyuan and Shiping. Ping is now having a love affair with Fourth Phoenix. Shiping, whom Puyuan has presumed dead for twenty-seven years, appears at the Zhous', and eventually all become aware of their interrelationships. Horrified to discover that the father-to-be of the child she is expecting is none other than her own half-brother, Fourth Phoenix rushes out of the house and is electrocuted by a faulty cable. Chong, chasing after her, is also electrocuted. Ping shoots himself.

To do justice to the complexity of the plot would require far more space. Moreover, such a short summary does not indicate the skill with which the dialogue is written, nor the deftness with which the many-threaded plot is handled. There are many other complications, and interwoven with the question of the personal relationships there is a conflict between rich and poor, privileged and unprivileged. There are also notes of assault on the traditional family and social system. The play was first staged by the Fudan University Drama Society in Shanghai under the direction of Ouyang Yuqian and Hong Shen, but its first public performance by a professional troupe was in 1936, when it was performed by the China Travelling Drama Troupe, founded in 1933. Audiences and the drama world greeted it with tremendous enthusiasm, and it gave the *huaju* movement as a whole a vital fillip to its self-confidence. In subsequent years Cao Yu wrote several other very successful plays.

The following excerpt from *Thunderstorm*, containing its dénouement, should give some brief impression of the extent to which Cao Yu, and some other dramatists, had learned from the West. The chopped, staccato, 'realistic' dialogue, the psychological minuteness with which both the speech and the stage directions are given, as well as the tenor of emotional interplay, are quite unlike the general run of traditional Chinese drama with its clearer rhythms of prose and poetry, its music, and its philosophical universalities and structural harmonies. As the excerpt begins, Fanyi has learned that Ping has made Fourth Phoenix pregnant and, bitterly furious at her own rejection by Ping, calls Zhou Puyuan in to confront the two young people.[29]

Thunderstorm by Cao Yu: Act Four

[. . .] (*Zhou Puyuan comes in from the study. Nobody moves, and it is as quiet and still as death.*)

ZHOU PUYUAN. (*In the doorway*) What were you shouting? Why don't you go upstairs to bed?

FANYI. (*Imperiously*) I wanted you to meet some nice relatives of yours.

ZHOU PUYUAN. (*Sees Shiping and Fourth Phoenix together. Astonished*) You, you – what are you two doing here?

FANYI. (*Pulling Fourth Phoenix towards Zhou Puyuan*) This is your daughter-in-law. Say hello to her. (*To Fourth Phoenix, pointing at Zhou Puyuan*) Say 'hello daddy'! (*To Zhou Puyan, pointing at Shiping*) And I'm sure you'd like to be introduced to this lady.

SHIPING. Madam!

FANYI. Ping, come over here. Now your father's present, come on, give your mother-in-law here a kowtow.

PING. (*Distressed*) Dad, I, I –

ZHOU PUYUAN. (*Realising*) How – (*To Shiping*) Shiping, so you've come back again after all.

FANYI. (*Startled*) What?

SHIPING. (*In a panic*) No, no, you've got things wrong.

ZHOU PUYUAN. (*Remorsefully*) I thought you might come back, Shiping.

SHIPING. No, no! (*Bows her head*) Oh, Heaven!

FANYI. (*Flabbergasted*) Shiping? What? Is she Shiping?

ZHOU PUYUAN. (*Irritably*) You don't have to deliberately repeat your question. Yes, she's young Ping's mother, the one who died thirty years ago.

FANYI. Oh, Heavens above!

(*There is a long pause. Fourth Phoenix lets out a wretched cry, then stares at her mother. Shiping is bowing her head in pain and anguish. Ping is staring in helpless stupefaction at his father and Shiping. Meanwhile, Fanyi gradually moves over to Chong's side. It is steadily dawning on her that certain other people's fates have been even more unfortunate than her own.*)

ZHOU PUYUAN. (*Heavy with grief*) Ping, lad, come over here. Your own flesh-and-blood mother didn't die. She's still in the land of the living.

PING. (*Half-crazily*) That's not her! Dad, that's not her!

ZHOU PUYUAN. (*Harshly*) You silly bugger! I'll have none of your nonsense! She may not have a high station in life, but she's your mother, all the same!

PING. (*In immense anguish*) Oh, dad!

ZHOU PUYUAN. (*Earnestly*) Don't think that because you and Fourth Phoenix come from the same mother and you feel it looks shameful, you can forget the innate bond between a son and his mother.

FOURTH PHOENIX (*In anguish*) Oh, mum!

ZHOU PUYUAN. (*Gravely*) Ping, lad, forgive me. This is the only thing I've made a mess of in my whole life. It had never even vaguely occurred to me that she might still be alive today and find her way here. As I see it, we can only put it down to fate. (*To Shiping, with a sigh*) I'm getting old now, so just now, after I'd told you to go, I felt full of remorse, and I was arranging to send you twenty thousand dollars. Now, since you're here, I think young Ping, being an obedient and loving son, will be able to take every care of you. He'll be able to make it up to you for the wrongs I've done you.

PING. (*To Shiping*) You – you're my –

SHIPING. (*Losing self-control*) Ping – (*Turns her head away, and sobs.*)

ZHOU PUYUAN. Ping, lad, kneel down! This isn't a dream: this is your very own mother.

FOURTH PHOENIX. (*In dazed bewilderment*) Mum, it can't be true. (*Shiping says nothing.*)

FANYI. (*To Ping, remorsefully*) Ping, I . . . I never for a moment imagined that – it was like this, Ping –

PING. (*To Zhou Puyuan*) Dad! (*To Shiping*) Mum!

FOURTH PHOENIX. (*She and Ping stare at one another, until she is suddenly unable to bear it any more*) Oh Heaven above! (*Runs off through central door. Ping flings himself face forward onto the sofa. Lu Shiping is standing dull and lifeless.*)

FANYI. (*Shouts worriedly*) Fourth Phoenix! Fourth Phoenix! (*Turns and says to Chong*) Chong dear, I don't like the way she looked. Hurry out and keep an eye on her for a moment.

(*Chong hurries out through the central door, shouting for Fourth Phoenix.*)

ZHOU PUYUAN. (*Going over in front of Ping*) Ping, what's the meaning of it all?

PING. (*Abruptly*) You should never have given me life! (*Runs off through dining room.*)

(*From the distance come the sounds of pitiful cries from Fourth Phoenix, and of Chong's frenzied calls of 'Fourth Phoenix! Fourth Phoenix!' After which Chong, too, lets out a terrible scream.*)

SHIPING. (*Calls out*) Fourth Phoenix, what's happened to you?

FANYI. (*Crying out simultaneously*) My son, my own dear Chong! (*Shiping and Fanyi rush out through the central door.*)

ZHOU PUYUAN. (*Hastening over to the window, and pulling aside the window curtain. In a trembling voice*) What's happened? What's happened?

(*Enter servant, rushing in through central door.*)

SERVANT. (*Panting*) Master!

ZHOU PUYUAN. Speak up, quickly: what's the matter?

SERVANT. (*In such a state that he can hardly get a sound out*) Fourth Phoenix . . . she's dead . . .

ZHOU PUYUAN. (*Horrified*) And what about young Master Chong?

SERVANT. He . . . he's dead, too.

ZHOU PUYUAN. (*In a trembling voice*) No, no, how . . . how did they . . . ?

SERVANT. Fourth Phoenix ran into that live electric cable. Young Master Chong didn't know about it, and straightway grabbed hold of her, and the two of them were electrocuted together there.

ZHOU PUYUAN. It couldn't happen. It, it – it's not possible, it's not possible!

(*Zhou Puyuan and servant rush off. Ping comes out from the dining room, his face ghastly pale, but with a suppressedly calm air about him. He walks up to the square table, opens the drawer, takes out a pistol, and walks into the study on the right. Outside there is a hubbub of voices, the noises of people crying, people shouting and people squabbling all mingled into one. Enter Shiping through the central door. An elderly servant follows her on, bearing an electric torch. Not uttering a sound, Shiping stands in the middle of the stage.*)

OLD SERVANT. (*Trying to comfort her*) Come on now, madam, don't just stand there in a daze. That's no good. You must cry, have a real good cry.

SHIPING. No, I, I – (*Stands stupefied.*)

(*The central door is opened wide, and there is Fanyi, with a crowd of servants surrounding her. One cannot tell whether she is crying or laughing.*)

SERVANT. (*From outside*) Go on in, madam – don't look!

(*Fanyi is ushered up to the central door by the servants. She leans in the doorway, laughing weirdly.*)

FANYI. My Chong, why have you got your mouth open like that? Why do you look as if you're smiling at me all the time? – Dear Chong, you silly boy, you.

(*Zhou Puyuan walks in through central door.*)

ZHOU PUYUAN. Fanyi, come in. My hands are numb. Don't you look at those two any more, either.

OLD SERVANT. Come in, won't you, madam. They've been burnt by the electricity. There's nothing that can be done about it now.

FANYI. (*Coming in, weeping tearlessly*) My Chong, my own dear son. Just now you were still alive and well. How could you die? How could you have died so horribly?

ZHOU PUYUAN. You must just try to calm yourself now. (*Wipes tears from his eyes.*)

FANYI. (*Laughs hysterically*) It was right that you should die, my Chong. It was right!

With a mother like me, you deserved to die!

(*Sounds from outside of servants fighting with Dahai.*)

ZHOU PUYUAN.   Who's that? Who's that fighting at a time like this?

(*Exit old servant to find out. Immediately another servant comes on.*)

ZHOU PUYUAN.   What on earth's happening outside?
SERVANT.   That Lu Dahai who came this morning – now he's come back again, and he's fighting with us.
ZHOU PUYUAN.   Tell him to come in here.
SERVANT.   He injured quite a few of us with his kicks and punches, master, and now he's already run off through the back gate.
ZHOU PUYUAN.   Run off?
SERVANT.   That's right, master.
ZHOU PUYUAN.   (*Suddenly*) Go after him. Go and bring him back here.
SERVANT.   Right, master.

(*He and the other servants go off together, and now there are only three poeple, Zhou Puyuan, Shiping and Fanyi left in the room.*)

ZHOU PUYUAN.   (*Brokenly*) I've lost one son. I can't lose another one.

(*Zhou Puyuan, Shiping, and Fanyi all sit down.*)

SHIPING.   Let them go, all of them. Might as well let him go. I know that lad of mine. He's full of bitterness now. I know he won't come back here.
ZHOU PUYUAN.   (*Feeling uneasy in the desolate quiet of it all*) The young ones have gone on ahead of us after all, and all that's left now is us old – (*Suddenly*) What about young Ping? Where's the young master of the house? Ping, . . . Ping lad! (*No reply.*) Come here, someone! Somebody come here! (*No reply.*) You both go and have a look. Where's my son and heir?

(*Sound of pistol shot from study. It becomes as still and silent as death in the room.*)

FANYI.   (*Suddenly*) Oh! (*Runs off into the study. Zhou Puyuan stands stock-still in stupefaction. Almost immediately, Fanyi comes rushing out of the study shouting frantically*) He . . . he . . .
ZHOU PUYUAN.   He . . . he . . .

(*Zhou Puyuan and Fanyi rush off together into the study.*)

END OF PLAY

By the Long March of 1934–5 the Communists established their main base in Shensi province. In July 1937 the Japanese launched large-scale attacks on China and the Chinese began their War of Resistance, not to end until 1945. An All-

China Drama-world Resist-the-enemy Federation came into being, its members including Ouyang Yuqian, Hong Shen, Xiong Foxi, Guo Moruo, Chen Baichen (1908–), Cao Yu, Lao She (1899–1966) and many other nationally celebrated writers who pledged their talents to the defence of China. Touring troupes were organised from Shanghai and elsewhere to carry out drama propaganda. When the Nationalist government moved to Chungking in Szechwan province, many leading writers continued to write plays there, while drama was also steadily fostered in the Communist areas to maintain morale and disseminate propaganda.

War produced and popularised a considerable amount of fiercely patriotic plays. Among them were such as *Put down your whip*, adapted in 1937 from a one-act play by Xia Yan (1903–) written several years earlier. Xia Yan's play was itself based on the novel *Wilhelm Meister* by Goethe. The new play transposed the action into contemporary China and made it a fire-spitting condemnation of the Japanese invaders. The themes of plays by the more widely known playwrights were often on a more general plane, concerned with more internal Chinese social issues, or with theories of patriotism and of family and personal relationships, and sometimes experimenting with new dramatic techniques. Cao Yu's *Peking man*, written in 1940, concerned the collapse of an old-style Chinese family. Guo Moruo wrote a number of plays, such as his *Qu Yuan* of 1942, based on ancient themes but with modern implications, or modern applications.

There were literally thousands of troupes active during the war, some local, some touring, some stemming from the old professionals and also a huge number of amateur composition, though these were sometimes led and directed by professionals. Students sometimes formed drama groups for the vacations, and there was even a widely known troupe made up of twenty-four refugee children between the ages of nine and nineteen. Many touring troupes performed anywhere they could, to soldiers and to farmers, even behind the Japanese lines, utilising open spaces, village streets or temple stages. A Western reporter describes such a performance at army headquarters in Shensi:

At five in the afternoon a pale sun was sinking over the dust-covered village which even three months of zero weather had not yet softened with snow. The air was still; there was no wind to raise the choking dust-storm of North China. Only the tread of hundreds of feet going towards the village temple stirred a powdery mist that rose high and slowly settled making a haze across the setting sun. The last light set aglow with colour the high curved roofs around the temple court. Inside the court some seven or eight hundred men found space to stand for the meeting: a few of the more venturesome perched informally on the roof. The only other seat was one bench fronting the stage, where sat Chu Teh [Commander-in-chief; his mother came from a family of itinerant actors], the Eighth Route generals, and the invited guests.

One side of the temple court was filled by the stage, a square box of a house from which the side facing the audience had been torn and only partly covered again by a crude curtain. There was no stage entrance. To reach the platform the actors had to pass in front of the audience and climb up about seven feet by a crude ladder. All of them did this together at the beginning of the programme; then they disappeared into the dark interior, hiding behind furniture and side curtains until their cues. Since an exit from the stage via the audience would have distracted attention during the performance, none of the actors left until the show was over; all waited in that dark box behind the scenery for the many hours of the entertainment; then all came to the front of the stage together and climbed down amid plaudits of farewell.

Under these crude conditions the two dramatic troupes put on their performances which held their audience spellbound for many hours. The sun went down and the winter stars shone on the village drama; kerosene lamps were brought to light the stage. Till after ten on a bitter January night the blue-grey soldiers stood watching, laughing and applauding. The dramas showed aspects of the war against Japan; they were portrayals of life as those soldiers knew it.[30]

Many such programmes were multiple bills, including ballads and other kinds of entertainment as well as drama. Simple one-act plays, moreover, were widely favoured for performance. Fairly mechanical formulas for the plots, and an intensification of the moral blacks and whites, made for very effective wartime propaganda. Sometimes they resembled English Morality Plays in their personifications of abstractions, but generally they were more straightforwardly and immediately relevant.

There was at this period a great distance between the loftier dramatists with their broad theorisations, subtleties and intellectual experiments and the on-the-spot creations of the wandering troupes in the battle areas. Similarly there was a chasm between the city intellectual *huaju* troupes and the more traditional, more countrified and more pragmatic dramatic groups and troupes. The war served to give *huaju* a much wider and closer experience of the rural living conditions of the vast majority of Chinese, and of their attitudes and tastes in entertainment. This was a vital step for the sinicisation and full national appropriation of the *huaju* drama, if such was ever to occur, and inevitably developments in the direction of sinicisation involved certain adjustments in the direction of the more wholly Chinese traditional entertainments which were more familiar to the ordinary populace. Perhaps there was even a fairly absolute requirement, in such a predominantly agricultural, scarcely mechanised society, for performance with song and dance.

One of the important developments from the later years of the war was the appearance of the *xin geju*, 'new opera'. The influences of both *huaju* and traditional forms of drama and music were clear in the form of the *xin geju*. Dealing with contemporary topics and containing very large portions of speech, it yet retained a considerable amount of song and poetic matter, and often utilised traditional kinds of music. At least in peacetime conditions, fairly literally realistic scenery was used. *Brother and sister pioneers*, generally regarded as the first *xin geju* or as its main ancestor, was based in form on a traditional, salacious singing act,[31] but dispensed with the salacity. It appeared in 1943. The first major creation, however, was *White-haired girl*, by Ding Yi and He Jingzhi, which was made public between January and April 1945. In five acts, the major part of it i dialogue, but there are many traditional features, such as the introductory songs at the beginning of scenes. It was based on a story then current, and set in the years 1935–38. Landlord Huang forces a tenant to give him his daughter, named Delightful Child, in payment of debts. He rapes her, and eventually she flees into the mountains. All the tragedies and ill-treatment she has endured turn her hair white, and the legend spreads of a wild-looking white-haired goddess roaming the area. Huang utilises the legend to play on superstitious fears, and finally two former neighbours of the girl's pursue her and bring her back to her village, which is by now under the control of Chinese Communist forces. Before a massed crowd she accuses Huang, in song, and he is committed for trial. This *xin geju* has repeatedly been performed, and has several times been heavily revised, since 1945.[32]

The war with the Japanese ended in 1945, but in 1946 full-scale internal warfare broke out in China, and by 1949 the Communists under Mao Tse-tung had established the People's Republic of China, while Chiang Kai-shek and his Nationalists had been confined to Taiwan for their Republic of China. A new era began for many aspects of Chinese society. It was some forty years since *La Dame aux camélias* and the Spring Willow Society. The *huaju* movement had undoubtedly undergone considerable changes, and had acquired a solid body of experience. It was established as a strong force in Chinese theatre and dramatic literature, and had accumulated a fairly large body of translations, native *huaju* dramas, theoretical writings and theatrical traditions. At least at the more intellectual levels, its connections with its Western origins remained strong and evident. In 1946, for instance, Cao Yu went to America for a year on a fellowship, and in 1949 his wartime translation of *Romeo and Juliet* was published. Beyond doubt *huaju* had not, and still has not, even begun to exhaust the possibilities of profiting from Western drama. At the same time, it is too early to tell whether it can survive as a permanent strong feature of Chinese drama without considerable adjustments to native forms of performance or to peculiarly Chinese conditions of performance.[33] The *xin geju* is but one of the signs of attempted compromise that have appeared in the past decades.

11
Traditional Drama in the Twentieth Century

Peking Opera, notwithstanding major vicissitudes, has remained a major force in the Chinese theatre of the twentieth century. Its standing among the intellectuals, or at least many of the younger ones, of those educated abroad and of those concerned with radical social and political change, became very low after 1917 or so, when increasing tendencies towards vernacularisation of literature in general and Western-style modernisation in many fields favoured *huaju* at certain levels and in certain spheres of society. The Japanese occupation of Peking and Shanghai (1937–1945), for all the Japanese efforts to foster Peking Opera, disrupted the existence and development of that drama, many actors motivated by patriotism refusing to perform under the enemy régime. The war and the ensuing civil war were not conducive to the flourishing of a kind of drama that in the complexities and sensitivities of its organisation and audiences was particularly unsuited to violently disturbed social conditions. All the same, Peking Opera, particularly during the earlier decades of this century, remained very much alive and exercised strong influence over other kinds of traditional and regional drama, and not infrequently over *huaju* too.

Towering over the world of Peking Opera for much of the present century was the actor Mei Lanfang (1894–1961).[1] Both his father and grandfather had been *dan* actors, and at the age of eight he himself embarked upon a severe and wide-ranging course of theatrical training. His most famous teacher, Wang Yaoqing (1882–1954), was a veteran in female roles.[2] Mei learned singing by repeating each passage to him twenty or thirty times. He acquired the extremely exacting skills of the *qingyi* actor, learning the appropriate way to walk, open and close doors, move the hands, point the fingers, flick and waft the sleeves, put on a slipper, throw up a hand in appeal to Heaven, raise the arm in lamentation, pace the stage, and faint into a chair. Walking on the short stilts or clogs (artificial feet designed to give the effect of feminine movements and small feet), a feature of acting that had been popularised by Wei Changsheng, required arduous practice. Mei even practised on the ice in winter. Through pain and blistered feet he neared perfection in that art. Later, under other teachers, he studied acrobatics, fighting and many other subjects. Performing as a *qingyi*, he first went on stage in 1904, when he was ten. Three years later he joined a famous troupe, although in

216

little more than an apprentice capacity. Early on during the Republic he made a great name for himself in Shanghai and was soon established as the brightest light of Peking Opera. By his performances in female roles, he did much to shift the emphasis of Peking Opera away from the *laosheng*.

Performing in major cities all over China, Mei became the object of great adulation, and by several tours abroad he also rendered his reputation international. He won the hearts of theatregoers in Japan in 1919 and 1925, and in 1930 performed in several cities in the United States.[3] There the reaction to him was enthusiastic, although the tour as a whole was a financial loss. He met Charlie Chaplin several times, and was the guest of Douglas Fairbanks and Mary Pickford in Hollywood. The following year he in turn acted as host to Fairbanks in Peking. Mei greatly admired Fairbanks's performance of D'Artagnan in *The Three Musketeers*, and respected Chaplin's comedy so much that he promoted certain comics in Peking Opera who displayed similar abilities in deadpan humour. 'From this,' remarked Mei, 'I came to the profound realisation that all arts of value, be they ancient or modern, Chinese or foreign, are all but different modes of expression capable of the same effect and to be enjoyed by everyone who has perception.' In 1935 Mei received a warm reception in Russia, and met Konstantin Stanislavsky and Bertolt Brecht.[4] He then went to Italy, France, Germany and England, but, because financial backing was lacking, was to his disappointment unable to perform in Europe. At the outbreak of the war with the Japanese in 1937, Mei was in Shanghai.[5] In mid-1938 he moved with his troupe to Hong Kong. The troupe shortly returned north, but he remained in Hong Kong. There he neglected his acting, devoting himself to the study of English and other pursuits. When the Japanese took Hong Kong in the last days of 1941, they made various attempts to persuade him to act again, but he refused, having grown a faint moustache to demonstrate his determination not to play *dan*.[6] In the summer of 1942 he returned to Shanghai. His continued refusal to act meant increasing financial difficulties, and he was obliged to sell many of his treasured possessions. He managed to earn some money at one point by exhibiting pictures that he had painted. On 15 August 1945, when the news of the Japanese surrender reached him, Mei wept, shaved his moustache, and from that day on took to practising his acting techniques every morning, retraining his voice every afternoon, and reading plays every evening. Two months after the surrender he was performing in public again. He was in great demand. In 1947 he starred in a colour film of his performance of *Bitter life and death*, a play he had taken into his repertoire just before the war.[7]

An important part of Mei's success in his early years was his cooperation with Qi Rushan (1876–1962), a scholar of high repute and wide interests,[8] and the most prolific literary dramatist of Peking Opera during the Republican period. He came of a family that had long been interested in the theatre, and during visits to Paris and London in the years 1908–13 he saw a great deal of European drama, which stimulated his eagerness to improve traditional Chinese drama.[9] In 1914 he joined with Mei Lanfang, and during the years of their partnership, which lasted until 1931, by writing anew and by revision of old plays, he created over twenty plays for Mei. Altogether in his life he wrote thirty-nine or more plays, as well as a score or so works on drama and the history of theatre.[10] For the first play that he created for Mei, *Chang E flees to the moon*, he sought to provide historical authenticity in the costumes and dances in place of the conventional stage dress and movements. In the 1930s he helped to promote drama and the study of theatre history by founding an association, a school and a museum for traditional theatre.

Although many of Mei Lanfang's plays were the literary creation of Qi Rushan, his own acting and singing skills and innovations were a vital part of the plays' success on stage, and as theatre the plays may be said to have been a joint creation. The importance of Mei's interpretations may be seen by looking at some of the written texts of the plays that he and others created for Peking Opera. For instance, his own favourite plays according to some statements were *Lady Yang gets drunk* and *Cosmos Point*. The first depicts a famous beautiful empress as she makes herself drunk in the despair of spurned love, and the second depicts a beautiful girl who feigns madness to avoid marrying an emperor. The written texts of both plays are at points extremely sparse, laconic almost to the point of pointlessness, and the drunkenness and madness require the most delicate portrayal of the highly complex emotions they involve if they are not to seem farcical. Mei's successful acting of both of them was a great testimony to his mastery of the art of acting.[11]

Mei's own copious writings and pronouncements on his career and on drama are ample evidence of the depth and breadth of his approach to his vocation. Forever eager to learn and to improve his art, he took everything he encountered as potentially a lesson for the further refinement of his acting. He kept pigeons, and the constant manipulation of the bamboo pole he used in directing their training strengthened him considerably for his more strenuous stage roles. He grew flowers, and the understanding of colour that this gave him assisted him with the use of colour in his play costumes. Painting lessons were likewise a great help in that direction. Among his friends was the master painter Qi Baishi (1863–1957), whose ingeniously sparse and spirit-capturing doodles of such small creatures as crabs, spiders, tadpoles, dragon-flies and shrimps have earned worldwide admiration. Mei culled points of inspiration for his acting from him, too.

Mei's humility towards his own art and his respect for the art of others stand out in a passage he wrote, which is also relevant to our understanding of his acting:

[. . .] At the time I studied the Kunqu opera *Peony pavilion* under the veteran Kunqu artist Qiao Huilian, Qiao had already long since given up the stage. My impression of him was of a wizened old man. But when he started to demonstrate gestures, I felt that the aged man wearing a fur coat had ceased to exist. I could only see the exquisite movements of the heroine of the play. I thought then, if someone ignorant of the art was watching, he would think it extremely funny.[12]

Mei Lanfang brought many technical innovations and new stylistic features to Peking Opera. Not only did he restore the prestige of *dan* roles, but he also broke with the tradition of specialising in only one type of *dan* role which was tending to stifle versatility.

Peking Opera continued to be chiefly characterised by its actors. There were many others of great repute, such as the *dan* actor Cheng Yanqiu (1903–59)[13] and the *sheng* actors Ma Lianliang (1901–) and Yu Zhenfei (1902–).[14] From the 1920s social pressures outside the theatre mounted against the playing of female parts by male actors, but Mei's reputation continued unimpaired, although this shift in public taste, together with others such as the dying of the custom of foot-binding for girls, and a certain relaxation of restrictions and prejudices against actresses, all had their effect on Peking Opera. In 1928 men and women appeared on the Peking Opera stage together. In 1930 a drama school, the Xiju Xuexiao, opened in Peking. The original intention was that it should be for both *huaju* and traditional drama, but it turned out to be mainly for Peking Opera. It trained both actors and actresses.[15] Many fine actresses, such as Xue Yanjin, who studied under Mei Lanfang, appeared. At first specialising in female roles, curiously enough some of the actresses later turned expert in male roles. There are precedents for such reversals in local drama, but it rings strangely in connection with Peking Opera. At various times there were attempts to 'modernise' Peking Opera,[16] and during the war against the Japanese there were increased attempts to adjust the genre to wartime ends, but Peking Opera's main contribution towards modernisation lay rather in its influence on other styles of drama.

While there is some justification for concentrating discussion of Chinese drama of recent centuries on Peking, there is not nearly as much as, let us say, for concentrating on London in discussing periods of British drama history. Numerous passing references have already been made to local and regional forms of play and drama. From some points of view, indeed, all kinds of traditional Chinese drama may quite fairly be viewed as regional rather than national, or, at least, rather than totally national. In the middle of the twentieth century it was estimated that China had probably more than three hundred kinds of local drama, without counting the many kinds of puppet play and shadow show.[17] The number of plays is countable in tens of thousands, though many of these duplicate each other's basic themes and stories. Some of these local drama forms are traceable back to the Sông dynasty.[18] Yuan *zaju*, *nanxi*, *chuanqi* and Kunqu were all in origin regional dramas. At least from the late Ming onwards there was a vigorous interaction and competition between various kinds of local drama, some of which influenced or themselves became more national kinds of drama and many of which were affected by each other and by the more national genres. For all its powerful cities and city cultures, China is essentially an agricultural country with frequently recurring strong tendencies towards regionalisation and localisation of culture and with vigorous rural communities, and conditions conducive to the birth of local dramas have persisted right into the present times. Even during the twentieth century new forms of local drama have emerged.[19]

The origins of some kinds of local drama are clearly traceable to structurally simpler kinds of show, such as the song acts and dances with stories that abounded in rural China, or to local folk-song and folk music. Since the beginning of history, and doubtless long before that, seasonal, celebratory and religious occasions in agricultural life have often been accompanied by music and song in one form or another, and in such music and song solemn aspirations and worship have frequently been inextricably associated with instruction, entertainment and levity. Into modern times there have abounded all over China the structurally rudimentary play performances or duo song-acts and so forth which the Chinese sometimes bundle together under term *minjian xiaoxi*, 'small folk plays', such as the *huaguxi*, 'flowery drum plays', and *huadengxi*, 'flowery lantern plays' of middle and southern China, and the *yanggexi*, 'rice-seedling planting-song plays', of northerly provinces. The *huaguxi* of Hunan province, for example, subdivide into a number of kinds of plays, each predominantly performed in a different area of the province: *caichaxi*, 'tea-picking plays', *madengxi*, 'horse-lantern plays', and *cherxi*, 'cart plays'. The *caichaxi* developed from folk-songs sung during the tea-picking in the early summer, and the other two kinds from popular airs sung at the Lantern festivals around the Chinese New Year.

The *minjian xiaoxi* would most often be performed by amateurs or part-time semi-professionals. The *yanggexi* of Ding county some 128 miles south of Peking, as performed in the 1920s, was fairly typical of many others in its conditions of performance. The county had thirty-six or so troupes of *yanggexi* actors, catering for hundreds of villages. Semi-professional groups of villagers, nearly all of them farmers during the growing and harvest seasons, would give plays to entertain the other villagers and to please the gods. A troupe usually consisted of fifteen or more men, including actors, musicians, and make-up and property men.

The winter lull in farming was the time for rehearsals and for the working out of new plays. A few of the more successful actors received wages, and some actors took on boys or young men as apprentices, for no fixed term. Most players being illiterate, they memorised their parts and music, and passed them on directly to other actors. Plays were usually performed at the lunar New Year, especially at the Lantern Festival, the fifteenth of the first lunar month, at the spring and autumn festivals, at the temple fairs and after the harvests. Sometimes there were permanent stages, but otherwise make-shift ones were readily and cheaply erected, being usually about thirty feet square with the back third curtained off as a dressing room. There was no scenery, only simple properties, and costumes were simple versions of those current in the more formal Chinese theatre. Most of the audience stood in the open space in front of the stage, but sometimes a mat-shed, thirty feet by sixty feet, or forty feet by eighty feet, and twenty feet high, would be hired to cover some of the spectators. There were no seats, but sometimes carts lined up alongside the matshed provided a privileged and decorously separate vantage-point for some of the women spectators. The number of women in the audiences was very large.

The performances were financed by contributions levied from the entire village, usually assessed according to the amount of land owned by each family, but the audience was not limited to the village and also came from surrounding villages. There was strong pressure, moral and otherwise, to pay the contribution or subscription, and sometimes when families refused the collector would threaten them with physical violence if any of their members were seen at the plays. The reason for refusal was generally that they considered the assessment too high, not, it seems, that the contents of the plays offended their moral principles.

The playing continued for three or four days, or sometimes for as long as ten days, which meant that the actors had to have a large repertoire. As many as eight or so plays might be shown in one evening. In the age-old tradition, the festivities were often accompanied by many other kinds of entertainment, especially at the New Year. An illuminated dragon, preceded by an illuminated 'pearl', would dance through the streets to the tempo of accompanying musicians. Lantern dancers, their lanterns decorated with flowers, butterflies, birds, writing and poems, danced from place to place repeating their dances till about midnight. A show of warrior acrobatics lasted from ten o'clock one morning till six in the evening on the fifteenth of the first lunar month. Some seventy or eighty players, individually and in groups of two, three or four, demonstrated their prowess, agility and muscular control with spears, lances, tridents, knives, swords, daggers and staves, and in exhibitions of Chinese boxing. There was also the commonly seen show involving men dressed as lions.[20] It opened with a group of clowns, one of them, dressed as an old man, pushing a wheelbarrow and another, dressed as an old woman, pulling it. On the barrow sat a clown disguised as an official, with black rings painted round his eyes. Then there came the passage of a boat made of willow twigs and bright cloth, and finally the lion dance, with two one-man or two-man lions, and a lion-tamer with a club. A well-to-do family would provide the entertainers of this show with rest and refreshments after it. The privilege of acting the lion was greatly prized.

Most of the performances of *yanggexi* were connected with religious activities of some sort, although of course that does not necessarily imply that religion was always their prime purpose (one notable secular exception was a kind of fair that had no temple associations). In general, if the stage was not near or in a temple, a temporary shrine would be built opposite the stage. The occasion for giving plays was often to please or propitiate the gods and seek their assistance, or to ask for rain or for protection against locusts and other disasters. All day long people would be burning incense and sacrificial paper money at the shrine, most of those doing so being women.

The *yanggexi* plays were given on a stage, in costume, with make-up, and with the music of orchestras variously composed of the *huqin*-fiddle, a flute, a shrill single-skin drum some two feet high and one foot in diameter at the ends, and also sometimes clappers and gongs. The plays often had only two or three characters but sometimes several, and involved much wholesomely bawdy humour and vig-

orous slapstick. Sex and humour were very prominent in the choice and treatment of themes. On an oddly recurrent note, the government authorities tried in
the 1920s to suppress the *yanggexi* on the grounds that they were a social and
moral menace. But Chinese rural society was too resilient for the prohibition to be
enforced. Some of the plays had subjects shared with Peking Opera and other
kinds of drama, but many were purely or largely local creations, it would seem.
The mark of country life and work was very strong on them, and the language and
song were intimately familiar to the audiences. This was one of the major virtues
of this kind of drama. It allowed for a much greater depth of appreciation in some
directions, since all the complexity of local traditions, social relationships,
humour, gesture, dialect and accent could be played upon. The plays themselves,
however, were very simple in plot and structure and generally very short.[21]

Such *minjian xiaoxi* dramas might appear and disappear, existing only
ephemerally, or they might long endure without much basic change in their
overall thematic scope or manner of performance, or they might enlarge their
scope and the region in which they were performed and become *daxing xiqu*,
'large-scale dramas'. Actively or passively, they might absorb elements of other
kinds of music and drama, reduce their more purely local qualities, widen their
repertoire and audience appeal, and spread to other villages, towns and provinces. The process of change in such cases could be constant and immensely
complex, with borrowings and reborrowings again and again from a huge variety
of sources, over centuries of time, and with many differences imposed by
relocalisations and other involved influences. Space allows mention here of but a
few of the many powerful forms of regional and local drama, with emphasis on
some common features.

The chief kinds of music current in the traditional dramas of twentieth-century
China are sometimes grouped as deriving from five systems or categories: Gao-
qiang, Kunshan-*qiang*, Bangzi-*qiang*, Liuzi-*qiang* and Pihuang. The first three may
be isolated as historically the more basic systems, Pihuang has already been mentioned in connection with Peking Opera, and Liuzi-*qiang* may be taken as a lesser
category. Gao-*qiang* is another name for the Yiyang-*qiang* system, and Bangzi-
qiang is basically the same as Qin-*qiang*. The kinds of music derived from these
five appear in very varied form under a bewildering variety of names, the
untangling of which is a major problem, and the occasion for not a little disagree-
ment among scholars. Some kinds of drama embrace two or more of the five, the
Chuanju drama of Szechwan province including all five in its repertoire. Outside
the five are many other kinds of local folk music and drama, such as the *yanggexi*,
various plays of shamanistic origin,[22] and others derived from narrative balladry
and story-telling. A modern writer typifies the three basic systems as follows:

From the point of view of style, if we say that Kun [shan]-*qiang*, excelling in its tender-
ness and warm sincerity, is especially coloured with the hues of the folk-song of the
southern Yangtse basin and may be taken as typical of the drama music of the south,
then Gao-*qiang*, dainty, refined, undulating, and with a slightly snooty air about it, may

very well be considered as typical of the drama music of Hunan, Kweichow and the south-west. As for Bangzi-*qiang*, it is obviously typical of the north, having always been celebrated for its bold, stirring emotions and exciting shrillness.[23]

As in the case of Peking Opera, known playwrights of local drama are exceedingly few in comparison to the volume of creation and revision. Among the many reasons for this are, again, the dominance of performance conditions over literary contribution, the existence of a considerable body of ancient plays of high quality, the frequently low social and literary standing of such drama, and the ingenuity and skill of the acting profession. The constant revision and adaptation of old plays to actual conditions of performance was one sign of the vitality of the drama, and produced a dazzling array of variations upon a theme. At the same time, there was an enormous number of plays peculiar to one kind of drama or another. We may now take a brief glance at certain of the main regional *daxing xiqu*, and at the same time at further varieties of *minjian xiaoxi*.

Hanju drama, the chief local drama of Hupeh province, was also performed in parts of Shensi, Kiangsi, Honan, Hunan and Anhwei provinces, being divided into four separate schools by geographical location and variations of dialect and accent. The name probably came into being between the years 1911 and 1917, but the drama has a much older history under various other names. Ultimately it seems to have come from plays using Yiyang-*qiang* music during the Ming dynasty. Like Peking Opera, but even earlier, it adopted Pihuang music, but it used no Kunshan-*qiang* in its singing. It had a great influence on the early developments of Peking Opera, and in this century in turn veered heavily towards the Peking Opera style of performance, differing from it, among other things, in the nomenclature of the role categories and in their detailed significance, in the measures and rhythms of some of its music, and in minor aspects of its orchestras. A guild for Hanju drama came into being around 1920, and at its height attained a membership of some seven thousand actors as registered members. By 1926 actresses were joining the guild. Later, a training troupe specially for women appeared. When they emerged from their apprenticeships, mixed troupes became widespread, and women came to make up a large proportion of the performers. During the years 1936–7 there was a brief vogue for mechanical scenery, and also for the performance of very long whole plays in long continuous sessions. During the war against the Japanese some troupes were formed to carry out wartime entertainment, propaganda and stimulation, using stirring old plays, and sometimes new plays on contemporary issues and acted in modern costume.

The other main drama of Hupeh is Chuju drama, which in the 1930s was more current within the province than Hanju. More rustic in character, its early roots lay in a form of folk-singing sung by people walking on high stilts. This became a duet between a man and a woman, then later the stilts were abandoned and a story was added. Then, as it became an indispensable part of festivals, a rough stage would be thrown up and rhythmic backing provided. It acquired the three role categories *xiaosheng*, *xiaodan* and *xiaochou*, and established itself as a kind of *huaguxi* drama, using folk-song and Gao-*qiang* music and, for its rhythmic backing, gongs, drums and cymbals. In common with many other kinds of local drama, it used a backstage chorus, which chimed in at the ends of lines of singing. In the earthiness and rich vulgarity of its stories and language it resembled *yang-gexi*. By the mid-nineteenth century some of the part-time actors had formed small full-time troupes of no more than nine or so men altogether. No doubt because of official attitudes, they performed somewhat clandestinely, very late at night. Adopting features from more sophisticated dramas such as Hanju, in about 1900 this *huaguxi* moved into the towns near to Hankow. A couple of years later it moved into the German concession of Hankow, then around 1911 to the French and Japanese concessions, too, where it prospered beyond the easy reach of Chinese law. More contact with Hanju drama and Peking Opera in the towns brought bigger casts, more intricate plots, richer costumes and more stylised manners of acting. Weakening of warlord power in the region around 1926 enabled it to move back into Chinese territory, changing its name to Chuju, and performing in a large theatre in the Chinese part of Hankow. The backstage choral backing of line endings gave way to *huqin*-fiddle passages. There was a tradition of blind fiddlers during the early years.

By 1929 Chuju had adopted Pihuang music from Hanju drama, but with the Peking Opera style of singing. In many ways it tended more and more to assimilate features of the more established drama forms. It increased its role categories to four with the addition of a *jing*. An *erhu*-fiddle was later added to the orchestra, and the natural-voiced and seductively gentle singing of the *dan* roles generally turned over to falsetto, though some performers retained it and left the falsetto singing to the *xiaosheng*. Heavily influenced by *huaju*, too, Chuju still retained traces of its origins, such as the great dominance of singing over speech[24] and various prosodic, thematic and stylistic features from folk-song and narrative ballads. There was some attempt during the War of Resistance to return to more pristine purity of form, but the influence from other kinds of drama, particularly Peking Opera, continued to increase, to the grave detriment of the distinctiveness of Chuju. It was not until after 1949 that actresses performed in Chuju drama.

Minju, the generic name for various kinds of drama in Fukien province and Taiwan, is frequently used to refer more specifically to the drama performed by the Fuzhou Troupes of eastern and northern Fukien. This latter arose from an amalgamation of strands from a number of kinds of drama: *pingjiang*, 'ordinary talk or flat talk', Rulin-ban, 'Confucian scholars troupes', and *laolao*, 'mumble-mumble' drama. *Pingjiang* drama was a typical form of *minjian xiaoxi*, performed after harvests by itinerant troupes at ground level with an area roped off by straw ropes serving for the stage. One view claims that it originated around 1800 and utilised the plays of earlier marionette and hand puppet shows. Its music derived partly from local folk-songs and professional balladry, and also from other provinces, quite possibly including some Yiyang-*qiang* music, but all appropriated into its own red-blooded manner and lusty mood. Polite gentlemen deplored its village vulgarity, one complaining in the early days around 1800, 'Their songs are vile and vulgar, their air and manner foul and filthy, and indeed one felt most strongly that they were quite unwatchable and that it was quite impossible for one to listen to them right through to the end.'[25]

By the mid-nineteenth century *pingjiang* drama was at the height of its popularity. In reaction against it, a certain Pu Zhishan cultivated a Rulin-ban, a troupe made up of 'handsome and intelligent young gentlemen actors' to perform at religious thanksgivings, birthday celebrations, and so forth. Initially they performed plays of a markedly moralistic nature and theme. A play called *Purple jade hairpin*, either by Pu or by a celebrity named Guo Boyin, later established a model for the genre by its tasteful elegance, moving plot and fine musical setting. The music of Rulin-ban drama was mainly Yiyang-*qiang*, modified by the local pronunciation and the effort to avoid 'vulgarity'. At first there was only percussive rhythmic backing and backstage chorus, but later various wind and stringed instruments were added to provide accompaniment, and the use of both accompaniment and chorus became a hallmark of the style. Great emphasis was placed on the tightness and logicality of plots, and such strictness of standards extended to the audience, who were according to one set of rules not allowed to be feasting during the performance. Troupes were small, with only half a dozen or so actors, and there were three main role categories, *sheng, dan* and *chou*, each with a main and secondary division. Achieving considerable popularity, Rulin-ban drama acquired twelve troupes which operated as going financial concerns.

During the nineteenth century troupes known as Huizhou Troupes performed in Fukien, probably brought into the province to entertain generals and viceroys from elsewhere on important occasions. They used Kunqu and other kinds of music, but since they also used outside dialects, their appeal to the local population was limited. Indeed the local people dubbed their singing '*laolao*', meaning 'mumble-mumble'. Both the Rulin-ban and *pingjiang* adopted some features of *laolao*, which was one of the things that eventually blurred the distinctions between the two former, basically opposed, kinds of drama. Even lofty literary dramatists began writing for both Rulin-ban and *pingjiang*. After 1911, deprived of official support, the *laolao* troupes slumped, and by 1916 they broke up, some of their actors joining the *pingjiang* troupes. Rulin-ban drama also declined, and veered towards *pingjiang*, some of its actors likewise entering the *pingjiang* troupes. Thus, with *pingjiang* troupes in the ascendancy and embracing the other two kinds of drama, a composite Minju drama arose. Eventually all three kinds of music and performance largely merged into one homogeneous style. The influence of Peking Opera, which early on had transformed *laolao* drama so considerably that some sources still refer to *laolao* as 'Peking Opera', became very strong, but Minju drama retained some distinctive musical and orchestral qualities, a great diversity of role categories, the use of the natural voice in singing (even for males acting *dan*), and a vivid technical terminology.

Other modern fashions made themselves felt. Early on, actresses were brought in, and with the May the Fourth Movement there arose a move to 'modernise' Minju. There were considerable influences from *wenmingxi* and *huaju*, and, especially during the war against the Japanese, there were some plays in contemporary costume. Such plays tended greatly to increase the proportion of speech. After the Japanese war, however, partly in response to desperate economic and political conditions, Minju turned strongly in favour of fantastic spectacle, performing mammoth plays on ancient themes, and utilising mechanical devices for supernatural and magical scenes. Perhaps it was the uneasy times, too, that gave the audience and actors a taste for the fiercely bombastic acting and violent stage fighting that became the order of the day, very often to the detriment of plot.

Chuanju is a generic term for the theatre of Szechwan province and embraces a number of still distinct kinds of drama: *dengxi*, Kunqu, Gao-*qiang*, Huqin-*qiang* and Tan-*qiang*.[26] All except the first originated from other provinces, but were appropriated as distinctive Szechwanese genres. *Dengxi*, 'lantern play', drama, a native *minjian xiaoxi*, seems to have originated with shamanistic performances for the purpose of exorcism and for various celebrations. Performed by peasants and artisans as well as by shamans, it persisted as a folk drama right into the 1930s, particularly in the mountainous regions of north Szechwan. The stage was bare ground or a mat, and the name derived from lanterns used to light evening performances. In the early days there were only three actors to a troupe, one of them acting female roles. At the beginning of this century some ten of the fifty existing *dengxi* plays found their way into the repertoire of the city theatres.

Actors from Kiangsi introduced Kunqu to the province, on the invitation of the governor-general Wu Tang (d. 1876), some time after 1862 and some time before 1876. Wu maintained a troupe which survived until about 1911, when most of the actors joined Huqin-*qiang* troupes. The Kunqu plays that endured were brief, comic ones, using Kunqu melodies, but largely Szechwan pronunciation, especially in the spoken parts.

Szechwan Gao-*qiang* music was a form of Yiyang-*qiang* music. It may have come into Szechwan in the seventeenth century with large-scale migrations into the province from eastern China, but some say that the playwright Yang Shengan (1488–1559), who certainly produced plays in Szechwan, introduced it there towards the end of his life. It adopted some of the local folk-song of rice-planters, boatmen and carters. With a predominantly percussive orchestra, it was further characterised by a choir of about six singers. This choir, which did not wear theatrical costume, would respond to the actor's singing, sometimes by repetition and sometimes by musical variation of what he had just sung. It was situated on the stage, and also sang while the actor mimed his part or pretended to sing at moments of tension or deep emotion.[27] Sometimes it commented on the action, dialogue and so forth, and sometimes it interrupted dialogues or songs with humorous or sympathetic comments. The Gao-*qiang* repertoire embodied plays of great antiquity, such as *Lute* and *Moon prayer pavilion*.

Tan-*qiang*, 'strum music', originated in the Bangzi-*qiang* or Qin-*qiang* music of northern China, perhaps introduced into Szechwan by the drama critic, dramatist and literatus Li Tiaoyuan (1734–1803) on his return to the province in 1784, or by actors from Shensi province. Besides percussion, its orchestra included fiddle and wind instruments. Li Tiaoyuan may also, along with the actor Wei Changsheng, have been responsible for bringing Pihuang music from Peking to Szechwan, which music served as the basis for Huqin-*qiang*. The most characteristic instrument of Huqin-*qiang* in modern times has been the *erhu*-fiddle, and its repertoire of plays, like that of Peking Opera, has been mostly of adaptations from nationally famous stories of ancient literature, history and legend.

Late last century and early in this century, several permanent theatres were established in Chengdu and other large cities in Szechwan. A theatre reform movement arose, with much cooperation between literati and actors, and rewriting of old plays. Prominent among the playwrights and rewriters of Chuanju was Huang Ji'an (1836–1924), who from 1901 to 1924 created and re-created over one hundred old plays.[28] In 1925 a guild or union came into being to promote Szechwan drama, and also in the 1920s the first independent theatrical company for this kind of drama was formed. Actresses were performing in Chuanju by the early decades of this century.

All provinces of the Chinese (Han nationality) part of China (the national minorities seem generally to entertain themselves more with dance-dramas, balladry and other forms of sung entertainment than with drama, although there are exceptions) have both *minjian xiqu* and *daxing xiqu*. The names that are applied to both kinds of drama are varied in nature and origin. Sometimes one kind of drama may have been known by three or more names, and much inconsistency of nomenclature still persists. Some names are of venerable antiquity, while others have been coined very recently, sometimes during the last twenty years. The latter, especially, often convey misleading impressions of clear-cut formal categories and sharp geographical distinctions. While often tending to hide specific differences, the names also tend to obscure widespread general similarities among the various kinds of drama in their manner of performance. The distinction between what are termed *minjian xiaoxi* and what are termed *daxing xiqu* is not always consistently defined, but one may make some generalisations about each which are true for a surprising proportion of dramatic genres. The former tend to use very few role categories, often just a *xiaodan*, a *xiaosheng* and a *xiaochou* (the *xiao* meaning 'little', implying 'folk-', 'local', etc.); their music is relatively simple in form or contains a large amount of folk-song or borrowings from traditional popular balladry; their range of instruments is small; their subject-matter is mostly love between man and woman, and commonplace social happenings; their language is very colloquial or dialectal; their costumes, make-up and range of stylised acting conventions are relatively restricted; their treatment of themes is often bawdy or coarsely humorous (although some rather stress vigorous action, and the *daoqixi* drama of Anhwei, for instance, has a large proportion of tragedies in its repertoire); they usually lack printed or even manuscript plays; and they lack elaborate stages or proper theatre buildings. This pattern, although obscured in recent times by heavy borrowings from *daxing xiqu* and other forms of drama, and by various conscious movements for reform and improvement, is often still discernible in many of the kinds of drama that are termed, or have in fairly recent history been so termed, *minjian xiaoxi*, such, for instance, as the *pingju* of Hupeh and the far north-east, the *errenchan* of the north-east, the *heheqiang* of Hupeh, the *wurenban* and Lüxi of Shantung, the Meihuju of Shensi and Shansi, the *quzixi* and Luoyang-*quzi* of Hunan, the Huangmeidiao and Sizhouxi of Anhwei, the Huju ('Shanghai drama'), Jianghuaixi and *tanhuang* of Kiangsu, the Yueju, Muju (also called *sanjiaoxi*, 'three-legged plays', because of the small number of actors required to act it), Shaoju and *tanhuang* of Chekiang, the various kinds of *huaguxi* and *huadengxi* of southern and mid-China, the various kinds of *yanggexi* in the north, and the *gezixi* of Taiwan.

Some of the *minjian xiaoxi* have had a very wide geographical range and considerable popularity, in both respects often surpassing some of the kinds of drama termed *daxing xiqu*. The latter are generally distinguished by converse characteristics and tendencies to those of the former. A large proportion of their music usually stems from the three main kinds of music or from Pihuang. Besides proper theatres, they often have guilds and other institutions to promote them. Very often they are strongly based in towns or cities. Their themes are of a more varied nature and wider range than those of *minjian xiaoxi*, and include a greater proportion of historical, antique, serious, tragic or emotionally complex topics. In some cases, however, the distinction seems to be made by Chinese writers, rather than from intrinsic qualities, as a contrast, in order to pick out the most complex and dominant form of drama in a given region by referring to it as *daxing xiqu*, although it may not be comparable in complexity to other *daxing xiqu* in other regions.

In recent decades there has been an increasing tendency to refer to the *daxing xiqu* and other fairly complex forms of drama by a term denoting a geographical region, indicating the region in which they originated or are chiefly found: thus Minju, 'Fukien drama', Guiju, 'Kwangsi drama', Yueju,* 'Kwangtung drama' ('Cantonese Opera'), Dianju, 'Yunnan drama', Ganju, 'Kiangsi drama', Qianju, 'Kweichow drama', Xiangju, 'Hunan drama', Yuju, 'Honan drama', Jinju, 'Shansi drama', and Chuanju, 'Szechwan drama'. In each of these names, the first syllable is a common abbreviated reference to the province, as in the case of Qin-*qiang*, a very old term, which refers to the 'music' and drama of Qin, i.e. Shensi province. Nowadays it generally means the drama current in Shensi, Kansu and other areas of north-west China. In some cases the reference of a name is wider than a province, as in Chuju, 'Hunan-Hupeh drama', or smaller than a province as in Chaoju, 'Chaozhou drama' (of Chaozhou in Kwangtung),

---

*Pronounced the same, but written in a different manner from the Yueju of Chekiang.

Qiongju, 'Hainan drama' (of Hainan Island), Wuju, 'River Wu drama' (of Kiangsi), Qiyangxi, 'Qiyang plays' (of Qiyang county in Hunan), Changdexi, 'Changde plays' (of Changde county in Hunan), Changxiju, 'Changxi drama' (of Changzhou and Wuxi counties in Kiangsu), and Yongju, 'Yong drama' (of Yong, i.e. Yin county in Chekiang). Sometimes the drama of a national minority is encompassed by a similar term, as in Baiju, 'Bai drama', the drama of the Bai people of Yunnan.[29] Often concealing a variety of forms of entertainment, these names are best viewed as convenient headings for discussing drama, rather than as wholly reliable guides to regional differences of performance.

Likewise, it should be stressed that the terms *minjian xiaoxi* and *daxing xiqu* must not be viewed as descriptive of a genre as a whole, but rather of two stages in the development of a genre. Most kinds of drama have passed through the former stage or are still in it, and some have returned to it, and any kind of drama may reach the latter stage. For instance, *pingju*, Shaoju and Weiyangxi, with the widening of their repertoires and technical range, have now come to be regarded as *daxing xiqu*. New *xiaoqing xiqu* have arisen recently, such as the *quju*, 'song drama', created from the ballads of Peking and elsewhere, and may well continue to appear. As long as a genre is not institutionally circumscribed or fixed by the weight of its written traditions, in a predominantly rural society the possibilities of its development remain very fluid.

A number of general features and recent historical changes that are observable in the development of many kinds of regional drama in China may now be reviewed. Local music merged with imported music, rustic drama with sophisticated drama, and dialect and accent very often added a distinctive local stamp to intensify local homogeneity. Rustic dramas moved to the towns, part-timers and amateurs became full-time professionals, and bigger theatres arose in the cities.[30] Rapid social and political changes increasingly affected drama. The decisive abolition of footbinding meant that more women were able to undertake the rigours of stage acting, although, of course, it was a decade or two before the abolition had its real effect. Regional dramas reorganised their financial bases, and formed guilds or unions and new-style training troupes, the better to protect and foster themselves and their arts. From each other, and from the more national kinds of drama, they received influences, often very strong, which adversely affected their distinctiveness, intimate community appeal and particular attractions as well as sometimes furthering their competitive capacity and range of performance. Much that was admirable and of age-old value gave way to imitation of *wenmingxi, huaju*, the cinema, and more particularly Peking Opera, of which the music, acrobatics and many other aspects were increasingly imitated by regional and local drama forms.[31] The War of Resistance served to associate many kinds of drama in the effort of wartime entertainment and propaganda and in some cases, no doubt beneficially or potentially so, to recall the advantages of their earlier structural and operational simplicities, but strong trends towards national uniformity continued.

One might easily imagine that, with the emergence of *huaju* and the influence of Western and 'modern' thought on a vast range of other aspects of Chinese life, the Chinese past was bound to become an ever fainter influence on Chinese drama during the twentieth century. But the situation was vastly more complex than that. In some ways the past actually underwent a vigorous revival, perhaps most notably in the renewal of scholarly interest in China's ancient drama. In the years 1908–11 the scholar Wang Guowei (1877–1927), one of the intellectual giants of twentieth-century China, produced a series of works on early Chinese drama, culminating in his *Examination of Sông and Yuan drama*,[32] which sought to trace the origins of Chinese drama and to outline its earliest known forms. In preceding centuries there had been a number of writers who had attempted to elucidate or put forward theories about these subjects, and Wang himself made use of their analyses. Recent writers often seem to ignore his predecessors, and thus to overestimate the novelty of his studies, but in the scope and breadth of his treatment, and indeed in much of his material, he did much to create a radically new epoch of research. Many other men of note also wrote on early drama, such as the Japanese scholar Yoshikawa Kōjirō and Chinese scholars such as Wu Mei, Sun Kaidi, Zhou Yibai, and many others. French and English writers, translators and scholars had shown eager interest in Yuan and other kinds of early Chinese drama during the Age of Enlightenment and the early nineteenth century, but twentieth-century Western studies lagged rather behind those of the Orient, and have only recently begun to appear in any quantity.

The unearthing of China's early dramatic past has occupied a great deal of the energies of modern Chinese scholars, and made possible a feedback into the living theatre and dramatic literature, although drama has far from fully exploited the possibilities. More important still perhaps has been the renewal, to which such studies have contributed, of respect for ancient Chinese drama, and for ancient literature in general. Many Chinese still have decidedly mixed feelings towards their ancient drama: is it a powerful justification of modern movements for vernacular, popular literature, or is it to be condemned for its out-of-date form and content? Many, too, undoubtedly have unmixed feelings of delight and enthusiasm, or of condemnation. There can, however, be little doubt but that the activities of scholars and publishers in the twentieth century have firmly ensured the richness and variety of possible sources of inspiration for drama.

12
Drama under the People's Republic

The advent of the People's Republic created another new epoch for Chinese drama. While many of the former conditions of dramatic creation and performance persisted without immediate radical alterations in Taiwan and South-East Asian Chinese communities, in mainland China a very different situation rapidly arose.[1] The régime's high degree of political cohesion, and the widespread consciousness and influence of its ideology, seemingly afforded greater possibilities both of fostering and of controlling drama than perhaps ever before. In the earlier years there was some leeway for a variety of approaches to drama, then with the Cultural Revolution, which was launched in 1966, drama was more firmly reined. It is convenient to deal first of all with the period before the Cultural Revolution.

A large proportion of the better-known playwrights remained in the People's Republic after 1949. Cao Yu, Tian Han, Hong Shen, Ouyang Yuqian and many others remained active and prominent in the world of drama, as did Mei Lanfang and a large number of celebrated actors. Previously, the very individualism and independence of some of the playwrights had sometimes served the general cause of opposition to the Nationalist government, but now that the new régime was in authority it sought to establish greater political conformity, with which literary individualism and independence often conflicted. Increasingly, though in an irregular wave motion rather than in a direct progression, dramatists and other writers came under pressure to conform more closely to official and Party concepts of Communist ideology. Statements by the Party leadership frequently set forth overall political and literary lines and limitations for writers, but the business of actually ensuring adherence to the lines, and of operating the limitations, was often conducted through debates and disputes at meetings and in literary media.

Various periodicals came into being to cater for different facets of drama, such as *Plays*, first published in January 1952, in which many new theatrical pieces appeared, *Theatre*,[2] first published on 24 January 1954 and containing articles on drama past and present, and *Drama research*, also containing scholarly articles, largely on ancient and traditional kinds of drama. Both in such periodicals and in the more general literary ones, and in book form, a host of dramas and works on

231

drama appeared. Numerous books on dramatic technique and on traditional and *huaju* theatre, actors' memoirs, including those of Mei Lanfang, and many new editions of earlier works were published. On ancient drama alone, for instance, during the years 1954–8, the vast collection of photolithographic reprints entitled *Compendia of ancient editions of drama* was issued, which was a treasury of a large proportion of the Yuan and Ming dramas and many Qing ones, and an invaluable reference work for anyone studying early Chinese drama. Yuan *zaju* not found in *Selection of Yuan songs* were conveniently published in a sequel to that venerable Ming collection. In 1958 there appeared a 1070-page critical edition of the complete poetical and dramatic works of Guan Hanqing, collating all surviving editions, a monument to painstaking scholarship. Also in 1958, there began the publication of the *Complete collection of Chinese local dramas*, a massive enterprise, which for the first time made hundreds of plays generally available as literature, sometimes bowdlerised, but otherwise, as far as one can tell, largely faithfully reproduced. In addition, there were many minutely annotated editions of early plays, including *Lute, Palace of Eternal Life, Peach blossom fan, West wing*, selections of Yuan *zaju*, selections of Ming *zaju*, and collections of excerpts from Ming and Qing *chuanqi*, as well as many editions of the whole plays, and no less than four or five annotated collections of some of Guan Hanqing's plays. Peking Opera was likewise well served in this respect, with numerous manuals of technique and with individual and compendious editions of plays, including a volume of Mei Lanfang's favourite pieces. There were books of reflections on the *huaju* movement, with personal reminiscences by some of the leading practitioners. The reprinting of early *huaju* plays, though not comparable in comprehensiveness with the reprinting of plays of the earlier forms of drama, and more ideologically selective, was not neglected. After Hong Shen's death in August 1955, a collection of his writings appeared.

The achievements in the realm of translation from foreign drama were less striking, and the range more restricted. Fairly little came from Western European or American literature, although Goldoni, Ibsen, Shaw, Shakespeare and, very belatedly, Brecht all appeared in translation. The translations of Shakespeare, published in 1954, were by Zhu Shenghao (1913–45). For most of the 1950s Russian was the most translated foreign literature, although even there the proportion of translations which were of dramas was very small. There was some turning to new fields, as instanced in the translation of the Sanskrit play *Shakuntula* by Kalidasa, which was actually performed in 1957, probably the first Indian classical drama to be staged in China, or in modern China at least.

With Peking re-established as the capital of China, and with the emergence there of strong, centralised political organisations, it was perhaps to be expected that the city would become more than ever the centre of cultural and theatrical developments. All over the country drama began to be transformed by new buildings and new institutions. In 1950 Guo Moruo described the situation in the realm of film and drama as follows:

China now has three state-owned motion picture studios in North-East China, Peking and Shanghai, which are capable of producing two thirds of the country's films. There are four important privately owned picture studios. Throughout China there are 467 cinemas of which 206 are publicly owned, 10 jointly owned and 251 privately owned. According to incomplete figures, in the 18 major cities below the Great Wall there are 151 theatres, while there are 82 theatres in the North-East. There are also 400 dramatic groups, with 40,000 actors, musicians, singers, dancers and other members throughout the country, including those attached to the People's Liberation Army and those directed by municipal and higher governments.[3]

The change in theatres was particularly marked in Peking.[4] Old ones were renovated, and new ones of much greater size were built. The Guanghelou was one notable ancient theatre to undergo radical change. It was there that Mei Lanfang had first appeared on stage. Early in the 1950s it became a modern building, with a square-built exterior very like that of many British theatres or cinemas, a state-owned theatre seating 1,400 people. One account of the change states: '[. . .] The stage does not project into the pit any more and the audience can watch a performance from any seat. There are proper seats instead of benches in the pit. There are no more tea-tables now that the show is the most important thing. The seats behind the wings are also a thing of the past [. . .]'[5] Several old theatres likewise took on a new shape and appearance, with seating capacity for a thousand or more. The old Tianqiao, 'Heavenly Bridge', theatre and entertainment quarter, noted in the past for its sleazy disorder, was thoroughly transformed.[6]

A number of brand-new theatres were also built. The Shoudu, 'Capital', Theatre built in 1956 in the middle of Peking seated over a thousand, had modern equipment, lighting and acoustics, and provided spacious wings on both sides of the revolving stage for scene-shifters, and comfortable dressing rooms backstage with accommodation for two hundred actors at a time. There were lounges where actors could relax, and at the back of the theatre were four rehearsal halls. Its dimensions, however, were dwarfed by those of some of the other new theatres. Not all were solely or even primarily used for the performance of plays; some catered for musical, acrobatic and other entertainments, and meetings as well. The Music Hall had a seating capacity of three thousand, and the Great Hall of the People a capacity of about eleven thousand in its main theatre with a stage that according to one calculation could take 1,700 or more actors, and a further 2,500 backstage. Such conditions, along with proscenium stages, naturally favoured grandly impressive, imposing spectacle rather than atmospheres of casual intimacy.

Similarly, new and powerful organisations arose to provide a framework for dramatic activities. A Chinese Dramatists' Society was established as early as July 1949, and like associations, regional, local or for specific genres of drama, also came into being all over China, notable among them the Peking Opera School founded in May 1952. A Central Dramatic Institute was set up in 1950, with some Russian advisers, and an emphasis upon the Stanislavsky approach to drama. Among the leading performers of *huaju* was the Peking People's Art Theatre, of which Cao Yu was the president, and which played mostly in the

Shoudu Theatre. Besides the more permanent organisations, there were national and local conferences, and drama festivals for various kinds of drama, sometimes on a massive scale. A sign of the priority of drama in the first years of the People's Republic is that as early as 1952 a National Festival of Classical Folk Drama was held in Peking, lasting from 6 October to 19 November. Over twenty different kinds of drama were represented, and although some of them showed only a couple of plays from their repertoires, it was a revelation for many Peking theatre experts and was followed by the setting up of a research group, which in turn led to the publication of materials on some of the regional drama forms. There was a second similar festival in 1957. In April 1955 there was a large-scale puppet show festival, demonstrating some of the wealth of surviving and resuscitated puppetry. The First All-China Festival of Huaju opened on 1 March 1956, and ended on 5 April, being held in Peking. At this festival Cao Yu was awarded first prize for a new play written in 1954. There were also many other festivals, some of them more local and regional, such as the Chuanju drama festivals in Szechwan province. Provincial drama troupes, *huaju* and traditional, also made separate, non-festival visits to Peking. Some of the more theoretical and ideological aspects of drama were brought up at various local and national conferences. Besides the larger structures, organisations and meetings, there were countless smaller ones throughout China. In very many areas Chinese drama continued to be performed under the same simple, makeshift physical conditions as ever.

Under the new régime the economic foundation and organisation of many of the larger troupes and companies underwent radical changes, which in many ways in itself created a fundamentally different theatre. In local and regional drama some troupes went over to a cooperative system of management, and some, such as the six major Minju troupes, united themselves into larger cooperative units. Sometimes, too, 'private-run government-assisted' troupes came into being, some of them termed 'experimental troupes'. Some of the larger organisations were more wholly state-supported, such as the state companies for Peking Opera and for the kind of drama known as *pingju*. It would be quite wrong to imagine that economic hardship had vanished for even the majority of actors. There was still often considerable privation and hardship in the acting profession,[7] but in many cases, particularly in the more prominent companies, the actor was personally more financially secure, and many of the former abuses of actors ceased to exist for a large proportion of them. The considerable transformation of the general economic climate and often of particular economic conditions changed the conditions of performance in certain ways. Ideological factors in particular became increasingly dominant over matters of economic competition and livelihood.[8] In addition to such organisations as those mentioned above, there were many dramatic organisations of an amateur nature, or belonging to another profession than that of drama, such as those of the armed services. The drama of the services became more and more prominent towards the time of the Cultural Revolution.

The situation as far as the creation of plays is concerned was much more complex than a first glance might lead one to imagine. Choice of theme and its form of expression were to be sure bounded by the confines allowed by the ideology of the new political order. Some overstepped these confines, deliberately and otherwise, but there were other aspects to the complexity. First of all, on such a complicated matter as literary creation almost inevitably is, it is perhaps to be expected that the representatives of orthodoxy would vary in their interpretations of that orthodoxy, or find themselves overtaken by shifts in the orthodoxy itself. They did not speak as one man; from time to time they gave expression to their own personal, mixed and complex feelings, and they did not, moreover, command the absolute power to impose their views. Besides which, an imaginative or subtle playwright could sometimes manage to go his own unorthodox or anti-orthodox way, however thematically or linguistically restricted he might be. Limitations of themes and of external forms of expression did not constitute an unbreachable barrier to wayward creativity.

Among the five or six most prominent literary figures of the early years of the People's Republic, who constantly jockeyed with one another as chairmen or vice-chairmen of a wide range of the most important cultural institutions, were Guo Moruo, Zhou Yang, Mao Dun and Lao She. Cao Yu was likewise prominent. Lao She, who had turned largely to play-writing before this period, was constantly getting himself into ideological trouble or being sharply prodded for his ideological shortcomings, yet he did not vanish from the scene but remained in the public eye, writing and continuing to create difficulties for himself. Dramatist Cao Yu sought to follow the set lines with some energy, but came under increasing criticism and self-criticism. The other three were more wholly representatives of orthodoxy. Playwright Guo Moruo, one-time vice-premier, and constantly the holder of other high positions, wrote plays that stood out among other things for the antiquity of their themes and their classical learning, one of them appearing in May 1959.[9] Mao Dun was dismissed as Minister of Culture in January 1965. Zhou Yang, chief and most prolific representative of orthodox literary criticism during the period, and deputy director of the Party propaganda department, came under fierce criticism in 1966, and fell to the Cultural Revolution.

Although there was more scope for unorthodox dramatic creation than might be expected, there were gigantic pressures and powerful urges towards creation along particular lines, and unorthodoxy must be measured in the light of these pressures and urges. Apart from the general atmosphere and ideological requirements, there were specific moves and campaigns to reform drama along the desired lines both in performance and in literary production. In 1949 there was an immediate temporary ban on fifty-five plays. As early as 11 July 1950, a Central Drama Reform Committee was set up under Zhou Yang, concerned mainly with traditional drama (usually referred to as *xiqu*), and in the following years there were further strong measures in support of the reform. From 1950 to 1952, for instance, the Ministry of Culture banned twenty-six plays, including fifteen Peking Operas, two Chuanju plays, seven *pingju* plays, and a further two that were not to be performed in the regions of the minority peoples. Complex argumentation lay behind many of the bans, but we may touch upon some of the more general reasons given.[10] Many of the banned plays were full of ghosts and demons, but there was no blanket prohibition on superstition, religion or the supernatural. Rather, bans were imposed for composite reasons. For instance, a play was prohibited because it was 'pessimistic', 'feudalistic', 'fatalistic' and 'superstitious', rather than for one of these reasons alone. Many plays concerning the supernatural, or containing prominent supernatural elements, continued to be performed, and to receive glowing praises for their overall messages and morals. The ban on sexual spice, lewdness and stage pornography was, however, more nearly complete. The depiction of brutality and murder, 'class mentality' and 'anti-historicity' were among the many detailed aspects attacked by the reforms.

The complexity of the reform movement even in the minds of some of the spokesmen of orthodoxy may be seen in a quotation from a 1952 speech by Zhou Yang:

> We respect myths because they have preserved within them both the naïve views our forebears had of the world and their visions of a beautiful, happy life in the future. But the anti-historicists stubbornly insist on distorting legends into reflections of present-day struggles. And so, for the simple reason that the dove is the symbol of the peace for which the people of the whole present-day world are struggling, doves have taken the place of magpies forming the bridge in *The Cowherd and the Weaving Maid*. One play-wright has been even more thoroughgoing: he makes the magpies symbolise peace; replaces the old ox that ploughs the field by a tractor; and brings Truman, aeroplanes and tanks all onto the stage as part of the story.[11]

The Cowherd and the Weaving Maid is an age-old legendary love story in which the two lovers, identified with two constellations, meet once a year on the seventh of the seventh lunar month across the Milky Way by means of a bridge formed of magpies.

Elaborate arguments were put forward in defence of many old popular plays that to a casual observer might seem quite incongruous or positively in conflict with the new order in its stricter senses. The general complexity of the period is further illustrated by such developments as the period of relaxation known by the name of the Hundred Flowers, when, for instance, on 17 May 1957 the above-mentioned ban on twenty-six plays was officially lifted, in accordance with the slogan 'Boldly let go the hand and give freedom to dramas', and for a brief period many of them were performed by troupes who, in one view, 'cast aside their glorious duties as "engineers of mankind's soul" and threw themselves utterly into the pursuit of box office receipts'.[12] Such motives are easily attributed, but how valid the attribution was in this case is difficult to ascertain.

In the case of *huaju* and other modern drama forms, it was more often a matter of guiding and restraining new productions than of banning or revising old plays, but similar considerations prevailed here too. There was a fairly strong orthodox distaste for humorous plays in general, and satire was unwelcome. There was constant exhortation, encouragement and pressure to adhere to the tenets of socialist realism,[13] with Soviet theory and practice as the major model. In general there was a strong tendency to write on modern themes (in some traditional forms of drama as well as in *huaju*), the war against the Japanese, the Korean war, railway construction, farm and factory life, modern Chinese social and domestic situations, and so forth. An often mentioned model play during the early years was *Test* by Xia Yan published in August 1954, set in an electrical machinery works and marked by frequent mention of the Soviet Union.

There were constant attempts to change the mentality of famous playwrights and to educate new playwrights along the desired paths. To this end many writers went to stay for brief periods in factories, on farms, and amid the soldiers in the Korean war areas. Cao Yu, for example, 'went down' in this manner in July 1950, Tian Han to Korea in early 1951, Cao Yu to the factories in March 1952, Lao She, Hong Shen, Xiong Foxi and others to Korea in October 1953.

Perhaps more than through translation the Chinese theatre world, or parts of it, maintained contacts with foreign drama, and in some ways increased such contacts, through the foreign troupes and dramatists who came to China and the Chinese dramatists who went abroad, as delegates to conferences and the like. For instance, Cao Yu attended a congress in Czechoslovakia in 1949, and Lao She a conference in New Delhi. Some foreign drama companies visited China, such as the Japanese *kabuki* company which went there in 1960 and 1966. Ballet, with its predominantly visual quality, proved particularly welcome, and was to have considerable effect on the development of some kinds of Chinese drama. As early as the 1920s, there had been interest in ballet in China, and it was taught by White Russians in Shanghai in the 1930s. In the early 1940s Dai Ailian (1916–), a lady with Western ballet experience, set up a Chinese Ballet Group concerned with Chinese folk dances. After 1949 folk dances were given considerable government encouragement, and in 1955 Dai Ailian was appointed principal of the Peking Dance School founded that year with the help of Russian advisers. As well as traditional Chinese dances, this school also taught some rudiments of Western ballet.[14] In addition to the influence and inspiration of Russian ballet, through visits by the state company and such peers of the art as Ulanova, described by Mei Lanfang as 'In form like the shining moon, her body as a gentle breeze', there were visits, for example, by a Bulgarian company in July 1956 and the British Ballet Rambert in 1957, and the Classical Ballet of France performed in Peking, Shanghai and other cities, their tour starting in May 1965. Tours by Oriental and East European song-and-dance ensembles served further to emphasise the role of dance for Chinese drama. The Chinese themselves established an experimental ballet troupe in 1959 with Soviet assistance. In addition to individual representatives, the Chinese sent some superb entertainment companies abroad, such as the Peking Opera Company which visited Britain in 1955, and companies which performed shadow shows and marionette shows in Paris in 1957.

By the mid-1950s a powerful tendency had developed to turn to the treasures of Chinese traditional drama, a tendency that received considerable impetus both from a general relaxation, for economic and other reasons, towards intellectual activities, and from events in the Soviet Union.[15] De-Stalinisation from 1956 encouraged a certain liberalisation in China, weakened uncritical views of the Soviet image there, and increased the confidence of the Chinese in their own destiny and past. The desire to veer towards the Chinese past was perhaps latently powerful in all kinds of Chinese people from the top to the bottom of society. The manifestations of this veering to the past were manifold, and we may mention only a few of those in the field of drama. It should be noted that even when, after a brief period, much of the liberalisation was reined in, the stress on the past remained clearly in evidence.

In early 1956 a Kunqu company, renamed that year as the Chekiang Kunqu Drama Company, performed *Fifteen strings of cash*, a revision of the Kunqu play by the early Qing playwright Zhu Suchen. An edition appeared in 1956[16], with articles from the pens of such notable theatre figures as Xia Yan, Mei Lanfang, Tian Han and Ouyang Yuqian. Fervent enthusiasm from a variety of directions greeted the performances.

The play is based on an old tale called *A joke over fifteen strings of cash brings uncanny disaster.* (The numbers parenthesised in the following summary of the plot refer to the illustration reproduced between pages 196 and 197.) One evening the butcher Bottle-gourd Yow returns home drunk, with a bundle of fifteen strings of cash. His step-daughter Su Xujuan (1) questions him, and he jokingly tells her that he has sold her, and that the money is his payment. Actually it is a loan to help his business. As he falls into a drunken sleep, the panic-stricken girl runs away to seek refuge with an aunt. A villainous, unsuccessful gambler, Rat Lou (2), passes Yow's shop at midnight, and enters it to steal something. He sees the money, but Yow wakes up. Rat hacks him to death with his own butcher's cleaver and runs off with the money. A young man called Xiong Yulan (3) is travelling to Suzhou with fifteen strings of cash belonging to his merchant master, when he meets Xujuan. Just then, Yow's neighbours rush up, find the money on him, and haul him and Xujuan off to court as the murderers. After a mockery of a trial conducted by the conceited incompetent magistrate of Wuxi, Guo Yuzhi (4), the two young people are sent to the death cell. The noble-minded Prefect of Suzhou, Kuang Zhong (5), is sent to supervise their execution, but, strongly suspecting injustice, he speeds overnight to his superior, Governor Zhou Chen. By desperate arguments Kuang persuades him to allow him to reinvestigate the case, and is grudgingly and with menaces granted a two weeks' time limit. By ingenious sleuthing he then pinpoints Rat as the major suspect (6). Rat escapes to the countryside, but Kuang and his helpers, including Bottle-gourd Yow's elderly, good-hearted neighbour Qin Guxin, trace him to his hideout. Disguised as a fortune-teller Kuang accosts Rat Lou in a temple, and by ingenious probing (7) manages to ascertain beyond all doubt that Rat is the murderer. He then tricks him on board his own boat, and ships him back to Suzhou for trial. The time limit has expired, and Kuang's career hangs in the balance, but in a tension-packed trial Rat is obliged by the sheer weight of evidence to confess, and the young man and girl are saved. The following is a translation of the celebrated scene in the temple during which Kuang as the fortune-teller cleverly and comically induces Rat to exhibit his own guilt. In performance, much of the dramatic appeal stems from Rat's visual portrayal of rattish traits.[17]

Fifteen strings of cash (1956): Scene Seven, 'Probing Rat'

(*In front of second curtain. The foot of Mount Hui, near the Temple of Eastern Yue. Enter porter, in guise of pedlar, and Qin Guxin.*)

QIN GUXIN.   I've been making enquiries here, there and everywhere for more than ten days, and now at last I've discovered that Rat Lou is living in that very thatched hut over there. (*Points it out to porter.*)
PORTER.   What does this Rat Lou look like, old uncle?
QIN GUXIN.   (*Does not reply. Stares fixedly ahead.*) Hey now, that man ahead of us looks like Rat Lou in person! Yes, it's him. Mustn't let him see me. I'll dodge out of sight. (*Exit.*)

(*Enter Rat Lou. Encounters porter. Porter taps his pedlar's drum. Rat gives a start of alarm. Exit porter.*)

RAT LOU.   Who's that? . . . What the . . . ? ! Phew! 'If your conscience is clear, the midnight knock occasions no fear!' Ever since that dratted Kuang Zhong fellow came to Wuxi, it's made me all nervy and edgy, and I can't relax for a moment or get a good night's sleep. These last ten days and more, I've been lying low out in the countryside here, and I can tell you it makes me feel proper hemmed-in and fed-up. The old priest in the Temple of Eastern Yue over there is an old acquaintance of mine, and often goes into town to purchase incense and candles, so what I must do is go and ask him for news of how the land lies. And while I'm at it, I'll ask for a divination lot, and find out whether I'm due for good or bad luck, ruin or joy.
> Hiding here in the countryside
> is a hell of a burden and bore,
> When Kuang Zhong pops back to his post,
> I'll pop out into action once more. (*Exit.*)

(*Enter Qin Guxin and porter again.*)

QIN GUXIN.   Yes, that was him. I'll hurry back while you stay here. (*Exit.*)
PORTER.   Much obliged. (*Seeing Rat Lou go into the temple*) My gaffer, His Worship, has been rigging himself up in disguise day after day, sleuthing here and enquiring there,

and now the time limit's nearly up, he's been really worked up and worried about things. Now that we've discovered where Rat Lou's gone to ground, you can bet he'll be delighted.

(*Enter first constable, in disguise.*)

FIRST CONSTABLE.   How are things going?
PORTER.   Rat Lou is in the Temple of Eastern Yue. Hurry off and report it to His Worship.
FIRST CONSTABLE.   Hang on, I'll go into the temple and arrest him.
PORTER.   His Worship said that although there are grave suspicions against Rat Lou, we still can't pin him down as the murderer, so his instructions were that we mustn't barge in and make a mess of things. I'll keep watch here, while you go down onto the boat and report to His Worship, and then we can think of the next step.

(*Exit first constable. Second curtain is withdrawn to reveal the interior of the Temple of Eastern Yue. Rat Lou emerges from the back.*)

RAT LOU.   The old priest's gone into town to buy some incense and candles, and he's still not back, so I'll just draw a divination lot and see what my fortune is while I'm waiting for him. Oh, Great God of Eastern Yue, oohh, Great God, if a smooth passage lies ahead, do your best for me, will you? (*Draws a lot. Enter Kuang Zhong disguised as a fortune-teller of the kind that interprets handwriting.*)
KUANG ZHONG.   Hoy! Good friend!
RAT LOU.   You made me jump out of my skin! What do you want?
KUANG ZHONG.   Do you want your fortune told?
RAT LOU.   I've come here to draw a lot. Tell my fortune? Not likely, none of that stuff for me!
KUANG ZHONG.   Drawing lots is sorcery – it isn't a patch on having your fortune told.
RAT LOU.   Eh? Is fortune-telling better then?
KUANG ZHONG.   Of course. If you've any doubts or perplexities on your mind that you can't resolve, or you want to know whether you're going to have good or bad luck during the coming year, all you have to do is have your fortune told. That clarifies everything, makes everything as plain as a pikestaff. If you want to alter any bad luck you may be heading for into good luck, or change your bothers into blessings, or find someone you've been looking for, or pull off some scheme or other that you're trying, or win when you're gambling, all you need to do is have your fortune told, and that'll put you completely in the picture. It never fails!
RAT LOU.   Oh . . . fortune-telling's the best, is it? (*Puts down the tube of divination lots.*) Would you mind telling me what line of fortune-telling you deal in?
KUANG ZHONG.   Try me and see.
            (*Sings*) For my graphology, my character-fathoming,
                    I am famed far and wide, all over the place.
RAT LOU.   Well, character-fathoming is fathoming characters, but what's all that about 'graphology'?
KUANG ZHONG.   Now, good friend, if you've got anything on your mind, all you have to do is write any old character that comes to you, and by looking at it we can judge whether you're going to have good luck or bad luck.

RAT LOU.   No you can't! No you can't!

KUANG ZHONG.   What do you mean? Why not?

RAT LOU.   I can't read a single character and I can't write a single character. So you can't tell my fortune, can you?

KUANG ZHONG.   Oh, it'll do if you just *say* a word. Any word that you think of.

RAT LOU.   Eh, it's all right if I just *say* a word? Any old word?

KUANG ZHONG.   Yes, that's right.

RAT LOU.   Look here, sir, my name, for what it's worth, is Rat Lou. Can you tell my fortune from the character for 'rat'?

KUANG ZHONG.   I can. I can indeed!

RAT LOU.   Let me fetch you a bench to sit on.

KUANG ZHONG.

> (*Sings*) On the pretext of fathoming characters, the truth I shall slowly trace,
>
> I only pray today that I may get to the bottom of this case.

RAT LOU.   Please sit down, sir.

KUANG ZHONG.   Now about what particular thing do you want me to fortune-tell from that character?

RAT LOU.   (*Looking round to right and left. In a whisper*) About a court case.

KUANG ZHONG.   I see! A court case?

(*Rat Lou covers up Kuang Zhong's mouth with his hand, making signs to him not to speak so loudly.*)

KUANG ZHONG.   (*Proceeding to interpret the character*) The character for 'rat' is composed of fourteen strokes. That's an even number, so it belongs to the dark hexagram line. And the rat, as an animal, also comes under the dark category. Darkness upon darkness is an indication of gloom and sombre confusion to come. If we're fortune-telling for a court case, there's no chance of its being cleared up in a hurry.

RAT LOU.   Oh, no, they never got it clear. What I want to know is whether any further trouble will crop up in connection with it in the future.

KUANG ZHONG.   Might I ask if it's for yourself that you want me to interpret this character, or for someone else?

RAT LOU.   Er, er, for someone else, somebody else, somebody else's fortune.

KUANG ZHONG.   From the look of the character though, I wouldn't have thought it was for someone else.

(*Rat Lou gives a start of alarm.*)

KUANG ZHONG.   (*Deliberately feigning consternation*) Oho, yes, rat's the root of the rot!

RAT LOU.   Eh, the lot of the loot?

KUANG ZHONG.   No, no, not the lot of the loot, the root of the rot, the prime source of the crime!

(*Rat shows great agitation.*)

KUANG ZHONG.   Yes, rat is the root, the prime one of the Twelve Cyclical Animals of the Horoscope, so it must be the root cause of calamity, mustn't it? Judging from the pattern of the character, one can ascertain beyond doubt that some theft from another person was what brewed this disaster. Is that so, good friend?

RAT LOU.   Reverend sir! You trot round the jetties, and I scrape my living in the gambling dens – we're birds of a feather, so there's no call for you to use that load of trade trick stuff on me. Cut out the tricks of the trade! Cut them out, will you! How can you tell that somebody's stolen something?

KUANG ZHONG.   Well, the rat's always a masterly thief. That's the only reason for our verdict. Now, another thing: wasn't the surname of the person who was robbed 'Yow'? (*Rat is so taken aback that he tumbles flat on the ground.*) Hey, watch yourself!

RAT LOU.   (*Gets up*) Phew, I told you not to use your tricks of the trade on me, and there you go again with your dodges. I don't believe you can tell the other bloke's name. How could you possibly know his name?

KUANG ZHONG.   I have my reasons.

RAT LOU.   What reasons?

KUANG ZHONG.   Doesn't the surname *Yow* sound the same as the word *yow* meaning 'oil'? And don't rats love stealing cooking oil?

RAT LOU.   That's right, they do. That's why there's the saying (*mimes a rat stealing oil*) 'rat stealing oil, the oil-stealing rat!' Look here, sir, let's forget about oil. Oil or salt, it makes no odds. Just you tell me whether you think I'm going to get tangled up in some nasty argy-bargy any time in the future?

KUANG ZHONG.   Not half you are! Any moment now, the lid will be taken off the whole affair.

RAT LOU.   How do you know?

KUANG ZHONG.   Look now, you asked me to tell a fortune by interpreting the character for 'rat'. Well, just now we're coming into the Month of the Rat, so the two things coincide, and the time is ripe. I'm afraid the case is about to be cleared up.

RAT LOU.   (*Speaking to himself*) Oh dear, oh dear. Cleared up! That's just what it mustn't be – cleared up! (*In such a fluster that he doesn't know which way to turn next.*)

KUANG ZHONG.   Tell me the truth now, good friend. Was it for yourself you wanted this fortune told, or for someone else? You'll have to make it quite plain to me, otherwise I shan't be able to give you any clear guidance as to what's to be done.

RAT LOU.   Wait a moment, sir. (*Walks to one side. Ponders over the matter. Stares all around him.*)

   (*Sings*) Him there . . . and me here . . .
   Sir, it's for somebody –

KUANG ZHONG. Eh? Come now, good friend, we're all brothers in this old world of ours. If you're in a fix, out with it, and perhaps I can help you lighten the burden of your troubles.

RAT LOU.   To tell you the honest truth, it's for myself!

KUANG ZHONG.   Ah, so it was for yourself you wanted it told?

RAT LOU.   (*Stops him, with signs that he must not talk so loudly.*) This star of ruination that's looming over my head, sir . . . do you think I can dodge it?

KUANG ZHONG.   Hm, if it's *your* fortune we're telling, then you mustn't miss a gap for yourself.

RAT LOU.   What do you mean by that?

ZUANG ZHONG.   Listen, if you put the character for 'rat' under the character for 'gap', it makes the character for 'scuttle', doesn't it!

RAT LOU.   What's that about 'skittle'?

KUANG ZHONG.   Scuttle! Scram, escape.

RAT LOU. Oh, do you think I can scuttle out of it, sir?

KUANG ZHONG. Of course you can, if you want to. The only trouble is that rats are always suspicious by nature, and if you start suspecting this and suspecting that, imagining you see bogies here and goblins there, I'm afraid you may cut off all your own retreats, leave yourself no way out. Then there'll be no chance of your scuttling anywhere.

RAT LOU. (*With respectful awe*) You really do have marvellous second sight, sir. Quite infallible! You know, I've always been over-suspicious, seeing snags everywhere when there aren't any at all. Now if I'm to follow your wonderful advice, when, in your opinion, would be the best time for me to move off?

KUANG ZHONG. If you're going to go at all, you'll have to set off today. By tomorrow you won't make it, if you try your hardest.

RAT LOU. Why not?

KUANG ZHONG. The top part of the character for 'rat' is the character for 'mortar', which in turn is made up of two halves of the character for 'day'. Put the two halves together, and you've got one whole day. If you wait until tomorrow, that'll count as two days. So it'll be one day too long, and you won't be able to escape.

RAT LOU. Oh deary me, and now it's getting dark already. How should I make my getaway then?

KUANG ZHONG. Let me see. Well, the rat's a creature that keeps hidden during the day and moves around at night, so if you made your escape tonight, that would do splendidly.

RAT LOU. And could I bother you to find out which direction I ought to take so as to get away safely without any hitches, sir?

KUANG ZHONG. Just let me work it out a minute: rat comes under the hexagram *xun*, and *xun* comes under the east. You'd do best going south-eastwards.

RAT LOU. South-east? . . . And if it's not too much trouble, sir, could you see which would be the safest route for me – by waterway or by road?

KUANG ZHONG. Let me do another little calculation then: rat comes under the Celestial Stem 'son', and 'son' comes under the influence of 'water'. Yes, by water would be best.

RAT LOU. Heading south-east, by waterway, it's through Wuxi, Wangting, Guanshang, Suzhou – (*Gives a start.*)*

KUANG ZHONG. Jiaxing, Hangzhou . . . now Hangzhou would be an ideal place!

RAT LOU. Oh dear, if only there was a boat available heading south-east, I'd jump slap-bang straight on board, and if it got under way at once . . . ah, that would be wonderful!

KUANG ZHONG. As it happens, I have a boat going that way, and we're due to sail this evening, heading for the Suzhou-Hangzhou area, so as to make the best of the New Year, businesswise. The only snag is . . .

RAT LOU. I beg you to do me a good turn, sir. Take me along with you, couldn't you? I'll pay plenty for my fare, you can rely on that.

KUANG ZHONG. Come, come, don't mention such things! Money's like muck, but kindness and nobility are worth a thousand golden guineas. The only snag is that the boat travels very slowly, but if you don't mind that, good friend, it's settled, you can share my vessel.

*Suzhou being the seat of Kuang Zhong's prefectureship, and the very place Rat most wants to avoid.

RAT LOU.   Well, I never! – You're no fortune-teller!

KUANG ZHONG.   Eh, what?

RAT LOU.   No, you're old Rat Lou's Divine Saviour, his Redeeming Bodhisattva! From now on, I put my life entirely in your hands!

KUANG ZHONG.   Then just you set your mind at rest, and I guarantee you a safe and uneventful voyage!

RAT LOU.   (*Sings*) Just like some fish from the net slipping free,
                    swimming hurry-scurry off into the mighty sea.

KUANG ZHONG.(*Continuing the song*)
                    May any troubles we meet now turn to joys instead,
                    may from this moment only plain-sailing lie ahead!

RAT LOU.   (*Continuing the song*)
                    Far far away I'll soar, to the end of the world I'll flee.
Hey, sir, where's your boat?

KUANG ZHONG.(*Leading Rat outside by the arm*) On the river just down there in front of us.

RAT LOU.   I live in that thatched hut right there on the other bank. Now here's your fee for the fortune-telling, and here's my fare for the boat. Please take it, and, if you don't mind, I'll just go and fetch some clothes and silver and then I'll be with you right away.

KUANG ZHONG.   Be quick then. I'll wait for you on board. (*Exit Rat Lou. Enter first constable and porter.*)

KUANG ZHONG.   (*To first constable*) Quickly, shadow him!

(*Exit first constable.*)

KUANG ZHONG.(*To porter*) You hurry off into town, fetch some government beadles, gather some local people, and go and make a search of Rat's house. If you discover any suspicious objects, bring them back to Suzhou tonight without fail!

(*Exit porter. Exit Kuang Zhong.*)

From 28 June to 23 July 1956 the first stage of formal discussions on the annotated edition of *Lute* took place. The Union of Dramatists invited specialists on the play from all over the country to the discussions, and a volume was published recording the proceedings of some of them.[18] The topic was debated until the end of the year. On 12 November 1957 there were commemorations in Shanghai and elsewhere of the 340th anniversary of the death of Tang Xianzu. On 28 June in Peking there commenced a memorial congress to celebrate the seven-hundredth anniversary of the death of Guan Hanqing. This was accompanied by a Guan Hanqing Exhibition, publication of works by and about him, and the first performance of a *huaju* play written by Tian Han and entitled *Guan Hanqing*.[19]

Guan Hanqing consisted of twelve scenes (comparable in length to the acts of *chuanqi*), and also showed other structural features akin to those of traditional Chinese dramas. It was an imaginative fantasy about the Yuan playwright, stressing his and his friends' qualities of fierce resistance to injustice. Historical events were woven into the plot, but the details and general outline stemmed largely from Tian Han. Incensed by the unjust execution of a young woman, Guan, with the encouragement of courtesan-actress Pearl Curtain Beauty, resolves to write a play condemning the evil men in power.[20] Meanwhile, in his capacity as a medical doctor, he cures the mother of Khublai Khan's Deputy Prime Minister, Akham, and, as a reward, is able to rescue a girl who has been forcibly pressed into service in Akham's household. Working day and night on his new play, he completes it, and it is performed. After the first performance, which calls forth the admiration of a certain Chinese military commander, Guan is ordered to make radical alterations to the script to tone it down for a performance before Akham. He refuses to do so. Akham stops the play, has Guan and Pearl Curtain Beauty thrown into jail, and puts out the eyes of another of the cast, the actress Vying-with Pearl Curtain. In jail, Guan learns the news that the commander has assassinated Akham. Refusing a chance to avoid execution by giving false evidence in favour of Akham's party, he manages to have a 'farewell' meeting with Pearl Curtain Beauty in jail. A change in the attitudes of the régime towards Akham and a petition signed by ten thousand people obtain the reduction of their sentences. Guan is banished, and takes sad leave of his beloved lady and his friends.

The following excerpt from his play contains one of the most active moments of the plot. Deputy Prime Minister Akham and company are watching Guan's play, which Akham has the day before ordered to be revised.[21]

Guan Hanqing by Tian Han: Scene Seven

(*The privileged seats of the auditorium of the Jade Angel Bower theatre. Deputy Prime Minister Akham is watching the play in the company of Grand Chancellor Horikhoson. Because Pearl Curtain Beauty is performing the play exactly as first written, without any revisions whatsoever, Hao Zhen and other officials who have responsibilities in the matter have several times tried to explain things to Akham, and to ask him for instructions as to what to do about it, but have been prevented from doing so, because Grand Chancellor Horikhoson is present, and his presence makes it awkward for them to say anything. Akham is by now so angry that he is hissing through his whiskers and glaring fiercely, but he is still trying his utmost to humour Horikhoson.*)

GRAND CHANCELLOR HORIKHOSON. Not a bad play, my lord Akham. No wonder Her Ladyship, Boyan's mother, appreciated it. The playwright is a man of considerable insight. I hear he's highly celebrated for his dramas. Is that so?

DEPUTY PRIME MINISTER AKHAM. Yes, that's right, Chancellor. Have you seen any of his plays before?

GRAND CHANCELLOR HORIKHOSON. Very few. As you know, I'm not much of a one for frequenting playhouses and sing-song quarters. That's why I couldn't come and enjoy the pleasure of your company here yesterday. But since today you have favoured me with repeated invitations, my lord Akham, I could hardly refuse!

DEPUTY PRIME MINISTER AKHAM. Come, come now, you flatter me. Yes, you're right, the author of this play does enjoy a certain reputation. Written fifty or sixty plays, so they tell me. Deprived of their imperial Civil Service examinations under our

dynasty, these Chinese with their modicum of education and book learning have no
longer been able to rise to the top at one go by becoming junior and senior optimes or
what have you. So they've shifted their attentions to this line of activity. Actually, it's not
such a bad thing either. After all, doesn't his Imperial Majesty tell us to try and devise
outlets for such people to dissipate their wits and talents? So I personally often come and
have a listen to their baubles. For one thing, it provides a little amusement, and, for
another, it enables me to investigate what they are really thinking.

GRAND CHANCELLOR HORIKHOSON.   You have the right approach, my lord Akham.
Next time there is such a fine play as this, you must let me come and see it. I shall
certainly be only too glad to keep you company.

DEPUTY PRIME MINISTER AKHAM.   Hm! Yes, but these little monkeys are devilish
awkward to handle. They never rest content with their lot for a single moment. Always
either saying how much better the past was than the present, or making roundabout
insinuations. And even if you tell them not to do something, it only makes them all the
more determined to do it. Didn't you hear just now how this play was getting in digs at
us government officials?

GRAND CHANCELLOR HORIKHOSON.   Yes, indeed, I did notice it. He had some very
weighty jabs at corrupt and venal officialdom. But how does that concern us, now?

DEPUTY PRIME MINISTER AKHAM.   You're too generous and fair-minded, Grand
Chancellor. – If he's capable of abusing them, he's capable of abusing us, too.

GRAND CHANCELLOR HORIKHOSON.   Let them have their bouts of abuse. It has certain advantages, helps to keep the administrative system in trim.

DEPUTY PRIME MINISTER AKHAM.   No, no, the one thing we can't do is let them talk.
As soon as you loosen your grip on them, they'll be up in rebellion. Be no limit to what
they might do! Terrible to imagine!

GRAND CHANCELLOR HORIKHOSON. . . .

(*For the moment, Horikhoson is unable to find any polite words with which to answer the overbearing,
wildly blustering Akham, and just at this juncture the play on stage re-enters their consciousness. Pearl
Curtain Beauty is playing the part of Dou Graceful.*)

DOU GRACEFUL.
            (*Sings*) These vows I now make are not frivolous ones,
                    – truly I am wronged most grievously!
                    And without some sign divine to prove it to mankind,
                    who'll believe a kind Heaven cares for me!
                    Let not one smallest drop of my blood
                    sprinkle the mortal dust below,
                    but all to the silken streamer there
                    atop the eight-foot flagpole it must flow.
                    And when they thus perceive,
                    then may all around believe
                    that I am as Chang Hong whose blood turned to emerald stone,*

*Chang Hong, an official during the Zhou dynasty, who, incidentally, was able to summon snow
making spirits. He was unjustly killed, and his blood, so it is said, turned to stone or green jade.

          like Emperor Gaze, whose soul within the nightjar bird makes
            moan.*

EXECUTIONER.   Have you got anything else you want to say? If you don't speak up with it to His Excellency the Execution Superintendent now, I don't know when you'll ever get the chance again!

DOU GRACEFUL.   Your Excellency, it is now the very height of summer. If I really am being done an injustice, as I claim, then when I am dead Heaven will send down three feet of snow as a sign, and it will cover my corpse.

EXECUTION SUPERINTENDENT.   In this hot summer weather, even if you had a Heaven-high heap of valid grievances, you could never bring down a single flake of snow. What nonsense you're talking!

DOU GRACEFUL.

       (*Sings*) You tell me this is warm summertime,
          not the kind of days for falling snow,
          – Haven't you heard how, for Zou Yan's sake,
          frost flew down one July long ago!†
          If, from deep inside me, true resentment
          spurts forth like fire into the air,
          surely Heaven in pity will send its snowflakes
          like July ice-flowers tumbling everywhere,
          so that thus my flesh and bones shall not lie bare.
          What need shall I have then of 'white horses and carriage pure
            pale'‡
          to send me off mid ancient paths, along the wilderness graveyard
            trail!

(*Kneels once more*) Your Excellency, if my death is really and truly an undeserved one, then from this day there will be a terrible drought here in Chu subprefecture for three years.

EXECUTION SUPERINTENDENT.   I'll slap your mouth! What are you thinking of, talking in that manner!

DOU GRACEFUL.

       (*Sings*) You think one can pin no hopes on Heaven,
          that the human heart cannot draw its sympathies,
          You are unaware that the Vast Celestial Realm
          can answer human prayers if so it please:
          Why otherwise did, in distant years gone by,
          for three years no sweet showers drop from out the sky,

*The Emperor Gaze, Du Yu, was ruler of Shu in the late Zhou dynasty, and abdicated his throne to become a hermit. It was said that he changed into a nightjar, and the sad call of that bird was interpreted as the sorrowful cries of his soul.

†Zou Yan was a minister of the Prince of Yan during the Zhou, and was imprisoned through others' slanders. Heaven is said to have caused frost to form in midsummer as a supernatural sign of his innocence.

‡Fan Shi and Zhang Shao of the Latter Han dynasty were very close friends. One year, when they were living far apart, Fan dreamed that Zhang came to him and told him of his death and the date of his funeral. Fan set off with white horses and white carriage to the funeral, but was a little late. Meanwhile, the coffin refused to budge. Only when Fan arrived and led it forward would it move on to its permanent place of rest. The friendship of Fan and Zhang was the subject of a Yuan *zaju*. The reference to white horses and white carriage was widely used in later times to allude to funerals.

> were it not for the wrong endured by the loving Daughter-in-law of
>   Donghai?*
> And now the turn of your Shangyang county† is nigh:
> all because the officials have no intention
> of adhering to justice or upholding the law,
> and thus leave the ordinary people no way,
> no ear for their grief, none to hear what they implore.

DEPUTY PRIME MINISTER AKHAM.   (*In a great rage, shouts*) Stop the play! I forbid you
to continue the performance any further!

IMPERIAL GUARDSMEN.   Stop the play! Forbidden to continue the performance!

DEPUTY PRIME MINISTER AKHAM.   This is intolerable! (*To Hao Zhen*) You, Hao
Zhen, is this the way you carry out your duties?

HAO ZHEN.   Yesterday evening, I did as you instructed, and told them to make revisions. And today, just before the performance started, Pearl Curtain Beauty assured me
that it had been revised. But as I was listening to them, I realised they hadn't changed
one single word.

DEPUTY PRIME MINISTER AKHAM.   (*With a false, evil smile*) You generally manage to
perform your tasks quite ably – how is it you've suddenly become an utter nincompoop!
Eh? Quickly grab that stinking whore Pearl Curtain Beauty and bring her here.

HAO ZHEN.   Grab Pearl Curtain Beauty and bring her here!

(*The guardsmen rush off, then return, marching Pearl Curtain Beauty, under arrest and still wearing
her stage convict's smock and skirt.*)

PEARL CURTAIN BEAUTY.   I kowtow to you, venerable Excellency.

DEPUTY PRIME MINISTER AKHAM.   Eh, what? So you're Pearl Curtain Beauty?

PEARL CURTAIN BEAUTY.   I am.

DEPUTY PRIME MINISTER AKHAM.   You're remarkably bold, I must say.
(*To Hao Zhen*) What message did you convey to them yesterday?

HAO ZHEN.   Your insignificant subordinate told them that if they didn't alter the play,
or refused to perform it, we'd have their heads.

DEPUTY PRIME MINISTER AKHAM.   And what about the one who drafted the play, that
Guan Hanqing? Is he here today?

PEARL CURTAIN BEAUTY.   No, he hasn't come.

DEPUTY PRIME MINISTER AKHAM.   Where's he got to?

PEARL CURTAIN BEAUTY.   I don't know. His mother is ill, so he may perhaps have
gone back to his home in the country.

DEPUTY PRIME MINISTER AKHAM.   We told you to revise the play, and you deliberately failed to make any alterations. What on earth can you have been thinking of?! Eh?

---

*This refers to the tale of the woman of the Latter Han dynasty who, widowed when still young, looked
after her mother-in-law most lovingly. The mother-in-law hung herself to avoid being a burden on her,
and her own daughter then accused the daughter-in-law of having murdered the dead woman. Examined
in court under torture, the daughter-in-law was sentenced to death. After she died there was no rain in the
region for three years, until the injustice was officially recognised. This tale was no doubt the main inspiration for the *zaju Injustice done to Dou Graceful* attributed to Guan Hanqing, of which the above is a quotation.

†In Chu subprefecture in Shantung province.

PEARL CURTAIN BEAUTY.   Mr Guan did actually revise the play, but as we had only half a day left for rehearsing, I didn't have time to manage to learn the new words. So there was nothing else for it, I just had to sing all the old words. I know it's a crime deserving of ten thousand deaths, and I can only beseech you, venerable Excellency, to have mercy upon me.

DEPUTY PRIME MINISTER AKHAM.   Couldn't learn the new words? Aren't you famous for your lightning powers of memorisation? You cover up well, and you take a lot upon your own shoulders, I must admit. In your attempts to save Guan Hanqing, just like Dou Graceful tries to save her mother-in-law, you try to carry the whole burden yourself. (*To Grand Chancellor Horikhoson*) A most touching and admirable episode, don't you agree, Grand Chancellor? (*Turning to Pearl Curtain Beauty*) Very well then, I shall grant you the fulfilment of your noble desires, I shall. You, here!

IMPERIAL GUARDSMEN.   Yessir!

DEPUTY PRIME MINISTER AKHAM.   Take Pearl Curtain Beauty out and chop off her head.

(*The guardsmen bind Pearl Curtain Beauty. Guan Hanqing rushes up.*)

GUAN HANQING.   Not so fast! (*To Deputy Prime Minister Akham*) Your Excellency, Lord Akham, it was I who refused to allow the play to be altered. Nothing whatsoever to do with Pearl Curtain Beauty.

DEPUTY PRIME MINISTER AKHAM.   (*To Hao Zhen*) Who is this man?

HAO ZHEN.   That's Guan Hanqing himself.

DEPUTY PRIME MINISTER AKHAM.   So, stepping forward and showing himself, so as not to let his whore pay for the crime all on her own. Yes, he has plenty of pluck, too, I'll give him that. Guan Hanqing, you have written a good number of other plays – are you trying to tell me that you are ignorant of the fact that the laws of this dynasty prohibit 'the wild and irresponsible composition of songs, attacking those in high position with abusive words'? And in addition to attacking those in high position with abusive words, this play commits the further crime of 'satirising other individuals'. So you should by rights already have had your head removed for it. It was only because I was taking into consideration your ability and reputation, meagre though they be, that I allowed you the chance to perform the play again, with certain revisions. Yet, you actually dared to disobey my commands and not alter the play, and, not content with that, even had your slut of a mistress perform it absolutely intact. Doesn't that indicate nothing more nor less than an attempt at rebellion? Very well, I shall grant you the fulfilment of what you seem to seek. Guards!

IMPERIAL GUARDSMEN.   Yessir!

DEPUTY PRIME MINISTER AKHAM.   Hustle them both outside and chop off their heads!

(*Fierce as wolves and tigers, the guardsmen bind Guan Hanqing with ropes. Grand Chancellor Horikhoson, who is sitting to one side, can no longer restrain himself, and rises to his feet.*)

GRAND CHANCELLOR HORIKHOSON.   My lord Akham, old dodderer that I am, I would like, if I may, to put in a word of mitigation. I wonder if you would condescend to lend me your ear for a moment?

[. . .]

A great deal of mention of Yuan *zaju* and Yuan playwrights, poets and singing girls comes into the play. There is much 'ancient' atmosphere, and much humour. Another, earlier version had a happy ending, with Guan Hanqing and singing girl reunited. The play made a considerable impact, was adapted into other kinds of drama, and filmed. Other playwrights of note also wrote plays on ancient themes during the next few years, and there were many signs of great interest in traditional Chinese theatre and the remoter Chinese past.[22] Ancient and regional kinds of drama were performed in Peking, and several traditional plays were made into films.

In addition to the renewed interest in Chinese traditional drama, the tendency to mix and amalgamate different kinds of drama gained momentum. Of course this had always been the practice, but such amalgamations now came more and more to the fore of national drama, and became much freer in their range of structural borrowings. A small number of *xin geju* appeared,[23] and there was a wide variety of other forms loosely termed *geju*, 'operas', *wuju*, 'dance dramas', or *gewuju*, 'song-and-dance dramas', which terms were also sometimes applied to traditional kinds of drama, and also embraced foreign and national minority forms of performance.[24] An experienced theatregoer described the situation as follows:

> Some people ask me: Was it an old play or a new play you saw? Very difficult indeed to answer, because the plays I see are truly a motley. Some have old form and new theme. Some have new form and old theme. Some old forms have now absorbed many new forms, and a number of new forms have evolved from old forms. The words 'new' and 'old' are no longer adequate to circumscribe dramatic art.[25]

The use of contemporary themes with old forms was greatly on the increase during the late '50s and early '60s, and there were a number of festivals of traditional drama with contemporary themes in 1964.

The force and potential of drama in China during these years were partly reflected in the sensitivity of politicians to drama, and in the fierce controversy to which some plays gave rise, among them *Bitterness in the Qing Palace* written by Yao Xinnong (1905–) and first performed in 1941,[26] or more particularly the film version of it, and the play *Dismissal of Hai Rui* by Wu Han (1909–), deputy mayor of Peking, published in January 1961.[27] Criticism in a newspaper of Wu Han's play was considered by many official organs as the opening shot fired in the Grand Proletarian Cultural Revolution, known more briefly as the Cultural Revolution.

The Cultural Revolution was many things at once, ideological, political, factional, and most certainly involved with 'culture' even in its narrower English connotations. The disputes, the origins of which may be traced back many years earlier, culminated in a confrontation between Mao Tse-tung, Chairman of the Chinese Communist Party, and Liu Shaoqi, President of the People's Republic of China and Vice-chairman of the Party. Even before this confrontation came to a head, Mao had already launched the Cultural Revolution, his major missile against a broad sweep of his political, ideological and other enemies generally branded as 'revisionist'. Much of the early sparring and fighting was conducted through the medium of literature, and more particularly the medium of drama. Wu Han was associated with leading literary and political groups opposed to Mao, and his play was seen as a satire in support of them and their ideas. On 10 November 1965 a Shanghai newspaper published an article by Yao Wenyuan (b. 1925) fiercely attacking the play and accusing Wu Han of using historical personalities to satirise contemporary people and events. This was the article that in effect opened the Cultural Revolution. Criticism of Wu Han, his play, and the group to which he adhered mounted during the months that followed. On 19 April 1966, the Cultural Revolution was formally announced in the *People's Daily* newspaper. The attacks from Mao's supporters widened their range to include many more political and intellectual figures, and by June had moved into open and more purely political combat at the highest levels of control. By 11 July a fierce campaign against Zhou Yang was under way. Political, academic and other leaders fell. In the early days of August, Liu Shaoqi was demoted, and on 18 August the Red Guards held their first public parade, a million strong, in Peking.

The Red Guards were mainly very young people mobilised by the Mao side as a major weapon against its opponents. They took action against individuals, institutions and physical structures in their attacks on 'bourgeois remnants, bureaucracy and vested interests', encouraging and obliging citizens of Peking, and later of other places, to make self-criticisms. They came into fierce conflict with factory workers and other large organisations. Later the army was brought more actively into the Revolution to stabilise matters. The powerful presence of the army was reflected in the literature and drama of the period. Meanwhile, in December 1966, Wu Han, Tian Han, who had also been attacked earlier in the year for a play he had written, and others were arrested, and some time towards the end of 1966 Lao She, so it is strongly rumoured, drowned himself in a lake in Peking. Another playwright to fall was Xia Yan. Indeed, of the better known playwrights and writers of long standing only Guo Moruo endured and continued to appear in print and at lofty functions.

Specialist writings on literature ceased to be published and only a limited amount of detailed information is available on many aspects of the history of Chinese drama during the last few years. Drama has occupied an important position in China during this period, but many accounts are presented in a generalised manner which affords no complete picture of what has been happening. Some outline may be essayed all the same. The continuing prestige of drama in China was amply reflected in the pride of place it occupied in many of the activities, speeches and writings of the Cultural Revolution. It was also reflected in the constant preoccupation of the government with drama creation and reform. In this latter respect it was Jiang Qing (c. 1914–), former Shanghai film actress and Mao Tse-tung's third wife, who was the guiding hand for the new theatre.[28]

Appointed Adviser on Cultural Work to the army, she was able to give direct instruction to the various Peking Opera and other entertainment companies which were taken over by the army. Already in July 1964 at a Festival of Peking Opera on Contemporary Themes Jiang Qing had expressed some very explicit views on drama:

> [. . .] According to rough statistics, there are three thousand drama troupes in China (not including amateur troupes and even less accounting for the 'black' unauthorised troupes). Among them are about ninety which are professional *huaju* troupes, and over eighty which are cultural troupes, while the remainder, over 2,800 of them, are traditional drama troupes. On the traditional drama stages we get nothing but emperors and kings, generals and prime ministers, talented scholars and beautiful young ladies, and ox-headed demons and snake-gods into the bargain. Even those ninety *huaju* troupes, you cannot rely on them to portray the workers, peasants and soldiers, either. Their principle, too, is 'bigness, foreignness and antiquity', and it is fair to say that the *huaju* stage too has been taken over by the ancients, Chinese and foreign. The theatre is a place for educating the people, but nowadays all we get on the stage is emperors and kings, generals and prime ministers, talented scholars and beautiful young ladies, all a load of feudalistic stuff, all a load of bourgeois stuff. Such conditions cannot provide protection for the basis of our economy, but may on the contrary serve to destroy the basis of our economy.[29]

Such objections to foreignness and antiquity were reflected in the themes and, more mixedly, in the structure and style of the new approved dramas.

Most publicity for drama in recent years has concerned those plays included among the 'eight models', which emerged as such in 1967, although some had been created years earlier. The models were five *geming xiandai jingju*, 'revolutionary modern Peking Operas', two *geming xiandai wuju*, 'revolutionary modern ballets', and one symphony. The events that immediately led to the founding of the new drama, which can partly be traced back to some of Mao Tse-tung's own promptings,[30] were a national conference on drama held in August 1963 and the East China Festival of Modern Drama held in Shanghai in late December 1963. More imposing was the Festival of Peking Opera on Contemporary Themes held in July 1964 in Peking, when Jiang Qing made her famous speech. Mao Tse-tung attended the performance of one of the new plays in the same month. Later in the year similar festivals were held in Kiangsi and Heilongkiang provinces.

The five model plays were as follows: *Taking Tiger Mountain by strategy*, *Sea harbour*, *Raid on the White Tiger Regiment*, *Shajiabang*, and *Red lantern*. All emerged in fairly approved form around 1964, but later underwent constant revisions. They were collectively created and revised by various Peking Opera troupes, from Peking, Shanghai and Shantung province, with a great deal of advice from Jiang

Qing. The first concerned the taking of a bandit's lair by an army unit in 1946; the second, the defeat of a saboteur in the docks in 1963; the third, a raid on the headquarters of a South Korean regiment in 1953; the fourth, an army unit's destruction of Japanese soldiers and of the Chinese who assisted them during the War of Resistance; and the fifth, the story of how the family of a railway switchman fought the Japanese during the same war. Some gestures, acrobatics and other features and conventions of traditional Peking Opera were used, but some of the gestures and other movements were newly devised, or derived from other sources. Modern uniforms were very prominent in four of the five, as indeed were modern weapons. The scenery was elaborate and fairly literally realistic. There was a general attempt, however, not to be too closely naturalistic and although sets, props, lighting and costumes were easily associable with what they represented, the aim was to present them 'on a higher plane than ordinary life'. Heroes and good people were often dressed in brilliant colours, villains in drab, murky colours. Patches on the clothing of the poor were not ragged, but were neatly placed. Sometimes vast panoramas were used to lend majesty to the action and to the heroes, towering straight pines, for instance, to emphasise the firmness, uprightness and strength of the hero. Great stress was placed on depicting the heroes as lofty, straightforward, simplified characters, much less complex than some of the most familiar heroes of traditional drama. The singing derived much from the traditional style, but the overall effect of the dramas was very distinct from that of traditional Peking Opera.

Many of the above characteristics were shared by the two ballets. *Red detachment of women*, presented in October 1964, depicted the struggle during the period 1927–37 of a women's company and other armed forces against a local tyrant. The other ballet, *White-haired girl*, created between 1964 and 1965 and based on the earlier play of the same name, greatly simplified the play's story to stress good and bad more blackly and whitely and gave the army a greater role. These ballets were often acclaimed as examples of making foreign things serve China, and the debt to Western and Russian ballet in the formal features of the choreography is unmistakable, although there was some borrowing from traditional Chinese dance and drama movements, and some innovation. *White-haired girl* even had a sung chorus to accompany the dancing. Orchestras combined Western and traditional Chinese instruments. The scenery, whilst fairly close to literal reality, also embodied features akin to traditional Chinese painting. The soft grace of many of the movements of Western ballet gave way, in accordance with the themes, to more vigorous and aggressive movements. The eighth of the models was the symphony *Shajiabang*, based on the play of the same name. Other examples of the taste for more purely musical versions of plays are *Red Lantern* of 1967, consisting of vigorous piano music with Peking Opera-style singing, and more recently the piano concerto *Yellow River*, to which much publicity has been given.

Something of the mixture of old and new, the obvious borrowings from traditional drama, the emphasis on action, and other typical features of the *geming xiandai geju* may be glimpsed in the following excerpt from the play *Shajiabang*, in which Chinese soldiers under Guo Jianguang, and militia under Sister Aqing, are advancing to attack the headquarters of 'puppet' forces collaborating with the Japanese. Zhang Songtao, Ye Sizhong and Seventh Dragon are all fighting on Guo's side.[31]

Shajiabang: Scene Eight, 'Rapid raid'

(*Three days later, before dawn. Out in the countryside. As the curtain opens, Zhang Songtao and Ye Sizhong enter, keeping a look-out as they patrol. Exeunt.*)

GUO JIANGUANG.
    (*Sings backstage*) The moon shines on the traveller's path, and the breeze sends brisk
        air . . .

(*Enter warriors and Guo Jianguang.*)

GUO JIANGUANG.
        (*Sings*) We have gone through the hills and rivers and the heavily sleeping
           villages.
        The branch unit has spread its encircling net,
        to destroy Hu Chuankuei's gang of traitors.
        A raiding platoon has been organised to advance at a forced march,
        and flying troops will make a miraculous assault on Shajiabang.
        We shall drive a sharp-pointed knife straight into the enemy's heart,
        hit him when he's least expecting it.
        And I guarantee we shall make his whole line collapse in confusion
           and lose all sense of direction,
        just like pouring hot water on an ants' nest or setting fire to a bee-
           hive!

(*Enter Zhang Songtao and Ye Sizhong.*)

YE SIZHONG. An enemy patrol!
SEVENTH DRAGON. Clobber them!
GUO JIANGUANG. Take cover!

(*All conceal themselves. The puppet army patrol walks past them.*)

GUO JIANGUANG. Platoon commander Ye! Zhang Songtao!
ZHANG SONGTAO and YE SIZHONG. Present!
GUO JIANGUANG. Look: there ahead of us lies Shajiabang. I command you two to continue your scouting.
ZHANG SONGTAO and YE SIZHONG. Right! (*Exeunt.*)
GUO JIANGUANG. Forward!
        (*Sings*) What's all that about 'a defensive cordon lined with sentry boxes
           and guard posts'?!

−As I see it, they are nothing but paper barriers and silk-muslin
walls!
Far far ahead Shajiabang is coming into my gaze,
and this time we go to pound the enemy nest and seize the brigands
and the brigand king! (*Exit. Curtain.*)

Scene Nine: 'Breaking through'

(*Closely following on the previous scene, outside the rear wall of the headquarters of the puppet Loyal
and Just National Salvation Army. As the curtain rises on a sentry post of the puppet army, a soldier of
the puppet army is standing there on sentry duty.*)

PUPPET SOLDIER.   The commander gets married, and he goes and invites the Japanese
to the wedding, and sends us to reinforce the guard! Pah! just my rotten luck!

(*Enter Ye Sizhong and others. They take the puppet soldier captive, and drag him off. Enter Guo
Jianguang with fighters of the raiding party, and Sister Aqing leading the militia.*)

SISTER AQING.   Instructor, immediately past this wall is Diao Deyi's* back yard!
       (*Sings*) There has been no change in the disposition of the enemy forces,
       −the intelligence map that was sent shows it all at a glance.
       Their main strength lies all to the eastern and western sides,
       and they have only one squad at the front gate.
       With their telephone line severed by the militia,
       the two flanks cannot come to their aid.
       In the courtyard a wedding party is being held,
       and, as they play guess-fingers and wine-forfeits, they are shaking
         the heavens with their noisy revelling.
       You leap over the wall, and strike right into the courtyard,
       and for certain you'll be able to slaughter all the crowd of vicious
         rogues together,
       at one rattle of the battle-drums.
GUO JIANGUANG.   Seventh Dragon!
(*Continues the song*)   You lead the fire-power group round to the front yard,
       and destroy the enemy's guard squad.
(*To Sister Aqing*)   You go and meet our main corps at the end of the village.

(*Exeunt Seventh Dragon leading some soldiers, and Sister Aqing leading the militia. Guo Jianguang
leads soldiers over the wall. Exeunt. Curtain.*)

During the last few years these models have constituted the major cultural
showpieces, rivalled sometimes by table tennis, and great efforts have been made
to advertise and popularise them both inside and outside China. They have been

---

*The chief of staff of the puppet army.

reproduced in an astonishing variety of media, in films, television, printed editions, translations, stamps, picture storybooks, postcards, calendars, pictures, magazines, pieces of embroidery, wood and jade sculptures, posters, gramophone records, and even machine-produced steel silhouettes.[32] The models have been used for entertainment on many important occasions and to welcome foreign delegations and dignitaries, including the President of the United States and Dom Mintoff of Malta.

Piano, ballet, symphony, imposing scenery, part-Western orchestras, wide picture stages, big casts . . . It is easy to see how such things may be suited to grand occasions, modern city theatres and the purposes of stirring, lofty moral elevation, but the problem of popularising them in outlying districts and remote villages is physically more difficult than with the more mobile kinds of traditional drama, which used light instruments, no scenery and generally small casts. Some of the performers have had to carry stage sets on their shoulders in their tours of the countryside, and ingenious collapsible scenery has been devised in an attempt to reduce the burden. One time-honoured way round the problems has been the performance of excerpts and isolated songs, sometimes involving only one *huqin*-player and a singer. Piano transportation has given a great deal of trouble, and for a while there were stories of heroic efforts to drag them to remote parts and rocky islands. Promotion of the piano was one of Jiang Qing's major enterprises, and from May 1967 it was publicly proclaimed as the musical instrument of the Cultural Revolution. Films, radio and television may, of course, solve many of the transport difficulties, but the carrying of film projectors by travellers on foot is no easy task. As and if villages acquire their own equipment, such problems will diminish.

Publications have mentioned details of few other plays besides the models.[33] The reasons for this are not altogether clear yet. Various reasons suggest themselves. It may be that the attempt has been made to impress the models with every thoroughness before a general expansion of dramatic creation is encouraged. On the other hand, there may have been a paucity of response, or acceptable response, to the new line on drama. The apparent lack of new plays has also no doubt been due partly to the government's continuing wariness of the hostile possibilities of drama. That this wariness has probably remained a potent factor seems to be borne out by the bitter criticisms, continuing into the '70s, of pre-Cultural Revolution drama and dramatists, and individuals connected with that drama. Zhou Yang, Tian Han, Xia Yan and another playwright Yang Hansheng were termed 'the four villains', and Lao She was condemned, mainly for his early novels, but among other things also for his 'vulgar language'. One of the repeated criticisms of Liu Shaoqi was that he was opposed to random changes in Peking Opera, and that he admired such ballets as *Swan Lake*. He was also accused of enjoying obscene plays. The opposition to flirtatious love, spicy romance or indeed any obvious sex at all has been especially strong during this latest period. Many of the criticisms delved deeply back into the early writings and pronouncements of those criticised.

There can be little doubt but that the new drama is a radical departure from traditional drama. The models have been adapted to some local styles of performance and some other plays on modern themes are performed in such styles, but how generally the traditional styles are now performed is not clear. The available publicity at least has been stressing the new kinds of show and the new forms of organisation, such as the small touring all-purpose propaganda teams, although very recently there has been more mention of regional and local styles of performance. It is quite feasible that the vast potential of traditional drama will be utilised more copiously again in time to come, and in the last year or two there have been some signs that certain traditional plays may be revived.[34] There have been renewed moves to encourage amateur acting in the '70s, which if they reinforce the general habit of acting and interest in drama could well bode favourably for the theatre in the future.[35] To some extent the Chinese communities outside China remain a reservoir of traditional theatre, and one cannot tell what influence they may some day exercise upon China itself. The future of the theatre in China depends on many factors, ideological, political, and otherwise, some of them peculiarly Chinese, some of them universal. For instance, it remains to be seen whether the theatre will maintain its significance and vigorous potentialities in the face of increasing industrialisation and the growth of television and other forms of competition, such as sport. There are indications that the piano and other Western instruments may not be the only challengers to the traditional music and instruments of drama, but that mechanisation of traditional instruments may also perhaps help to transform traditional dramatic music in possibly fundamental ways. What is beyond all doubt is that drama at present continues to be an important part of life in China.[36] For what lies ahead, the imponderables are legion and prediction is vain, but when one recalls the energy and appeal of Chinese drama throughout the centuries, it is difficult not to feel that it will also have its vital part in the Chinese future.

NOTES

LIST OF WORKS CITED

LIST OF TRANSLATIONS OF CHINESE
DRAMAS INTO WESTERN LANGUAGES

INDEX

260

Abbreviations Used in Notes, List of Works Cited and List of Translations

BJXB: *Biji xiaoshuo daguan xubian*, 'Sequel to the "Grand view of jottings and stories"', Taipei, Xinxing Shuju, 1966.

CL: *Chinese Literature* [periodical: Peking]

CSJB: *Congshu jicheng jianbian*, 'Concise version of the "Assembled collectaneas"', compiled by Wang Yunwu (1888–), Taipei, Shangwu, 1966.

DJWS: *Dong-jing meng-hua lu (wai sizhong)*, 'Reminiscences of the Eastern Capital (and four other works)', Shanghai, Gudian Wenxue, 1957.

GXJB: *Guoxue jiben congshu*, 'Basic collectanea of National Learning', compiled by Wang Yunwu, Taipei, Zhong Hua Shuju, 1958.

JDZG: *Jindai Zhongguo shiliao congkan*, 'Collection of historical materials on China in recent ages', compiled by Shen Yunlong and others, Taipei, Wenhai, 1966–8.

QDYD: *Qingdai Yandu liyuan shiliao*, 'Historical materials on the theatre in Qing-dynasty Peking' (1934; vol. 4, '*xubian*', 1937), compiled by Zhang Cixi, in *Zhongguo shixue congshu*, Taipei, Xuesheng Shuju, 1964.

QYSQ: *Quan Yuan sanqu*, 'Complete collection of Yuan non-dramatic *qu*', compiled by Sui Shusen, Peking, Zhong Hua Shuju, 1964.

SBBY: *Sibu beiyao*, 'Complete collection of important works of the four literary categories' (1936), compiled by Guo Maoqian, Taipei, Zhong Hua Shuju, 1965.

SBXB: *Sibu congkan xubian*, 'Sequel to the "Collectanea of the four literary categories"' (1934), compiled by Zhang Yuanji (1866–1959) and others, Taipei, no publisher given, 1966.

XFHZ: *Xiao-fang-hu-zhai yu-di cong-chao*, 'Little Square Pot Study's collected manuscripts of the world' (1891–7), compiled by Wang Xiqi (1855–1913), Shanghai, no publisher given, 1891.

XHLB: *Xue-hai lei-bian*, 'Classified analecta from the sea of learning' (first printed in 1831), compiled by Cao Rong (1613–85), revised and enlarged by his pupil Tao Yue, Taipei, Wenyuan Shuju, 1964.

XYCS: *Xiang-yan cong-shu*, 'Collectanea of the fragrant and spicily bewitching' (1909–11), compiled by Chong Tianzi (late nineteenth–early twentieth century), Taipei, Guting Shuju, 1969.

YLDD: *Yong-le da-dian*, 'Grand repository of Eternal Joy' (1403–7), compiled by Xie Jin (1369–1415) and others, remnant volumes, Peking, Zhong Hua Shuju, 1960.

ZBZZ: *Zhi-bu-zu-zhai cong-shu*, 'Can't-be-satisfied Study's collectanea' (1776–1823), compiled by Bao Tingbo (1728–1814) and son, Taipei, Xingzhong Shuju, 1964.

ZGFZ: *Zhongguo fangzhi congshu*, 'Collectanea of Chinese local gazetteers', Taipei, Chengwen, 1966.

ZGGD: *Zhongguo gudian xiqu lunzhu jicheng*, 'Collection of writings on Chinese classical drama', Peking, Zhongguo Xiju, 1959.

Notes

Chapter 1: Antecedents of Drama and Tang Plays

1. Shamanism and masked dances are often seen as the origin of various forms of drama, e.g. Korean. cf. Zŏng In-sŏb, *An Introduction to Korean Literature*, pp. 201–21. For the songs in translation, with comment, see Waley, *The Nine Songs*, and Hawkes, *Ch'u Tz'u* (esp. pp. 35–6). On origins of drama, cf. Zucker, *The Chinese Drama*, and Hightower, *Topics in Chinese Literature*, pp. 94–101.

2. Dolby and Scott, *Warlords*, pp. 159–68, translate biographies of Meng and other jesters.

3. cf. Ricks, *English Drama*, p.21.

4. See *Xi-jing za-ji*, p.5, and *Xi-jing fu*, pp. 43–4.

5. cf. Appiah, *The Pineapple Child*, p. 163.

6. Keith, *The Sanskrit Drama*, p. 170, says Xuanzang visited Kanchipuram, capital of Pallava. The ruler, Mahendra Varman, was a brilliant dramatist.

7. See Liu Jung-en, *Six Yuan Plays*, introduction, p.13.

8. For arguments that it did, see Xu Dishan, 'Fanju tili jiqi zai Hanjushangde diandian-didi'.

9. *Jiu Tang-shu* ch. 29, p.8b, says that puppets were originally a music/entertainment (*yue*) used at funerals, and were not used at celebrations until near the end of the Han; that Gao Wei, ruler of Qi (r. 565–77), was fond of them; and that Emperor Xuanzong (r. 712–56), as they and other such 'plays of the ordinary populace' (*sanyue*) were 'unregulated music', set up a Music Academy in the Inner Palace to provide an institution for them. It remarks that puppets (*kuleizi*, also called *kuileizi*) were 'plays performed with models made to resemble humans, which sing and dance most skilfully'.

10. It is unsound to assume that they were automata rather than fantoccini, but the former is more likely. *San-guo zhi* vol. 3, ch. 29, p. 807, note by Pei Songzhi (372–451) quoting Fu Xuan (217–78), says that Ma Jun (famed as the inventor of a waterwheel) at the request of Emperor Mingdi (r. 227–39) made wooden figures that were able to dance, play drums and pipes, juggle with balls and swords, climb ropes, do handstands, stroll to and fro, pound grain, cock-fight, etc., seemingly operated by water (waterwheel?). *He-shuo fang-gu ji*, ch. 2, pp. 99–100, says that in 559–60 a certain Cui Shishun made life-like musicians, monks, a Buddha, bodhisattvas and guardian gods, seemingly water-operated, who performed on a boat. These were probably different from Ming dynasty and Vietnamese water-puppets operated by hand and strings. *Sui-shu* vol. 3, ch.

58, p.5b, says that Emperor Yangdi (r. 605–17) had a model of his beloved Liu Bian (537–605) carved from wood and mechanically enabled to sit, stand, bow and prostrate itself, which in Bian's absence kept him company in his moonlight drinking and revels. The same emperor, according to *Da-ye shi-yi* pp. 74–6, had a certain Huang Gun make wooden, silk-clad and bejewelled people that were able to move as if alive round a pool and angle for fish. They were able also to perform altogether seventy-two pageants (*shi*, or tableaux) on aquatic themes such as *Zhou Chu slaying the dragon*, *Qiu Hu's wife jumps in the river*, etc. Likewise operated by water-driven mechanisms, there were boat-borne wooden entertainers, too, who performed Hundred Games, juggled swords, turned cartwheels(?), climbed poles, and did rope-dancing(?).

11. See Pei Song's note, quoting Sima Shi (3rd century AD), to 'Annals of the King of Qi', in *San-guo zhi*, vol. 1, p. 129.

12. cf. Edwards, *Chinese Prose Literature*, vol. 1, ch. VI, pp. 60–72.

13. *Jiao-fang ji*, p.17, says that this dance was a 'play' (*xi*) 'also made into a song'. *Yue-fu za-lu*, pp. 44–5, says that the players of the *Mask* (or the whole performance associated with it) wore purple robes and golden belts and held whips or maces. *Tai-ping yu-lan* ch. 569, p. 2702, and *Jiu Tang-shu*, ch. 29, p. 8b, both mention this, seemingly quoting from some fuller, non-extant version of *Yue-fu za-lu*.There is a detailed study of *Yue-fu za-lu*: Gimm, *Das Yüeh-fu tsa-lu des Tuan An-chieh*.

14. *Yue-fu za-lu*, p. 45, says that the players (*xizhe*) of this wore their hair loose, were clad in white mourning garments, and wailed as if bereaved.

15. See *Jiao-fang ji*, p.18, and *Yue-fu za-lu*, p.45. *Tai-ping yu-lan*, ch. 573, p. 2717, claims to quote from the latter, but has a much larger account.

16. According to *Jiao-fang ji*, p. 18.

17. According to 'Tan Rong-niang', poem by Chang Feiyue, in *Quan Tang-shi*, pt. 3, vol. 9, p. 1155.

18. *Yue-fu za-lu*, pp. 44–5, 'Drum-stand section', which also includes *Sheep's-head huntuo* (probably a dance in strange headgear), *Nine-headed lion*, and 'playing *White horse increases the money*'. The music for this section was clappers, flute and drums, and it may have been the main common characteristic of the various items.

19. See *Jiu Tang-shu*, ch. 17, p. 6a.

20. See *Yu-quan-zi zhen-lu*, p. 222.

21. With Li Keji as the main performer. See *Tang-que shi*, ch. 2, p. 43.

22. e.g. *Jiang-nan yu-zai*, ch. 1, p. 2898, gives a slightly post-Tang skit, concerning the Xu Zhixun mentioned later in this chapter. An actor in it wore a green costume and mask.

23. See *Yue-fu za-lu*, p.49.

24. See *Tai-ping yu-lan*, ch. 569, p. 2702.

25. See *Yue-fu za-lu*, p. 49.

26. Her singing could move one to tears; see *Yun-xi yu-yi*, ch. 2, pp. 115–16.

27. See *Yue-fu za-lu*, p.49.

28. The poem is 'Yong Wu-ji', in *Quan Tang-shi*, pt. 9, vol. 2, p. 3416.

29. See *Yin-hua lu*, ch. 1, pp. 1-2, and *Nan-bu xin-shu*, ch. 6, p. 43.

30. cf. Mo She, 'Hangdang', for general discussion of role categories.

31. cf. Hanan, 'The Development of Fiction and Drama', esp. pp. 136–7.

32. The poem is 'Jiao-er', in *Xi-xi cong-yu*, ch. 1, p. 45.

33. See *Xin Wu-dai shi*, ch. 61, p. 6a.

34. See *Xi-xi cong-yu*, ch. 1, p. 45.

35. Hu Ji, *Song Jin zaju kao*, p. 122, takes 'pillar' as meaning the prime role, the principal

initiator of action, on a parallel with similar terms used in gambling that mean something like 'banker', 'croupier', etc.

36. See *Chuo-geng lu*, ch. 25, p. 366.

37. *Tai-he zheng-yin pu*, p. 53.

38. Sông writers were aware of the historical traditions of the *canjunxi*. *Tiao-xi yu-yin cong-hua*, ch. 16, p. 3b, tells that the famous Zhang Jing (970–1018), punished by being awarded the sinecure of Adjutant of Fangzhou (place in Hupeh), complained in a *Memo on the wall of my room* that it made him the object of scorn and that actors were making humiliating plays about him. The account then quotes the *Yue-fu za-lu*, and observes: 'People have made skits thus mocking the Adjutant since the Han. It did not start with the Tang. And during the Five Dynasties under Wang Jian (d. 902, Emperor of Former Shu dynasty, 891–925, in Szechwan), Wang Zongkan, when appointed Census Adjutant of Weizhou as a punishment, declared: "If you want my head, take it! Do you think I'm going to take such a paltry post and let the actors play the Adjutant!" '

39. See *Tang hui-yao*, ch. 33, p. 919.

40. See *Yan-shi jia-xun*, ch. 6, p. 165; *Yue-fu za-lu*, p. 62; *Jiu Tang-shu*, ch. 29, p. 8b; and *You-yang za-zu*, ch. 8, p. 59. *Zi-zhi tong-jian*, ch. 194, p. 8b, says that during January or early February 634, a Minister of Works named Duan Lun introduced an ingenious inventor named Yang Siqi to the emperor, and as proof of his ability had him make puppets. For such wanton frivolity, Duan was demoted. These puppets must have been automata.

41. See *Liu Bin-ke jia-hua lu*, p. 126.

42. This poem, 'Nong kuilei', is found in *Quan Tang-shi*, pt. 1, vol. 1, p. 73, attributed to Minghuang, and pt. 3, vol. 8, p. 1152, attributed to Liang Huang (Tang, dates unknown). *Ming-huang za-lu*, p. 3a, associates it with Minghuang, providing background.

43. See *Bei-meng suo-yan*, ch. 3, as in Sun Kaidi, *Kuileixi kaoyuan*, p. 39.

44. See *Jiu Tang-shu*, ch. 177, p. 3b.

45. See *Feng-shi jian-wen ji*, ch. 6, pp. 3258–9.

46. See *Jiu Tang-shu*, ch. 28, p. 8a, and *Xin Tang-shu*, ch. 22, p. 2b.

47. See *Ce-fu yuan-gui* , ch. 857, p. 10182.

48. See *Yin-hua lu*, ch. 6, p. 39.

49. See 'Lou-xia guan sheng-ji *fu*' by Zhang Chujin (seventh-eighth century), as cited in Zhou Yibai, *Zhongguo xiqu lunji*, p. 130.

50. See *Du-yi zhi* by Li Kang (Tang), as cited in Zhou Yibai, op. cit., p. 130. *Nan-bu xin-shu*, p. 78, says twenty-eight people were carried. See also *Jiao-fang ji*, p. 22.

51. The story *You-xian ku*.

52. For tentative translation of term *bianwen*, see Guan Dedong, 'Lueshuo "bian"-zide laiyuan'. Waley, *Ballads and Stories from Tunhuang*, p. 245, suggests that it means 'incident texts'.

53. See *Yue-fu za-lu*, p. 60, and *Yin-hua lu*, ch. 4, p. 25.

54. Waley, op. cit., pp. 216–35, translates part of one from a text copied down in AD 921. On p. 234, Waley appends an account of a sixteenth-century Maudgalyāyana play.

55. cf. Liu Dajie, *Zhongguo wenxue fazhan shi*, vol. 2, p. 45. Zhao Jingshen in his 'Qiu Hu xiqude yanbian' discusses the evolution of the Qiu Hu plays, but does not mention *bianwen*.

Chapter 2: Sông and Jin Plays

1. Bradbrook, *The Rise of the Common Player*, p. 97.

264

2.   *Xin Wu-dai shi*, ch. 37, pp. 1b–2b, tells how Zhuangzong once mocked his wife, who was ashamed of her social origins, by impersonating her father as the herb-pedlar he formerly was. She, furious, caned their son, who was also taking part in the skit, and chased them both away. The emperor gave himself the stage-name of 'Li World', alluding to his real-life capacity, and his preoccupation with play-acting is said to have occasioned his downfall.

3.   See *Dong-jing meng-hua lu*, ch. 5, pp. 137–8, and ch. 7, p. 202.

4.   See *San-chao bei-meng hui-bian*, ch. 20, pp. 139–146, referring to the Liao.

5.   See *Wu-lin jiu-shi*, ch. 1, pp. 350–1.

6.   On meaning of *yuanben*, cf. Hu Ji, *Song Jin zaju kao*, pp. 8–10, and Feng Yuanjun, *Guju shuohui*, p. 41, note 39. *Tai-he zheng-yin pu*, p. 53, says: 'This *yuanben* means the text (*ben*) of the entertainers [or actors, or their quarters; *hangyuan*]'.

7.   Seemingly just before 1116, a certain Meng Jiaoqiu, Grand Commissioner of the Music Academy, wrote a *zaju* text (*zaju benzi*). See *Du-cheng ji-sheng*, p. 97. *Song-shi*, ch. 142, p. 9b, says: 'Zhenzong [r. 998–1022] did not delight in lascivious music, but he sometimes composed words [lyrics ?] for *zaju*. They were never disclosed outside the palace.' Hu Ji, op. cit., p. 11, doubts that the emperor himself wrote the words, but the statement seems to say so.

8.   On *shuhui*, see Feng Yuanjun, op. cit., pp. 57–8, and Sun Kaidi, *Yeshiyuan gujin zaju kao*, pp. 388–95.

9.   See *Wu-lin jiu-shi*, ch. 3, pp. 377–8.

10.   See *Dong-jing meng-hua lu*, ch. 8, p. 218. cf. Dudbridge, *The Hsi-yu chi*, pp. 43–44.

11.   Gernet, *La Vie quotidienne*, describes late Sông society.

12.   See *Dong-jing meng-hua lu*, ch. 2, p. 67.

13.   See *Du-cheng ji-sheng*, pp. 95–6, *Fan-sheng lu*, pp. 123–4, *Meng-liang lu*, ch. 19, p. 298, and *Wu-lin jiu-shi*, ch. 6, p. 440.

14.   See *Wu-lin jiu-shi*, ch. 6, p. 440.

15.   See *Xian-chun Lin-an zhi*, ch. 19, pp. 222–3.

16.   The Sông court Music Academy was abolished in 1161. See *Du-cheng ji-sheng*, p. 96. From 1164 onwards it became the custom to call in market entertainers for palace celebrations. See *Song-shi*, ch. 142, pp. 11a–11b.

17.   See *Ji-lei bian*, ch. 1, p. 17.

18.   Liu Nianzi, 'Yuan zaju yanchu xingshi', p. 75, gives a photograph of a temple stage built on the site of a Yuan stage, itself built, in 1271, on the site of an earlier, roofless, brick, stone or earthen-based stage.

19.   *Qi-dong ye-yu*, ch. 20, p. 704, tells how Emperor Huizong (r. 1101–25) and his minister Cai You (1047–1126) some time during 1119–25 acted a 'jester play' (*youxi*), the emperor as *canjun* flogging Cai with a whip (and seemingly reversing the usual *canjun* function). *Ting-shi*, ch. 10, p. 2162, mentions a performance in 1180 of the 'green-robed *canjun*'. Clearly the *canjunxi* continued, and had affinities with what little we know of the Sông *zaju*, which were also often akin to the jester skits.

20.   The household of Song Qi (998–1061), eminent politician and historian. See *Qu-Wei jiu-wen*, ch. 6, p. 7257.

21.   See *Za-cuan xu* by Wang Zhi (fl. c. AD 1126), as quoted in Hu Ji, *Song Jin zaju kao*, p. 29.

22.   The poet was Huang Tingjian (1045–1105) criticising the poetry of Qin Guan (1049–1101). See *Gui-sou shi-hua* by Wang Zhifang (c. 1055–1105), as quoted in *Qu-lü* (Wang Jide), p. 141.

23. See note 21 (by Deng Zhicheng) to *Dong-jing meng-hua lu*, p. 237.
24. See *Meng-liang lu*, ch. 20. pp. 308–9, and *Du-cheng ji-sheng*, p. 96.
25. See *Meng-liang lu*, ch. 20, p. 309, and *Du-cheng ji-sheng*, p. 97.
26. See *Wu-lin jiu-shi*, ch. 6, pp. 458–9.
27. See *Meng-liang lu*, ch. 20, p. 309.
28. Such songs are collected in Liu Yongji, *Songdai gewu juqu luyao*, with introduction.
29. See Hu Ji, op. cit., pp. 44–51.
30. Discussed by Hu Ji, op. cit., pp. 64, 187, and Zhou Yibai, *Zhongguo xiqu lunju*, p. 384. The list is found in *Wu-lin jiu-shi*, ch. 10, pp. 508–13.
31. See Zhou Yibai, op. cit., pp. 376–83.
32. 'Zhuang-jia bu-shi gou-lan' by Du Renjie (c. 1190–1270), QYSQ, vol. 1, pp. 31–2. Translations in Crump, 'Yuan-pen', Hawkes, 'Reflections', and Idema, 'de opvoering', pp. 94–7.
33. 'Sang-dan hang-yuan', by Gao Andao (late thirteenth–early fourteenth century), QYSQ, vol. 2, pp. 1109–11. Translation by Idema, op cit., pp. 97–100.
34. See *Chuo-geng lu*, ch. 25, pp. 366–85.
35. Trans. from *Lü Dong-bin hua-yue shen-xian hui*, pp. 3b–4b.
36. Given in Hu Ji, op. cit., pp. 80–92.
37. *Sheng-chao tong-shi shi-yi*, ch. 6, p. 40b, is only partly correct in stating: 'Those called "*guojin*", for instance, resembled the entertainments of the jester actors of antiquity, providing good counsel by means of a comic skit on a topical subject.' cf. Hu Ji, op. cit., pp. 106–8. *Ci-yu cong-hua*, p. 284, says that on the advent of the Qing, *guojin* ceased to be performed.
38. See *Du-cheng ji-sheng*, p. 96, and *Chuo-geng lu* , ch. 25, p. 366.
39. The *qu* 'Ke-gua' by Li Boyu (late Yuan), QYSQ, vol. 2, p. 1222, says: 'A wooden heart [lit. womb, matrix] felt-padded – for it must be tender – wrapped inside the softest leather. Without it in my hand, I'm mighty ill-at-ease, but once my fingers round it close, the world's smartest clown won't dodge my blows. With such a prop, and a powder-cheeked chap around, we freely shall make merry and laughter will abound.' See also poem on the *fujing* in *Ci-nue*, pp. 282–3.
40. See *Nan-ci xu-lu*, p. 239.
41. cf. Hu Ji, op. cit., pp. 59–60.
42. Trans. from *Zhang Xie zhuang-yuan*, pp. 13b–15a.
43. See *Dong-jing meng-hua lu*, ch. 5, p. 137 and ch. 7, p. 206; *Du-cheng ji-sheng*, p. 97; *Fan-sheng lu*, pp. 116 and 123; *Meng-liang lu*, ch. 20, p. 311; and *Wu-lin jiu shi*, ch. 2, pp. 371–2. There were water-puppets (*shui kuilei*), similar to those of the Sui, and 'herb-puppets' (*yao kuilei*) or 'herb-started puppets' (*yaofā kuilei*) or 'herb-method puppets' (*yaofā kuilei*). (The 'herb' may be translated as 'powder', too.) The latter seem to have involved the use of gunpowder and fireworks. cf. Sun Kaidi, *Cangzhou ji*, vol. 1, p. 316.
44. See *Dong-jing meng-hua lu*, p. 137.
45. See *Meng-liang lu*, ch. 20, p. 311.
46. See *Du-cheng ji-sheng*, p. 97, and *Meng-liang lu*, ch. 20, p. 311. On the *yaici*, cf. Ye Dejun, *Song Yuan Ming jiangchang wenxue*, pp. 28–38.
47. *Shi-wu ji-yuan* , ch. 9, p. 351, attributes their origin to Gong Yu (124–44 BC), who by means of a screen and lighting conjured an image of the Emperor Wudi's wife for him. This cannot have been the source of any regular entertainment, as far as we know. On p. 352 it is said that during the reign of Renzong (r. 1023–63) someone adapted market story-tellers' tales of Three Kingdoms warfare for performance with shadow-men (*yingren*).

48. Also eleventh century. See *Ming-dao za-zhi*, ch. 2, pp. 3395–6. The tale adds that the puppeteer (*nongzhe*) tricked the young man into paying him for placatory sacrifices when they at last slew Guan, and at the sacrificial feast the false friends made him distribute the sacrificial silverware among them.

49. See *Du-cheng ji-sheng*, pp. 97–8, and *Wu-lin jiu-shi*, ch. 2, p. 370.

50. See *Wu-lin jiu-shi*, ch. 6, p. 456. *Dong-jing meng-hua lu*, ch. 5, p. 138, mentions a *qiao-yingxi* ('deception shadow-show'?, 'farcical shadow-show'?).

51. *Du-cheng ji-sheng*, p. 97, says they were performed with (or by?) little boys and young men.

52. See Zhou Yibai, *Zhongguo xiqu lunji*, pp. 63–6.

53. See Sun Kaidi, *Kuileixi kaoyuan*, pp. 52 ff.

54. See *Dong-jing meng-hua lu*, ch. 5, p. 138, and *Du-cheng ji-sheng*, p. 96.

55. Doleželová-Velingerova and Crump, *Ballad of the Hidden Dragon*, translate a fragmentary *zhugongdiao*.

56. Trans. from *Dong Jie-yuan xi-xiang ji*, ch. 2, pp. 37–9.

57. *You-yang za-zu*, ch. 4, p. 211, mentions a market man towards the end of the Taihe period (827–35) who had been telling market-men's tales (*shiren xiaoshuo*), apparently professionally, for at least twenty years.

58. *Qi-xiu lei-gao*, ch. 22, p. 331, states that it originated under Renzong. *Dong-po zhi-lin*, ch. 1, pp. 5–6, quoting Wang Peng (1067–92), mentions urchins being kept quiet by professional story-tellers and applauding the defeat of Cao Cao.

59. See *Dong-jing meng-hua lu*, ch. 5, pp. 137–8; *Du-cheng ji-sheng*, p. 98; *Meng-liang lu*, ch. 20, pp. 312–13: and *Wu-lin jiu-shi*, ch. 6, pp. 454–5.

60. See *Zui-weng tan-lu*, pp. 1–3, list of titles. Titles are analysed by Tan Zhengbi, *Huaben yu guju*, pp. 13–37 and 93–104. On the complex problems of early story-telling, cf. Hanan, 'Sung and Yüan Vernacular Fiction'.

Chapter 3: Yuan *Zaju* Drama

1. See *Yuan-shi*, ch. 24, p. 15a, and ch. 81, pp. 2b–3a, and *Chuo-geng lu*, ch. 1, p. 33.

2. See *Die-shan ji*, ch. 6, pp. 3a–5b. cf. Wang Liqi, 'Yuan Ming Qing tongzhi jieji'.

3. See *Chuo-geng lu*, ch. 4, pp. 63–9, on Yang Lianzhenjia, Khublai-Khan's Comptroller of Buddhism.

4. e.g. *Yao-shan tang qu-ji*, p. 2a.

5. From Boyle, *The History of the World Conqueror*, vol. 1, ch. XXXVII, p. 207.

6. See *Chuo-geng lu*, ch. 25, p. 366.

7. cf. Dolby, 'Kuan Han-ch'ing', p. 39.

8. For biography, see Dolby, op. cit.

9. cf. Tan Zhengbi, *Yuanqu liu dajia luezhuan*, pp. 175–220.

10. cf. ibid., pp. 221–66.

11. cf. ibid., pp. 119–74.

12. Trans. from *Xi-xiang ji*, pp. 17–21.

13. cf. Tan Zhengbi, op. cit., pp. 267–310.

14. Mostly preserved in *Lu-gui bu*. For a modern collection of biographies of dramatists, with lists of their plays and editions, see Fu Xihua, *Yuandai zaju quanmu*.

15. *Tai-he zheng-yin pu*, p. 24, lists twelve thematic categories of *zaju* (the notes in brackets

are mine): *shenxian daohua* (immortality and Taoistic transformation); *yin-ju le-dao* (living in reclusion and rejoicing in the Way), also known as *lin-quan qiu-huo* (forests, springs, hills and valleys); *zhongchen lieshi* (loyal ministers and gentlemen of ardent honour); *xiao-yi lian-jie* (filiality, honour, incorruptibility and integrity); *chi-jian ma-chan* (rebuking treachery and reviling calumny); *zhuchen guzi* (banished ministers and orphaned sons); *po-dao gan-bang* (swordplay and staff-plying), i.e. *tuobo* (bare-arm) *zaju*; *feng-hua xue-yue* (wind and flowers, snow and moon, i.e. airy romantic themes); *bei-huan li-he* (sorrows of parting and joys of union); *yan-hua fen-dai* (mist-flowers and powder-kohl, i.e. love affairs involving courtesans or adventurously amorous beauties), i.e. *huadan* (gay woman) *zaju*; and *shentou guimian* (god-head demon-face), i.e. *shenfo* (gods and buddhas) *zaju*. *Qing-lou ji*, pp. 19, 20, 21, 22, 24, 26, etc. also mentions *jiatou* (throne) *zaju* (concerning monarchs); *guiyuan* (boudoir repinings) *zaju* (on the love affairs of genteel maidens); *lülin* (greenwood) *zaju* (on robbers and brigands); and *ruan moni* (soft *moni*, i.e. on genteel or effete young scholars?). cf. Feng Yuanjun, *Guju shuohui*, pp. 59–63, and Luo Jintang, *Xiancun Yuanren zaju benshi kao*, pp. 419–23, on these categories and their limitations.

16. Many of the plots are found in Lowe, *Stories from Chinese drama*.
17. I discussed this at length in my thesis, chs. 4–7. On structure of Yuan *zaju*, cf. Yao, 'The Theme and Structure of the Yuan Drama', Crump, 'The Elements of Yüan Opera', and Crump, 'The Conventions and Craft of Yüan Drama'.
18. For some general and poetic comparisons, see Liu, 'Elizabethan and Yuan'.
19. cf. Zhao Jingshen, *Du-qu xiao-ji*, pp. 15–16, and Yang and Yang, 'Poetic Songs of the Yuan'.
20. See *Chang-lun*, pp. 160–1 for a list of the keys and associated moods. Actual usage is difficult to match, but Aoki, *Genjin zatsugeki josetsu*, pp. 25–6, gives some examples of moods matching acts. cf. also, Muramatsu, 'Chugoku gikyoku no ongaku', pp. 1–4, and Picken, 'Chinese Music', pp. 223, 229, 243, on the music of *zaju* in general.
21. On the structure of *qu*, cf. Schlepp, *San-ch'ü*, Dolby, thesis, chs. 8–10, and Johnson, 'The prosody of Yuan drama'.
22. See *Zhong-yuan yin-yun*, pp. 224–31.
23. See *Qu-lü* (by Wang Jide), ch. 3, pp. 153–4.
24. The *Discourse on singing* (*Chang-lun*) by Zhi-an was composed in the early or middle Yuan, but it is for the most part extremely laconic and imprecise.

Chapter 4: Performers and the Theatre World during the Yuan Dynasty

1. e.g. Yan Shanxiu. See *Qing-lou ji*, p. 39.
2. Many of these biographies are translated in Waley, 'The Green Bower Collection'; also in Waley, *The Secret History*, pp. 89 ff.
3. See *Qing-lou ji*, p. 29.
4. ibid., p. 20.
5. ibid., p. 32. On Ni, see Dolby, 'Ni Tsan'.
6. Zhao Zhenqing sang Shang Dao's revision of Zhang Wuniu's *zhugongdiao*. See *Qing-lou ji*, p. 19.
7. See ibid., p. 27.
8. i.e. *huadan zaju*. See ibid., pp. 31–2.
9. On this mural, see Liu Nianzi, 'Yuan zaju yanchu xingshi', and Zhou Yibai, *Zhongguo*

xiqu lunji, pp. 393–400. The mural is on the wall facing the image of the temple god, Mingyingwang, water god of Huo Stream. Plays must have been performed at the temple during festivities from the 18th of the third lunar month each year, and probably also at the mid-autumn festival.

10. See 'Yong-gu' by Sui Xuanming (13th or early 14th century), QYSQ, vol. 1, pp. 547–8. There is a translation by Idema, 'de opvoering', pp. 100–2.

11. On Chinese drama costume, tracing it back to the Zhou, see Li Xin, 'Lun xiqu fuzhuangde yanbian yu fashan'. He attempts some deductions for the Yuan on the basis of palace dance costumes. cf. also Feng Yuanjun, *Guju shuohui*, pp. 74–82, 33–85, but using Ming material. Various clay figurines of actors have been discovered in recent years.

12. See *Lan Cai-he*. There is a translation by Idema, 'Lan Cai-he'.

13. Sun Kaidi, *Yeshiyuan gujin zaju kao*, pp. 383–8, explains *luqi* as actors not officially registered as such. *Wu-lin jiu-shi*, ch. 6, p. 441 mentions *luqi* who 'do not enter the *goulan*, but just perform in bustling open spaces'. Either this does not mean *all luqi*, or the term later acquired a broader application, for *luqi* certainly did act in *goulan* during the Yuan and Ming.

14. See 'Xin-jian jiao-fang gou-lan qiu-zan' by Tang Shi (late fourteenth–early fifteenth century), QYSQ, vol. 2, pp. 1494–6. There is a translation by Idema in his 'de opvoering', pp. 89–94.

15. See *Chuo-geng lu*, ch. 24, pp. 345–6. The date is open to doubt, but the event certainly occurred during the late Yuan.

16. See Liu Nianzi, 'Yuan zaju yanchu xingshi', pp. 74–5, with photographs.

17. On such attitudes and measures concerning the novel, see Lévy, 'La condamnation du roman en France et en Chine'. Most of the measures are collected in Wang Xiaochuan, *Yuan Ming Qing*.

18. See Wang Xiaochuan, op. cit., pp. 3–8, for this and following bans, etc.

19. On the early novels, cf. Hsia, *The Classic Chinese Novel*.

20. The earliest biography of Luo Guanzhong, thought to be the same person as Luo Ben, is, as far as I know, that in *Lu-gui bu xu-bian*, p. 281, a work fairly reliably attributed to the playwright Jia Zhongming (1343–post 1422). It refers to Luo as such a good friend that 'he and I forgot the difference in age between us'. Parted, presumably by late Yuan rebellions, they met again in 1364, but again parted and had not met again by the time the biography was written, in or around 1422. Jia says that he did not 'know what became of him in the end'. The biography only mentions Guanzhong as a playwright, etc., with no mention of novels, which is perhaps strange, but possibly he wrote novels after 1364 and possibly they did not become nationally famous till after 1422. *Qi-xiu lei-gao*, ch. 22, p. 331, mentions Luo (by both names) as the author of the novels *Three Kingdoms* and *Song Jiang* (i.e. *Fenlands*), but says that the latter was also attributed to Shi Naian. The same work moots the possibility that these novels were based on Yuan *zaju* plays. Shi Naian was early considered to be the same person as the playwright Shi Hui (late thirteenth–early fourteenth century).

Chapter 5: *Nanxi* Drama, *Chuanqi* drama, and the Beginnings of Kunqu Drama

1. I refer to the plays (not originally printed as a collection) contained in *Jiaoding Yuankan zaju sanshizhong*.

2. See *Lu-gui bu*, pp. 134–5.

3. See *Zhong-yuan yin-yun*, p. 220.

4. See Qian Nanyang, *Song Yuan xiwen jiyi*, for most fragments.

5. See *Nan-ci xu-lu*, p. 239, and *Shao-shi shan-fang bi-cong*, ch. 41, p. 555. A love comedy called *Jewelled stone* was a popular play in Kiangsu during the thirteenth century; see *Shan-zhong bai-yun ci*, pp. 91–2.

6. See *Qian-tang yi-shi*, ch. 6, pp. 3427–8.

7. The priest, Zu Jie, was an associate of the notorious Yang Lianzhenjia, the Comptroller of Buddhism. See Zhou Yibai, *Zhongguo xijushi jiangzuo*, pp. 108–9 (deriving from *Gui-xin za-shi* by Zhou Mi, lived 1232–98).

8. Found in London by railway administrator Ye Gongchuo (1881–?). Smith, *China in Convulsion*, vol. 1, pp. 283–4, gives a contemporary account of the destruction of much of the collection (the *Yong-le da-dian*).

9. cf. Hu Ji, *Song Jin zaju kao*, p. 61.

10. See *Lu-gui bu*, pp. 134–5.

11. From *Cheng-zhai yue-fu* by Zhu Youdun, as quoted in Li Diankui, *Yuan Ming sanqu zhi fenxi yu yanjiu*, p. 573.

12. From *Nan-ci xu-lu*, p. 245.

13. From *Qu-lü* (Wang Jide), p. 57. cf. also *Qu-zao*, p. 27, *Qu-lü* (Wei Liangfu), p. 7, and *Yue-fu chuan-sheng*, pp. 164–5 and 175.

14. See *Lu-gui bu*, p. 121.

15. Attributions open to doubt. There was more than one early version of some of these plays. On *nanxi* playwrights, see Zhao Jingshen, *Yuan Ming nanxi kaolue*, pp. 11–16, idem, *Xiqu bitan*, pp. 29–42, and 159, and Zhou Yibai, op. cit., pp. 119–20.

16. See *Qu-hua*, ch. 2, p. 257.

17. See *Xian-ju ji*, ch. 5, pp. 297–8.

18. The *Yong-le da-dian*.

19. See *Xian-ju ji*, ch. 5, pp. 297–8.

20. See ibid., and *Jin-ling suo-shi sheng-lu* by Zhou Hui (sixteenth century), ch. 2, as quoted in Wang Xiaochuan, *Yuan Ming Qing*, p. 10.

21. See *Jin-ling suo-shi sheng-lu*, ch. 1, as quoted in Wang Xiaochuan, op. cit., p. 10.

22. See *Ci-yu cong-hua*, ch. 3, pp. 282–4.

23. See Wang Xiaochuan, op. cit., pp. 11–13, for these bans, etc.

24. See *Nan-ci xu-lu*, p. 239.

25. See ibid.

26. Trans. from *Ming Qing chuanqi*, pp. 20–26, and *Pi–pa ji*, pp. 208–11.

27. See *Nan-ci xu-lu*, p. 240.

28. See *Xiao Sun-tu*, p. 1a.

29. See *Cuo li-shen*, p. 54b.

30. Trans. from *Pi–pa ji*, pp. 1–2.

31. See ibid., p. 96.

32. See *Nan-ci xu-lu*, p. 245.

33. See *Ju-shuo*, p. 100.

34. There seems to have been a corresponding lull for *nanxi* during the first few decades of the Ming. cf. Zheng Zhenduo, *Chatuben Zhongguo wenxue shi*, vol. 4, p. 769.

35. Originally called Yang Xian, but he must have had a Mongol name. See *Lu-gui bu xu-bian*, p. 284.

36. Author of *Tian-yi-ge Lu-gui bu*, and most probably of *Lu-gui bu xu-bian*. The latter,

p. 292, contains his laudatory (auto)biography.

37. Presumably this was the major source of the great number of extra Yuan *zaju* play-titles found in the *Tian-yi-ge Lu-gui bu*.

38. His *Great Peace tables for correcting sounds*, published in 1398. In the same year he published a *Jewelled Grove refined rhymes*, on the rhymes of *qu*. He was a leading figure in the major military and political events of his age. See biography in *Ming-shi*, ch. 117, *Lie-chao shi-ji xiao-zhuan*, vol. 1, pp. 6–7, and *Guo-chao xian-zheng lu*, ch. 1, pp. 47–8. cf. also Zhao Jingshen, *Du-qu xiaoji*, pp. 22–7. For modern biographies of Ming *zaju* dramatists, see Fu Xihua, *Ming-dai zaju quanmu*. See also Hung, *Ming Drama*.

39. See *Nan-ci xu-lu*, p. 243, and *Qu-lun* (Xu Fuzha), p. 236.

40. Fu Xihua, *Mingdai chuanqi quanmu*, provides biographies of Ming *chuanqi* playwrights.

41. See *Yi-yuan zhi-yan* by Wang Shizhen (1526–90), as quoted in Fu Xihua, op. cit., p. 5.

42. See *Nan-ci xu-lu*, p. 252.

43. See *Qu-lun* (He Liangjun), p. 6, *Gu-qu za-yan*, p. 204, and *Du-qu xu-zhi*, ch. 1, p. 239.

44. *Tan-qu za-zha*, p. 254, remarks: 'Authors of recent times such as Tang Yinai [i.e. Tang Xianzu] are very skilled at imitating the men of the Yuan.'

45. For some discussions, see Zhou Yibai, *Zhongguo xijushi jiangzuo*, pp. 140–72; idem, *Zhongguo xiqu lunji*, pp. 204–29; Ouyang Yuqian, *Zhongguo xiqu yanjiu ziliao chuji*, intro. pp. 5–20; Xia Ye, *Xiqu yinyue yanjiu*; and Mackerras, 'The Growth of Chinese Regional Drama in the Ming and Ch'ing'.

46. The *Diaoqiangxi* plays of Kiangsu. See Zhou Yibai, *Zhongguo xijushi jiangzuo*, p. 143.

47. *Gu-qu za-yan*, p. 212, says: 'In Wu [i.e. Kiangsu] the only one known for excelling in northern *qu* is Zhang Yetang'. A Kunshan-*qiang* had existed at least as early as the Yuan, seemingly created by one Gu Jian. See *Nan-ci yin-zheng*. And many people were involved in the revisions of Kunshan-*qiang* during the sixteenth century.

48. *Nan-ci xu-lu* (written in 1559), p. 242, remarks on the wide predominance and popularity of Kunshan-*qiang*, presumably Wei's new version. Thus the new music may have been devised round 1550 or earlier. On Kunqu in general, cf. Ts'iang Un-kai, *K'ouen K'iu*, Yao Hsin-nung. 'The Rise and Fall of K'un Ch'ü', and anon., 'Kunchu Opera'.

49. Xu Fuming, 'Liang Chenyu he ta chuangzuo *Wan-sha ji* de yitu', gives his date of birth as 1508. *Bi-tan* by Zhang Yuanchang (Ming), as quoted in *Ju-shuo* ch. 2, p. 117, states: 'Wei Liangfu [. . .] was an able musicologist, and such as Zhang Xiaoquan, Ji Jingpo and Dai Meichuan vied to be his pupil. Liang Bolong [i.e. Chenyu] appeared and emulated them, did research into Yuan drama, and himself produced new music, composing the songs of *Jiangdong white boehmeria* [a collection of non-dramatic *qu*] and *Washing silk*'. But most probably Liang made much use of Wei's music and the vogue that it had created.

50. *Nan-ci xu-lu*, p. 242, refers to it as 'old music made more rich and gorgeous', so perhaps it was even more florid than earlier southern music.

51. See Huang Zhigang, 'Tang Xianzu nianpu', pt. 3, pp. 113–15.

52. e.g. *Qu-lü* (Wang Jide), p. 165.

53. Trans. from *Mu-dan ting*, pp. 45–8.

54. See *Qu-lun* (Xu Fuzha), p. 240.

55. His friend Wang Jide termed him, 'truly an unfetterable songster'. See *Qu-lü* (Wang Jide), p. 168. cf. also *Ming-shi*, ch. 288, pp. 2a–3a, and *Xu Wen-chang san-ji*, pp. 37–58.

56. *Gun* seems to imply rapidity of delivery, as in some popular ballads. For an example, see Zhao Jingshen, *Xiqu bitan*, pp. 101–2.

57. Anthologies of Qingyang-*qiang* plays were published as early as 1573. It was already then a rival to Kunshan-*qiang*. cf. Zhao Jingshen, op. cit., pp. 87–104.

Chapter 6: The Theatre World during the Ming Dynasty

1. See *Long-tan-shi zhi-tan* by Qian Chengzhi (1612–93), as quoted in Zhou Yibai, *Zhongguo xijushi jiangzuo*, p. 195, and *Ju-shuo*, ch. 6, p. 199 (quoting from *Xi-po lei-gao* by Song Luo, lived 1634–1713/4).
2. See *Tao-an meng-yi*, ch. 7, p. 64.
3. See 'Zhou Tie-dun zhuan' by Zheng Fujiao (1596–1675), as quoted in Zhou Yibai, op. cit., p. 174.
4. See *Shu-yuan za-ji*, ch. 10, pp. 112–13.
5. For more detail, see Li Xin, 'Lun xiqu fuzhuangde yanbian he fazhan', pp. 74–6.
6. See Feng Yuanjun, *Guju shuohui*, pp. 242–360. *Qu-lü* (Wang Jide) says of these: 'But it is no longer possible nowadays to identify any of the various kinds of hats, clothes and properties named.' Pictures, various editions of Ming plays, and numerous writings give firm indications of the Ming concern for stage costume. *Tao-an meng-yi*, ch. 4, p. 29, describing a temple theatre performance, says: 'The actors absolutely had to resemble the characters in the play [. . .] Even pieces of brocade worth scores of taels were not deemed too expensive.' ibid., ch. 8, p. 69, tells of the minute care that Ruan Dacheng took over costume.
7. See Cao Juren, *Renshi xinyu*, pp. 311–12.
8. See Zhang Jing, *Ming Qing chuanqi daolun*, pp. 122–5.
9. See Hua Chuanhao, *Wo yan Kunchou*, pp. 23–40.
10. For the foregoing, see Wang Xiaochuan, *Yuan Ming Qing*, pp. 335–6, and for following bans etc., see ibid., pp. 144, 152–3, 171, 178–81.
11. See ibid., p. 144.
12. From ibid., p. 179.
13. ibid.
14. See *Ying-mei-an yi-yu*, p. 9a.
15. See *Ban-qiao za-ji*, ch. 1, p. 3a.
16. See *Zhou Tie-dun zhuan*, as quoted in Zhou Yibai, op. cit., p. 183.
17. See *Ci-nue*, pp. 353–4.
18. See *Zhuang-hui-tang wen-ji*, ('Wenji' section), ch. 5, pp. 13a–13b.
19. See *Ci-nue*, p. 353.
20. See *Tao-an meng-yi*, ch. 6, pp. 47–8.
21. See *Ju-shuo*, p. 207.
22. cf. Sun Kaidi, *Yeshiyuan gujin zaju kao*, for early history of these.
23. The 'authenticity' of Zang's collection is a topic which arouses oddly fierce passions, but to doubt the earliness of much of its material surely insults no one's honour and casts no slur upon its literary value, since indeed such doubts may enable us all the better to perceive and admire Zang's contribution to literature. cf. Yan Dunyi, *Yuanju zhenyi*, Iwaki Hideo, 'Genkan kokon zatsugeki sanjūshu no ryuden', pp. 74–5, and Xu Fuming, 'Zang Maoxun yu Yuan-qu xuan'. In a letter in his *Fu-bao-tang ji*, ch. 4, pp. 91–2, Zang mentions having borrowed 300 plays (the basis of the *Selection*) from a certain Liu Yanbo, and says: 'Recently, becoming daily more senile and idle, I for amusement took out the *zaju* and removed untidy and confused parts from them, altering unsuitable parts as I myself thought fit, and I consider myself to have indeed mastered the knacks and techniques of the Yuan authors.' *Qu-lü* (Wang Jide), p. 170, notes: 'Recently the learned doctor Zang Jinshu [i.e. Zang Maoxun] of Wuxing has collated and printed a total of 100 Yuan dramas in two parts, [. . .] But [. . .] many of the phrases and words have been altered, somewhat

272

departing from the original sources.' *Ci-yu cong-hua*, p. 254, quotes Ye Tang (early Qing) as making some sharp criticisms of Zang's editing of the plays, but Zang's contribution to drama and literature was undeniably great.

Chapter 7: A Diversity of Dramatic Styles during the Early Qing

1. See *Ju-shuo*, ch. 4, p. 158, and Wu Weiye's preface to *Yi-li-an Bei-ci guang-zheng pu*.
2. Aoki, *Zhongguo jinshi xiqu shi*, vol. 1, p. 328, views Li's *Northern lyrics compendious correction tables* and Shen Jing's *Nine southern keys qu tables* as the 'twin jade orbs of *qu* prosody', but Yan Dunyi, *Yuanju zhenyi*, vol. 2, p. 656, talks of 'confusions and errors' in Li's work. Used with discretion, it is a valuable work.
3. *Qu-hua*, p. 269, and *Ci-yu cong-hua*, pp. 246–7, tell how he wrote a play to embody the sad events when a magistrate (an elder brother of Wu Weiye) and all his family were killed in military disturbances.
4. For a biography, see Hummel, *Eminent Chinese*, pp. 495–7.
5. See *Xian-qing ou-ji*, p. 55.
6. *Ci-yu cong-hua*, p. 262, sums up grounds for the blame, but praises him as a supreme dramatist.
7. He says, in *Xian-qing ou-ji*, pp. 54–5, 'The flourishing of the spoken parts in plays really began with me. Half the world applauds me for it, while half condemns me for it. My admirers say: "Until now, dramatic speech was always regarded as just talking, something to be uttered just as the mood takes one at the time. But Liweng creates dramatic speech as literature, making a real effort, and weighing the pros and cons of every single word. [. . .]" My critics say: "[. . .] the songs should be the main thing. [. . .] What is the point of [. . .] making the tree bigger than the roots?" ' Elsewhere, ibid., p. 104, he says: 'There must be 2 or 3 in every 10 actors who excel in singing, but, as for those skilled in spoken delivery, there can be only 1 or 2 in every 100.' Translations of his dramatic theory are also found in Helmut, *Li Liweng über das Theatre*.
8. See biography in Hummel, op. cit., pp. 935–6.
9. See *Ju-shuo*, p. 172.
10. For a biography, see Hummel, op. cit., pp. 434–5.
11. *Qu-hua*, pp. 271–2: 'He slept and ate the Yuan playwrights, [. . .] Wu Xuefang declares that he was the best of those sixty years, and that is truly a statement of insight.'
12. For a biography, see Hummel, op. cit., pp. 628–30.
13. cf. Guan Dechen, *Quyi lunji*, pp. 76–85.
14. See *Zai-yuan za-zhi*, ch. 3, pp. 109–10.
15. According to Zhou Yibai, *Zhongguo xijushi jiangzuo*, pp. 220–5.
16. There is a biography in Hummel, op. cit., p. 375.
17. *Ju-shuo*, p. 154, says: 'In writing the *Palace of Eternal Life* he assembled all the tales of Tang fiction and lines of poetry from various [Tang] poets [. . .] then picked out certain splendid passages from dramas ancient and modern and adorned them, and thus became the foremost among modern dramatists.' *Ju-shuo*, we note, calls the play a *zaju*, and quotes Mao Qiling (1623–1716) who calls it a *yuanben*. The variations of terminology still flourished.
18. Trans. from *Ming Qing chuanqi*, pp. 67–76.
19. There is a biography in Hummel, op. cit., pp. 434–5. See also, Fan Ning, '*Tao-hua shan* zuozhe Kong Shangren'.

20. See *Ci-yu cong-hua*, p. 251.
21. Trans. from *Tao-hua shan*, pp. 236–9.
22. See 'Shu Xiang-sheng shi', *Fan-xie-shan-fang quan-ji*, 'Wen-ji' section, ch. 8, pp. 13a–13b.
23. See Zhou Yibai, op. cit., p. 213.
24. See ibid., p. 195.
25. Shoberl, *The World in Miniature: China*, pp. 109–11.
26. cf. biography in Hummel, op. cit., p. 864.
27. cf. ibid., pp. 164–6.
28. Cranmer-Byng, *An Embassy to China*, pp. 136–7.
29. ibid., p. 140.
30. ibid., pp. 203–4.
31. See ibid., p. 365.
32. See Bland and Backhouse, *China Under the Empress Dowager*, p. 149.
33. For following bans, etc., see Wang Xiaochuan, *Yuan Ming Qing*, pp. 19–48.
34. cf. Goodrich, *The Literary Inquisition of Ch'ien-long*, and Hummel, op. cit. (numerous instances of the inquisition throughout).
35. Wang Xiaochuan, *Yuan Ming Qing*, pp. 45–6.
36. ibid., pp. 336–7.
37. e.g. ibid., pp. 89–98.
38. ibid., pp. 90–1.
39. The variety of religious uses was very great. e.g. to propitiate the gods of the Yellow River (cf. tales in Wilhelm, *Chinese Folktales*, pp. 105–11); to propitiate the dead (see Gray, *China*, vol. 1, p.36); on the building of a bridge (see ibid., p. 104); in return for recovery from illness (see ibid., p. 377); for the goddess of navigation (see Ellis, *Journal*, p. 127); to snake gods or elfin fox deities in return for rain and the end of an epidemic respectively (see Douglas, *Society in China*, p. 375); Gray, op. cit., p. 382 mentions marionette and puppet-shows in honour of goddesses, held in front of temples and usually only attended by women, and plays in honour of the god of the markets.
40. Wang Xiaochuan, op. cit., p. 94.
41. ibid., pp. 96–8.
42. ibid., p. 107.
43. See *Lü-yuan cong-hua*, ch. 1, pp. 13b–14a.
44. ibid.
45. cf. (somewhat later) Ellis, *Journal*, p. 155: 'In splendour of appearance, the Mandarins did not stand any competition with the actors, who were blazing with gold.'
46. There is a biography in Hummel, op. cit., pp. 24–5.
47. ibid., pp. 925–6.
48. Detailed analysis in Zhao Jingshen, *Ming Qing qutan*, pp. 154–62.
49. See Cranmer-Byng, op. cit., pp. 137–8.
50. See *Yan-pu za-ji* by Zhao Yi (1727–1814), as quoted in Zhou Yibai, *Zhongguo xijushi jiangzuo*, p. 219.
51. Mackerras, *The Rise and Growth of Peking Opera*, pp. 49–80, and 116–24, discusses court theatre and Yangzhou merchants.
52. See *Ci-yu cong-hua*, p. 275.
53. Dates according to Zhou Miaozhong, 'Yang Chaoguan he tade "Yin-feng ge"'. This anecdote is told in *Ju-shuo*, ch. 5, p. 194.
54. There is a biography in Hummel, op. cit., pp. 141–2.

55. In 1751. See *Qu–hua*, p. 273. Plays commissioned by Kiangsi gentry and commoners.
56. See *Yu-cun qu-hua*, p. 27.
57. The preface to *Meng-zhong yuan* (the play that Zhang Jian wrote when he was eighteen) tells how northern audiences would disperse at the sound of Kunqu. *Yan-lan xiao-pu*, ch. 2, p. 4a, says: 'Kunqu is not liked by northerners'. cf. Aoki, *Zhongguo jinshi xiqu shi*, pp. 446–8.
58. See *Yan-lan xiao-pu*, ch. 5, p. 5b.
59. See *Teng-yin za-ji*, ch. 5, p. 1810.
60. Barrow, *Travels in China*, pp. 147–8, notes the widespread taste for boys among the literati that 'many of the first officers of state seemed to make no hesitation in publicly avowing'. The matter is of great importance for Qing and theatrical society, but how it affected stage performance and the content of plays, and to what extent, are complex problems. It is clear that audiences often accepted the stage portrayals of femininity without reservation, and the topics were often intensely 'heterosexual'. It is also clear that the actors often, if not generally, identified themselves very deeply with their feminine roles (some jokes told of them having pregnancies and miscarriages as a result! See *Ju-shuo*, p. 209). The social aspects are reflected in many works, such as *Yang-zhou hua-fang lu*, written in 1794, and the novel *Pin-hua bao-jian*, written in 1849. Aoki, *Zhongguo jinshi xiqu shi*, pp. 447–8, makes comparisons with the *kagema* of the Genroku era (1688–1704). Of course, Elizabethan and other theatres used boys to act the parts of women. By way of not entirely facetious comparison, we note that Moges, *Recollections*, pp. 88–9, tells of French plays aboard the warships *Nemesis* and *Audacieuse* at Hong Kong in 1857, with French sailors clad in 'left-off' crinolines and 'emulating the sweet and gentle voice of woman', and the audience being 'shocked neither by the big hands nor the shaven chins of the performers'.
61. e.g. the *Yan-lan xiao-pu* published in 1785 was a treatise on actors, but devoted to the *dan* performers.
62. See *Hua-bu nong-tan*, p. 225.
63. See *Ting-chun xin-yong*, pt. 3, pp. 4a–4b.
64. e.g. *Xiuding pingju xuan*, 10th series, pp. 65–71.
65. Trans. from *Zhui bai-qiu*, pt. 6, fol. 2, pp. 72–6.
66. In Yangzhou, and later more generally, Kunqu was termed *yabu*, 'refined section', and all other, more local, kinds of drama, were called *huabu*, 'flowery (gaily lascivious?) section'.
67. From Zhou Yibai, *Zhongguo xijushi jiangzuo*, pp. 231–2. For 1785, see also Zhang Cixi, *Beijing liyuan zhanggu*, pp. 2a–2b.

Chapter 8: The Nineteenth Century and the Emergence of Peking Opera

1. For a biography, see Hummel, *Eminent Chinese*, vol. 1, p. 573.
2. For these remarks, bans, etc., see Wang Xiaochuan, *Yuan Ming Qing*, pp. 50–82.
3. See ibid., p. 60.
4. Her reply is translated in Bland and Backhouse, *China Under the Empress Dowager*, pp. 86–7. For her theatrical activities, see also Carl, *With the Empress Dowager of China*.
5. From Bland and Backhouse, op. cit., pp. 359–61.
6. See Wang Xiaochuan, op. cit., pp. 108–36, for this and following bans, etc.
7. See Wang Xiaochuan, op. cit., p. 117.
8. ibid., p. 135. cf. Dudbridge, *The Hsi-yu chi*, pp. 165–6 (quoting J. J. M. de Groot), on

coarse farcical presentations of Maudgalyāyana.

9.   See *Yan-jing za-ji*, p. 13a.

10.   See *Jin-tai can-lei ji*, ch. 3, p. 1b. For later in the century, Gray, *China*, vol. 1, pp. 378–9, has some generalisations: 'In every large town there are several companies of actors, each consisting of ten, twenty or a hundred persons. [. . .] When boys, they are bought by the conductors of companies, and sent to dramatic schools, [. . .] They are very harshly treated at these seminaries [. . .] Should a youth die under the hands of a master, no notice is taken by those whose duty it is to administer justice. [. . .] The usual period of instruction is one year, at the close of which the youths are expected to take part in any plays which may be performed. They are regarded by their purchasers as little better than beasts of burden, and receive for their services only food and clothing. Their period of servitude, however, lasts only for six years, after which they may claim their discharge. If sufficiently influential they form companies of their own; otherwise, they engage them- selves to managers at a tolerably remunerative salary. As a rule, women are not allowed to appear on stage. Female parts are well sustained by men, and their presence does not seem required. There are, however, schools in which females, generally of dissolute habits, are instructed for the stage.

'The usual hire for a company of players is from twenty to one hundred dollars a day. They are frequently rewarded during the performance of a play by presents of food, such as roast pigs, or offerings of money. I have seen a present of roast pigs carried across the stage by the servant of the donor at the very time the most pathetic part of the play was being performed. The gifts are no sooner received than one of the performers not engaged in the play attires himself as a deity, and coming before the audience with a graceful salutation, unfolds a scroll with an inscription in large characters expressive of the thanks of the company for the presents received. These substantial expressions of approbation may remind the reader of the *corollarium*, or reward given to actors among the ancient Romans.' There existed much less formal and humbler conditions of employ, too.

11.   Interspersed with short, often farcical *zaju*; see *Jin-tai can-lei ji*, ch. 3, p. 4b, and Aoki, *Zhongguo jinshi xiqu shi*, pp. 486–7.

12.   See *Lü-yuan cong-hua*, ch. 12, p. 12b.

13.   See *Ding-nian yu-sun zhi*, pp. 6b–7a.

14.   See *Pin-hua bao-jian*, ch. 4.

15.   e.g. *Tian-zhi ou-wen*, ch. 7, pp. 524–5: 'Towards the end of the Daoguang period [1821–50], Erhuang-*qiang* suddenly became very popular. Its music was louder and faster than Yi[yang-*qiang*], and its words were all market slang and low vulgarisms, with nothing of the refined elegance of Kun[shan-*qiang*] and Yi[yang-*qiang*] there any more.'

16.   From *Du-men za-yong* (1845) by Yang Jingting, as quoted in Zhang Cixi, *Beiping liyuan zhuzhici huibian*, p. 3a.

17.   The novel was *Three Kingdoms*; see *Li-yuan jiu-hua*, pp. 3a–3b.

18.   See Cao Chousheng, *Zhongguo yinyue wudao xiqu*, p. 155 (quoting *Qingdai shengse zhi*). cf. also Chen Yanheng, *Jiuju congtan*, p. 27a.

19.   From *Du-men za-yong* (1864) by Banhuazhai, as quoted in Zhang Cixi, op. cit., p. 4b.

20.   See Zhang Cixi, *Yandu mingling zhuan*, p. 1b; Chen Jiantan, *Yiling zhuan*, p. 1a; and *Li- yuan jiu-hua*, p. 2a.

21.   See *Li-yuan jiu-hua*, p. 2b.

22.   From *Du-men xin zhu-zhi-ci* (1853) by Zhilanshi-zhuren, as quoted in Zhang Cixi, *Beiping liyuan zhuzhici huibian*, p. 4a.

23.   See *Li-yuan jiu-hua*, p. 2b.

24. See Luo Chunrong, *Jubu congtan*, p. 13a.
25. See ibid., p. 12b.
26. For fuller story see Zhang Cixi, *Yandu mingling zhuan*, p. 5b.
27. His great-grandson Tan Yuanshou (1930–) was playing *laosheng* in the Peking Opera troupe that performed in Hong Kong in 1963.
28. See biography in Zhang Cixi, *Yandu mingling zhuan*, pp. 9b–11a.
29. See Cao Chousheng, op. cit., p. 131.
30. See ibid., p. 81; Xu Jiuye, *Liyuan yiwen*, pp. 2b–3a; *Li-yuan jiu-hua*, pp. 4a–4b; and Zhang Cixi, *Yandu mingling zhuan*, pp. 7b–9b.
31. Translated from *Xiuding pingju xuan*, pt. 2, pp. 21–6.
32. See Cao Chousheng, op. cit., p. 240. cf. also Luo Chunrong, *Jubu congtan*, p. 9b; *Ju-bu qun-ying*, p. 5a; and Zhang Cixi, *Yandu mingling zhuan*, pp. 3b–5a.
33. cf. Zhang Cixi, *Yandu mingling zhuan*, pp. 6a–6b, on actors in the palace.
34. See ibid., pp. 17a–18b, and Zhou Yibai, *Zhongguo xijushi jiangzuo*, p. 261.
35. Standard works in English include Scott, *The Classical Theatre of China*, and Halson, *Peking Opera*. See also: Yang, Daniel Shih-p'êng, *An Annotated Bibliography*.
36. Guo Jianying, *Xiqu longtao jiaocai*. It gives numerous categories of *longtao*. Etymologically the word means 'dragon-suit'.
37. Plays are translated with detailed description of performance in Scott, *Traditional Chinese Plays*. Tape available.
38. cf. Zung, *Secrets of the Chinese Drama*.

Chapter 9: Theatres and Playwrights

1. Some of the bigger troupes were very heavily equipped, and touring was a cumbersome business for them. Smith, *Village Life in China*, p. 62, says: 'In inland regions where it is necessary to use animals, it requires a great many carts to move about so much lumber, [. . .] The carts for this hauling are provided by the village which is to enjoy the exhibition, being often selected by lot. Sometimes, however, a small tax is levied on all the land in the village, and the carts are hired.'
2. Many accounts note the rich silk costumes. Even poor actors were often particular about costume, but colour and magnificence were sought rather than historical accuracy or naturalistic reality. cf. *Ju-shuo*, p. 200, and *Xian-qing ou-ji*, p. 109. Gordon Cummings, *Wandering in China*, p. 190, notes the contrast between the principal actors and effects-men, etc.: 'The service of the play is all done by men in the commonest blue coolie dress! It is so odd to see them moving about among the gorgeously arrayed principal actors. There is no attempt at stage illusion – no curtain, no shifting of scenes, beyond the most primitive alterations in the stage furniture. If a culprit is to be killed by fire from heaven, you see a coolie climb up and scatter an inflammable powder, to which he sets fire.'
3. But some information is available from building inscriptions, such as those of the Qing Dynasty reproduced in Zhang Cixi, *Beijing liyuan jinshi wenzi lu*.
4. Gray, *China*, vol. 1, pp. 377–8. He mentions one fire disaster of 1844 in which two thousand spectators lost their lives. Williams, *The Middle Kingdom*, vol. 2, pp. 820–1, specifics on the matter of construction of temple matshed theatres: 'The erection of sheds for playing constitutes a separate branch of the carpenter's trade; one large enough to accommodate two thousand persons can be put up in the southern cities in a day, and almost the only part of the materials which is wasted is the rattan which binds the posts

and mats together. One large shed contains the stage, and three smaller ones before it enclose an area, and are furnished with rude seats for the paying spectators. The subscribers' bounty is acknowledged by pasting red sheets containing their names and amounts on the walls of the temple.'

5.   Fortune, *A Journey to the Tea Countries of China*, pp. 74–6.

6.   Fortune, *A Residence Among the Chinese*, pp. 256–7.

7.   Aoki, *Zhongguo jinshi xiqu shi*, pp. 515–16.

8.   ibid.

9.   Gordon Cummings, *Wanderings in China*, pp. 187–91, 'Temple Theatres'.

10.   Cao Juren, *Renshi xinyu*, pp. 420–1.

11.   Gray, *China*, vol. 1, pp. 72–4, concerns tea-houses and the *qingchang*, 'pure singing' (singing of plays without costume, etc.), that was commonly performed in them. Preceded by a discussion of guilds and guild halls.

12.   *Meng-hua suo-bu*, p. 2b.

13.   ibid., p. 7a. cf. also *Jin-tai can-lei ji*, ch. 2, p.7b.

14.   *Meng-hua suo-bu*, p. 7a, and *Jin-tai can-lei ji*, ch. 3, p. 4a.

15.   One purpose of the volume of sound from the stage is pointed out by Lin Yutang, *My Country and my People*, p. 249: '[. . .] the actors had to compete with the pedlars' cries, the barbers' tuning forks, the malt-sugar sellers' small gongs, the shouting of men, women and children and the barking of dogs. Above such a din, only a thin falsetto keyed in a high pitch could have been heard, as anybody may verify for himself. The gongs and drums were also used as a means of attracting attention; they always preceded the plays and could be heard a mile away, thus serving the purpose of street posters for the movies.' This is perhaps truer of some conditions in the outdoor theatres, but it may also partly explain the volume of stage sound in some of the indoor theatres with bustling audiences. But more purely dramatic factors, such as the creation of tension, the emphasis of action, and the division of scenes, also played their part.

16.   cf. Lin Yutang, *Imperial Peking*, p. 150, on the Guanghelou: '[. . .] the benches were rickety, ventilation was almost nil and breathing was almost impossible. But the surroundings did not seem to matter. There was noise and laughter in the audience; refreshments were served, and ushers, or more strictly waiters, sent wrung-out hot towels flying in the air across the heads of the audience.'

17.   For my views of the Globe, I rely largely on Adams, *The Globe Playhouse*.

18.   A detailed account of this theatre as it was is found in Zhang Cixi, *Yanguilaiyi suibi*, pp. 7b–9b.

19.   There is a biography in Hummel, *Eminent Chinese*, pp. 661–2.

20.   See *Ou-bo yu-hua*, ch. 1, pp. 5328–9.

21.   There is a biography in Hummel, op. cit., pp. 503–5.

22.   On early dramas from the novel, see *Ju-shuo*, pp. 265–6.

23.   From *Hua-bu nong-tan*, preface, p. 225. There is a biography of Jiao in Hummel, op. cit., pp. 144–5.

Chapter 10: The Appearance of Western-style Drama

1.   The psychological link in many minds between the national humiliation and the uses of drama is seen in many writings around the turn of the century. An anonymous 'Account of play-watching' of 1903 (given in A Ying, *Wan Qing wenxue congchao (xiaoshuo xiqu yanjiu*

zhuan, pp. 67–72) urges reform of the contents and musical instruments of Chinese drama, and calls for tragic and violent, bloody plays, on the example of French plays performed after the Franco-Prussian War, and for heroic plays on the Japanese model. There were frequent calls for tragedies, to stir patriotism. cf. also the remarks of Xiao Lu, a dramatist, in 1906, as given in A Ying, op.cit., p. 192.

2. An anonymous preface of 1908, in A Ying, op. cit., p. 306, calls a French play 'a brief simple *zaju*'. Plays were still often referred to as *zaju* and *chuanqi*.

3. He was the earliest to make extensive use of Peking Opera for such modern purposes. His plays and others of the period are listed in A Ying, *Wan Qing xiqu xiaoshuo mu*. Huang Jilian (1836–1924) was another prolific adaptor and creator of traditional drama for modern aims. New drama societies also played a role, such as the Yisushe founded in 1912 and the Chuanju Gailiang Gonghui founded early this century.

4. See Bertuccioli, *La Letteratura Cinese*, pp. 319–25 (including a translation of *New Rome*). A lecture by Professor Bertuccioli in 1960 first drew my attention to *New Rome*. Liang actually preferred the novel as a medium of propaganda, as did many other scholars of that time. See Zhu Meishu, 'Liang Qichao yu xiaoshuojie geming', p. 111.

5. From A Ying, *Wan Qing wenxue congchao (chuanqi zaju juan)*, vol. 2, pp. 518–51.

6. Launching China's first drama periodical, *Great twentieth century stage*, in 1904, Liu Yazi shows how relevant some Chinese considered the history of some Western nations to be to China's situation. '[. . .] What we must do now is press the blue-eyes and purple-beards [i.e. Westerners] into the garb of Jester Meng [i.e. Chinese drama], and set forth their history, so that the French Revolution, American Independence, the glorious revivals of Italy and Greece, and the cruel destruction of India and Poland may all be imprinted on the minds of our compatriots.' See A Ying, *Wan Qing wenxue congchao (xiaoshuo xiqu yanjiu juan)*, pp. 176–7.

7. Japanese inspiration and the inadequacies of traditional Chinese drama (for cultivating modern attitudes to warfare) as arguments for the introduction of Western-style drama are found in remarks made by Jiang Guanyun in 1904, as given in A Ying, *Wan Qing wenxue congchao (xiaoshuo xiqu yanjiu juan)*, pp. 50–2. (He also quotes Napoleon as saying, 'Tragedy is good for rousing the spirit'.)

8. cf. Okazaki, *Japanese Literature in the Meiji Era*.

9. Various Shanghai schools performed Western, Western-style or otherwise *xinju* plays: St John's University (from 1899); Nanyang Public School (in 1900); Xuhuai Public School (from 1902); Yucai Academy (in 1903); Nanyang Middle School and National Middle School (both in 1904); Mingde School, Shanghai Academy, the Y.M.C.A., and Nanxiang Primary School (all in or from 1906). These plays were often in English or French, and included Western classics such as *Merchant of Venice*. Societies also arose in Shanghai. Wang Zhongxian (Wang Yuyu, d. 1911), a pupil of the National Middle School, founded the first *xinju* society in 1905, the Literary Friends Society. Various others were founded in 1906 and 1907, by Li Shutong (Li Xishuang), Wang Zhongxian, Zhu Shuangyun, Ren Tianshu, Jin Yinggu, and others. cf. Ouyang Yuqian, 'Tan wenmingxi'. Zhu Shuangyun, *Xinju shi*, says that St John's plays began in 1902 and Nanyang Public School's in 1903.

10. Organised by Zeng Cunwu, Li Shutong, and others. Its initial declaration acknowledges the Japanese inspiration and uses Japanese terms: *shimpa*, 'new school', to refer to Western-style drama, and *kyūpa*, 'old school, to refer to Chinese traditional dramas. In Japan, the *shimpa* were, like *New Rome*, often new in theme but old in style, and often acted like *kabuki*. The adoption of the term *shingeki*, 'new drama' might have been more consistent, but in China the various terms for 'new drama' and 'new style' have been applied

both loosely, to apply to any drama new in form, presentation or content, and specifically, to drama new in all these respects. Li Shutong was later a famous Buddhist monk. See A Ying, *Wan Qing wenxue congchao (xiaoshuo xiqu yanjiu juan)*, pp. 635–8 for the declaration, which pointedly notes the esteem accorded to Henry Irving in Britain and America.

11.   Wang Ziren translated it into the vernacular for his friend Lin to render into the classical language. Lin was the first major Chinese translator of Western fiction, and later a vigorous opponent of vernacularisation. His involvement in the first two important *huaju* is rather ironic in view of the latter fact.

12.   Zeng Xiaogu composed a full written text. Unlike the traditional dramas it had no interludes, recitation, song, asides, or soliloquies, but was pure *huaju* in form. See Ouyang Yuqian, 'Huiyi Chunliu'.

13.   Among them *Calling out for justice*, a translation of a French play (Courteline, *L'Article 330*? Not Molière as sometimes suggested, if I understand the preface in A Ying, *Wan Qing wenxue congchao (xiaoshuo xiqu yanjiu juan)*, pp. 306–7). This and a Polish(?) play (under the title *Night is still young*) both translated by Li Shizeng and published in 1908, are considered the earliest published *huaju*.

14.   Zhu Shuangyun, *Xinju shi*, lists over seventy *xinju* troupes, often very short-lived, that arose between 1902 and 1914, mostly in Shanghai, but after 1908 or so also in Peking, Anqing, Suzhou, and elsewhere. The number greatly increased in 1911 and 1912, and from 1912 touring with *xinju* became a widespread habit. Some probable 'firsts': in 1907 Nanyang Public School performed the first historical *xinju* in entirely contemporary costume; in 1907 the Spring Sunlight Society (of Shanghai, founded by Wang Zhongsheng) was the first to use full scenery; in 1908 the newly founded Keshe drama society started a new-style *xinju* using a lot of singing; in Shanghai in May 1912 the Women's Suffrage Society were the first women to perform *xinju*. Ouyang Yuqian, 'Tan wenmingxi', p. 50, says that the Tokyo performance of *La Dame aux camélias* was the first to use the curtain to divide the play into acts (*mu*) and the first to use scenery, and that *Black slave's cry to Heaven* was the first to do so in China, when performed by Wang Zhongsheng and others in Shanghai in 1907.

15.   cf. Ouyang Yuqian, op. cit., pp. 88–96.

16.   The earliest terms in general use seem to have been *xinju*, and, less frequent, *xinxi*. The word *kaiming* was popular in the early years of this century. Zhu Shuangyun and others formed an Enlightenment (*Kaiming*) Society in 1906. *Wenming* seems to have come into use to imply plays of higher moral quality than some early *xinju*, but was later used undifferentiatedly for any Western-style drama. By the twenties it had acquired connotations of low quality.

17.   Hong Shen, introduction to vol. 9 of *Zhongguo xin wenxue daxi*, pp. 14–15 (quoting himself from a newspaper article of 1929), attributes the lull to poor training, histrionic failings and off-stage immorality in the theatre world. He says: 'The so-called *wenmingxi* had completely crumbled [. . .] And so the better people went elsewhere, to seek another way.' Film competition may have been another cause. The New People Film Company founded in 1913 for a brief while drew some *wenmingxi* actors away from the living stage.

18.   An article by Hu Shi (1891–1962) was a major initial step in the movement. He later wrote on 'Ibsenism' (see his 'Yibusheng zhuyi' of 1918) and was the author of a short *huaju*: *Life's great event.*

19.   Perhaps the theatre has dominated the cinema more in China than anywhere. The first motion pictures there (first referred to as *xiyang yingxi*, 'Western shadow-shows', later as *dianying*, 'electric shadows') were shown in Shanghai in 1896, in between conjuring,

fireworks and other entertainments. In 1897 an American showed short comic, documentary and other films there. Tea-house theatres were often used in the early years. A Spanish businessman began shows in 1899, but soon sold his equipment to the Spaniard A. Ramos, who in 1909 built China's first cinema, seating 250. In Peking, too, a Westerner showed films as early as 1899, and in 1900 the merchant Li Zhusan became the first Chinese to show films in China. The British envoy gave the empress dowager a projector and films in 1904, but it exploded. By 1911 films had become so popular that regulations appeared in Shanghai, proscribing such things as men and women sitting together in the audiences. The first narrative film made in China was a 1905 daylight filming of Tan Xinpei in selections of Peking Operas. Westerners and Western films dominated cinema in China for many years. In 1909 the French company Pathé filmed parts of various Peking Operas. Also in 1909, the American Benjamin Brasky founded China's first film-making company, the Asia Company. In 1911 it came under two other Americans, who in 1913 with Zheng Zhengqiu (d. 1935) and other *wenmingxi* actors filmed the first Chinese film with an integral plot, *Husband and wife in a plight*, script by Zheng. About ten films were made in 1913, mostly based on plays. Filmed stage performances have been very important in the Chinese cinema to the present day. The Commercial Press Motion Picture Section was founded in 1918. Its first two non-documentary films, made in 1919–20, were traditional plays starring Mei Lanfang. Its first films in modern costume, from 1921, were acted by *wenmingxi* actors. Not till the Lian Hua Film Enterprise Company was founded in 1930 did the industry draw free of *wenmingxi* plays and actors. The cinema expanded greatly during the twenties, with a 'golden age of silent films' from about 1924. In 1931 came the first talkies made in China: *Singing-girl Red Peony* (scenario by Hong Shen); *Yu the Beautiful* (story from a Peking Opera); *Clear sky after rain*; *Spring in the singsong house* (from a stage play); and *Metropolis of old* (scenario by Hong Shen). Talkies gradually prevailed, and the cinema reared more of its own writing and acting talent, with stars such as Hudie (Miss Butterfly), but the link with the theatre remained strong, especially through the scenario writers, often prominent theatremen, such as Zheng Zhengqiu, Hong Shen, Xia Yan, A Ying, Ouyang Yuqian, Zheng Boqi, Tian Han, Yang Hansheng, Wang Zhongxian, and Song Zhidi. cf. Yisha, introduction to *Zhongguo xin wenxue daxi xubian*, Scott, *Literature and the Arts*, and Du Yunzhi, *Zhongguo dianying shi*, vol. 1.

20.　*Wenmingxi* were often performed with *muwaixi*, 'beyond-the-curtain plays', short plays in front of the closed curtain between acts or scenes to prevent audience impatience. The intervals were also used to further elucidate the plot of the main play, by direct spoken explanations.

21.　Up to 1921, translated plays (sometimes rather in the nature of adaptations) included dramas by Hugo, Shakespeare, Scribe, Shaw, Wilde, Galsworthy, Lady Gregory, Brieux, Ibsen, Bjørnson, Gogol, Ostrovsky, Turgenyev, L. N. Tolstoy, Chekhov, Schiller, Sudermann, Maeterlinck, the brothers Álvarez Quintero, Tagore, Mushakōji Saneatsu, etc. cf. list in Lu Qian, *Zhongguo xiju gailun*, pp. 152–3. Thirty to forty Western plays were translated between 1918 and 1927. The volume of translation was much greater during the twenties, and individual anthologies for Japanese drama, Russian drama, Ibsen, Hugo, and others appeared.

22.　Some utterly rejected it, some recommended reform. e.g. see correspondence in the periodical *Xin qingnian*, June 1958, pp. 620–5, and Hong Shen's introduction to vol. 9 of *Zhongguo xin wenxue daxi*, pp. 16–23. Liu Fu (1891–1934) urged reform. Qian Xuantong (1887–1939) asked: '[. . .] just how many farthings are China's old plays worth as literature?' cf. also Liu Ts'un-yen, 'Lu Xun yu Mei Lanfang' on many scholars' unfavourable view of the old theatre.

23. Trans. from Hong Shen, op. cit., p. 23.

24. cf. Tian Han, 'Nanguoshe shilue'.

25. e.g. the June 1918 volume of *Xin qingnian* was devoted to Ibsen, with a biography, an article, and three translations.

26. See Hong Shen, op.cit., p. 52. On Tian Han, cf. Häringova, 'The development of T'ien Han's dramatic writings during the years 1920–37'.

27. See Hong Shen, 'Xiju Xieshe pianduan'.

28. On the influence of Ibsen and other Westerners on Cao Yu, see Hsiao Ch'ien, 'Ibsen in China', and J. S. M. Lau, *Ts'ao Yü*.

29. Trans. from Cao Yu, *Cao Yu juben xuan*, pp. 159–64.

30. Strong, *China Fights for Freedom*, pp. 156–7.

31. A *yangge* of northern Shensi. On *yangge*, cf. next chapter. *Brother and sister pioneers* had only two roles, and was still essentially a singing act. There were many others of the same kind. See Liu Shouzhong, *Zhongguo xin wenxueshi chugao*, vol. 2, pp. 177–8.

32. On drama revision, cf. Zhao Cong, *Zhongguo dalude xiqu gaige 1942–1967*.

33. The problem of adjustment persists. Jin Jian, 'Mantan nongmin kan huaju' (1963) begins, 'Some people say that peasants like *xiqu* and are unwilling to watch *huaju*', and ends, 'How to facilitate peasant acceptance of *huaju* is a vital problem to be solved at the moment [. . .]'.

Chapter 11: Traditional Drama in the Twentieth Century

1. cf. Scott. *Mei Lan-fang*, Boorman, *Biographical Dictionary*, vol. 3, pp. 26–9, and Mei's own writings: *Mei Lanfang xiju sanlun, Wutai shenghuo sishinian, Mei Lanfang wenji*, etc.

2. There is a biography in Boorman, op. cit., vol. 3, pp. 98–9. Wang, a former stage partner of Tan Xinpei's, was himself an innovator in his techniques of acting and singing, and was one of the first teachers to train actresses.

3. He was awarded honorary degrees by two American colleges. On the way back, he also acted in Hawaii. On the tour, cf. Qi Rushan, *Mei Lanfang you Mei ji*.

4. Brecht wrote an article in 1936 entitled, 'Verfremdungseffekte in der chinesischen Schauspielkunst'. Tso Lin, 'The Chinese and Western Theatres', compares the theories of Mei, Brecht and Stanislavsky.

5. For Mei's wartime life, see Xu Yuanlai, 'Kangzhan banianzhongde Mei Lanfang'.

6. See photograph in Xu Yuanlai, op. cit., p. 49. To help his portrayal of *dan* roles, Mei had earlier tweezered his moustache, but a few hairs still remained.

7. During the fifties he made films of some more plays. cf. Mei Lanfang, *Wode dianying shenghuo*.

8. cf. Scott, *Literature and the Arts*, pp. 160–1.

9. Boorman, op. cit., vol. 1, pp. 299–301, gives details of Qi in France.

10. cf. Deng Suining, *Zhongguo xiju shi*, pp. 109–10, and Qi Rushan, *Qi Rushan chuanji*.

11. cf. Qi Rushan, *Mei Lanfang yishu yiban*.

12. Yang Chin-sheng, 'My Life on the Stage – by Mei Lan-fang'. See also, Ma Shao-po, 'Mei Lan-fang and Chou Hsin-fang'.

13. There is a biography in Boorman, op. cit., vol. 1, pp. 292–3. For early days, see biography in Zhang Cixi, *Yandu mingling zhuan*, pp. 18b–20b. See also Cheng Yanqiu, *Cheng Yanqiu wenji*. There is a comparison of Mei and Cheng in Zhang Huoshi, 'Mei

Lanfang yu Cheng Yanqiu'. A Manchu, Cheng was a student of both Wang Yaoqing and Mei. In 1919 he went with Mei to Japan, and in 1932 visited France, Germany, Italy, Switzerland and England to study theatre and opera. He performed briefly in Berlin and Nice, and in Geneva held a course in *taijiquan* boxing. In the late twenties, Cheng, Mei, Xun Huisheng, and Shang Xiaoyun were known as the Four Great Famous Dans.

14. A vivid insight into the life of a Peking Opera *laosheng* actor (Gai Tianjiao, 1888–?) is given in He Man and Gong Yijiang, *Fenmo chunqiu.*

15. See Scott, *The Classical Theatre of China*, pp. 60–4, 70–1.

16. In 1914 Mei Lanfang attempted *Waves of the sea of sin* and other plays in contemporary costume, akin to the *wenmingxi*, but after 1916 concentrated on traditional drama. In *Waves of the sea of sin* he appeared in modern dress and seated before a Singer sewing machine. See Scott, *Literature and the Arts*, pp. 37–8.

17. For puppetry in recent times, see Scott, *Literature and the Arts*, pp. 56–60, Wimsatt, *Chinese Shadow Shows*, and Obratsov, *The Chinese Puppet Theatre.*

18. e.g. Puju or Puxianxi from Fukien. See Hu Ji, *Song Jin zaju kao*, pp. 303–10.

19. e.g. the Yueju drama of Chekiang (and later of Kiangsu and elsewhere), created from popular songs in 1912. Banned for its bawdiness, it was fostered by local gentry and acquired first a proper theatre in the county capital, then in 1923 a foothold in Shanghai, where it broadened its range of instruments and techniques, and became one of the most vigorous regional kinds of drama. *Bengbengxi (Luozi, pingxi, pingju)* drama of the north-east is another powerful form, originating from folk songs, ballads, and other entertainments around the turn of the century. It is well documented: see Hu Sha, *Pingju jianshi.*

20. Bowers, *Theatre in the East*, p. 8, links lion dances with Indian Buddhist influence.

21. See Chao Wei-pang, 'Yang-ko', and Gamble, *Chinese Village Plays.*

22. e.g. the *nuoxi* drama of Anhwei, possibly with roots in the Han. It seems first to have been propitiatory or exorcistic dances, but became more purely an entertainment, with both dances and plays. Its music is mainly of Yiyang-*qiang* tradition, and uses only percussive instruments.

23. Xia Ye, *Xiqu yinyue yanjiu*, p. 146.

24. Zhou Yibai, *Zhongguo xiqu lunji*, p. 354, notes that some Hupeh *huaguxi* were initially all singing.

25. See Zhou Yibai, op.cit., p. 364 footnote.

26. See Kalvodová, 'The Origin and Character of the Szechwan Theatre'. Anon., 'Szechuan Opera Festival', says that Szechwan drama has a repertoire of over 1,900 plays.

27. Deng Suining, *Zhongguo xiju shi*, p. 125 (quoting Hai Ge, *Chuanxi*), says: 'The mode of singing in Gao-qiang is extremely simple: all that is needed is drums, *ban*-clappers and singers. But the drummers are exceedingly important because they have to perform the *bangqiang* [i.e. the choral repetition]. In the *bangqiang*, when the [main] singer has nearly reached the final line of his verse, the drummers take over the singing, while he just mimes the meaning, sometimes for as long as two or three lines.' This equates choir with orchestra.

28. See You Guoen et alia, *Zhongguo wenxue shi*, vol. 4, p. 1244.

29. Xia Guoyun, 'Shanchuan xiuli renwu fengliu', p. 39, mentions the dramas of the minorities in Yunnan, Kweichow, Szechwan, Kwangsi and Kwangtung: Baiju, Daiju and Zhuangju with a history of more than a hundred years, and Yiju a new form.

30. The history of Yongju drama clearly illustrates the progress from village to town to big city. Out of rustic songs of the Ningpo area came a springtime amateur entertainment with peasants, fishermen, carpenters, tanners, tailors, etc., forming all-male troupes

(called *madengban*, 'horse-lantern troupes') as small as two *dan* and two male-role actors. Love was their usual theme. Troupes grew as big as twelve *dan* and twelve male-role actors, and included professionals. Around 1910, Wu Shilai, viewed as the founder of Yongju, took this half-ballad half-drama play-acting into Ningpo itself. Called Ningpo-*tanhuang*, around 1915 it moved into Shanghai, where performing in over twenty tea-house theatres it enriched its repertoire and was influenced by *wenmingxi*, but grew vulgarly erotic and commercialised. With moves to reform it, in 1930 it gained the name *siming wenxi*, 'four enlightenments refined plays', and the ballad elements gave way to more wholly dramatic form. It gained many more plays, mostly from *wenmingxi*, Peking Opera and Yueju, and by 1940, now called *gailiang* ('reformed') Yongju, had largely lost its solid rustic simplicity. cf. Ma Yanxiang, 'Cong liangchu haoxi tan Yongjude fazhan'.

31.   *Pingju*, for instance, imitated *wenmingxi*, foreign plays, *huaju* (including Cao Yu's *Thunderstorm*) and cinema. The amount of interchange between ancient, modern traditional and foreign genres this century has been enormous. Actors and writers have moved with great freedom. cf. Hu Sha, *Pingju shi*, pp. 52, and 212–13. Hong Shen, Tian Han and Ouyang Yuqian created *pingju* and Peking Opera, etc.

32.   This and his other important works on Chinese drama are found in Wang Guowei, *Wang Guowei xiqu lunwen ji*.

Chapter 12: Drama under the People's Republic

1.   For theatre in Chinese communities outside the People's Republic, see Scott, *Literature and the Arts*, pp. 162–3, 169–73 and 175–6. They include many fertile fields for the study of traditional drama. The Chinese Republic in Taiwan presents a varied scene, with much Peking Opera (accomplished troupes have been sent to Europe and North America), *huaju* and regional drama, the latter including both a wide range of mainland traditional forms and some more wholly Taiwanese forms (such as the *gezixi*, 'little song plays', that can be traced from pristine work-song origins to the present fairly sophisticated form of performance). Puppetry also abounds in Taiwan. Numerous troupes have been formed in both *huaju* and traditional drama-forms, some in the armed forces, and there has been a fair amount of publication and republication of plays and of writings on drama (by such scholars as Qi Rushan, Zheng Qian, and others). Those communities furthest removed from Western and modern Chinese influence, such as those in Thailand, become increasingly valuable to the student of traditional drama as innovation continues apace in China, and Western modernisation elsewhere. Chinese in Singapore and Malaya (cf. Fang Xiu, *Ma Hua xin wenxue daxi*, vol. 5, pp. 1–19) have a history of *huaju* movements, although these have often reflected events and developments in China.

2.   Sometimes as the result of competitions. e.g. in 1954 *Theatre* attracted 667 entries for a one-act-play competition. In 1963 *Plays* received 1,947 entries for another competition (1,403 *huaju*, and 544 *geju* and *xiqu*).

3.   *Culture and Education in China*, p. 8.

4.   Twenty-four Peking cinemas and twenty-five theatres, with their locations, are listed in *Peking*, pp. 152–4.

5.   'The Broad Harmony Theatre', CL, 3, 1956, pp. 213–15.

6.   Zhang Henshui, *Ti-xiao yin-yuan* (a novel of the twenties), p. 3 et seq., gives the liveliest description of the old Tianqiao theatre area, the wild hubbub and vivid chaos, wood-plank theatres, gaudy posters, barrows and stalls, scruffy food-vendors (cooking 'boiled sheep's

284

intestines': 'strip on strip of extenuated lacquer-black things the image of dead de-scaled snakes, smelling stinking and frowzy, forever rearing from the pan'), bustling alleys of clothes, shoe and tinkers' shops, the broad, blue, muddy, evil-odoured ditch, and the more savoury pavilions with their entertainers. Cao Juren, *Renshi xinyu*, p. 291, describes the contrast in the fifties: the mirror-like broad highways, the luxuriant green trees, modern theatre, cinema, tidy restaurants and tea-houses ('with not a fly or mosquito to be seen'), and the department store where the ditch used to be.

7. For example see Hsia, *A History of Modern Chinese Fiction (1917–1957)*, p. 339.

8. Economic competition continued to exist. e.g. a letter to *Xijubao*, 2, 1958, p. 8, from a reader in Shantung, talks of actors earning as much as 1,850 dollars a month; a troupe making a loss because it relied on guest stars (the letter viewing this as a device for evading 'going down into the countryside' on unremunerative, uncomfortable tours); and an actress constantly pestering for wage increases and twice changing troupes to obtain them.

9. The first edition of this play bears an article (Guo Moruo, 'Ti Cao Cao fan-an') attempting to reverse the traditional verdict on Cao Cao, the arch-villain of Chinese theatre and popular history.

10. Mei Lanfang, 'Zhongguo xiqu yishude xin fangxiang', outlines many of the reforms expected of the theatre, and mentions difficulties over actor and audience nostalgia. *Fenlands* plays were prominent objects of reform. Zhang Zhen, *Xiqu renwu sanlun*, pp. 66–9, touches on the difficulties of reforming stage heroes whose images have become fixed in the public mind over centuries.

11. Zhou Yang, 'Gaige he fazhan minzu xiqu yishu', p. 7.

12. Shen Yao, 'Jinxi qiantan', p. 21.

13. Yan Yong, 'Xiqu biaoxian xiandai shenghuode zhuangkuang he wenti', pp. 18–19, mentions some of the difficulties some people encountered in the quest for more stage realism. In one play actors ate a real meal on stage to demonstrate better living conditions; a Peking Opera troupe, in place of symbolic or acrobatic fighting, used such realistic wrestling that arms were broken; an old-style actor, finding no use for his stylised gestures in new plays, simply stuck his hands in his pockets (his 'air-raid shelters' people called them) throughout each play; and another old actor complained: 'The one thing that scares me is those forums. When we act *huaguxi*, the peasants give us a fine reception, and all the players are happy. Everybody says, that's real *huagu*[*xi*], and I feel all relaxed. But as soon as we start these forums, somebody straightway says this thing "isn't real" and that thing "doesn't look right", and I get all muddled up.'

14. In England from 1931–40, she studied at the Jooss School of Ballet, worked under Anton Dolin and Margaret Craske, and took part in film- and stage-acting. In wartime China, she pursued her interest in local dance-forms, and taught at the National Academy of Opera, in Chungking, and other institutions. During 1946–7 she performed in the United States. From 1949 she was a leading figure in the revival of traditional dances in China. See Boorman, *Biographical Dictionary*, vol. 3, pp. 198–9, and Scott, *Literature and the Arts*, pp. 52–6.

15. cf. Fokkema, *Literary Doctrine in China*, pp. 82–118.

16. Including photographs of stage performances.

17. Trans. from *Shi-wu guan*, pp. 49–56.

18. *Pi-pa ji taolun zhuankan.*

19. Some of Guan's plays were turned into other styles of drama: five Peking Operas, three *pingju* plays, a Yueju (drama of Chekiang) play, etc.

20. The play, *Injustice done to Dou Graceful*, was first attributed to Guan in a Ming work:

Tai-he zheng-yin pu, p. 28.

21.   Trans. from Tian Han, *Guan Hanqing*, pp. 56–61.

22.   Wei Xun, 'Beijing Renyi ye bu zhongshi xiandai jumu' (1958), p. 17, accuses the Peking People's Art Theatre of disrespect for modern plays, giving the statistics that in 1957 only three of its fourteen plays were post-1949 and that they took up only a small part of its total performances. A play based on a novel by Lao She (*Ricksha boy*) was most performed, and two early Cao Yu plays were prominent items of the year. Wei's article is followed by others with titles such as 'Where have the modern plays gone?', 'Audiences like modern plays', 'Why are *huaju* troupes indifferent towards modern plays?' and 'Priority should be given to modern plays'. The problem concerned both modern creation and modern themes.

23.   An Bo, 'Guanyu xin gejude tigao wenti' (1962), p. 2, says that since 1949 'some 13 or so nationally famous *xin geju* have been produced'. A big conference on *xin geju* was held in 1956–7, and from 1961 various national periodicals gave the genre renewed close attention.

24.   A key debate in 1962 was on the form of the new operas, and whether they should be all singing, in the Western fashion (as was Zheng Lücheng's *Wang-fu yun geju* of 1962). This involved discussion of Western opera. *Xin geju* (often referred to as '*huaju* with singing added') was, however, the model generally preferred. Chinese interest in Western opera seems to have been small and sporadic (such early studies as Feng Kai, 'Geju yu yueju' (1925), seem to have aroused little active interest), and few Western operas have been performed in China. In 1962 fuel was added to the debate by a performance of Tchaikovsky's *Eugene Onegin* by the Central Experimental Opera and Dance-drama Theatre. During the early sixties there seems to have been yet increasing emphasis on national minority music, dance and dramas, as well as on regional dramas, which may have reinforced the role of music and song in the more national forms of Chinese theatre, too.

25.   Cao Juren, *Renshi xinyu*, p. 129.

26.   cf. Ingalls, introduction to trans. *The Malice of Empire*, by Yao.

27.   cf. Gray and Cavendish, *Chinese Communism in Crisis*, pp. 153–8, and Ansley (trans.), *The Heresy of Wu Han*.

28.   For background, cf. Gray and Cavendish. op. cit., pp. 69–113, and Fokkema, *Report from Peking*, pp. 47–50.

29.   *Zhiqu Weihushan*, pp. 1–2.

30.   See *Zhiqu Weihushan*, p. 1.

31.   Trans. from *Shajiabang*, pp. 62–5.

32.   See Mehnert, *China Returns*, p. 145.

33.   'How the Opera "Half a basket of peanuts" Came to be Written', CL, 5, 1973, pp. 102–4, concerns an example of a new play, in regional drama. Like a number of other new ones, it is short, roughly the length of an act of the usual four-act *huaju*. There seems to be a growing policy of promoting the short play as especially suitable for performance in factories and the countryside. This is a continuation or revival of tendencies in evidence just before the Cultural Revolution. cf., for instance, various articles in *Xijubao*, 1965, first issue of the year.

34.   See Mackerras, 'Chinese Opera after the Cultural Revolution'.

35.   cf. Mackerras, op. cit., esp. pp. 500–6, and idem, 'Amateur Theatre in China, 1949–1966'.

36.   In mid-1974 a fierce campaign of criticism was being waged in the national press and elsewhere against the Shansi opera *Thrice ascending Peach Peak*.

List of Works Cited

Pre-1900 Chinese works (listed by title)

Ban-qiao za-ji by Yu Huai (1616–96), XYCS, pt. 13, fo. 3, pp. 1a–18a.
Bei-meng suo-yan by Sun Guangxian (d. A.D. 968), *Shuo-fu*, fo. 48.
Bi-hu za-ji by Xie Fangde (1226–89), XHLB, pp. 3480–2.
Ce-fu yuan-gui by Wang Qinruo (962–1025), Taipei, Zhong Hua Shuju, 1967.
Chang-lun by Zhi-an (thirteenth century), ZGGD, vol. 1.
Chuo-geng lu by Tao Zongyi (mid-fourteenth century), CSJB, vol. 13.
Ci-nue (during 1556–93) by Li Kaixian (1521–93), ZGGD, vol. 3.
Ci-yu cong-hua (1877) by Yang Enshou (1834–post 1885), ZGGD, vol. 9.
Cuo li-shen, anon. (Yuan), YLDD, fo. 13991, pp. 54b–60a.
Da-ye shi-yi (between 627 and 649) by Du Bao, XYCS, vol. 2.
Die-shan ji by Xie Fangde (1226–89), SBXB, vol. 87.
Ding-nian yu-sun zhi (1842) by Yang Maojian (fl. c. 1831), QDYD, vol. 2.
Dong Jie-yuan xi-xiang ji by Dong Jie-yuan (fl. c. 1190–1208), annotated by Ling Jingyan, Peking, Renmin Wenxue, 1962.
Dong-jing meng-hua lu (1147) by Meng Yuanlao (fl. c. 1120–50), annotated by Deng Zhicheng, Hong Kong, Shangwu, 1961.
Dong-po zhi-lin by Su Shi (1036–1101), CSJB, vol. 134.
Du-cheng ji-sheng (c. 1235?) by Naideweng, DJWS.
Du-qu xu-zhi (between 1639 and 1645) by Shen Chongsui (d. c. 1645), ZGGD, vol. 5.
Fan-sheng lu (shortly after 1252) by Xihu-laoren, DJWS.
Fan-xie-shan-fang quan-ji by Li E (1692–1752), SBBY, vols. 541–2.
Feng-shi jian-wen ji by Feng Yan (Tang), XHLB, pp. 3233–73.
Fu-bao-tang ji by Zang Maoxun (d. 1621), Shanghai, Gudian Wenxue, 1958.
Gu-qu za-yan by Shen Defu (1578–1642), ZGGD, vol. 4.
Guo-chao xian-zheng lu by Jiao Hong (1541–1620), Taipei, Xuesheng Shuju, 1964.
He-shuo fang-gu ji by Naxin (or Naixian, Yuan dynasty), *Shiliao congbian*, vol. 19.
Hua-bu nong-tan (1819) by Jiao Xun (1763–1820), ZGGD, vol. 8.
Ji-lei bian by Zhang Chuo (fl. c. 1126), CSJB, vol. 135.
Jiang-nan yu-zai by Zheng Wenbao (953–1013), ZBZZ, pt. 11, pp. 2895–906.
Jiao-fang ji (shortly after 762) by Cui Lingqin (fl. c. 749), ZGGD, vol. 1.
Jin-tai can-lei ji (1829) by Zhang Jiliang (1799–1843), QDYD, vol. 1.
Jiu Tang-shu (945) by Liu Xu (887–946) and others, SBBY.
Ju-bu qun-ying (1873) by Hanjiang-xiaoyouxianke, QDYD, vol. 2.

286

Ju-shuo (1805) by Jiao Xun (1763–1820), ZGGD, vol. 8.

Lan Cai-he, anon. (late Yuan or early Ming), *Yuan-qu xuan waibian*, vol. 2, pp. 971–80.

Lie-chao shi-ji xiao-zhuan (1652) by Qian Qianyi (1582–1664), Shanghai, Zhong Hua Shuju, 1961.

Li-yuan jiu-hua by Wu Tao (fl. c. 1876), QDYD, vol. 3.

Liu Bin-ke jia-hua lu by Wei Xuan (fl. c. 840), *Shuoku*, vol. 1, pp. 124–8.

Liu Dong-bin hua-yue shen-xian hui (1429) by Zhu Youdun (1379–1439), *Guben Yuan Ming zaju*, vol. 3.

Lu-gui bu (first version 1330) by Zhong Sicheng (c. 1279–post 1360), ZGGD, vol. 2.

Lu-gui bu xu-bian (1422) by Jia Zhongming (1343–1422 or later), ZGGD, vol. 2.

Lü-yuan cong-hua (1825) by Qian Yong (1759–1844), Shanghai, Wenming Shuju, no date given.

Meng-hua suo-bu (1842) by Yang Maojian (fl. c. 1830), QDYD, vol. 2.

Meng-liang lu (c. 1280) by Wu Zimu, DJWS, pp. 129–328.

Meng-zhong yuan (1699) by Zhang Jian (1681–post 1771), *Yu-yan-tang si-zhong qu*, 1750.

Ming-dao za-zhi by Zhang Lei (1052–1112), XHLB, vol. 6, pp. 3385–402.

Ming-huang za-lu by Zheng Chuhui (fl. c. 844), *Gan-zhu ji*, fo. 2.

Ming-shi (1739) by Zhang Tingyu (1672–1755) and others, SBBY.

Mu-dan ting (1598) by Tang Xianzu (1550–1617), Peking, Zhong Hua Shuju, 1959.

Nan-bu xin-shu by Qian Yi (fl. c. 1017), *Yue-ya tang*, vol. 1, pt. 1.

Nan-ci xu-lu (1559) by Xu Wei (1521–93), ZGGD, vol. 3.

Nan-ci ying-sheng by Wei Liangfu (mid-sixteenth century), *Xijubao*, 1961, no. 56.

Nan jiu-gong (*shi-san-diao*) *qu-pu* by Shen Jing (1553–1610), Peking, Peking University, c. 1921?

Ou-bo yu-hua by Ye Tingguan (1791–?), BJXB, pp. 5320–71.

Pi-pa ji by Gao Ming (c. 1301–c. 1370), Peking, Zhong Hua Shuju, 1960.

Qi-dong ye-yu by Zhou Mi (1232–98), *Shuoku*, pp. 625–704.

Qi-xiu lei-gao by Lang Ying (1487–1566 or later), Peking, Zhong Hua Shuju, 1959.

Qian-tang yi-shi by Liu Yiqing (Yuan), *Wu-lin zhang-gu cong-bian*, pp. 3396–456.

Qing-lou ji (1356) by Xia Tingzhi (c. 1300–post 1368), ZGGD, vol. 2.

Qu-hua (1825) by Liang Tingnan (1796–1861), ZGGD, vol. 8.

Qu-lü (1610) by Wang Jide (?–1623), ZGGD, vol. 4.

Qu-lü by Wei Liangfu (mid-sixteenth century), ZGGD, vol. 5.

Qu-lun by He Liangjun (fl. c. 1566), ZGGD, vol. 4.

Qu-lun by Xu Fuzha (1560–1630 or after), ZGGD, vol. 4.

Qu-Wei jiu-wen by Zhu Bian (d. 1154), ZBZZ, pt. 27, pp. 7223–82.

Qu-zao (1580?) by Wang Shizhen (1526–90) ZGGD, vol. 4.

San-chao bei-meng hui-bian (post 1162) by Xu Mengxin (1126–1207), Taipei, Wenhai, 1962.

San-guo zhi by Chen Shou (233–97), Peking, Zhong Hua Shuju, 1959.

Shan-zhong ba-yun ci by Zhang Yan (1248–c. 1320), GXJB, vol. 224.

Shao-shi shan-fang bi-cong by Hu Yinglin (fl. c. 1590), Peking, Zhong Hua Shuju, 1958.

Sheng-chao tong-shi shi-yi by Mao Qiling (1623–1716), XYCS, pt. 4, folios 3–4.

Shi-wu guan by Zhu Suchen (fl. c. 1644), modern revised version by Chen Si and others, Hong Kong, Sanlian Shudian, 1956.

Shi-wu ji-yuan by Gao Cheng (Sòng), CSJB, vol. 73.

Shu-yuan za-ji by Lu Rong (1436–94), CSJB, vol. 22.

Song-shi (1345) by Ouyang Xuan (1273–1357) and others, SBBY.

Sui-shu by Wei Zheng (580–643) and others, SBBY.

288

Tai-he zheng-yin pu (1398) by Zhu Quan (d. 1448), ZGGD, vol. 3.

Tai-ping guang-ji (977) by Li Fang (925–96) and others, Taipei, Xinxing Shuju, 1962.

Tai-ping yu-lan by Li Fang (925–96) and others, Taipei, 1968.

Tan-qu za-zha by Ling Mengchu (1580–1644), ZGGD, vol. 4.

Tang hui-yao by Wang Pu (922–82), GXJB, vols. 75–6.

Tang-que shi by Gao Yanxiu (874–post 944), ZBZZ, pt. 1, pp. 23–54.

Tao-an meng-yi by Zhang Dai (1597–1684 or 1689), CSJB, vol. 136.

Tao-hua shan (1689?–99) by Kong Shangren (1648–1718), Hong Kong, Hongzhi Shudian, 1973?

Teng-yin za-ji (1796) by Dai Lu (1739–1806), *Shuoku*, pp. 1792–821.

Tian-qi gong-ci by Jiang Zhiqiao (early–mid-seventeenth century), XYCS, pt. 3, fo. 4, pp. 28a–42a.

Tian-yi-ge (lan-ge xie-ben zheng-xu) Lu-gui bu (1422) by Jia Zhongming (1343–1422 or after), Shanghai, Zhong Hua Shuju, 1960.

Tian-zhi ou-wen (1896) by Zhenjun (fl. c. 1900), JDZG, vol. 219.

Tiao-xi yu-yin cong-hua by Hu Zi (fl. c. 1147), SBBY.

Ting-chun xin-yong (1810) by Liuchunge-xiaoshi, QDYD, vol. 1.

Ting-shi by Yue Ke (1183–1234), BJXB, pp. 2134–78.

Wu-lin jiu-shi (1280 or after) by Zhou Mi (1232–98), DJWS.

Xi-jing fu (97–107) by Zhang Heng (78–139), *Wen-xuan*, fo. 2, pp. 25–46.

Xi-jing za-ji by Ge Hong (c. 250–c. 330), BJXB, pp. 1–12.

Xi-xi cong-yu by Yao Kuan (d. 1161), CSJB, vol. 20.

Xi-xiang ji by Wang Shifu (Yuan), Hong Kong, Zhong Hua Shuju, 1960.

Xian-chun Lin-an zhi (1268) by Qian Shuoyou (fl. c. 1240–80), supplemented version (1830–1) by Wang Yuansun (1759–1835), ZGFZ, pt. E, no. 49.

Xian-ju ji (1556) by Li Kaixian (1501–68), in *Li Kaixian ji*, Peking, Zhong Hua Shuju, 1959.

Xian-qing ou-ji (1671) by Li Yu (1611–85), ZGGD, vol. 7.

Xiao Sun-tu, anon. (Yuan), YLDD, fo. 13991, pp. 1a–13b.

Xin Tang-shu (1060) by Ouyang Xiu (1007–72) and others, SBBY.

Xin Wu-dai shi by Ouyang Xiu (1007–72), SBBY.

Xu Wen-chang san-ji by Xu Wei (1521–93) Taipei, Guoli Zhongyang Tushuguan, 1968.

Yan-jing za-ji, anon. (late eighteenth or early nineteenth century), XFHZ, pt. 6.

Yan-lan xiao-pu (1785) by Wu Changyuan (fl. c. 1770), QDYD, vol. 1.

Yan-shi jia-xun by Yan Zhitui (531–post 591), GXJB, vol. 68.

Yao-shan-tang qu-ji by Jiang Yikui (late sixteenth–early seventeenth century), *Xin quyuan*.

Yi-li-an Bei-ci guang-zheng pu by Li Yu (c. 1590–c. 1660), Peking, Peking University, 1931?

Yin-hua lu by Zhao Lin (fl. c. 844), CSJB, vol. 134.

Ying-mei-an yi-yu by Mao Xiang (1611–93), XYCS, fo. 1, pp. 1a–22b.

You xian-ku by Zhang Zhuo (c. 660–741), *Tangren xiaoshuo* pp. 19–36.

You-yong za-zu by Duan Chengshi (d. AD 863), CSJB, vol. 19.

Yu-cun qu-hua (1784) by Li Tiaoyuan (1734–1803), ZGGD, vol. 8.

Yu-quan-zi zhen-lu, anon. (Tang), *Shuo-fu*, fo. 11.

Yuan-shi (1370) by Wang Yi (1321–72) and others, SBBY.

Yue-fu chuan-sheng (1743) by Xu Dachun (1693–1771), ZGGD, vol. 7.

Yue-fu za-lu (probably during 894–906) by Duan Anjie (fl. c. 894), ZGGD, vol. 1.

Yun-xi you-yi by Fan Shu (fl. c. AD 877), BJXB, vol. 1, pp. 100–3.

Zai-yuan za-zhi by Liu Tingji (fl. c. 1673), JDZG, vol. 379.

Zhang Xie zhuang-yuan, anon. (late thirteenth or early fourteenth century), YLDD, fo. 13991, pp. 13b–54b.

Zhong-yuan yin-yun (1324) by Zhou Deqing (c. 1270–post 1324), ZGGD, vol. 1.

Zhuang-hui-tang wen-ji by Hou Fangyu (1618–54), SBBY, vol. 525.

Zi-zhi tong-jian (1085) by Sima Guang (1019–86), SBBY.

Zui-weng tan-lu by Luo Ye (late Sòng or Yuan), Shanghai, Gudian Wenxue, 1957.

Collections, collective works, etc. (listed by title)

Chūgoku koten bungaku senshu, Tokyo, Heibonsha, 1958–61.

Culture and Education in China, Peking, Foreign Languages Press, 1960.

Gan-zhu ji, anon. Southern Sòng compiler, Taipei, 1970.

Guben Yuan Ming zaju (1941), comp. Wang Jilie, Peking, Zhongguo Xiju, 1958.

Jiaoding Yuankan zaju sanshizhong, ed. Zheng Qian, Taipei, Shijie Shuju, 1962.

Ming Qing chuanqi (1955), ed. and annotated by Zhao Jingshen and Hu Ji, Hong Kong, Jindai Tushu Gongsi, no date given.

Peking, Peking, Foreign Languages Press, 1960.

Pi-pa ji taolun zhuankan, Peking, Renmin Wenxue, 1956.

Quan Tang-shi (1707), comp. Peng Dingqiu (1645–1719) and others, Taipei, Fuxing Shuju, 1967.

Shajiabang, Peking, Renmin Wenxue, 1967.

Shiliao congbian (1924), comp. Luo Zhenyu (1866–1940), Taipei, Guangwen Shuju, 1968.

Shuo-fu, comp. Tao Zongyi (mid-fourteenth century), Taipei, Xinxing Shudian, 1963.

Shuoku (1915), comp. Wang Wenru, Taipei, Xinxing Shuju, 1963.

Tangren xiaoshuo, Hong Kong, Zhong Hua Shuju, 1966.

Wen-xuan, comp. Xiao Tong (501–31), Hong Kong, Shangwu, 1965.

Wu-lin zhang-gu cong-bian, comp. Ding Bing (1832–99), Taipei, Tailian Guofeng, 1967.

Xin quyuan, comp. Ren Ne, Shanghai, Zhong Hua Shuju, 1940.

Xiuding pingju xuan (1948), comp. Cheng Xubai, Taipei, Guoli Bianyiguan, 1958.

Yuan Ming Qing xiqu yanjiu lunwen ji, Peking, Zuojia, 1957.

Yuan-qu xuan waibian, comp. Sui Shusen, Peking, Zhong Hua Shuju, 1959.

Yue-ya-tang cong-shu (1850–75), comp. Tan Ying (1800–71) and Wu Chongyue (1810–63) and son, Taiwan, Huawen Shuju, 1965.

Zhiqu Weihushan, Peking, Renmin Wenxue, 1968.

Zhongguo huaju yundong wushinian shiliao ji: 1907–1957, Peking, Zhongguo Xiju, 1958.

Zhongguo xin wenxue daxi (1935), comp. Zhao Jiabi, Hong Kong, Wenxue Yanjiu She, 1962.

Zhongguo xin wenxue daxi xubian, Hong Kong, Wenxue Yanjiu She, 1968.

Zhui bai-qiu (1770), comp. Wanhua-zhuren (mid-eighteenth century) and Qian Decang, Taipei, Zhong Hua Shuju, 1967.

Western and modern Oriental writings (listed by author)

A Ying: (1) *Wan Qing xiqu xiaoshuo mu,* Shanghai, Wenyi Lianhe, 1954; (2) *Wan Qing wenxue congchao (chuanqi zaju juan),* Peking, Zhong Hua Shuju, 1962; (3) *Wan Qing wenxue congchao (xiaoshuo xiqu yanjiu juan),* Peking, Zhong Hua Shuju, 1960.

Adams, J. C., *The Globe Playhouse,* London, Constable; New York, Barnes and Noble, 1961.

An Bo, 'Guanyu xin gejude tigao wenti', *Renmin yinyue* (Peking),* no. 3, 1962, pp. 2–4.

Anon., 'Kunchu Opera', CL, 11, 1961, pp. 101–2.

Anon., 'Szechwan Opera Festival', CL, 4, 1955, pp. 166–7.

Aoki Masaru: (1) *Genjin zatsugeki josetsu*, Tokyo, Kōbundō, 1937; (2) *Shina kinsei gikyoku shi* (1930), trans. as *Zhongguo jinshi xiqu shi* by Wang Gulu, Peking, Zuojia, 1958.

Appiah, Peggy, *The Pineapple Child and Other Tales From Ashanti*, London, André Deutsch, 1969; as *Ananse the spider: Tales from an Ashanti Village*, New York, Pantheon, 1966.

Bertuccioli, Giuliano, *La Letteratura Cinese*, Milan, Sansoni, 1968.

Bland, J. O. P. and Backhouse, E., *China Under the Empress Dowager*, London, Heinemann, 1911; New York, Paragon, 1966.

Boorman, Howard L., *Biographical Dictionary of Republican China*, New York and London, Columbia University Press, 1970.

Bowers, Faubion, *Theatre in the East* (1956), New York, Grove Press, 1960; London, Evergreen, 1961.

Boyle, John Andrew (tr.), *The History of the World-Conqueror* by 'Ata-Malik Juvaini, Manchester University Press, 1958; as *Successors of Genghis Khan*, New York, Columbia University Press, 1971.

Bradbrook, M. C., *The Rise of the Common Player*, London, Chatto and Windus; Cambridge, Harvard University Press, 1962.

Cao Chousheng, *Zhongguo yinyue wudao xiqu renming cidian*, Peking, Shangwu, 1959.

Cao Juren, *Renshi xinyu*, Hong Kong, Yi Chuin, 1963.

Cao Yu, *Cao Yu juben xuan*, Hong Kong, Jianwen Shuju, 1961.

Carl, Katherine A., *With the Empress Dowager of China*, New York, Eveleigh Nash, 1906.

Chao Wei-pang, 'Yang-ko, the Rural Theatre in Ting-hsien, Hopei', *Folklore Studies* (Peiping), no. 3, 1944, pp. 17–38.

Chen Jiantan, *Yiling zhuan* (c. 1910), QDYD, vol. 3.

Cheng Yanqiu, *Cheng Yanqiu wenji*, Peking, Zhongguo Xiju, 1959.

Cranmer-Byng, J. L. (ed), *An Embassy to China: Lord Macartney's Journal 1793–1794*, London, Longmans; New York, Arcon, 1962.

Crump, J. I. : (1) 'The Elements of Yüan Opera', *The Journal of Asian Studies* (Michigan), no. 17, 1957–8, pp. 417–34; (2) 'Yüan-pen, Yüan Drama's Rowdy Ancestor', *Literature East and West* (Austin, Texas), vol. 14, no. 4, 1970, pp. 473–90; (3) 'The Conventions and Craft of Yüan Drama', *Journal of the American Oriental Society* (New Haven, Conn.), vol. 91, 1971, pp. 14–29.

Deng Suining, *Zhongguo xiju shi*, Taiwan, Zhong Hua Wenhua, 1956.

Dolby, W. : (1) 'Kuan Han-ch'ing', unpublished thesis, Cambridge, 1967; (2) 'Kuan Han-ch'ing', *Asia Major* (London), vol. 16, pts. 1–2, 1971, pp. 1–60; (3) 'Ni Tsan, an unconventional artist of the Yuan dynasty', *Oriental Art* (London), Winter 1973, pp. 429–32; (4) (with John Scott), *Warlords*, Edinburgh, Southside, 1974.

Doleželová-Velingerova, M. and Crump, J. I. (trs.), *Ballad of the Hidden Dragon: Liu Chi-yüan chu-kung-tiao*, Oxford, Clarendon Press; New York, Oxford University Press, 1971.

Douglas, Robert K., *Society in China*, London, A. D. Innes, 1894.

Du Yunzhi, *Zhongguo dianying shi*, Taiwan, Shangwu, 1972.

Dudbridge, Glen, *The Hsi-yu chi: A Study of the Antecedents to the Sixteenth Century Chinese Novel*, Cambridge and New York, Cambridge University Press, 1970.

*The place of publication of periodicals is given in brackets.

Edwards, E. D., *Chinese Prose Literature of the T'ang Period 618–906*, London, Probsthain; New York, AMS Press, 1937–8.

Ellis, Henry, *Journal of the Proceedings of the Late Embassy to China*, London, John Murray, 1818.

Fan Ning, ' "Tao-hua shan" zuozhe Kong Shangren', *Yuan Ming Qing xiqu yanjiu lunwen ji*, pp. 381–8.

Fang Xiu, *Ma Hua xin wenxue daxi*, Singapore, Shijie Shuju, 1971.

Feng Kai, 'Geju yu yueju', *Dongfang zazhi* (Shanghai), Dec. 1925, pp. 96–109.

Feng Yuanjun, *Guju shuohui* (1947), Peking, Zuojia, 1956.

Fokkema, D. W. : (1) *Literary Doctrine in China and Soviet Influence 1956–60*, The Hague, Mouton, 1965; (2) *Report From Peking: Observations of a Western Diplomat on the Cultural Revolution*, London, C. Hurst, 1971; McGill, Queen's University Press, 1972.

Fortune, Robert: (1) *A Journey to the Tea Countries of China*, London, John Murray, 1852; (2) *A Residence Among the Chinese*, London, John Murray, 1857; Wilmington, Scholarly Resources Inc., 1972.

Fu Xihua: (1) *Yuandai zaju quanmu*, Peking, Zuojia, 1957; (2) *Mingdai zaju quanmu*, Peking, Zuojia, 1958; (3) *Mingdai chuanqi quanmu*, Peking, Renmin Wenxue, 1959.

Gamble, S. D. (ed.), *Chinese Village Plays*, Amsterdam, Philo Press, 1970; New York, Schram, 1972.

Gernet J., *La Vie quotidienne en Chine à la veille de l'invasion Mongole, (1250–1276)*, Paris, Hachette, 1959.

Gimm, Martin, *Das Yüeh-fu tsa-lu des Tuan An-chieh*, Wiesbaden, Asiatische Fschgn., 1966.

Goodrich, L. C., *The Literary Inquisition of Ch'ien-lung*, Baltimore, Waverly Press, 1935.

Gordon Cummings, C. F., *Wanderings in China*, Edinburgh, Blackwood, 1888.

Gray, Jack, and Cavendish, Patrick, *Chinese Communism in Crisis*, London, Pall Mall Press; New York, Praeger, 1968.

Gray, John Henry, *China: A History of the Laws, Manners and Customs of the People*, London, Macmillan; New York, AMS Press, 1878.

Guan Dedong, 'Lueshuo "bian"-zide laiyuan', in his *Quyi luncong*, Peking, Zhong Hua Shuju, 1958, pp. 1–4.

Guo Jianying, *Xiqu longtao jiaocai*, Shanghai, Wenyi, 1962.

Guo Moruo, 'Ti Cao Cao fan-an', in his *Cai Wenji*, Peking, Wenwu, 1959, pp. 100–9.

Halson, Elizabeth, *Peking Opera: A Short Guide*, Oxford and New York, Oxford University Press, 1966.

Hanan, Patrick: (1) 'The Development of Fiction and Drama', in *The Legacy of China*, ed. Raymond Dawson, Oxford and New York, Oxford University Press, 1964, pp. 115–43; (2) 'Song and Yüan Vernacular Fiction: A Critique of Modern Methods of Dating', *Harvard Journal of Asiatic Studies* (Cambridge, Mass.), no. 30, 1970, pp. 159–84.

Häringova, Yarmila, 'The development of T'ien Han's Dramatic writings during the years 1920–37', in *Studien zur modernen Chinesischen Literatur*, ed. Jaroslav Prusek, Berlin, 1964, pp. 131–58.

Hawkes, David: (1) *Ch'u Tz'u: The Songs of the South*, Oxford, Oxford University Press, 1959; Boston, Beacon Press, 1962; (2) 'Reflections on some Yuan tsa-chü', *Asia Major* (London), vol. 16, pts. 1–2, Jan. 1971, pp. 69–81.

He Man and Gong Yijiang (eds.), *Fenmo chunqiu*, Peking, Zhongguo Xiju, 1959.

Helmut, Martin, *Li Liweng über das Theater*, unpublished thesis, Heidelberg, 1966.

Hightower, J. R., *Topics in Chinese Literature* (1950), revised ed., Cambridge, Mass.,

Harvard-Yenching Institute, 1953.

Hong Shen: (1) Introduction to vol. 9 of *Zhongguo xin wenxue daxi*; (2) 'Xiju Xieshe pianduan', *Zhongguo huaju yundong wushinian shiliao ji*, pp. 109–12.

Hsia, C. T. : (1) *A History of Modern Chinese Fiction (1917–1957)*, London and New Haven, Yale University Press, 1961; (2) *The Classic Chinese Novel: A Critical Introduction*, London and New York, Columbia University Press, 1968.

Hsiao Ch'ien, 'Ibsen in China (And the Chinese Annoyance at Bernard Shaw)', in his *The Dragon Beards versus the Blueprints*, London, Pilot Press, 1944.

Hu Ji, *Song Jin zaju kao*, Shanghai, Gudian Wenxue, 1957.

Hu Sha, *Pingju jianshi*, Peking, Tongsu Wenyi, 1958.

Hu Shi, 'Yibushengzhuyi', *Xin qingnian* (Peking and Shanghai), no. 15, June 1918, pp. 489–507.

Hua Chuanhao, *Wo yan Kunchou*, Shanghai, Shanghai Wenyi, 1961.

Huang Zhigang, 'Tang Xianzu nianpu', in three parts in *Xiqu yanjiu* (Shanghai), 1957, nos. 2–4.

Hummel, Arthur, *Eminent Chinese of the Ch'ing period (1644–1912)*, Washington, U.S. Government Printing Office, 1943–44.

Hung, Josephine Huang, *Ming Drama*, Taipei, Heritage Press, 1966.

Idema, W. L., 'de opvoering van de Yuan-komedie', in *forum der letteren*, Amsterdam, Arbeiderspers, Dec. 1972, pp. 80–107.

Iwaki Hideo, 'Genkan Kokon zatsugeki sanjūshu no ryuden', *Chūgoku bungaku hō* (Kyoto), vol. 14, April 1961, pp. 67–89.

Jin Jian, 'Mantan nongmin kan huaju', *Xijubao* (Peking), no. 2, 1963, pp. 17–19.

Johnson, Dale R., 'The Prosody of Yüan Drama', *T'oung Pao* (Leiden), vol. 56, pts. 1–3, 1970, pp. 96–146.

Kalvodová, D., 'The Origin and Character of the Szechwan Theatre', *Archiv Orientální* (Prague), no. 34, 1966, pp. 505–23.

Keith, A. Berriedale, *The Sanskrit Drama*, Oxford and New York, Clarendon Press, 1924.

Lau, J. S. M., *Ts'ao Yü: The Reluctant Disciple of Chekhov and O'Neill. A Study in Literary Influence*, Hong Kong, Hong Kong University Press, 1970.

Lévy, André, 'La condamnation du roman en France et en Chine' (1968), *Études sur le conte et le roman chinois*, Paris, l'École Française D'Extrème Orient, 1971, pp. 1–13.

Li Diankui, *Yuan Ming sanqu zhi fenxi yu yanjiu*, Taipei, Zhongguo Wenhua Xueyuan, 1965.

Li Xin, 'Lun xiqu fuzhuangde yanbian yu fazhan', *Xiqu yanjiu* (Shanghai), 1958, no. 3, pp. 69–82.

Lin Yutang: (1) *My Country and my People*, London, Heinemann, 1936, revised ed. 1943; (2) *Imperial Peking*, London, Elek Books; New York, International Publications Service, 1961.

Liu Dajie, *Zhongguo wenxue fazhan shi*, Shanghai, Gudian Wenxue, 1958.

Liu, James J. Y., 'Elizabethan and Yüan, a Brief Comparison of Some Conventions in Poetic Drama', London, Occasional Papers of the China Society, no. 8, 1955.

Liu Nianzi, 'Yuan zaju yanchu xingshide jidian chubu kanfa – Mingyingwangdian Yuandai xiju bihua diaocha zhaji', *Xiqu yanjiu* (Shanghai), 1957, no. 2, pp. 66–85.

Liu Shouzhong, *Zhongguo xin wenxueshi chugao*, Peking, Zuojia, 1956.

Liu Ts'un-yen, 'Lu Xun yu Mei Lanfang', *Renwu tan*, Hong Kong, Dagong Shuju, 1952, pp. 24–30.

Liu Yongji, *Songdai gewu juqu luyao*, Shanghai, Gudian Wenxue, 1957.

Lowe, H. Y., *Stories from Chinese Drama*, Peking, Peking Chronicle Press, 1942.

Lu Qian (Lu Jiye) *Zhongguo xiju gailun*, in *Zhongguo wenxue balun*, Hong Kong, Nanguo, 1961, no. 6.

Luo Chunrong, *Jubu congtan*, QDYD, vol. 3.

Luo Jintang, *Xiancun Yuanren zaju benshi kao*, Taipei, Zhongguo Wenhua Shiye, 1960.

Ma Shao-po, 'Mei Lan-fang and Chou Hsin-fang', CL, no. 3, 1955, pp. 142–8.

Ma Yanxiang, 'Cong liangchu haoxi tan Yongjude fazhan', *Xijubao* (Peking), no. 5, 1962, pp. 51–5.

Mackerras, C. P. : (1) 'The Growth of Chinese Regional Drama in the Ming and Ch'ing', *Journal of Oriental Studies* (Hong Kong University), 1971, vol. 9, no. 1, pp. 58–91; (2) *The Rise of the Peking Opera: 1770–1870*, New York and Oxford, Oxford University Press, 1972; (3) 'Amateur Theatre in China, 1949–1966', Contemporary China Papers no. 5, Canberra, Australian National University Press, 1973; (4) 'Chinese Opera after the Cultural Revolution (1970–72)', *The China Quarterly*, (London), no. 55, July-September 1973, pp. 478–510.

Mehnert, Klaus, *China Returns*, New York, Dutton; as *China Today*, London, Thames and Hudson, 1972.

Mei Lanfang: (1) 'Zhongguo xiqu yishude xin fangxiang', *Wenyibao* (Peking), 1952, no. 16, pp. 10–14; (2) *Mei Lanfang xiju sanlun*, Peking, Zhongguo Xiju, 1959; (3) *Wode dianying shenghuo*, Peking, Zhongguo Dianying, 1962; (4) *Mei Lanfang wenji*, Peking, Zhongguo Xiju, 1962; (5) *Wutai shenghuo sishinian* (1952–4), Peking, Zhongguo Xiju, 1957.

Mo She, 'Hangdang', *Xijubao* (Peking), no. 2, 1958, pp. 34–5.

Moges, Marquis de, *Recollections of Baron Gros's Embassy to China and Japan in 1857–8* (authorised translation), London, Griffin, Bohn and Company, 1861.

Muramatsu Kazuya, 'Chūgoku gikyoku no ongaku[ichi]', monthly bulletin of the *Chūgoku koten bungaku senshu*, no. 20.

Obratsov, Sergey Vladimirovich, *The Chinese Puppet Theatre*, tr. from the Russian by J. T. MacDermott, London, Faber and Faber, 1961; Boston, Plays Inc., 1975.

Okazaki Yoshie, *Japanese Literature in the Meiji Era*, tr. V. H. Viglielmo, Tokyo, Ōbunsha, 1955.

Ouyang Yuqian: (1) 'Tan wenmingxi', *Zhongguo huaju yundong wushinian shiliao ji*, pp. 48–108; (2) 'Huiyi Chunliu', ibid. pp. 13–47; (3). (ed.), *Zhongguo xiqu yanjiu ziliao chuji*, Peking, Yishu, 1956.

Picken, Laurence, 'Chinese Music', *Grove's Dictionary of Music and Musicians,* ed. Eric Blom, London, Macmillan; New York, St Martin's Press, 1954, vol. 2, pp. 219–48.

Qi Rushan: (1) *Mei Lanfang you Mei ji*, Peiping, Shangwu, 1933; (2) *Mei Lanfang yishu yiban*, Peiping, Peiping Guoju Xuehui, 1935; (3) *Qi Rushan quanji*, Taipei, 1964.

Qian Nanyang, *Song Yuan xiwen jiyi*, Shanghai, Gudian Wenxue, 1956.

Ricks, Christopher (ed.), *English Drama to 1710*, London, Sphere, 1971.

Schlepp, Wayne, *San-ch'ü: Its Technique and Imagery*, Madison, University of Wisconsin Press, 1970.

Scott, A. C.: (1) *The Classical Theatre of China*, London, George Allen and Unwin, 1957; (2) *Mei Lan-fang, Leader of the Pear Garden*, Hong Kong, Hong Kong University Press, 1949; (3) *Literature and the Arts in Twentieth Century China*, New York, Anchor Books, 1963; (4) *Traditional Chinese Plays*, London and Madison, University of Wisconsin Press, 1967.

Shen Yao, 'Jinxi qiantan', *Xiqu yanjiu* (Shanghai), no. 4, 1957, p. 21.

Shoberl, Frederic (ed.), *The World in Miniature: China*, London, R. Ackermann, 1823.

Smith, Arthur H. : (1) *Village Life in China*, Edinburgh and London, Oliphant, Anderson

294

and Ferrier, 1900; New York, Haskell, 1899; (2) *China in Convulsion*, Edinburgh and London, Oliphant, Anderson and Ferrier; New York, AMS Press, 1901.

Strong, Anna Louise, *China Fights for Freedom*, London, Lindsay Drummond; as *China's Millions: Revolutionary Struggles from 1927–1935*, New York, Books for Libraries Press, 1939.

Sun Kaidi: (1) *Kuileixi kaoyuan*, Shanghai, Shangza, 1952; (2) *Yeshiyuan gujin zaju kao*, Shanghai, Shangza, 1953; (3) *Cangzhou ji*, Peking, Zhong Hua Shuju, 1965.

Tan Zhengbi: (1) *Yuanqu liu dajia luezhuan*, Shanghai, Wenyi Lianhe, 1955; (2) *Huaben yu guju*, Shanghai, Gudian Wenxue, 1956.

Tian Han: (1) 'Nanguoshe shilue', *Zhongguo huaju yundong wushinian shiliao ji*, pp. 113–38; (2) *Guan Hanqing*, Peking, Zhongguo Xiju, 1960.

Tsiang Un-kai, *K'ouen k'iu: le Théâtre chinois ancien*, Paris, E. Leroux, 1933.

Tso Lin, 'The Chinese and Western Theatres: A Study in Contrasting Techniques', CL, no. 8, 1962, pp. 101–11.

Waley, Arthur: (1) *The Nine Songs*, London, George Allen and Unwin, 1955; San Francisco, City Lights, 1973; (2) 'The Green Bower Collection', *Oriental Art* (London), no. 3, 1957, pp. 50–54 and 107–9; (3) *Ballads and Stories From Tun-Huang*, London, George Allen and Unwin, 1960; New York, Macmillan, 1961; (4) *The Secret History of the Mongols and Other Pieces*, London, George Allen and Unwin, 1963; New York, Barnes and Noble, 1964.

Wang Guowei, *Wang Guowei xiqu lunwen ji*, Peking, Zhongguo Xiju, 1957.

Wang Liqi, 'Yuan Ming Qing tongzhi jieji duidai xiaoshuo xiqude taidude kaocha', *Wenxue yichan zengkan 5*, Peking, Zhong Hua Shuju, 1957, pp. 208–38.

Wang Xiaochuan, *Yuan Ming Qing sandai jinhui xiaoshuo xiqu shiliao*, Peking, Zuojia, 1958.

Wei Xun, 'Beijing Renyi ye bu zhongshi xiandai jumu', *Xijubao* (Peking), no. 2, 1958, p. 17.

Wilhelm, Richard, *Chinese Folktales* (1958, as *Chinesische Märchen*) transl. into English, London, G. Bell and Sons, 1971; New York, Transatlantic Arts Inc., 1974.

Williams, S. Wells, *The Middle Kingdon*, London, W. H. Allen, 1883; New York, Paragon, 1966.

Wimsatt, Genevieve B., *Chinese Shadow Shows*, Cambridge, Mass., Harvard University Press, 1936.

Xia Guoyun, 'Shanchuan xiuli renwu fengliu – mantan Yunnansheng minzu xiju guanmo yanchu', *Xijubao* (Peking), no. 3, 1962, pp. 39–41.

Xia Ye, *Xiqu yinyue yanjiu*, Shanghai, Wenyi, 1959.

Xu Dishan, 'Fanju tili jiqi zai Hanjushangde diandiandidi', *Zhongguo wenxue yanjiu*, ed. Zheng Zhenduo, Shanghai, Shangwu, 1927.

Xu Fuming: (1) 'Zang Maoxun yu Yuan-qu xuan', *Yuan Ming Qing xiqu lunwen ji*, 2nd series, Peking, Zuojia, 1959, pp. 55–63; (2) 'Liang Chenyude shengping he ta chuangzuo "Wan-sha ji" – de yitu', *Wenxue yichan zengkan 9*, Peking, Zhong Hua Shuju, 1962, pp. 25–34.

Xu Jiuye, *Liyuan yiwen*, QDYD, vol. 3.

Xu Yuanlai, 'Kangzhan banianzhongde Mei Lanfang', *Xijubao* (Peking), nos. 21–2, 1961, pp. 44–53.

Yan Dunyi, *Yuanju zhenyi*, Peking, Zhong Hua Shuju, 1960.

Yang Chin-sheng, (tr.) 'My Life on the Stage – by Mei Lan-fang', CL, no. 11, November 1961, pp. 3–35.

Yang, Daniel Shih-p'êng, *An Annotated Bibliography of Materials for the Study of the Peking*

Theatre, Wisconsin China Series, no. 2, Madison, 1967.

Yang, Richard, Liang, David, and Yang, Myrtle, 'Poetic Songs of the Yüan', *Chinese Culture* (Taipei), vol. 2, no. 1, 1970.

Yao Hsin-nung: (1) 'The Theme and Structure of the Yuan Drama', *Tien Hsia Monthly* (Shanghai), no. 1, January 1935, pp. 388–403; (2) 'The Rise and Fall of the K'un Ch'ü', *Tien Hsia Monthly* (Shanghai), no. 2, January 1936, pp. 63–84.

Ye Dejun, *Song Yuan Ming jiangchang wenxue*, Shanghai, Gudian Wenxue, 1957.

Yisha, Introduction to *Xin wenxue daxi xubian*, vol. 10 (cinema).

You Guoen, *Zhongguo wenxue shi*, Peking, Renmin Wenxue, 1964.

Zhang Cixi: (1) *Beijing liyuan zhanggu changbian*, QDYD, vol. 4; (2) *Beijing liyuan jinshi wenzi lu*, QDYD, vol. 3; (3) *Yanguilaiyi suibi*, QDYD, vol. 4, (4) *Yandu mingling zhuan*, QDYD, vol. 4; (5) *Beiping liyuan zhuzhici huibian*, QDYD, vol. 4.

Zhang Henshui, *Ti-xiao yin-yuan*, Hong Kong, Lezhi, 1960.

Zhang Huoshi, 'Mei Lanfang yu Cheng Yanqiu', *Zhongwai zazhi* (Taipei), vol. 10, no. 4, October 1971, pp. 29–37.

Zhang Jing, *Ming Qing chuanqi daolun*, Taipei, Dongfang Shudian, 1961.

Zhang Zhen, *Xiqu renwu sanlun*, Peking, Yishu, 1956.

Zhao Cong, *Zhongguo dalude xiqu gaige 1942–1967*, Hong Kong, Hong Kong University Press, 1969.

Zhao Jingshen: (1) *Ming Qing qutan*, Shanghai, Gudian Wenxue, 1957; (2) *Du-qu xiaoji*, Peking, Zhong Hua Shuju, 1959; (3) *Xiqu bitan*, Peking, Zhong Hua Shuju, 1962; (4) 'Qiu Hu xiqude yanbian', in *Du-qu xiaoji*, pp. 56–60 *passim*.

Zheng Zhenduo, *Chatuben Zhongguo wenxue shi*, Peking, Zuojia, 1957.

Zhou Miaozhong, 'Yang Chaoguan he tade "Yin-feng ge"', *Wenxue yichan zengkan 9*, Peking, Zhong Hua Shuju, 1962, pp. 43–61.

Zhou Yang, 'Gaige he fazhan minzu xiqu yishu', *Wenyibao* (Peking), 1952, no. 24, pp. 3–8.

Zhou Yibai: (1) *Zhongguo xijushi jiangzuo*, Peking, Zhongguo Xiju, 1958; (2) *Zhongguo xiqu lunji*, Peking, Zhongguo Xiju, 1960.

Zhu Meishu, 'Liang Qichao yu xiaoshuojie geming', *Wenxue yichan zengkan 9*, Peking, Zhong Hua Shuju, 1962, pp. 111–29.

Zhu Shuangyun, *Xinju shi*, as found in Lu Qian, *Zhongguo xiju gailun*, pp. 148–50 *passim*.

Zŏng In-sŏb, *An Introduction to Korean Literature*, Seoul, Hyangnin-Sa, 1970.

Zucker, A. E., *The Chinese Theater*, Boston, Little, Brown and Co., 1925.

Zung, Cecilia, *Secrets of the Chinese Drama: A Complete Explanatory Guide to Actions and Symbols as Seen in the Performance of Chinese Dramas*, London and Shanghai, Kelly and Walsh; New York, Blom, 1937.

Some Translations of Chinese Dramas into Western Languages

The list given below is primarily intended to provide a sample of what has appeared in translation and suggestions towards some further reading. It is by no means complete, and is largely restricted to collections of translations, to extensive selections, and to whole, usually longish, plays. It omits such things as retranslations from one European language into another, and where a translation has appeared both in a journal and as a separate edition, only the latter is listed. Other translated plays and excerpts of plays may be found in various journals, such as the *T'ien Hsia Monthly, Journal Asiatique* and *Chinese Literature*, as well as in a number of general works on Chinese drama. A much fuller list of translations, synopses, and reviews of translations in Western languages is found in Martha Davidson, *A List of Published Translations From Chinese into English, French and German*, 2 vols, Michigan, Ann Arbor, 1952, vol. 1, pp. 135–79. There are many excellent Japanese translations of Chinese plays, including such as Aoki Masaru, *Genjin zatsugeki*, Tokyo, Shunjūsha, 1957; idem, *Gikyoku shū*, Tokyo, Heibonsha, 1959; Yoshikawa Kōjirō, *Gengyoku Kinsen ki*, Tokyo, Tsukuma Shobō, 1943; and idem, *Gengyoku Kokukan tei*, Tokyo, Tsukuma Shobō, 1948.

Ansley, Clive, *The Heresy of Wu Han: his play 'Hai Jui's Dismissal' and its role in China's Cultural Revolution*, London and Toronto, Toronto University Press, 1971.

Arlington, L. C. : (1) *The Chinese Drama from the Earliest Times Until Today*, Shanghai, Kelly and Walsh Ltd., 1930; (2) (with Harold Acton), *Famous Chinese Plays*, Peiping, Henri Vetch, 1937; reissued New York, Russell and Russell, 1963.

Barnes, A. C. : (1) (with Wang Tso-liang), *Thunderstorm* by Tsao Yu, Peking, Foreign Languages Press, 1958; (2) *Sunrise*, Peking, Foreign Languages Press, 1960.

Bazin, Antoine, and Pierre, Louis: (1) *Tchao-mei-hiang, ou les intrigues d'une soubrette, comédie en prose et en vers*, Paris, l'Imprimerie royale, 1835; (2) *Théâtre chinois ou choix de pièces de théâtre composées sous les empereurs mongols traduites pour la première fois sur le texte original précédées d'une introduction et accompagnées de notes*, Paris, l'Imprimerie royale, 1838; (3) *Le Pi-Pa-Ki, ou l'histoire du luth, drame chinois de Kao-tong-kia représentée à Pékin en 1404 avec les changements de Mao-tseu*, Paris, l'Imprimerie royale, 1838.

Bertuccioli, G., 'Il sogno della farfalla', *Cina* (Rome), no. 5, 1959.

Chang Pei-chi, *Bright Skies* by Tsao Yü, Peking, Foreign Languages Press, 1960.

Chen Ta-jen, 'A night in Peiping – One-act Play', *Far Eastern Mirror* (Hong Kong), vol. 1, no. 8, 1938, pp. 63–75.

Crump, J. I., 'Li K'ui Carries Thorns', *Anthology of Chinese Literature* (ed. by Cyril Birch) (1965), Harmondsworth, Penguin, 1967, pp. 395–421; New York, Grove Press, 1965.

297

Davis, J. F. : (1) *Laou-seng-urh, or 'An Heir in His Old Age'*, a Chinese Drama, London, J. Murray, 1817; (2) *Han koong tsew, or the Sorrows of Han*, a Chinese Tragedy, London, Oriental Translation Fund, 1829.

Eichhorn, W. : (1) 'Ein Einakter von Hiung Fu-hsi', *Sinica* (Frankfurt am Main), no. 12, 1937, pp. 161–72; (2) *Chinesisches Bauernleben: drei Stücke aus dem chinesischen Landleben*, Tokyo, 1938.

Forke, Alfred: (1) 'Vaterlandsliebe', *Orient et Occident* (Geneva), vol. 2, nos. 11–12, 1936, pp. 416–35; (2) *Der Kreidekreis*, Leipzig, Philipp Reclam, no. 768, 1927.

Gamble, Sidney D. (ed.), *Chinese Village Plays*, Amsterdam, Philo Press, 1970; New York, Schram, 1972.

Hart, Henry H., *The West Chamber, A Mediaeval Drama*, California, Stanford University Press; London, H. Milford, Oxford University Press, 1936.

Hsiung, S. I. : (1) 'Mammon', *The People's Tribune* (Shanghai), vol. 8, no. 2, January 1935, pp. 125–51; (2) *Lady Precious Stream*, New York, Liveright; London, Methuen and Co., 1935; (3) 'Mencius Was a Bad Boy', *The People's Tribune* (Shanghai), vol. 9, no. 3, May 1935, pp. 191–200; (4) *The Romance of the Western Chamber*, London, Methuen, 1935; reissue (with additional, critical introduction by C. T. Hsia), New York and London, Columbia University Press, 1968.

Hsü Meng-hsiung, 'An Unhappy Reunion. One-act play', *China Forum* (Hankow and Chungking), no. 2, 3 September 1938, pp. 272–82.

Hsu, S. N., *Par sa propre faute; drame en cinq actes*, Peiping, Impr. de *La Politique de Pékin*, 1935.

Hundhausen, Vincenz: (1) *Das Westzimmer. Ein chinesisches Singspiel in deutscher Sprache*, Peking and Leipzig, Pekinger Verlag, 1926; (2) *Die Laute, von Gau Ming. Ein chinesisches Singspiel in deutscher Sprache*, Peking and Leipzig, Pekinger Verlag, 1930; (3) *Tang Hsiaen-Dsu. Der Blumengarten. Ein chinesisches Singspiel in deutscher Sprache*, Peking, Pekinger Verlag, 1933; (4) *Die Rückkehr der Seele, ein romantisches Drama von Tang Hsiän Dsu in deutscher Sprache*, Zürich and Leipzig, Rascher Verlag, 1937.

Idema, W. L. : (1) 'Lan Cai-he: een anonieme chinese komedie uit de 14e eeuw', *forum der letteren*, Amsterdam, Arbeiderspers, December 1972, pp. 108–32; (2) (with D. R. Jonker), *Vermaning door een dode hond*, Amsterdam, Arbeiderspers, 1974.

Imbault-Huart, Camille, 'Les deux soles, ou acteur par amour, drame chinois en prose et en vers', *Journal Asiatique* (Paris), no. 136, 1890, pp. 483–92.

Ingalls, Jeremy, *The Malice of Empire* by Yao Hsin-nung, translated with an introduction by Jeremy Ingalls, London, Allen and Unwin; Berkeley, University of California Press, 1970.

Julien, Stanislas: (1) *Hoei Lan Ki, ou l'histoire du cercle de craie, drame en prose et en vers*, London, Oriental Translation Fund, 1832; (2) *Tchao Chi Kou Eul, ou l'Orphelin de la Chine, drame en prose et en vers accompagné des pièces historiques qui ont fourni le sujet, de nouvelles, et de poésies chinoises*, Paris, Moutardier, 1834; (3) *Si-siang-ki, ou l'histoire du pavillon d'occident, comédie en seize actes*, Geneva, T. Mueller, 1872–80.

Kao, George, 'Fruits in the Spring', *China Monthly* (New York), vol. 17, no. 3, 1947, pp. 37–53; no. 4, 1947, pp, 38–48; no. 5, 1947, pp, 38–50; no. 6, 1947, pp. 38–48.

Keene, Donald, 'Autumn in the Palace of Han', *Anthology of Chinese Literature* (ed. Cyril Birch) (1965), Harmondsworth, Penguin, 1967, pp. 421–45; New York, Grove Press, 1965.

Klabund, *Der Kreidekreis*, Berlin, I. M. Spaeth, 1925.

Kwei Chen, 'Three Chinese Folk-dramas', *Theatre Arts Monthly* (New York), vol. 14, November 1930, pp. 967–78.

Laloy, Louis: (1) *Le Chagrin dans le Palais de Han*, Dramė chinois orné par René Piot et publié par la Société littéraire de France, 10 rue de l'Odéon à Paris, 1921; (2) *Le Rêve du millet jaune, drama taoiste du xiiie siècle*, Paris, Desclée de Brouwer, 1935.

Li Pi-lien, 'The Doomed Battalion', *The People's Tribune* (Shanghai), vol. 25, nos. 3 and 4, pp. 121–8.

Li Tche-houa, *Le signe de patience et autres pièces du théâtre des Yüan*, Paris, 1963.

Liao Bao-seing, 'Dschan-Yu – der Kriegskamerad, ein Einakter von Tiën Han', *Sinica* (Frankfurt am Main), no. 15, 1939, pp. 165–92.

Liu Jung-en, *Six Yuan Plays*, New York and Harmondsworth, Penguin, 1972.

Lu Yung, 'An Unexpected Reunion', *Far Eastern Mirror* (Hong Kong), 10 August 1938, pp. 60–70.

Prémare, Joseph, 'L'Orphelin de la Maison de Tschao', *Description géographique, historique, chronologue, politique, et physique de l'empire de la Chine et de la tartarie chinoise*, (ed. Du Halde), Paris, 1735.

Robertson, Pax, *Lew Yuen Wae*, London, Chelsea Publ. Co., 1923.

Rudelsberger, Hans, *Altchinesische Liebeskomödien*, Wien, Anton Schroll and Co., 1922.

Scott, A. C., *Traditional Chinese Plays*, London and Madison, University of Wisconsin Press, 1967.

Shih Chung-wen, *Injustice to Tou O [Tou O Yüan], A Study and a Translation*, Cambridge, Cambridge University Press, 1972; Princeton, Cambridge University Press, 1973.

Soulié de Morant, G. C.: (1) *Essai sur la littérature chinoise*, Paris, Editions Véga, 1912, pp. 331–51; (2) *Théatre et musique modernes en Chine*, Paris, P. Geuthner, 1924, pp. 55–67. 157–74; (3) *L'Amoureuse Oriole, jeune fille, roman d'amour chinois du xiiime siècle*, Paris, E. Flammarion, 1928.

Stanton, William, *The Chinese Drama*, Hong Kong, Kelly and Walsh, 1899, pp. 19–53, 55–101, 103–21.

Stent, G. C.: (1) *Jen Kuei's Return – A Play*, Shanghai, Da Costa and Co., 1873; reprinted in *The Jade Chaplet*, London, Trübner and Co., 1974, pp. 72–112; (2) 'The Yellow Stork Tower', *Far East* (Omaha), 1 September 1876, pp. 57–66 and October 1876, pp. 81–9.

Tang Sheng and others, *Saturday Afternoon at the Mill, and other one-act plays* by Tsui Te-chih and others, Peking, Foreign Languages Press, 1957.

Tcheng Mien: (1) *Le Théâtre chinois moderne*, Paris, Les Presses modernes, 1929; (2) *Répertoire Analytique du Théâtre chinois moderne*, Paris, Jouve et Cie Editeurs, 1929.

Tisseau, Bernard, 'La neige au milieu de l'été', *Théâtre populaire* (Paris), 3e trimestre 1961, no. 43.

Tu Kwei-ying, 'Serenade, One Act Play', *Far Eastern Mirror* (Hong Kong), 25 August 1938, pp. 68–77.

Van der Veer, Ethel, 'The Chalk Circle', *World Drama* (ed. Barrett H. Clark), New York and London, D. Appleton and Co., 1933, pp. 227–58.

Wilhelm, Richard: (1) 'Der gespaltene Sarg', *Chinesische Blätter für Wissenschaft und Kunst* (Frankfurt am Main), vol. 1, no. 3, 1926, pp. 49–87; (2) 'Der verwechselte Bräutigam', *Chinesische Blätter für Wissenschaft und Kunst* (Frankfurt am Main), vol. 1, no. 4, 1927, pp. 5–58.

Wimsatt, Genevieve B., *Chinese Shadow Shows*, Cambridge Mass., Harvard University Press, 1936, pp. 62–8.

Wollheim da Foncesca, A. E., *Der Kreide Kreis*, Leipzig, Philipp Reclam, 1876.

Yang, Gladys: (1) *The Runaway Maid (A Cantonese Opera)*, Peking, Foreign Languages Press, 1958; (2) *War Drums on the Equator (a play in seven scenes)* by Li Huang and others of the Drama Group of the Political Department of the Navy of the People's Liberation Army, CL, no. 7, 1965, pp. 3–72.

Yang Hsien-yi: (1) 'A Princess Gets Smacked (A Shansi Opera)', CL, no. 10. 1961, pp. 83ff; (2) 'Footprints in the Snow (A Szechuan Opera)', CL, no. 10, 1961, pp. 76–91.

Yang Hsien-yi and Yang, Gladys: (1) *Chu Yuan* by Kuo Mo-jo, Peking, Foreign Languages Press, 1953; (2) *The White-haired Girl* by Ting Yi and Ho Ching-chih, Peking, Foreign Languages Press, 1954; (3) *The Palace of Eternal Youth* by Hung Sheng, Peking, Foreign Languages Press, 1955; (4) *Love Under the Willows: Liang Shan-po and Chu Ying-tai (A Szechuan Opera)*, Peking, Foreign Languages Press, 1956; (5) *Fifteen Strings of Cash (A Kunchu Opera)*, original libretto by Chu Su-shen, revised by Chou Chuan-ying and others, final version by Chen Sze, Peking, Foreign Languages Press, 1957; (6) *Selected Plays of Kuan Han-ching*, Peking, Foreign Languages Press, 1958; (7) *The Forsaken Wife (A Pingchu Opera)*, Peking, Foreign Languages Press, 1958; (8) 'The Faithless Lover (Szechuan Opera)' CL, no. 10, 1961, pp. 67–75.

Yang, Richard F. S., *Four Plays of the Yuan Drama*, Taipei, 1972.

Yao Hsin-nong: (1) 'Madam Cassia', *T'ien Hsia Monthly* (Shanghai), no. 1, 1935, pp. 537–84; (2) 'The Right to Kill', *T'ien Hsia Monthly* (Shanghai), no. 2, 1936, pp. 468–507; (3) 'Thunder and Rain', *T'ien Hsia Monthly* (Shanghai), no. 3, 1936, pp. 270–95, 363–411, 486–530; and no. 4, 1937, pp. 61–95, 176–221, 270–83; (4) 'When the Girls Come Back', *T'ien Hsia Monthly* (Shanghai), no. 7, 1938, pp. 94–120.

Ying Yu, '"The Test" by Hsia Yen', CL, no. 4, 1955, pp. 3–69.

Yonge, H., *The Sunrise, a Play in Four Acts by Tsao Yu*, Changsha, Commercial Press, 1940.

Some other translations by anonymous translators:

1. *The Riverside Pavilion*, adapted by Wu Po-chi from the original play by Kuan Han-ching. Staged by the Szechuan Opera Company of Chengtu. Peking, Foreign Languages Press, 1958.
2. *The White Snake (A Peking Opera)*, Peking, Foreign Languages Press, 1957.
3. *The Ruse of the Empty City: A Peking Opera Recorded in China*, Folkways Records Album, FW 8882, New York, 1960 (A famous *ching-hsi* drama recorded on one long-playing record with English translation of the libretto.)
4. *Kuan Han-ching*, a play by Tian Han, Peking, Foreign Languages Press, 1961.
5. 'Taking the Bandits' Stronghold', CL, no. 8, 1967, pp. 129–81.
6. 'Raid on the White Tiger Regiment', CL, no. 10, 1967, pp. 12–58.
7. 'Shachiapang', CL, no. 11, 1967, pp. 3–53.
8. 'Sea Battle at Night', CL, no. 3, 1968, pp. 13–60; and no. 4, 1968, pp. 48–9.
9. 'The Army and the People Are One Family (an Operetta)' by Yung Chun, CL, no. 9, 1968, pp. 93–104.
10. 'On the Docks', CL, no. 1, 1969, pp. 3–53.
11. 'Red Detachment of Women', CL, no. 5, 1969, pp. 3–14.
12. 'Taking Tiger Mountain by Strategy (October 1969 script)', CL, no. 1, 1970, pp. 3–57.
13. 'A Cock Crows at Midnight (a puppet film scenario)', CL, no. 4, 1970, pp. 39–54.
14. 'The Red Lantern (May 1970 script)', CL, no. 8, 1970, pp. 8–53.
15. 'Shachiapang (May 1970 script)' CL, no. 11, 1970, pp. 3–62.
16. 'Red Detachment of Women' [ballet], CL, no. 1, 1971, pp. 2–80.

17. 'On the Docks (revised script by "On the Docks" Group of the Peking Opera Troupe of Shanghai)', CL, no. 5, 1972, pp. 52–98.
18. 'Song of the Dragon River', CL, no. 7, 1972, pp. 3–52.

Index

As an aid to the student and as a check against the possible inaccuracies or idiosyncrasies of some of my translations, romanisations of Chinese titles, terms and institutions are included. Chinese and Japanese words are listed by order of the first syllable. Italicised page numbers indicate major references.

301